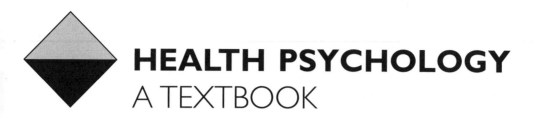

HEALTH PSYCHOLOGY
A TEXTBOOK

Second Edition

Jane Ogden

Open University Press
Buckingham · Philadelphia

Open University Press
Celtic Court
22 Ballmoor
Buckingham
MK18 1XW

email: enquiries@openup.co.uk
world wide web: www.openup.co.uk

and
325 Chestnut Street
Philadelphia, PA 19106, USA

First published 1996. Reprinted 1997, 1998 (twice)

This edition published 2000

A catalogue record of this book is available from the British Library

ISBN 0 335 20596 8 (pb) 0 335 20597 6 (hb)

Library of Congress Cataloging-in-Publication Data
Ogden, Jane, 1966–
Health psychology : a textbook / Jane Ogden. – 2nd ed.
p. cm.
Includes bibliographical references and index.
ISBN 0–335–20596–8 (PB) – ISBN 0–335–20597–6 (HB)
1. Clinical health psychology. I. Title.
R726.7.O37 2000
616′.001′9–dc21 99–056965

Typeset by Graphicraft Limited, Hong Kong
Printed in Great Britain by Biddles Ltd, Guildford and King's Lynn

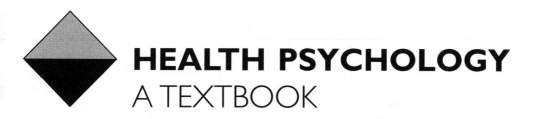

HEALTH PSYCHOLOGY
A TEXTBOOK

Second Edition

Jane Ogden studied for a PhD in eating behaviour at the Institute of Psychiatry, London. She then became a lecturer in health psychology at Middlesex University where she set up a health psychology course. Jane is a Reader in Health Psychology at Guy's, King's and St. Thomas's School of Medicine, University of London, where she carries out research into health related behaviours and teaches health psychology to both medical and psychology students.

Contents

Chapter 12 The interrelationship between beliefs, behaviour and health – the example of placebos 271

Chapter 13 Psychology throughout the course of illness: the examples of HIV, cancer and coronary heart disease 292

List of figures and tables

Figures

Tables

Preface to the second edition

It is now four years since I submitted the first edition of this book and it seemed time for an update. This second edition includes an additional chapter on the measurement of health status and quality of life (Chapter 14) and new sections on the following: professional issues in health psychology (Chapter 1), recent developments within the fields of health beliefs and social cognition models (Chapter 2), illness cognitions and health outcomes (Chapter 3), agreement in the consultation (Chapter 4), dieting and body dissatisfaction (Chapter 6) and psycho neuroimmunology (Chapter 10). In addition, it has been updated throughout. My thanks again go to my psychology and medical students and to my colleagues over the years for their comments and feedback.

CHAPTER 1

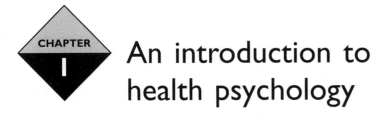

An introduction to health psychology

Chapter overview

This chapter examines the background against which health psychology developed in terms of (1) the traditional biomedical model of health and illness that emerged in the nineteenth century, and (2) changes in perspectives of health and illness over the twentieth century. The chapter highlights differences between health psychology and the biomedical model and examines the kinds of questions asked by health psychologists. Then the possible future of health psychology in terms of both clinical health psychology and becoming a professional health psychologist is discussed. Finally, this chapter outlines the aims of the textbook and describes how the book is structured.

This chapter covers:

- The background to health psychology
- What is the biomedical model?
- What are the aims of health psychology?
- What is the future of health psychology?
- What are the aims of this book?

The background to health psychology

During the nineteenth century, modern medicine was established. Man (the nineteenth-century term) was studied using dissection, physical investigations and medical examinations. Darwin's thesis, *The Origin of Species*, was published in 1856 and described the theory of evolution. This revolutionary theory identified a place for Man within Nature and suggested that we were part of nature, that we developed from nature and that we were biological beings. This was in accord with the biomedical model of medicine, which studied Man in the same way that other members of the natural world had been studied in earlier years. This model described human beings as having a biological identity in common with all other biological beings.

What is the biomedical model?

The biomedical model of medicine can be understood in terms of its answers to the following questions:

- *What causes illness?* According to the biomedical model of medicine, diseases either came from outside the body, invaded the body and caused physical changes within the body, or originated as internal involuntary physical changes. Such diseases may be caused by several factors such as chemical imbalances, bacteria, viruses and genetic predisposition.
- *Who is responsible for illness?* Because illness is seen as arising from biological changes beyond their control, individuals are not seen as responsible for their illness. They are regarded as victims of some external force causing internal changes.
- *How should illness be treated?* The biomedical model regards treatment in terms of vaccination, surgery, chemotherapy, and radiotherapy, all of which aim to change the physical state of the body.
- *Who is responsible for treatment?* The responsibility for treatment rests with the medical profession.
- *What is the relationship between health and illness?* Within the biomedical model, health and illness are seen as qualitatively different – you are either healthy or ill, there is no continuum between the two.
- *What is the relationship between the mind and the body?* According to the biomedical model of medicine, the mind and body function independently of each other. This is comparable to a traditional dualistic model of the mind–body split. From this perspective, the mind is incapable of influencing physical matter and the mind and body are defined as separate entities. The mind is seen as abstract and relating to feelings and thoughts, and the body is seen in terms of physical matter such as skin, muscles, bones, brain and organs. Changes in the physical matter are regarded as independent of changes in state of mind.

- *What is the role of psychology in health and illness?* Within traditional biomedicine, illness may have psychological consequences, but not psychological causes. For example, cancer may cause unhappiness but mood is not seen as related to either the onset or progression of the cancer.

The twentieth century

Throughout the twentieth century, there have been challenges to some of the underlying assumptions of biomedicine. These developments have included the emergence of psychosomatic medicine, behavioural health, behavioural medicine and, most recently, health psychology. These different areas of study illustrate an increasing role for psychology in health and a changing model of the relationship between the mind and body.

Psychosomatic medicine

The earliest challenge to the biomedical model was psychosomatic medicine. This was developed at the beginning of the century in response to Freud's analysis of the relationship between the mind and physical illness. At the turn of the century, Freud described a condition called 'hysterical paralysis', whereby patients presented with paralysed limbs with no obvious physical cause and in a pattern that did not reflect the organization of nerves. Freud argued that this condition was an indication of the individual's state of mind and that repressed experiences and feelings were expressed in terms of a physical problem. This explanation indicated an interaction between mind and body and suggested that psychological factors may not only be consequences of illness but may contribute to its cause.

Behavioural health

Behavioural health again challenged the biomedical assumptions of a separation of mind and body. Behavioural health was described as being concerned with the maintenance of health and prevention of illness in currently healthy individuals through the use of educational inputs to change behaviour and lifestyle. The role of behaviour in determining the individual's health status indicates an integration of the mind and body.

Behavioural medicine

A further discipline that challenged the biomedical model of health was behavioural medicine, which has been described by Schwartz and

Weiss (1977) as being an amalgam of elements from the behavioural science disciplines (psychology, sociology, health education) and which focuses on health care, treatment and illness prevention. Behavioural medicine was also described by Pomerleau and Brady (1979) as consisting of methods derived from the experimental analysis of behaviour, such as behaviour therapy and behaviour modification, and involved in the evaluation, treatment and prevention of physical disease or physiological dysfunction (e.g. essential hypertension, addictive behaviours and obesity). It has also been emphasized that psychological problems such as neurosis and psychosis are not within behavioural medicine unless they contribute to the development of illness. Behavioural medicine therefore included psychology in the study of health and departed from traditional biomedical views of health by not only focusing on treatment, but also focusing on prevention and intervention. In addition, behavioural medicine challenged the traditional separation of the mind and the body.

Health psychology

Health psychology is probably the most recent development in this process of including psychology into an understanding of health. It was described by Matarazzo in 1980 as the 'aggregate of the specific educational, scientific and professional contribution of the discipline of psychology to the promotion and maintenance of health, the promotion and treatment of illness and related dysfunction' (p. 815). Health psychology again challenges the mind–body split by suggesting a role for the mind in both the cause and treatment of illness but differs from psychosomatic medicine, behavioural health and behavioural medicine in that research within health psychology is more specific to the discipline of psychology.

Health psychology can be understood in terms of the same questions that were asked of the biomedical model:

- *What causes illness?* Health psychology suggests that human beings should be seen as complex systems and that illness is caused by a multitude of factors and not by a single causal factor. Health psychology therefore attempts to move away from a simple linear model of health and claims that illness can be caused by a combination of biological (e.g. a virus), psychological (e.g. behaviours, beliefs) and social (e.g. employment) factors. This approach reflects the *biopsychosocial model of health and illness,* which was developed by Engel (1977, 1980) and is illustrated in Fig. 1.1. The biopsychosocial model represented an attempt to integrate the psychological (the 'psycho') and the environmental (the 'social') into the traditional biomedical (the 'bio') model of health as follows: (1) The *bio* contributing factors included genetics, viruses, bacteria and structural defects. (2) The *psycho* aspects of health and illness were described in terms of cognitions (e.g. expectations of health), emotions (e.g. fear of treatment), and behaviours (e.g. smoking, diet, exercise or alcohol consumption). (3) The *social* aspects of health were

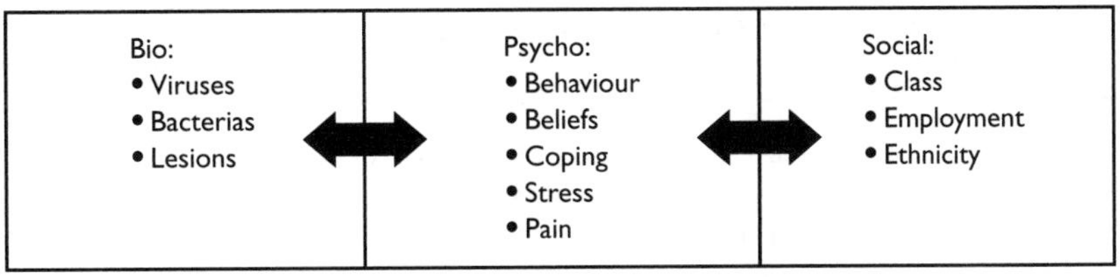

Figure 1.1 The biopsychosocial model of health and illness

described in terms of social norms of behaviour (e.g. the social norm of smoking or not smoking), pressures to change behaviour (e.g. peer group expectations, parental pressure), social values on health (e.g. whether health was regarded as a good or a bad thing), social class and ethnicity.

- *Who is responsible for illness?* Because illness is regarded as a result of a combination of factors, the individual is no longer simply seen as a passive victim. For example, the recognition of a role for behaviour in the cause of illness means that the individual may be held responsible for their health and illness.
- *How should illness be treated?* According to health psychology, the whole person should be treated, not just the physical changes that have taken place. This can take the form of behaviour change, encouraging changes in beliefs and coping strategies and compliance with medical recommendations.
- *Who is responsible for treatment?* Because the whole person is treated, not just their physical illness, the patient is therefore in part responsible for their treatment. This may take the form of responsibility to take medication, responsibility to change beliefs and behaviour. They are not seen as a victim.
- *What is the relationship between health and illness?* From this perspective, health and illness are not qualitatively different, but exist on a continuum. Rather than being either healthy or ill, individuals progress along this continuum from healthiness to illness and back again.
- *What is the relationship between the mind and body?* The twentieth century has seen a challenge to the traditional separation of mind and body suggested by a dualistic model of health and illness, with an increasing focus on an interaction between the mind and the body. This shift in perspective is reflected in the development of a holistic or a whole person approach to health. Health psychology therefore maintains that the mind and body interact. However, although this represents a departure from the traditional medical perspective, in that these two entities are seen as influencing each other, they are still categorized as separate – the existence of two different terms (the mind/the body) suggests a degree of separation and 'interaction' can only occur between distinct structures.
- *What is the role of psychology in health and illness?* Health psychology regards psychological factors not only as possible consequences of illness but as contributing to its aetiology.

What are the aims of health psychology?

Health psychology emphasizes the role of psychological factors in the cause, progression and consequences of health and illness. The aims of health psychology can be divided into (1) understanding, explaining, developing and testing theory and (2) putting this theory into practice.

1 *Health psychology aims to understand, explain, develop and test theory by*:
   (a) Evaluating the role of behaviour in the aetiology of illness. For example:
   - ◆ Coronary heart disease is related to behaviours such as smoking, cholesterol level, lack of exercise, high blood pressure and stress.
   - ◆ Many cancers are related to behaviours such as diet, smoking, alcohol and failure to attend for screening or health check-ups.
   - ◆ A stroke is related to smoking, cholesterol and high blood pressure.
   - ◆ An often overlooked cause of death is accidents. These may be related to alcohol consumption, drugs and careless driving.

   (b) Predicting unhealthy behaviours. For example:
   - ◆ Smoking, alcohol consumption and high fat diets are related to beliefs.
   - ◆ Beliefs about health and illness can be used to predict behaviour.

   (c) Understanding the role of psychology in the experience of illness. For example:
   - ◆ Understanding the psychological consequences of illness could help to alleviate physical symptoms such as pain, nausea and vomiting.
   - ◆ Understanding the psychological consequences of illness could help alleviate psychological symptoms such as anxiety and depression.

   (d) Evaluating the role of psychology in the treatment of illness. For example:
   - ◆ If psychological factors are important in the cause of illness they may also have a role in its treatment.
   - ◆ Treatment of the psychological consequences of illness may have an impact on longevity.

2 *Health psychology also aims to put theory into practice. This can be implemented by*:
   (a) Promoting healthy behaviour. For example:
   - ◆ Understanding the role of behaviour in illness can allow unhealthy behaviours to be targeted.
   - ◆ Understanding the beliefs that predict behaviours can allow these beliefs to be targeted.
   - ◆ Understanding beliefs can help these beliefs to be changed.

   (b) Preventing illness. For example:
   - ◆ Changing beliefs and behaviour could prevent illness onset.

- Behavioural interventions during illness (e.g. stopping smoking after a heart attack) may prevent further illness.
- Training health professionals to improve their communication skills and to carry out interventions may help to prevent illness.

What is the future of health psychology?

Health psychology is an expanding area in the UK, across Europe, in Australia and New Zealand and in the USA. For many students this involves taking a health psychology course as part of their psychology degree. For some students health psychology plays a part of their studies for other allied disciplines, such as medicine, nursing, health studies and dentistry. However, in addition, to studying health psychology at this preliminary level, an increasing number of students carry out higher degrees in health psychology as a means to develop their careers within this field. This has resulted in a range of debates about the future of health psychology and the possible roles for a health psychologist. To date these debates have highlighted two possible career pathways: the clinical health psychologist and the professional health psychologist.

The clinical health psychologist

A clinical health psychologist has been defined as someone who merges 'clinical psychology with its focus on the assessment and treatment of individuals in distress . . . and the content field of health psychology' (Belar and Deardorff 1995). In order to practise as a clinical health psychologist, it is generally accepted that someone would first gain training as a clinical psychologist and then later acquire an expertise in health psychology, which would involve an understanding of the theories and methods of health psychology and their application to the health care setting (Johnston and Kennedy 1998). A trained clinical health psychologist would tend to work within the field of physical health, including stress and pain management, rehabilitation for patients with chronic illnesses (e.g. cancer, HIV or cardiovascular disease) or the development of interventions for problems such as spinal cord injury and disfiguring surgery.

A professional health psychologist

A professional health psychologist is someone who is trained to an acceptable standard in health psychology and works as a health psychologist. Within the UK, the British Psychological Society has recently sanctioned the term 'Chartered Health Psychologist'. Across Europe, Australasia and the USA, the term 'professional health psychologist' or simply 'health psychologist' is used (Marks *et al.* 1998). Although still being considered by a range of committees, it is now generally agreed that a professional health psychologist should have experience in three areas: research, teaching and consultancy. In addition, they should be able to show a suitable knowledge base of academic health psychology normally by completing a higher degree in Health Psychology. Having demonstrated that they meet the required standards, a professional/chartered health psychologist could work as an academic within the higher education system, within the health promotion setting, within schools or industry, and/or work within the health service. The work could include research, teaching and the development and evaluation of interventions to reduce risk-related behaviour.

What are the aims of this book?

Health psychology is an expanding area in terms of teaching, research and practice. Health psychology *teaching* occurs at both the undergraduate and postgraduate level and is experienced by both mainstream psychology students and those studying other health-related subjects. Health psychology *research* also takes many forms. Undergraduates are often expected to produce research projects as part of their assessment, and academic staff and research teams carry out research to develop and test theories and to explore new areas. Such research often feeds directly into *practice*, with intervention programmes aiming to change the factors identified by research. This book aims to provide a comprehensive introduction to the main topics of health psychology. The book will focus on psychological theory supported by research. In addition, how these theories can be turned into practice will also be described.

The contents of this book

Health psychology emphasizes the role that *beliefs* and *behaviours* play in health and illness. The contents of this book reflect this emphasis and illustrate how different sets of beliefs relate to behaviours and how both these factors are associated with illness.

Chapters 2–4 emphasize beliefs. Chapter 2 examines changes in the causes of death over the twentieth century and why this shift suggests an increasing role for beliefs and behaviours. The chapter then assesses theories of health beliefs and the models that have been developed to describe beliefs and predict behaviour. Chapter 3 examines beliefs individuals have about illness and Chapter 4 examines health professionals' health beliefs in the context of doctor–patient communication.

Chapters 5–9 examine health-related behaviours. Chapter 5 describes theories of addictive behaviours and the factors that predict smoking and alcohol consumption. Chapter 6 examines theories of obesity, dieting and body dissatisfaction under- and over-eating and how eating behaviour relates to the individual's cognitive state. Chapter 7 describes the literature on exercise behaviour both in terms of its initiation and methods to encourage individuals to continue exercising. Chapter 8 examines sexual behaviour and the factors that predict self-protective behaviour both in terms of pregnancy avoidance and in the context of HIV. Chapter 9 examines screening as a health behaviour and assesses the psychological factors that relate to whether or not someone attends for a health check and the psychological consequences of screening programmes.

Chapters 10–14 examine the interrelationship between beliefs and behaviour and illness. Chapter 10 examines research on stress and the relationship between stress and illness, and assesses the possible effects of stress on illness via behaviour change. Chapter 11 focuses on pain and evaluates causes of pain perception and the role of beliefs and behaviour in pain perception. Chapter 12 specifically examines the interrelationships between beliefs, behaviour and health using the example of placebo effects. Chapter 13 illustrates this interrelationship in the context of illness, focusing on HIV, cancer and coronary heart disease. Chapter 14 explores the problems with measuring health status and the issues surrounding the measurement of quality of life.

Finally, Chapter 15 examines some of the assumptions within health psychology that are described throughout the book.

The structure of this book

This book takes the format of a complete course in health psychology. Each chapter could be used as the basis for a lecture and/or reading for a lecture and consists of the following features:

- A chapter overview, which outlines the content and aims of the chapter.
- A set of questions for seminar discussion or essay titles.
- Recommendations for further reading.
- Diagrams to illustrate the models and theories discussed within the text.
- A 'Focus on research' section, which aims to illustrate two aspects of health psychology: (1) 'testing a theory', which examines how a theory can be turned into a research project with a description of the background, methods used (including details of measures), results and conclusions for each paper chosen; and (2) 'putting theory into practice', which examines how a theory can be used to develop an intervention. Each 'Focus on research' section takes one specific paper that has been chosen as a good illustration of either theory testing or practical implications.
- An 'assumptions in health psychology' section, which examines some of the assumptions that underlie both the research and practice in health psychology, such as the role of methodology and the relationship

between the mind and body. These assumptions are addressed together in Chapter 15.

In addition, there is a glossary at the end of the book, which describes terms within health psychology relating to methodology.

Questions

1 To what extent does health psychology challenge the assumptions of the biomedical model of health and illness?

2 Discuss the interactions described by the biopsychosocial model of health.

3 Discuss the role of the whole person in health psychology.

4 What are the implications of health psychology for the mind–body debate?

5 Design a research study to evaluate the role of the biopsychosocial model in predicting an illness of your choice.

For discussion

Consider the last time you were ill (e.g. flu, headache, cold, etc.). Discuss the extent to which factors other than biological ones may have contributed to your illness.

Further reading

Carroll, D., Bennett, P. and Davey Smith, G. (1993) Socio-economic health inequalities: their origins and implications, *Psychology and Health*, 8: 295–316.
This paper discusses the problematic relationship between inequality and health status and illustrates an integration of psychological factors with the wider social world.

Johnston, M. and Weinman J. (1995) Health Psychology, in *British Psychological Society: Professional Psychology Handbook*, pp. 61–8. Leicester: BPS Books.
This chapter describes the different skills of a health psychologist, where they might be employed and the types of work they might be involved in.

Kaplan, R.M. (1990) Behaviour as the central outcome in health care, *American Psychologist*, 45: 1211–20.
This paper provides an interesting discussion about the aims of health psychology and suggests that rather than focusing on biological outcomes, such as longevity and cell pathology, researchers should aim to change behaviour and should therefore evaluate the success of any interventions on the basis of whether this aim has been achieved.

Maes, S. and Kittel, F. (1990) Training research health psychologists, *Psychology and Health*, 4: 39–50.

This paper discusses the interrelationship between research, theory and practice in health psychology and focuses on the specific skills involved in being a research health psychologist.

CHAPTER 2

Health beliefs

Chapter overview

Changes in causes of death throughout the twentieth century can in part be explained in terms of changes of behaviour-related illnesses, such as coronary heart disease, cancers and HIV. This chapter examines theories of health behaviours and the extent to which health behaviours can be predicted by health beliefs such as the attributions about causes of health and behaviour, perceptions of risk and the stages of change model. In particular, the chapter describes the integration of these different types of health beliefs in the form of models (health belief model, protection motivation theory, theory of planned behaviour, health action process approach). In addition, it explores new developments within social cognition models in terms of new variables that predict behavioural intentions and studies that address the gap between behavioural intentions and actual behaviour. Finally, there is an examination of lay theories of health.

This chapter covers:

- What are health behaviours?
- Why study health behaviours?
- What factors predict health behaviours?
- Social cognition models
- New developments
- The intention–behaviour gap
- Lay theories about health

What are health behaviours?

Kasl and Cobb (1966) defined three types of health-related behaviours. They suggested that:

- a *health behaviour* was a behaviour aimed to prevent disease (e.g. eating a healthy diet);
- an *illness behaviour* was a behaviour aimed to seek remedy (e.g. going to the doctor);
- a *sick role behaviour* was any activity aimed to get well (e.g. taking prescribed medication, resting).

Health behaviours were further defined by Matarazzo (1984) in terms of either:

- *health impairing habits*, which he called 'behavioural pathogens' (e.g. smoking, eating a high fat diet), or
- *health protective behaviours*, which he defined as 'behavioural immunogens' (e.g. attending a health check).

In short, Matarazzo distinguished between those behaviours that have a negative effect (the behavioural pathogens, such as smoking, eating foods high in fat, drinking large amounts of alcohol) and those behaviours that may have a positive effect (the behavioural immunogens, such as tooth brushing, wearing seat belts, seeking health information, having regular check-ups, sleeping an adequate number of hours per night).

Generally health behaviours are regarded as behaviours that are related to the health status of the individual.

Why study health behaviours?

Over the past century health behaviours have played an increasingly important role in health and illness. This relationship has been highlighted by McKeown (1979).

McKeown's thesis

The decline of infectious diseases

In his book *The Role of Medicine* (1979) Thomas McKeown examined the impact of medicine on health since the seventeenth century. In particular, he evaluated the widely held assumptions about medicine's achievements and the role of medicine in reducing the prevalence and incidence of infectious illnesses, such as tuberculosis, pneumonia, measles, influenza, diphtheria, smallpox and whooping cough. McKeown argued that the commonly held view was that the decline in illnesses, such as TB, measles, smallpox and whooping cough, was related to medical interventions such

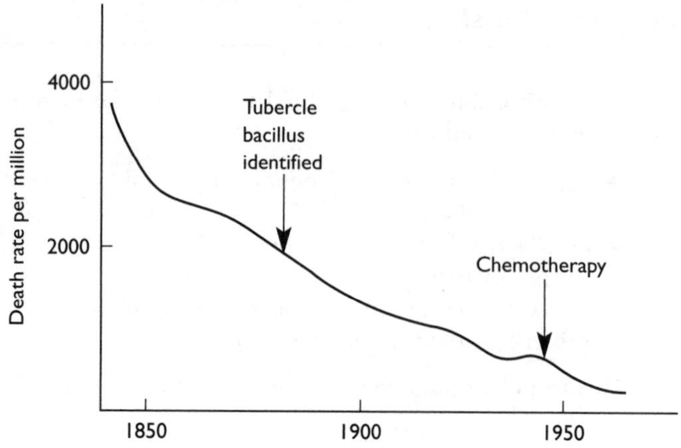

Figure 2.1 Decline in mortality from tuberculosis

as chemotherapy and vaccinations; for example, that antibiotics were responsible for the decline in illnesses such as pneumonia and flu. He showed, however, that the reduction in such illnesses was already underway before the development of the relevant medical interventions. This is illustrated in Fig. 2.1 for tuberculosis.

McKeown therefore claimed that the decline in infectious diseases seen throughout the past three centuries is best understood not in terms of medical intervention, but in terms of social and environmental factors. He argued that:

> The influences which led to [the] predominance [of infectious diseases] from the time of the first agricultural revolution 10,000 years ago were insufficient food, environmental hazards and excessive numbers and the measures which led to their decline from the time of the modern Agricultural and Industrial revolutions were predictably improved nutrition, better hygiene and contraception.
>
> (McKeown 1979: 117)

The role of behaviour

McKeown also examined health and illness throughout the twentieth century. He argued that contemporary illness is caused by 'influences . . . which the individual determines by his own behaviour (smoking, eating, exercise, and the like)' (p. 118) and claimed that 'it is on modification of personal habits such as smoking and sedentary living that health primarily depends' (p. 124). To support this thesis, McKeown examined the main causes of death in affluent societies and observed that most dominant illnesses, such as lung cancer, coronary heart disease, cirrhosis of the liver, are caused by behaviours.

Behaviour and mortality

It has been suggested that 50 per cent of mortality from the ten leading causes of death is due to behaviour. This indicates that behaviour and lifestyle have a potentially major effect on longevity. For example, Doll and Peto (1981) reported estimates of the role of different factors as causes for all cancer deaths. They estimated that tobacco consumption accounts for 30 per cent of all cancer deaths, alcohol 3 per cent, diet 35 per cent and reproductive and sexual behaviour 7 per cent. Accordingly, approximately 75 per cent of all deaths due to cancer are related to behaviour. More specifically, lung cancer, which is the most common form of cancer, accounts for 36 per cent of all cancer deaths in men and 15 per cent in women in the UK. It has been calculated that 90 per cent of all lung cancer mortality is attributable to cigarette smoking, which is also linked to other illnesses such as cancers of the bladder, pancreas, mouth, larynx and oesophagus and coronary heart disease. The impact of smoking on mortality was shown by McKeown when he examined changes in life expectancies in males from 1838–54 to 1970. His data are shown in Fig. 2.2, which indicate that the increase in life expectancy shown in non-smokers is much reduced in smokers. The relationship between mortality and behaviour is also illustrated by bowel cancer, which accounts for 11 per cent of all cancer deaths in men and 14 per cent in women. Research suggests that bowel cancer is linked to behaviours such as a diet high in total fat, high in meat and low in fibre.

Longevity: Cross-cultural differences

The relationship between behaviour and mortality can also be illustrated by the longevity of people in different countries. For example, in the USA and the UK, only three people out of every 100,000 live to be over 100. However, in Georgia, among the Abkhazians, 400 out of every 100,000 live to be over 100, and the oldest recorded Abkhazian is 170 (although this is obviously problematic in terms of the validity of any written records in the early 1800s). Weg (1983) examined the longevity of the Abkhazians and suggested that their longevity relative to that in other countries was due to a combination of biological, lifestyle and social factors including:

- Genetics.
- The Abkhazians maintain vigorous work roles and habits.
- The Abkhazians have a diet low in saturated fat and meat and high in fruit and vegetables.
- The Abkhazians drink no alcohol, nor smoke nicotine.
- The Abkhazians have a high level of social support.
- They report low stress levels.

Analysis of this group of people suggests that health behaviours may be related to longevity and are therefore worthy of study. However, such cross-sectional studies are problematic to interpret, particularly in terms

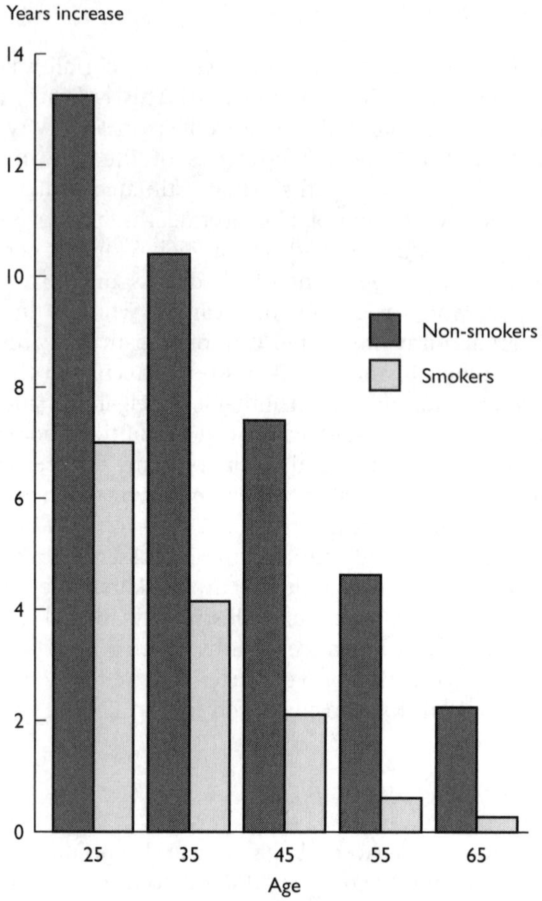

Figure 2.2 The effect of smoking on increase in expectation of life: Males, 1838–1970

of the direction of causality: Does the lifestyle of the Abkhazians cause their longevity or is it a product of it?

Longevity: The work of Belloc and Breslow

Belloc and Breslow (1972), Belloc (1973) and Breslow and Enstrom (1980) examined the relationship between mortality rates and behaviour among 7000 people. They concluded from this correlational analysis that seven behaviours were related to health status. These behaviours were:

1 sleeping 7–8 hours a day;
2 having breakfast every day;
3 not smoking;
4 rarely eating between meals;
5 being near or at prescribed weight;

6 having moderate or no use of alcohol;
7 taking regular exercise.

The sample was followed up over $5^1/2$ and 10 years in a prospective study and the authors reported that these seven behaviours were related to mortality. In addition, they suggested for people aged over 75 who carried out all of these health behaviours, health was comparable to those aged 35–44 who followed less than three.

Health behaviours seem to be important in predicting mortality and the longevity of individuals. Health psychologists have therefore attempted to understand and predict health-related behaviours.

What factors predict health behaviours?

Several correlational studies have attempted to predict these behaviours. For example, Kristiansen (1985) carried out a correlational study looking at the seven health behaviours defined by Belloc and Breslow and their relationship to a set of beliefs. She reported that these seven health behaviours were correlated with (1) a high value on health, (2) a belief in world peace and (3) a low value on an exciting life. Obviously there are problems with defining these different beliefs, but the study suggested that it is perhaps possible to predict health behaviours.

Leventhal *et al.* (1985) described factors that they believed predicted health behaviours:

- social factors, such as learning, reinforcement, modelling and social norms;
- genetics, suggesting that perhaps there was some evidence for a genetic basis for alcohol use;
- emotional factors, such as anxiety, stress, tension and fear;
- perceived symptoms, such as pain, breathlessness and fatigue;
- the beliefs of the patient;
- the beliefs of the health professionals.

Leventhal *et al.* suggested that a combination of these factors could be used to predict and promote health-related behaviour.

In fact, most of the research that has aimed to predict health behaviours has emphasized beliefs. Approaches to health beliefs include attribution theory, the health locus of control, unrealistic optimism and the stages of change model.

Attribution theory

The development of attribution theory

The origins of attribution theory can be found in the work of Heider (1944, 1958), who argued that individuals are motivated to see their social world as predictable and controllable – that is, a need to understand causality. Kelley (1967, 1971) developed these original ideas and proposed a clearly defined attribution theory suggesting that attributions about causality were structured according to causal schemata made up of the following criteria:

- *Distinctiveness*: the attribution about the cause of a behaviour is specific to the individual carrying out the behaviour.
- *Consensus*: the attribution about the cause of a behaviour would be shared by others.
- *Consistency over time*: the same attribution about causality would be made at any other time.
- *Consistency over modality*: the same attribution would be made in a different situation.

Kelley argued that attributions are made according to these different criteria and that the type of attribution made (e.g. high distinctiveness, low consensus, low consistency over time, low consistency over modality) determine the extent to which the cause of a behaviour is regarded as a product of a characteristic internal to the individual or external (i.e. the environment or situation).

Since its original formulation, attribution theory has been developed extensively and differentiations have been made between self-attributions (i.e. attributions about one's own behaviour) and other attributions (i.e. attributions made about the behaviour of others). In addition, the dimensions of attribution have been redefined as follows:

- *internal vs external* (e.g. my failure to get a job is due to my poor performance in the interview vs the interviewer's prejudice);
- *stable vs unstable* (e.g. the cause of my failure to get a job will always be around vs was specific to that one event)
- *global vs specific* (e.g. the cause of my failure to get the job influences other areas of my life vs only influenced this specific job interview)
- *controllable vs uncontrollable* (e.g. the cause of my failure to get a job was controllable by me vs was uncontrollable by me).

Brickman *et al.* (1982) have also distinguished between attributions made about the causes of a problem and attributions made about the possible solution. For example, they claimed that whereas an alcoholic may believe that he is responsible for becoming an alcoholic due to his lack of willpower (an attribution for the cause), he may believe that the medical profession is responsible for making him well again (an attribution for the solution).

Attributions for health-related behaviours

Over recent years, attribution theory has been applied to the study of health and health-related behaviour. Herzlich (1973) interviewed 80 people about the general causes of health and illness and found that health is regarded as internal to the individual and illness is seen as something that comes into the body from the external world.

More specifically, attributions about illness may be related to behaviours. For example, Bradley (1985) examined patients' attributions for responsibility for their diabetes and reported that perceived control over illness ('is the diabetes controllable by me or a powerful other?') influenced the choice of treatment by these patients. Patients could either choose (1) an insulin pump (a small mechanical device attached to the skin, which provides a continuous flow of insulin), (2) intense conventional treatment, or (3) a continuation of daily injections. The results indicated that the patients who chose an insulin pump showed decreased control over their diabetes and increased control attributed to powerful doctors. Therefore, if an individual attributed their illness externally and felt that they personally were not responsible for it, they were more likely to choose the insulin pump and were more likely to hand over responsibility to the doctors. A further study by King (1982) examined the relationship between attributions for an illness and attendance at a screening clinic for hypertension. The results demonstrated that if the hypertension was seen as external but controllable by the individual then they were more likely to attend the screening clinic ('I am not responsible for my hypertension but I can control it').

Health locus of control

The internal versus external dimension of attribution theory has been specifically applied to health in terms of the concept of a health locus of control. Individuals differ as to whether they tend to regard events as controllable by them (an internal locus of control) or uncontrollable by them (an external locus of control). Wallston and Wallston (1982) developed a measure of the health locus of control which evaluates whether an individual regards their health as controllable by them (e.g. 'I am directly responsible for my health'), whether they believe their health is not controllable by them and in the hands of fate (e.g. 'whether I am well or not is a matter of luck'), or whether they regard their health as under the control of powerful others (e.g. 'I can only do what my doctor tells me to do'). Health locus of control has been shown to be related to whether an individual changes their behaviour (e.g. gives up smoking) and to the kind of communication style they require from health professionals. For example, if a doctor encourages an individual who is generally external to change their lifestyle, the individual is unlikely to comply if they do not deem themselves responsible for their health. The health locus of control is illustrated in **Focus on research 9.1** (pages 215–18).

Although, the concept of a health locus of control is intuitively interesting, there are several problems with it:

- Is health locus of control a state or a trait? (Am I always internal?)
- Is it possible to be both external and internal?
- Is going to the doctor for help external (the doctor is a powerful other who can make me well) or internal (I am determining my health status by searching out appropriate intervention)?

Unrealistic optimism

Weinstein (1983, 1984) suggested that one of the reasons why people continue to practise unhealthy behaviours is due to inaccurate perceptions of risk and susceptibility – their unrealistic optimism. He asked subjects to examine a list of health problems and to state 'compared to other people of your age and sex, what are your chances of getting [the problem] greater than, about the same, or less than theirs?' The results of the study showed that most subjects believed that they were less likely to get the health problem. Weinstein called this phenomenon unrealistic optimism as he argued that not everyone can be less likely to contract an illness. Weinstein (1987) described four cognitive factors that contribute to unrealistic optimism: (1) lack of personal experience with the problem; (2) the belief that the problem is preventable by individual action; (3) the belief that if the problem has not yet appeared, it will not appear in the future; and (4) the belief that the problem is infrequent. These factors suggest that perception of own risk is not a rational process.

In an attempt to explain why individuals' assessment of their risk may go wrong, and why people are unrealistically optimistic, Weinstein (1983) argued that individuals show selective focus. He claimed that individuals ignore their own risk-increasing behaviour ('I may not always practise safe sex but that's not important') and focus primarily on their risk-reducing behaviour ('but at least I don't inject drugs'). He also argues that this selectivity is compounded by egocentrism; individuals tend to ignore others' risk-decreasing behaviour ('my friends all practise safe sex but that's irrelevant'). Therefore, an individual may be unrealistically optimistic if they focus on the times they use condoms when assessing their own risk and ignore the times they don't and, in addition, focus on the times that others around them don't practise safe sex and ignore the times that they do.

In a recent study, subjects were required to focus on either their risk-increasing ('unsafe sex') or their risk-decreasing behaviour ('safe sex'). The effect of this on their unrealistic optimism for risk of HIV was examined (Hoppe and Ogden, 1996). Heterosexual subjects were asked to complete a questionnaire concerning their beliefs about HIV and their sexual behaviour. Subjects were allocated to either the risk-increasing or risk-decreasing condition. Subjects in the risk-increasing condition were asked to complete questions such as 'since being sexually active how often have you asked about your partners' HIV status?' It was assumed that only a few subjects would be able to answer that they had done this frequently, thus making them feel more at risk. Subjects in the risk-decreasing condition were asked questions such as 'since being sexually active how often have you tried to select your partners carefully?' It was believed that most subjects would answer that they did this, making them feel less at risk. The results showed that focusing on risk-decreasing factors increased optimism by increasing perceptions of others' risk. Therefore, by encouraging the subjects to focus on their own healthy behaviour ('I select my partners carefully'), they felt more unrealistically optimistic and rated themselves as less at risk compared with those who they perceived as being more at risk.

The stages of change model

The transtheoretical model of behaviour change was originally developed by Prochaska and DiClemente (1982) as a synthesis of 18 therapies describing the processes involved in eliciting and maintaining change. It is now more commonly known as the stages of change model. Prochaska and DiClemente examined these different therapeutic approaches for common processes and suggested a new model of behaviour change based on the following stages:

1 *Precontemplation*: not intending to make any changes.
2 *Contemplation*: considering a change.
3 *Preparation*: making small changes.
4 *Action*: actively engaging in a new behaviour.
5 *Maintenance*: sustaining the change over time.

These stages, however, do not always occur in a linear fashion (simply moving from 1 to 5) but the theory describes behaviour change as dynamic and not 'all or nothing'. For example, an individual may move to the preparation stage and then back to the contemplation stage several times before progressing to the action stage. Furthermore, even when an individual has reached the maintenance stage, they may slip back to the contemplation stage over time.

The model also examines how the individual weighs up the costs and benefits of a particular behaviour. In particular, its authors argue that individuals at different stages of change will differentially focus on either the costs of a behaviour (e.g. stopping smoking will make me anxious in company) or the benefits of the behaviour (e.g. stopping smoking will improve my health). For example, a smoker at the action (I have stopped smoking) and the maintenance (for four months) stages tend to focus on the favourable and positive feature of their behaviour (I feel healthier because I have stopped smoking), whereas smokers in the precontemplation stage tend to focus on the negative features of the behaviour (it will make me anxious).

The stages of change model has been applied to several health-related behaviours, such as smoking, alcohol use, exercise and screening behaviour (e.g. DiClemente *et al.* 1991; Marcus *et al.* 1992). If applied to smoking cessation, the model would suggest the following set of beliefs and behaviours at the different stages:

1 *Precontemplation*: 'I am happy being a smoker and intend to continue smoking'.
2 *Contemplation*: 'I have been coughing a lot recently, perhaps I should think about stopping smoking'.
3 *Preparation*: 'I will stop going to the pub and will buy lower tar cigarettes'.

4 *Action*: 'I have stopped smoking'.
5 *Maintenance*: 'I have stopped smoking for 4 months now'.

This individual, however, may well move back at times to believing that they will continue to smoke and may relapse (called the revolving door schema). The stages of change model is illustrated in **Focus on research 5.1** (pages 106–13).

The stages of change model is increasingly used both in research and as a basis to develop interventions that are tailored to the particular stage of the specific person concerned. For example, a smoker who has been identified as being at the preparation stage would receive a different intervention to one who was at the contemplation stage. However, the model has recently been criticized for the following reasons (Weinstein *et al.* 1998; Sutton, in press):

- It is difficult to determine whether behaviour change occurs according to stages or along a continuum: the absence of qualitative differences between stages could either be due to the absence of stages or because the stages have not been correctly assessed and identified.
- Changes between stages may happen so quickly as to make the stages unimportant.
- Interventions that have been based on the stages of change model may work because the individual believes that they are receiving special attention, rather than because of the effectiveness of the model *per se*.
- Most studies based on the stages of change model use cross-sectional designs to examine differences between different people at different stages of change. Such designs do not allow conclusions to be drawn about the role of different causal factors at the different stages (i.e. people at the preparation stage are driven forward by different factors than those at the contemplation stage). Experimental and longitudinal studies are needed for any conclusions about causality to be valid.

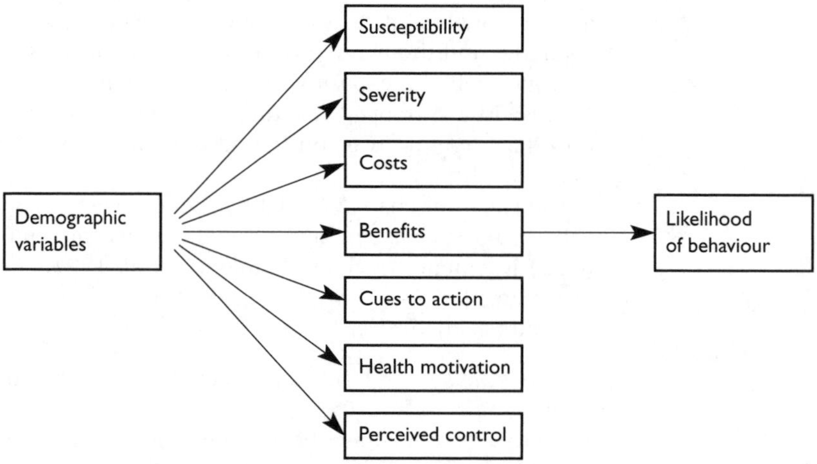

Figure 2.3 Basics of the health belief model

Integrating these different health beliefs: developing models

In summary, attribution theory and the health locus of control emphasize attributions for causality and control, unrealistic optimism focuses on perceptions of susceptibility and risk and the stages of change model emphasizes the dynamic nature of beliefs, time and costs and benefits. These different aspects of health beliefs have been integrated into structured models of health beliefs and behaviour. For simplicity, these models are often all called *social cognition models* as they regard cognitions as being shared by individuals within the same society. However, for the purpose of this chapter these models will be divided into *cognition models* and *social cognition models* in order to illustrate the varying extent to which the models specifically place cognitions within a social context.

Cognition models

Cognition models examine the predictors and precursors to health behaviours. They are derived from subjective expected utility (SEU) theory (Edwards 1954), which suggested that behaviours result from a rational weighing up of the potential costs and benefits of that behaviour. Cognition models describe behaviour as a result of rational information processing and emphasize individual cognitions, not the social context of those cognitions. This section examines the health belief model and the protection motivation theory.

The health belief model

The health belief model (HBM; see Fig. 2.3) was developed initially by Rosenstock (1966) and further by Becker and colleagues throughout the 1970s and 1980s in order to predict preventative health behaviours and also the behavioural response to treatment in acutely and chronically ill patients. However, over recent years, the health belief model has been used to predict a wide variety of health-related behaviours.

Components of the HBM

The HBM predicts that behaviour is a result of a set of core beliefs, which have been redefined over the years. The original core beliefs are the individual's perception of:

- susceptibility to illness (e.g. 'my chances of getting lung cancer are high');
- the severity of the illness (e.g. 'lung cancer is a serious illness');
- the costs involved in carrying out the behaviour (e.g. 'stopping smoking will make me irritable');

- the benefits involved in carrying out the behaviour (e.g. 'stopping smoking will save me money');
- cues to action, which may be internal (e.g. the symptom of breathlessness), or external (e.g. information in the form of health education leaflets).

The HBM suggests that these core beliefs should be used to predict *the likelihood that a behaviour will occur*. In response to criticisms the HBM has been revised originally to add the construct 'health motivation' to reflect an individual's readiness to be concerned about health matters (e.g. 'I am concerned that smoking might damage my health'). More recently, Becker and Rosenstock (1987) have also suggested that perceived control (e.g. 'I am confident that I can stop smoking') should be added to the model.

Using the HBM

If applied to a health-related behaviour such as screening for cervical cancer, the HBM predicts regular screening for cervical cancer if an individual perceives that she is highly susceptible to cancer of the cervix, that cervical cancer is a severe health threat, that the benefits of regular screening are high, and that the costs of such action are comparatively low. This will also be true if she is subjected to cues to action that are external, such as a leaflet in the doctor's waiting room, or internal, such as a symptom perceived to be related to cervical cancer (whether correct or not), such as pain or irritation. When using the new amended HBM, the model would also predict that a woman would attend for screening if she is confident that she can do so and if she is motivated to maintain her health. Using the HBM to predict screening behaviour is described in **Focus on research 9.1** (pages 215–18).

Support for the HBM

Several studies support the predictions of the HBM. Research indicates that dietary compliance, safe sex, having vaccinations, making regular dental visits and taking part in regular exercise programmes are related to the individual's perception of susceptibility to the related health problem, to their belief that the problem is severe and their perception that the benefits of preventative action outweigh the costs (e.g. Becker 1974; Becker *et al.* 1977; Becker and Rosenstock 1984).

Research also provides support for individual components of the model. Norman and Fitter (1989) examined health screening behaviour and found that perceived barriers are the greatest predictors of clinic attendance. Several studies have examined breast self-examination behaviour and report that barriers (Lashley 1987; Wyper 1990) and perceived susceptibility (Wyper 1990) are the best predictors of healthy behaviour.

Research has also provided support for the role of cues to action in predicting health behaviours, in particular external cues such as informational input. In fact, health promotion uses such informational input to change beliefs and consequently promote future healthy behaviour. Information in the form of fear-arousing warnings may change attitudes and health behaviour in such areas as dental health, safe driving and smoking (e.g. Sutton 1982; Sutton and Hallett 1989). General information regarding the negative consequences of a behaviour is also used both in the prevention and cessation of smoking behaviour (e.g. Sutton 1982; Flay 1985). Health information aims to increase knowledge and several studies report a significant relationship between illness knowledge and preventive health behaviour. Rimer *et al.* (1991) report that knowledge about breast cancer is related to having regular mammograms. Several studies have also indicated a positive correlation between knowledge about breast self-examination (BSE) and breast cancer and performing BSE (Alagna and Reddy 1984; Lashley 1987; Champion 1990). One study manipulated knowledge about pap tests for cervical cancer by showing subjects an informative videotape and reported that the resulting increased knowledge was related to future healthy behaviour (O'Brien and Lee 1990).

Conflicting findings

However, several studies have reported conflicting findings. Janz and Becker (1984) found that healthy behavioural intentions are related to low perceived seriousness, not high as predicted, and several studies have suggested an association between low susceptibility (not high) and healthy behaviour (Becker *et al.* 1975; Langlie 1977). Hill *et al.* (1985) applied the HBM to cervical cancer, to examine which factors predicted cervical screening behaviour. The results suggested that barriers to action was the best predictor of behavioural intentions and that perceived susceptibility to cervical cancer was also significantly related to screening behaviour. However, benefits and perceived seriousness were not related. Janz and Becker (1984) carried out a study using the health belief model and found that the best predictors of health behaviour are perceived barriers and perceived susceptibility to illness. However, Becker and Rosenstock (1984) in a review of 19 studies using a meta-analysis that included measures of the health belief model to predict compliance, calculated that the best predictors of compliance are the costs and benefits and the perceived seriousness.

Criticisms of the HBM

The HBM has been criticized for these conflicting results. It has also been criticized for several other weaknesses, including:

- Its focus on rational processing of information. (Is tooth brushing really determined by weighing up the pros and cons?)
- Its emphasis on the individual. (What role does the social and economic environment play?)

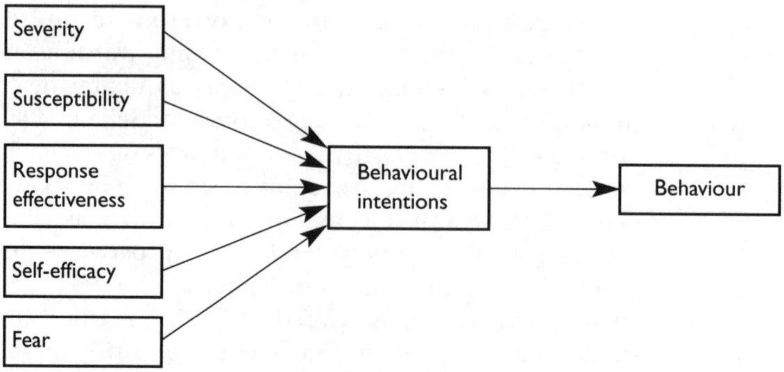

Figure 2.4 Basics of the protection motivation theory

- The interrelationship between the different core beliefs. (How should these be measured and how should they be related to each other? Is the model linear or multifactorial?)
- The absence of a role for emotional factors such as fear and denial.
- It has been suggested that alternative factors may predict health behaviour, such as outcome expectancy and self-efficacy (Seydel *et al.* 1990; Schwarzer 1992).
- Schwarzer (1992) has further criticized the HBM for its static approach to health beliefs and suggests that within the HBM, beliefs are described as occurring simultaneously with no room for change, development or process.
- Leventhal *et al.* (1985) have argued that health-related behaviour is due to the perception of symptoms rather than to the individual factors as suggested by the HBM.

Although there is much contradiction in the literature surrounding the HBM, it might be concluded that elements of this model may predict screening for hypertension, screening for cervical cancer, genetic screening, exercise behaviour, decreased alcohol use, changes in diet and smoking cessation.

The protection motivation theory

Rogers (1975, 1983, 1985) developed the protection motivation theory (PMT) (see Fig. 2.4), which expanded the HBM to include additional factors.

Components of the PMT

The original protection motivation theory claimed that health-related behaviours are a product of four components:

1 Severity (e.g. 'Bowel cancer is a serious illness');
2 Susceptibility (e.g. 'My chances of getting bowel cancer are high').

3 Response effectiveness (e.g. 'Changing my diet would improve my health');
4 Self-efficacy (e.g. 'I am confident that I can change my diet');

These components predict *behavioural intentions* (e.g. 'I intend to change my behaviour'), which are related to behaviour. Recently, Rogers has also suggested a role for a fifth component, fear (e.g. an emotional response), in response to education or information. The PMT describes severity, susceptibility and fear as relating to *threat appraisal* (i.e. appraising to outside threat) and response effectiveness and self-efficacy as relating to *coping appraisal* (i.e. appraising the individual themselves). According to the PMT, there are two types of sources of information, environmental (e.g. verbal persuasion, observational learning) and intrapersonal (e.g. prior experience). This information influences the five components of the PMT (self-efficacy, response effectiveness, severity, susceptibility, fear), which then elicit either an 'adaptive' coping response (i.e. behavioural intention) or a 'maladaptive' coping response (e.g. avoidance, denial).

Using the PMT

If applied to dietary change, the PMT would make the following predictions: information about the role of a high fat diet in coronary heart disease would increase fear, increase the individual's perception of how serious coronary heart disease was (perceived severity) and increase their belief that they were likely to have a heart attack (perceived susceptibility/susceptibility). If the individual also felt confident that they could change their diet (self-efficacy) and that this change would have beneficial consequences (response effectiveness), they would report high intentions to change their behaviour (behavioural intentions). This would be seen as an adaptive coping response to the information. The PMT is illustrated in **Focus on research 2.1** (pages 28–9).

Support for the PMT

Rippetoe and Rogers (1987) gave women information about breast cancer and examined the effect of this information on the components of the PMT and their relationship to the women's intentions to practise breast self-examination (BSE). The results showed that the best predictors of intentions to practise BSE were response effectiveness, severity and self-efficacy. In a further study, the effects of persuasive appeals for increasing exercise on intentions to exercise were evaluated using the components of the PMT. The results showed that susceptibility and self-efficacy predicted exercise intentions but that none of the variables were related to self-reports of actual behaviour. In another study, Beck and Lund (1981) manipulated dental students' beliefs about tooth decay using persuasive communication. The results showed that the information increased fear and that severity and self-efficacy were related to behavioural intentions.

FOCUS ON RESEARCH 2.1

TESTING A THEORY – PREDICTING SEXUAL BEHAVIOUR

A study to predict sexual behaviour and behavioural intentions using the protection motivation theory (van der Velde and van der Pligt 1991)

This study integrates the protection motivation theory (PMT) with other cognitions in order to predict sexual behaviour in the context of HIV. It highlights the possibility of adapting models to fit the specific factors related to a specific behaviour. This study is interesting as it represents an attempt to integrate different models of health behaviour.

Background

Since the identification of the HIV virus, research has developed means to predict and therefore promote safer sexual behaviour. The PMT suggests that behaviour is a consequence of an appraisal of the threat and an appraisal of the individual's coping resources. It suggests that these factors elicit a state called 'protection motivation', which maintains any activity to cope with the threat. This study examines the role of the PMT in predicting sexual behaviour and in addition examines the effect of expanding the PMT to include variables such as coping styles, social norms and previous behaviour.

Methodology

Subjects 147 homosexual and 84 heterosexual subjects with multiple partners in the past 6 months took part in the study. They were recruited from Amsterdam through a variety of sources including informants, advertisements and a housing service.
Design Subjects completed a questionnaire (either postal or delivered).
Questionnaire The questionnaire consisted of items on the following areas rated on a 5-point Likert scale:

1 *Sexual behaviour and behavioural intentions*: the subjects were asked about their sexual behaviour during the previous 6 months, including the number and type of partners, frequencies of various sexual techniques, condom use and future intentions.
2 *Protection motivation variables*: (a) perceived severity, (b) perceived susceptibility, (c) response efficacy, (d) self-efficacy, (e) fear.
3 *Additional beliefs*: (a) social norms, (b) costs, (c) benefits, (d) knowledge, (e) situational constraints.

4 In addition, the authors included variables from Janis and Mann's (1977) conflict theory: (a) vigilance, (b) hypervigilance, (c) defensive avoidance.

Results

The results were analysed to examine the best predictors of sexual behaviour in both homosexual and heterosexual subjects. It was found that although the variables of the PMT were predictive of behaviour and behavioural intentions in both populations, the results were improved with the additional variables. For example, when social norms and previous behaviour were also considered, there was improved associations with future behaviour. In addition, the results suggested that although there was a relationship between fear and behavioural intentions, high levels of fear detracted from this relationship. The authors suggested that when experiencing excess fear, attention may be directed towards reducing anxiety, rather than actually avoiding danger through changing behaviour.

Conclusion

The results from this study support the use of the PMT to predict sexual behaviour in the context of HIV. Further, the model is improved by adding additional variables. Perhaps, rather than developing models that can be applied to a whole range of behaviours, individual models should be adapted for each specific behaviour. Furthermore, the results have implications for developing interventions, and indicate that the health education campaigns which promote fear may have negative effects, with individuals having to deal with the fear rather than changing their behaviour.

Criticisms of the PMT

The PMT has been less widely criticized than the health belief model; however, many of the criticisms of the HBM also relate to the PMT. For example, the PMT assumes that individuals are rational information processors (although it does include an element of irrationality in its fear component), it does not account for habitual behaviours, nor does it include a role for social and environmental factors. Schwarzer (1992) has also criticized the PMT for not explicitly examining behaviours in terms of process and change.

Social cognition models

Social cognition models examine factors that predict behaviour and/or behavioural intentions and in addition examine why individuals fail to maintain a behaviour to which they are committed. Social cognition theory was developed by Bandura (1977, 1986) and suggests that behaviour is governed by expectancies, incentives and social cognitions. Expectancies include:

- Situation outcome expectancies: the expectancy that a behaviour may be dangerous (e.g. 'smoking can cause lung cancer').
- Outcome expectancies: the expectancy that a behaviour can reduce the harm to health (e.g. 'stopping smoking can reduce the chances of lung cancer').
- Self-efficacy expectancies: the expectancy that the individual is capable of carrying out the desired behaviour (e.g. 'I can stop smoking if I want to').

The concept of *incentives* suggests that a behaviour is governed by its consequences. For example, smoking behaviour may be reinforced by the experience of reduced anxiety, having a cervical smear may be reinforced by a feeling of reassurance after a negative result.

Social cognitions are a central component of social cognition models. Although (as with cognition models) social cognition models regard individuals as information processors, there is an important difference between cognition models and social cognition models – social cognition models include measures of the *individual's representations of their social world.* Accordingly, social cognition models attempt to place the individual within the context both of other people and the broader social world. This is measured in terms of their normative beliefs (e.g. 'people who are important to me want me to stop smoking').

Several models have been developed using this perspective. This section examines the theory of planned behaviour (derived from the theory of reasoned action) and the health action process approach.

The theory of planned behaviour

The theory of reasoned action (TRA) (see Fig. 2.5) was extensively used to examine predictors of behaviours and was central to the debate within social psychology concerning the relationship between attitudes and behaviour (Fishbein 1967; Ajzen and Fishbein 1970; Fishbein and Ajzen 1975). The theory of reasoned action emphasized a central role for social cognitions in the form of subjective norms (the individual's beliefs about their social world) and included both beliefs and evaluations of these beliefs (both factors constituting the individual's attitudes). The TRA was therefore an important model as it placed the individual within the social context and in addition suggested a role for value which was in contrast to the traditional more rational approach to behaviour. The theory of

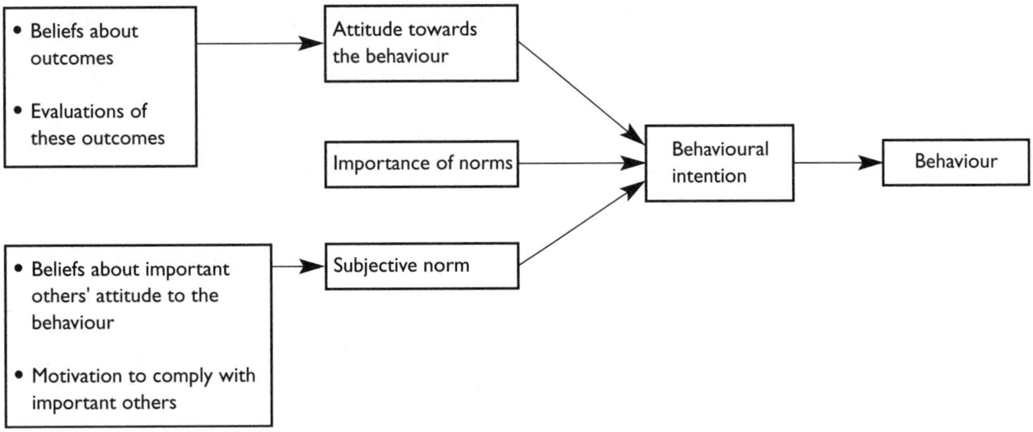

Figure 2.5 Basics of the theory of reasoned action

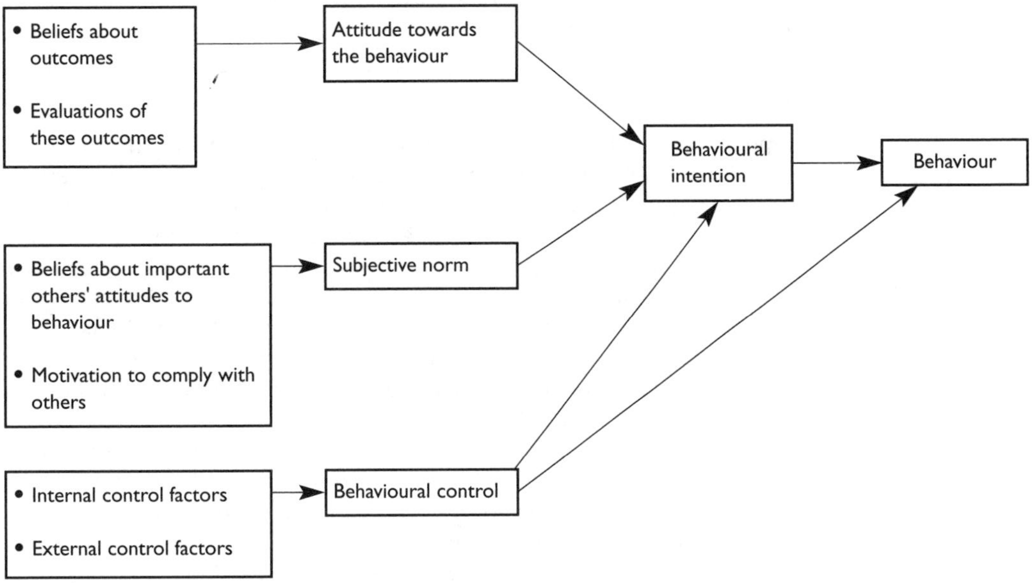

Figure 2.6 Basics of the theory of planned behaviour

planned behaviour (TPB) (see Fig. 2.6) was developed by Ajzen and colleagues (Ajzen 1985; Ajzen and Madden 1986; Ajzen 1988) and represented a progression from the TRA.

Components of the TPB

The TPB emphasizes *behavioural intentions* as the outcome of a combination of several beliefs. The theory proposes that intentions should be conceptualized as 'plans of action in pursuit of behavioural goals' (Ajzen and Madden 1986) and are a result of the following beliefs:

- Attitude towards a behaviour, which is composed of both a positive or negative evaluation of a particular behaviour and beliefs about the outcome of the behaviour (e.g. 'exercising is fun and will improve my health').
- Subjective norm, which is composed of the perception of social norms and pressures to perform a behaviour and an evaluation of whether the individual is motivated to comply with this pressure (e.g. 'people who are important to me will approve if I lose weight and I want their approval').
- Perceived behavioural control, which is composed of a belief that the individual can carry out a particular behaviour based upon a consideration of internal control factors (e.g. skills, abilities, information) and external control factors (e.g. obstacles, opportunities), both of which relate to past behaviour.

According to the TPB, these three factors predict behavioral intentions, which are then linked to behaviour. The TPB also states that perceived behavioural control can have a direct effect on behaviour without the mediating effect of behavioural intentions.

Using the TPB

If applied to alcohol consumption, the TPB would make the following predictions: if an individual believed that reducing their alcohol intake would make their life more productive and be beneficial to their health (attitude to the behaviour) and believed that the important people in their life wanted them to cut down (subjective norm), and in addition believed that they were capable of drinking less alcohol due to their past behaviour and evaluation of internal and external control factors (high behavioural control), then this would predict high intentions to reduce alcohol intake (behavioural intentions). The model also predicts that perceived behavioural control can predict behaviour without the influence of intentions. For example, if perceived behavioural control reflects actual control, a belief that the individual would not be able to exercise because they are physically incapable of exercising would be a better predictor of their exercising behaviour than their high intentions to exercise. Using the TPB to predict exercise is described in **Focus on research 7.2** (pages 177–9).

Support for the TPB

The theory of planned behaviour has been used to assess a variety of health-related behaviours. For example, Brubaker and Wickersham (1990) examined the role of the theory's different components in predicting testicular self-examination and reported that attitude towards the behaviour, subjective norm and behavioural control (measured as self-efficacy) correlated with the intention to perform the behaviour. A further study evaluated the TPB in relation to weight loss (Schifter and Ajzen 1985). The results showed that weight loss was predicted by the components of the model; in particular, goal attainment (weight loss) was linked to perceived behavioural control.

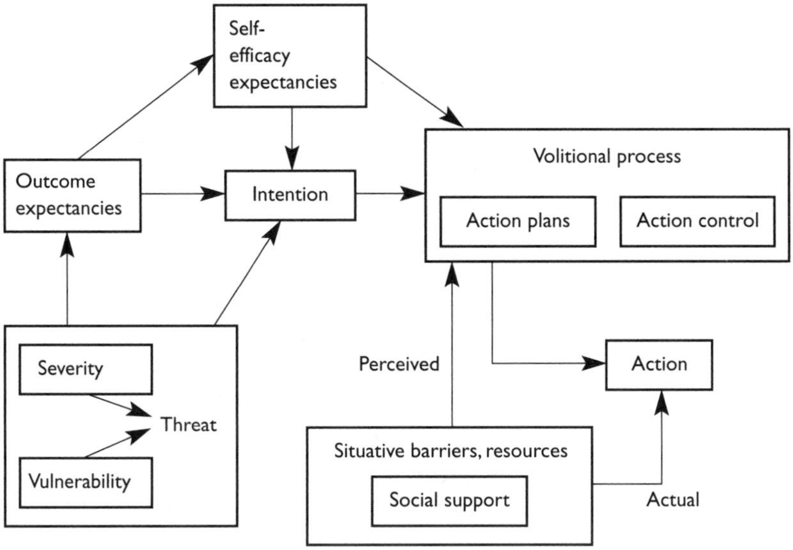

Figure 2.7 The health action process approach

Criticisms of the TPB

Schwarzer (1992) has criticized the TPB for its omission of a temporal element and argues that Ajzen does not describe either the order of the different beliefs or any direction of causality. However, in contrast to the HBM and the PMT, the model includes a degree of irrationality (in the form of evaluations) and attempts to address the problem of social and environmental factors (in the form of normative beliefs). In addition, it includes a role for past behaviour within the measure of perceived behavioural control.

The health action process approach

The health action process approach (HAPA) (see Fig. 2.7) was developed by Schwarzer (1992) following his review of the literature, which highlighted the need to include a temporal element into the understanding of beliefs and behaviour. In addition, it emphasized the importance of *self-efficacy* as a determinant of both behavioural intentions and self-reports of behaviour. The HAPA includes several elements from all previous theories and attempts to predict both behavioural intentions and actual behaviour.

Components of the HAPA

The main addition made by the HAPA to the existing theories is the distinction between a decision-making/motivational stage and an action/

maintenance stage. Therefore, the model adds a temporal and process factor to understanding the relationship between beliefs and behaviour and suggests individuals initially decide whether or not to carry out a behaviour (the *motivation* stage), and then make plans to initiate and maintain this behaviour (the *action* phase).

According to the HAPA, the motivation stage is made up of the following components:

- self-efficacy (e.g. 'I am confident that I can stop smoking');
- outcome expectancies (e.g. 'stopping smoking will improve my health'), which has a subset of social outcome expectancies (e.g. 'other people want me to stop smoking and if I stop smoking I will gain their approval');
- threat appraisal, which is composed of beliefs about the severity of an illness and perceptions of individual vulnerability.

According to the HAPA the end result of the HAPA is an intention to act.

The action stage is composed of cognitive (volitional), situational and behavioural factors. The integration of these factors determines the extent to which a behaviour is initiated and maintained via these self-regulatory processes. The cognitive factor is made up of action plans (e.g. 'if offered a cigarette when I am trying not to smoke I will imagine what the tar would do to my lungs') and action control (e.g. 'I can survive being offered a cigarette by reminding myself that I am a non-smoker'). These two cognitive factors determine the individual's determination of will. The situational factor consists of social support (e.g. the existence of friends who encourage non-smoking) and the absence of situational barriers (e.g. financial support to join an exercise club).

Schwarzer (1992) argued that the HAPA bridges the gap between intentions and behaviour and emphasizes self-efficacy, both in terms of developing the intention to act and also implicitly in terms of the cognitive stage of the action stage, whereby self-efficacy promotes and maintains action plans and action control, therefore contributing to the maintenance of the action. He maintained that the HAPA enables specific predictions to be made about causality and also describes a process of beliefs whereby behaviour is the result of a series of processes.

Support for the HAPA

The individual components of the HAPA have been tested providing some support for the model. In particular, Schwarzer (1992) claimed that self-efficacy was consistently the best predictor of behavioural intentions and behaviour change for a variety of behaviours such as the intention to dental floss, frequency of flossing, effective use of contraception, breast self-examination, drug addicts' intentions to use clean needles, intentions to quit smoking, and intentions to adhere to weight loss programmes and exercise (e.g. Beck and Lund 1981; Seydal *et al.* 1990).

Criticisms of the HAPA

Again, as with the other cognition and social cognition models, the following questions arise when assessing the value of the HAPA in predicting health behaviours:

1 Are individuals rational processors of information? Although the model includes measures of value, the role of other less rational factors, such as emotion, is neglected.
2 What role do social and environmental factors play? The social cognition models attempt to address the problem of the social world in their measures of normative beliefs. However, such measures only access the individual's cognitions about their social world.
3 Do these cognitive states exist or are they simply created by social cognitive theorists? That is, do terms such as 'action control', 'self-efficacy' and 'subjective norms' describe thoughts that individuals have prior to the theories or do the theories create these thoughts?

New developments

Therefore, cognition and social cognition models provide a structured approach to understanding health beliefs and predicting health behaviours. However, over recent years it has become clear that these models are not as useful as hoped. In particular, two main observations have been made. First, it has been suggested these models are not that successful at predicting behavioural intentions and that they should be expanded to incorporate new cognitions. Second, it has been argued that they are even less successful in predicting actual behaviour. This second criticism has resulted in research exploring the intention–behaviour gap.

Predicting intentions: the need to incorporate new cognitions

Sutton (1998) argued that studies using models of health beliefs only manage to predict between 40 and 50 per cent of the variance in behavioural intentions. Therefore, up to 50 per cent of the variance remains unexplained. Some new variables have been developed to improve the effectiveness of the models.

Moral norms

The theory of reasoned action and the theory of planned behaviour include measures of social pressures to behave in a particular way – the subjective norms variable. However, it has been suggested that they should also assess moral norms. For example, the intention to carry out behaviours that have an ethical or moral dimension such as donating blood, donating organs for transplant, committing driving offences or eating genetically produced food may result not only from general social norms but also moral norms. Some research has shown the usefulness of including a moral norms variable (e.g. Sparks 1994; Parker *et al.* 1995). However, moral norms may only be relevant to a limited range of behaviours (Norman and Conner 1996).

Anticipated regret

The protection motivation theory explicitly includes a role for emotion in the form of fear. Researchers have argued that behavioural intentions may be related to anticipated emotions. For example, the intention to practise safer sex 'I intend to use a condom' may be predicted by the anticipated feeling 'If I do not use a condom I will feel guilty'. Some research has shown that anticipated regret is important for predicting behavioural intentions (Richard and van der Pligt 1991).

Self-identity

The third variable which has been presented as a means to improve the model's ability to predict behavioural intentions is self-identity. It has been argued that individuals will only intend to carry out a behaviour if that behaviour fits with their own image of themselves. For example, the identity 'I am a healthy eater' should relate to the intention to eat healthily. Further, the identity 'I am a fit person' should relate to the intention to carry out exercise. Some research has supported the usefulness of this variable (Sparks and Shepherd 1992). However, Norman and Conner (1996) suggested that, as with moral norms, this variable may also only have limited relevance.

Predicting behaviour: exploring the intention–behaviour gap

Sutton (1998) argued that although structured models are ineffective at predicting behavioural intentions they are even less effective at predicting actual behaviour. In fact, he suggested that studies using these models only predict 19–38 per cent of the variance in behaviour. Some of this failure to predict behaviour may be due to the behaviour being beyond the control of the individual concerned. For example, 'I intend to study at university' may not be translated into 'I am studying at university' due to economic or educational factors. Further, 'I intend to eat healthily' may not be translated into 'I am eating healthily' due to the absence of healthy food. In such instances, the correlation between intentions and behaviour would be zero. However, for most behaviours the correlation between intentions and behaviour is not zero but small, suggesting that the individual does have some control over the behaviour. Psychologists have addressed the problem of predicting actual behaviour in three ways: (1) the concept of behavioural intentions has been expanded; (2) past behaviour has been used as a direct predictor of behaviour; and (3) variables that bridge the intention–behaviour gap have been studied.

Expanding behavioural intentions

Much of the research that uses models to predict health behaviours focuses on behavioural intentions as the best predictor of actual behaviour. However, recent researchers have called for additional variables to be added which expand behavioural intentions. These include the following:

- *Self-predictions* – Sheppard *et al.* (1988) argued that rather than just measuring behavioural intentions (i.e. 'I intend to start swimming next week') it is also important to assess an individual's own prediction that this intention is likely to be fulfilled (e.g. 'It is likely that I will start swimming next week'). They suggested that such self-predictions are more likely to reflect the individual's consideration of those factors that may help or hinder the behaviour itself. To date, some research supports the usefulness of this new variable (Sheppard *et al.* 1988) whilst some suggests that the correlation between intentions and self-predictions is too high for self-predictions to add anything extra to a model of health behaviour (Norman and Smith 1995).
- *Behavioural willingness* – Along similar lines to the introduction of self-predictions, researchers have called for the use of behavioural willingness. For example, an individual may not only intend to carry out a behaviour (e.g. 'I intend to eat more fruit') but is also willing to do so (e.g. 'I am willing to eat more fruit'). Gibbons *et al.* (1998) explored the usefulness of both intentions and willingness, and suggested that willingness may be of particular importance when exploring adolescent behaviour, as adolescents may behave in a less reasoned way, and be unwilling to carry out behaviour that is unpleasant ('I intend to stop smoking').
- *Perceived need* – It may not only be intentions to behave, or self-predictions or even willingness that are important. Paisley and Sparks (1998) argued that it is the perception by an individual that they need to change their behaviour which is critical. For example, an intention 'I intend to stop smoking' may be less influential than a perceived need to stop smoking 'I need to stop smoking'. They examined the role of perceived need in predicting expectations of reducing dietary fat and argued for the use of this variable in future research.

Therefore, by expanding behavioural intentions to include self-predictions, behavioural willingness and/or perceived need it is argued that the models will be become better predictors of actual behaviour.

The role of past behaviour

Most research assumes cognitions predict behavioural intentions, which in turn predict behaviour. This is in line with the shift from 'I think therefore I intend to do therefore I do'. However, it is possible that behaviour is not predicted by cognitions but by behaviour. The TPB includes a role for past behaviour. Much research has highlighted the central importance of this variable. Along these lines, individuals are more likely to eat healthily tomorrow if they ate healthily today. Further, they are more likely to go to the doctor for a cervical smear if they have done so in the past. Research has supported the role of past behaviour in terms of cycle helmet use (Quine *et al.* 1998), breast self-examination (Hodgkins and Orbell 1998) and attendance at health checks (Norman and Conner 1993). Therefore, including past behaviour may increase a model's ability to predict actual behaviour. In addition, past behaviour may itself predict cognitions that then predict behaviour (Gerrard *et al.* 1996).

Bridging the intention–behaviour gap

The third approach to address the limited way in which research has predicted behaviour has been to suggest variables that may bridge the gap between intentions to behave and actual behaviour. In particular, some research has highlighted the role of plans for action, health goals commitment and trying as a means to tap into the kinds of cognitions that may be responsible for the translation of intentions into behaviour (Bagozzi and Warshaw 1990; Schwarzer 1992; Bagozzi 1993). Most research, however, has focused on Gollwitzer's (1993) notion of implementation intentions. According to Gollwitzer, carrying out an intention involves the development of specific plans as to what an individual will do given a specific set of environmental factors. Therefore, implementation intentions describe the 'what' and the 'when' of a particular behaviour. For example, the intention 'I intend to stop smoking' will be more likely to be translated into 'I have stopped smoking' if the individual makes the implementation intention 'I intend to stop smoking tomorrow at 12.00 when I have finished my last packet'. Further, 'I intend to eat healthily' is more likely to be translated into 'I am eating healthily' if the implementation intention 'I will start to eat healthily by having an apple tomorrow lunchtime' is made. Some experimental research has shown that encouraging individuals to make implementation intentions can actually increase the correlation between intentions and behaviour for behaviours such as taking a vitamin C pill (Sheeran and Orbell 1998), performing breast self-examination (Orbell *et al.* 1997) and writing a report (Gollwitzer and Brandstatter 1997). This approach is also supported by the goal-setting approach of cognitive behavioural therapy. Therefore, by tapping into variables such as implementation intentions it is argued that the models may become better predictors of actual behaviour.

Lay theories about health

Other studies of health beliefs have also been developed which do not use the specific structure outlined by the above models. Such research has examined lay theories about health and has tended to use a qualitative methodology rather than a quantitative one.

In particular medical sociologists and social anthropologists have examined beliefs about health in terms of lay theories or lay representations. Using in-depth interviews to encourage subjects to talk freely, studies have explored the complex and elaborate beliefs that individuals have. Research in this area has shown that these lay theories are at least as elaborate and sophisticated as medicine's own explanatory models, even though they may be different. For example, medicine describes upper respiratory tract infections such as the common cold as self-limiting illnesses caused by viruses. However, Helman (1978) in his paper, 'Feed a cold starve a fever', explored how individuals make sense of the common cold and other associated problems and reported that such illnesses were analysed in terms of the dimensions hot–cold, wet–dry with respect to their aetiology and possible treatment. In a further study, Pill and Stott (1982) reported that working-class mothers were more likely to see illness as uncontrollable and to take a more fatalistic view of their health. In a recent study, Graham (1987) reported that, although women who smoke are aware of all the health risks of smoking, they report that smoking is necessary to their well-being and an essential means for coping with stress (see Chapter 4 for a further discussion of what people think health is). Lay theories have obvious implications for interventions by health professionals; communication between health professional and patient would be impossible if the patient held beliefs about their health that were in conflict with those held by the professional (see Chapter 4 for a discussion of communication).

To conclude

The role of health beliefs in predicting health-related behaviours has become increasingly salient with the recent changes in causes of mortality. Theories such as attribution theory, health locus of control, unrealistic optimism and the stages of change model have been adapted to examine beliefs about health and resulting behaviours. Psychologists have also developed structured models to integrate these different beliefs and to predict health behaviours such as the health belief model, the protection motivation theory, the theory of planned behaviour and the health action process approach. These models consider individuals to be processors of information and vary in the extent to which they address the individual's cognitions about their social world. The models can be used to predict health behaviours quantitatively and have implications for developing methods to promote change. Alternative views of health beliefs have emphasized lay theories, which present individuals as having complex views and theories about their health which influence their behaviour. This perspective regards individuals as less rational and examines lay theories in a relatively unstructured format using a qualitative approach.

Questions

1 Recent changes in mortality rates can be explained in terms of behaviour related illnesses. Discuss.

2 Discuss the contribution of attribution theory to understanding health behaviours.

3 Health beliefs predict health behaviours. Discuss with reference to two models.

4 Discuss the role of the social world in understanding health behaviours.

5 Human beings are rational information processors. Discuss.

6 Discuss the argument that changing an individual's beliefs would improve their health.

7 Models can only predict behavioural intentions, not actual behaviour. Discuss.

8 Design a research project to promote non-smoking in a group of smokers using two models of health beliefs.

For discussion

Consider a recent change in your health-related behaviours (e.g. stopped/started smoking, changed diet, aimed to get more sleep, etc.). Discuss your health beliefs that relate to this change.

Assumptions in health psychology

Research into health beliefs highlights some of the assumptions in health psychology:

1 *Human beings as rational information processors.* Many models of health beliefs assume that behaviour is a consequence of a series of rational stages that can be measured. For example, it is assumed that the individual weighs up the pros and cons of a behaviour, assesses the seriousness of a potentially dangerous illness and then decides how to act. This may not be the case for all behaviours. Even though some of the social cognition models include past behaviour (as a measure of habit), they still assume some degree of rationality.

2 *Cognitions as separate from each other.* The different models compartmentalize different cognitions (perceptions of severity, susceptibility, outcome expectancy, intentions) as if they are discrete and

separate entities. However, this separation may only be an artefact of asking questions relating to these different cognitions. For example, an individual may not perceive susceptibility (e.g. 'I am at risk from HIV') as separate to self-efficacy (e.g. 'I am confident that I can control my sexual behaviour and avoid HIV') until they are asked specific questions about these factors.

3 *Cognitions as separate from methodology*. In the same way that models assume that cognitions are separate from each other they also assume they exist independent of methodology. However, interview and questionnaire questions may actually create these cognitions.

4 *Cognitions without a context*. Models of health beliefs and health behaviours tend to examine an individual's cognitions out of context. This context could either be the context of another individual or the wider social context. Some of the models incorporate measures of the individuals' representations of their social context (e.g. social norms, peer group norms), but this context is always accessed via the individuals' cognitions.

Further reading

Conner, M. and Norman, P. (1996) *Predicting Health Behaviour*. Buckingham: Open University Press.

This book provides an excellent overview of the different models, the studies that have been carried out using them and the new developments in this area.

Conner, M. and Norman, P. (eds) (1998) Special issue: Social cognition models in Health Psychology, *Psychology and Health*, 13: 179–85.

This special issue presents recent research in the area of social cognition models. The editorial provides an overview of the field.

Schwarzer, R. (1992) Self efficacy in the adoption and maintenance of health behaviours: Theoretical approaches and a new model, in R. Schwarzer (ed.), *Self Efficacy: Thought Control of Action*, pp. 217–43. Washington, DC: Hemisphere.

This chapter provides an interesting overview of the different models and emphasizes the central role of self-efficacy in predicting health-related behaviours. It illustrates a quantitative approach to health beliefs.

Woodcock, A., Stenner, K. and Ingham, R. (1992) Young people talking about HIV and AIDS: Interpretations of personal risk of infection, *Health Education Research: Theory and Practice*, 7: 229–47.

This paper illustrates a qualitative approach to health beliefs and is a good example of how to present qualitative data.

CHAPTER 3

Illness cognitions

Chapter overview

Chapter 2 described health beliefs and the models that have been developed to evaluate these beliefs and their relationship to health behaviours. Individuals, however, also have beliefs about illness. This chapter examines what it means to be 'healthy' and what it means to be 'sick' and reviews these meanings in the context of how individuals cognitively represent illness (their illness cognitions/illness beliefs). The chapter then places these beliefs within Leventhal's self-regulatory model and discusses the relationship between illness cognitions, symptom perception and coping behaviour. Finally, it examines the relationship between illness cognitions and health outcomes.

This chapter covers:

- What does it mean to be healthy?
- What does it mean to be ill?
- What are illness cognitions?
- Leventhal's self-regulatory model of illness cognitions
- Symptom perception
- Coping
- Illness cognitions and health outcomes

What does it mean to be healthy?

For the majority of people living in the Western world, being healthy is the norm – most people are healthy for most of the time. Therefore, beliefs about being ill exist in the context of beliefs about being healthy (e.g. illness means not being healthy, illness means feeling different to usual, etc.). The World Health Organization (1947) defined good health as 'a state of complete physical, mental and social well being'. This definition presents a broad multidimensional view of health that departs from the traditional medical emphasis on physical health only. Over recent years this multidimensional model has emerged throughout the results of several qualitative studies that have asked lay people the question 'what does it mean to be healthy?' For example, from a social anthropological perspective, Helman (1978) explored the extent to which beliefs inherent within the eighteenth century's humoral theory have survived alongside those of conventional medicine. In particular, he focused on the saying 'feed a cold and starve a fever', and argued that lay constructs of health could be conceptualized according to the dimensions 'hot/cold' and 'wet/dry'. For example, problems with the chest were considered either 'hot and wet' (e.g. fever and productive cough) or 'cold and wet' (e.g. cold and non-productive cough). Likewise, problems could be considered 'hot and dry' (e.g. fever, dry skin, flushed face, dry throat, non-productive cough) or 'cold and dry' (e.g. cold, shivering, rigor, malaise, vague muscular aches). In a similar vein, medical sociologists have also explored lay conceptions of health. For example, Herzlich (1973) interviewed 80 French subjects and categorized their models of health into three dimensions: 'health in a vacuum', implying the absence of illness; 'the reserve of health', relating to physical strength and resistance to illness; and 'equilibrium' indicating a full realization of the individual's reserve of health. Likewise, Blaxter (1990) asked 9000 individuals to describe someone whom they thought was healthy and to consider 'what makes you call them healthy?' and 'what is it like when you are healthy?' A qualitative analysis was then carried out on a subsample of these individuals. For some, health simply meant not being ill. However, for many health was seen in terms of a reserve, a healthy life filled with health behaviours, physical fitness, having energy and vitality, social relationships with others, being able to function effectively and an expression of psycho-social well being. Blaxter also examined how a concept of health varied over the life course and investigated any sex differences. Furthermore, Calnan (1987) explored the health beliefs of women in England and argued that their models of health could be conceptualized in two sets of definitions: positive definitions including energetic, plenty of exercise, feeling fit, eating the right things, being the correct weight, having a positive outlook and having a good life/marriage; and negative definitions including don't get coughs and colds, only in bed once, rarely go to the doctor and have check-ups – nothing wrong.

The issue of 'what is health?' has also been explored from a psychological perspective with a particular focus on health and illness cognitions.

For example, Lau (1995) found that when young healthy adults were asked to describe in their own words 'what being healthy means to you', their beliefs about health could be understood within the following dimensions:

- *Physiological/physical,* e.g. good condition, have energy.
- *Psychological,* e.g. happy, energetic, feel good psychologically.
- *Behavioural,* e.g. eat, sleep properly.
- *Future consequences,* e.g. live longer.
- *The absence of,* e.g. not sick, no disease, no symptoms.

Lau (1995) argued that most people show a positive definition of health (not just the absence of illness), which also includes more than just physical and psychological factors. He suggested that healthiness is most people's normal state and represents the backdrop to their beliefs about being ill. Psychological studies of the beliefs of the elderly (Hall *et al.* 1989), those suffering from a chronic illness (Hays and Stewart 1990) and children (Normandeau *et al.* 1998) have reported that these individuals also conceptualize health as being multidimensional. This indicates some overlap between professional (WHO) and lay views of health (i.e. a multidimensional perspective involving physical and psychological factors).

What does it mean to be ill?

In his study of the beliefs of young healthy adults, Lau (1995) also asked 'what does it mean to be sick?' Their answers indicated the dimensions they use to conceptualize illness:

- *Not feeling normal,* e.g. 'I don't feel right'.
- *Specific symptoms,* e.g. physiological/psychological.
- *Specific illnesses,* e.g. cancer, cold, depression.
- *Consequences of illness,* e.g. 'I can't do what I usually do'.
- *Time line,* e.g. how long the symptoms last.
- *The absence of health,* e.g. not being healthy.

These dimensions of 'what it means to be ill' have been described within the context of illness cognitions (also called illness beliefs or illness representations).

What are illness cognitions?

Leventhal and his colleagues (Leventhal *et al.* 1980, 1997; Leventhal and Nerenz 1985) defined illness cognitions as 'a patient's own implicit common sense beliefs about their illness'. They proposed that these cognitions provide patients with a framework or a schema for *coping with* and *understanding their illness*, and *telling them what to look out for if they are becoming ill*. Using interviews with patients suffering from a variety of different illnesses, Leventhal and his colleagues identified five cognitive dimensions of these beliefs:

- *Identity*: This refers to the label given to the illness (the medical diagnosis) and the symptoms experienced (e.g. I have a cold, 'the diagnosis', with a runny nose, 'the symptoms').
- *The perceived cause of the illness*: These causes may be biological, such as a virus or a lesion, or psychosocial, such as stress or health-related behaviour. In addition, patients may hold representations of illness that reflect a variety of different causal models (e.g. 'My cold was caused by a virus', 'My cold was caused by being run down').
- *Time line*: This refers to the patients' beliefs about how long the illness will last, whether it is acute (short-term) or chronic (long-term) (e.g. 'My cold will be over in a few days').
- *Consequences*: This refers to the patient's perceptions of the possible effects of the illness on their life. Such consequences may be physical (e.g. pain, lack of mobility), emotional (e.g. loss of social contact, loneliness) or a combination of factors (e.g. 'My cold will prevent me from playing football, which will prevent me from seeing my friends').
- *Curability and controllability*: Patients also represent illnesses in terms of whether they believe that the illness can be treated and cured and the extent to which the outcome of their illness is controllable either by themselves or by powerful others (e.g. 'If I rest, my cold will go away', 'If I get medicine from my doctor my cold will go away').

Evidence for these dimensions of illness cognitions

The extent to which beliefs about illness are constituted by these different dimensions has been studied using two main methodologies – qualitative and quantitative research.

Qualitative research

Leventhal and his colleagues carried out interviews with individuals who were chronically ill, had been recently diagnosed as having cancer and healthy adults. The resulting descriptions of illness suggest underlying beliefs that are made up of the above dimensions. Leventhal and his colleagues argued that interviews are the best way to access illness cognitions as this methodology avoids the possibility of priming the subjects. For example, asking a subject 'to what extent do you think about your illness in terms of its possible consequences' will obviously encourage them to regard consequences as an important dimension. However, according to Leventhal, interviews encourage subjects to express their own beliefs, not those expected by the interviewer.

Quantitative research

Other studies have used more artificial and controlled methodologies, and these too have provided support for the dimensions of illness cognitions. Lau *et al.* (1989) used a card sorting technique to evaluate how subjects conceptualized illness. They asked 20 subjects to sort 65 statements into piles that 'made sense to them'. These statements had been made previously in response to descriptions of 'your most recent illness'. They reported that the subjects' piles of categories reflected the dimensions of identity (diagnosis/symptoms), consequences (the possible effects), time line (how long it will last), cause (what caused the illness) and cure/control (how and whether it can be treated).

A series of experimental studies by Bishop and colleagues also provided support for these dimensions. For example, Bishop and Converse (1986) presented subjects with brief descriptions of patients who were experiencing six different symptoms. Subjects were randomly allocated to one of two sets of descriptions: high prototype in which all six symptoms had been previously rated as associated with the same disease, or low prototype in which only two of the six symptoms had been previously rated as associated with the same disease. The results showed that subjects in the high prototype condition labelled the disease more easily and accurately than subjects in the low prototype condition. The authors argued that this provides support for the role of the identity dimension (diagnosis and symptoms) of illness representations and also suggested that there is some consistency in people's concept of the identity of illnesses. In addition, subjects were asked to describe in their own words 'what else do you think may be associated with this person's situation'. They reported that 91 per cent of the given associations fell into the dimensions of illness representations as described by Leventhal and his colleagues. However, they also reported that the dimensions consequences (the possible effects) and time line (how long it will last) were the least frequently mentioned.

There is also some evidence for a similar structure of illness representations in other cultures. Weller (1984) examined models of illness in English-speaking Americans and Spanish-speaking Guatemalans. The results indicated that illness was predominantly conceptualized in terms of contagion and severity. Lau (1995) argued that contagion is a version of the cause dimension (i.e. the illness is caused by a virus) and severity is a combination of the magnitude of the perceived consequences and beliefs about time line (i.e. how will the illness effect my life and how long will it last) – dimensions which support those described by Leventhal and his colleagues.

Measuring illness cognitions

Although it has been argued that the preferred method to access illness cognitions is through interview, interviews are time consuming and can only involve a limited number of subjects. In order to research further into individuals' beliefs about illness, researchers in New Zealand and the UK have developed the Illness Perception Questionnaire (IPQ) (Weinman *et al.* 1996). This questionnaire asks subjects to rate a series of statements about their illness. These statements reflect the dimensions of identity (e.g. a set of symptoms such as pain, tiredness), consequences (e.g. 'My illness has had major consequences on my life'), time line (e.g. 'My illness will last a short time'), cause (e.g. 'Stress was a major factor in causing my illness') and cure/control (e.g. 'There is a lot I can do to control my symptoms'). This questionnaire has been used to examine beliefs about illnesses such as chronic fatigue syndrome, diabetes and arthritis and provides further support for the dimensions of illness cognitions (Weinman and Petrie 1997). Along similar lines, Horne *et al.* (1999) developed a questionnaire to assess beliefs about medicine which was conceptualized along two dimensions: 'necessity' (to reflect whether their medicine is seen as important) and 'concerns' (to reflect whether the individual is concerned about side effects). The authors argued that not only do individuals have beliefs about their illness but they also have beliefs about the medicines they take, or are asked to take.

In summary, it appears that individuals may show consistent beliefs about illness that can be used to make sense of their illness and help their understanding of any developing symptoms. These illness cognitions have been incorporated into a model of illness behaviour to examine the relationship between an individual's cognitive representation of their illness and their subsequent coping behaviour. This model is known as the 'self-regulatory model of illness behaviour'.

Leventhal's self-regulatory model of illness cognitions

Leventhal incorporated his description of illness cognitions into his self-regulatory model of illness behaviour. This model is based on approaches to problem-solving and suggests that illness/symptoms are dealt with by individuals in the same way as other problems (see Chapter 4 for details of other models of problem solving). It is assumed that given a problem or a change in the *status quo* the individual will be motivated to solve the problem and re-establish their state of normality. Traditional models describe problem solving in three stages: (1) interpretation (making sense of the problem); (2) coping (dealing with the problem in order to regain a state of equilibrium); and (3) appraisal (assessing how successful the coping stage has been). According to models of problem solving these three stages will continue until the coping strategies are deemed to be successful and a state of equilibrium has been attained. In terms of health and illness, if healthiness is an individual's normal state, then any onset of illness will be interpreted as a problem and the individual will be motivated to re-establish their state of health (i.e. illness is not the normal state).

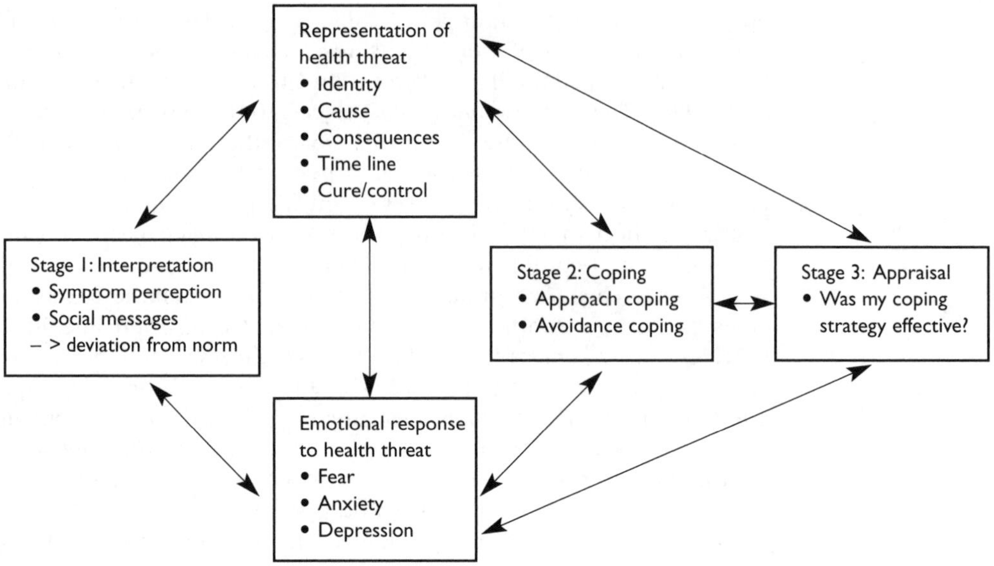

Figure 3.1 Leventhal's self-regulatory model of illness behaviour

These stages have been applied to health using the self-regulatory model of illness behaviour (see Fig. 3.1) as follows.

Stage 1: Interpretation

An individual may be confronted with the problem of a potential illness through two channels: *symptom perception* (I have a pain in my chest), or *social messages* (the doctor has diagnosed this pain as angina).

Once the individual has received information about the possibility of illness through these channels, according to theories of problem solving, the individual is then motivated to return to a state of 'problem-free' normality. This involves assigning meaning to the problem. According to Leventhal, the problem can be given meaning by accessing the individual's illness cognitions. Therefore, the symptoms and social messages will contribute towards the development of illness cognitions, which will be constructed according to the following dimensions: identity, cause, consequences, time line, cure/control. These cognitive representations of the 'problem' will give the problem meaning and will enable the individual to develop and consider suitable coping strategies.

However, a cognitive representation is not the only consequence of symptom perception and social messages. The identification of the problem of illness will also result in changes in emotional state. For example, perceiving the symptom of pain and receiving the social message that this pain may be related to coronary heart disease may result in anxiety. Therefore, any coping strategies have to relate to both the illness cognitions and the emotional state of the individual.

Stage 2: Coping

The next stage in the self-regulatory model is the development and identification of suitable coping strategies. Coping can take many forms, which will be discussed in detail later. However, two broad categories of coping have been defined that incorporate the multitude of other coping strategies: approach coping (e.g. taking pills, going to the doctor, resting, talking to friends about emotions) and avoidance coping (e.g. denial, wishful thinking). When faced with the problem of illness, the individual will therefore develop coping strategies in an attempt to return to a state of healthy normality.

Stage 3: Appraisal

The third stage of the self-regulatory model is appraisal. This involves individuals evaluating the effectiveness of the coping strategy and determining whether to continue with this strategy or whether to opt for an alternative one.

Why is the model called self-regulatory?

This process is regarded as self-regulatory because the three components of the model (interpretation, coping, appraisal) interrelate in order to maintain the *status quo* (i.e. they regulate the self). Therefore, if the individual's normal state (health) is disrupted (by illness), the model proposes that the individual is motivated to return the balance back to normality. This self-regulation involves the three processes interrelating in an ongoing and dynamic fashion. Therefore, interactions occur between the different stages. For example:

- Symptom perception may result in an emotional shift, that may exacerbate the perception of symptoms (e.g. 'I can feel a pain in my chest. Now I feel anxious. Now I can feel more pain as all my attention is focused on it.').
- If the individual opts to use denial as their coping strategy, this may result in a reduction in symptom perception, a decrease in any negative emotions and a shift in their illness cognition (e.g. 'This pain is not very bad' (denial); 'Now I feel less anxious' (emotions); 'This pain will not last for long' (time line); 'This illness will not have any serious consequences for my lifestyle' (consequences)).
- A positive appraisal of the effectiveness of the coping strategy may itself be a coping strategy (e.g. 'My symptoms appear to have been reduced by doing relaxation exercises' may be a form of denial).

Problems with assessment

This dynamic, self-regulatory process suggests a model of cognitions that is complex and intuitively sensible, but poses problems for attempts at assessment and intervention. For example:

1 If the different components of the self-regulatory model interact, should they be measured separately? For example, is the belief that an illness has no serious consequences an illness cognition or a coping strategy?
2 If the different components of the self-regulatory model interact, can individual components be used to predict outcome or should the individual components be seen as co-occurring? For example, is the appraisal that symptoms have been reduced a successful outcome or is it a form of denial (a coping strategy)?

The individual processes involved in the self-regulatory model will now be examined in greater detail.

Stage 1: Interpretation

Symptom perception

Individual differences in symptom perception

Symptoms such as a temperature, pain, a runny nose or the detection of a lump may indicate to the individual the possibility of illness. However, symptom perception is not a straightforward process and Pennebaker (1983) has argued that there are individual differences in the amount of attention people pay to their internal states. Whereas some individuals may sometimes be internally focused and more sensitive to symptoms, others may be more externally focused and less sensitive to any internal changes. However, Pennebaker suggested that this difference is not consistent with differences in accuracy. In a study evaluating the accuracy of detecting changes in heart rate, Pennebaker (1983) reported that individuals who were more focused on their internal states tended to overestimate changes in their heart rate compared with subjects who were externally focused. Being internally focused has also been shown to relate to a perception of slower recovery from illness (Miller *et al.* 1987). Being internally focused may result in an exaggerated perception of symptom change, not a more accurate one.

Mood, cognitions, environment and symptom perception

Skelton and Pennebaker (1982) have also suggested that symptom perception is influenced by factors such as mood, cognitions and the social environment. The role of mood in symptom perception is particularly apparent in pain perception with anxiety increasing self-reports of the

FOCUS ON RESEARCH 3.1

TESTING A THEORY – ILLNESS REPRESENTATIONS AND COPING

A study to examine the relationship between illness representations, coping and psychological adjustment in sufferers of chronic fatigue syndrome (Moss-Morris *et al.* 1996).

This study examined the interrelationship between illness representations, coping and psychological adjustment in the context of chronic fatigue syndrome (CFS). The aim of the study was to test directly elements of Leventhal's self-regulatory model and to examine whether the way an individual makes sense of their illness (their illness representation) and the way they cope with their illness (their coping strategies) relates to their level of functioning (the outcome measure).

Background

Chronic fatigue syndrome (sometimes called myalgic encephalomyelitis (ME) or post-viral fatigue syndrome) has interested psychologists for over a decade as it appears to have no apparent simple organic origin or to be a psychiatric disorder. Recent theorists have suggested that CFS is best characterized as an interaction between psychological and physical factors with cognitive and behavioural responses mediating between an acute organic illness and a chronic syndrome. Because of the hypothesized role of cognitions in the maintenance/progression of CFS, Moss-Morris *et al.* aimed to examine the role of illness cognitions and coping strategies in sufferers' level of functioning.

Methodology

Subjects 520 members of the Australian and New Zealand Myalgic Encephalomyelitis Society were sent an invitation to take part in the study, of whom 308 returned the consent forms and were sent a questionnaire. A total of 233 CFS sufferers (189 female and 44 male) completed and returned the questionnaire and were included in the data analysis. These subjects ranged in age from 18 to 81, 61 per cent were married, 55 per cent had received tertiary education and the mean length of illness was 10.8 years.

Design The study involved a cross-sectional design with all subjects completing a questionnaire once.

Measures Subjects were sent a questionnaire consisting of the following measures:

1 *The Illness Perception Questionnaire*. This questionnaire measured illness representations and included items reflecting the following aspects of illness representations:

- *Identity*: This consisted of a set of 12 core symptoms (e.g. pain) and 13 symptoms specific to CFS (e.g. tiredness). Subjects were asked to rate each symptom according to how often they experienced them from 'never' to 'all the time'.
- *Time line*: This consisted of items relating to the subjects' predicted length of their illness (e.g. 'My CFS will last a long time').
- *Control/cure*: This consisted of items relating to the degree to which the subjects believed that their illness could be controlled/cured (e.g. 'There is a lot I can do to control my symptoms').
- *Consequences*: Subjects were asked to rate statements concerning the perceptions of the possible consequences (e.g. 'My illness has strongly affected the way I see myself as a person').
- *Cause*: subjects also rated statements relating to the cause of their illness (e.g. 'Stress was a major factor in causing my illness').

2 *Coping strategies*. Subjects completed a shortened version of the COPE Inventory (Carver *et al.* 1989), which has been designed to measure aspects of coping. The authors included items relating to *problem-focused* coping (e.g. active coping, planning, suppression of competing activities, seeking support for instrumental reasons), *emotion-focused* coping (e.g. positive reinterpretation and growth, venting emotions, seeking emotional support), *behavioural disengagement* coping (e.g. using substances for distraction) and *mental disengagement* coping (e.g. wishful thinking).

3 *Level of functioning:* Subjects completed the five-item mental health scale (MHI5) as a measure of psychological adjustment, a four-item vitality scale (Ware and Sherbourne 1992) as a measure of subjective well-being and the Sickness Impact Profile (Bergner *et al.* 1981) as a measure of dysfunction.

Results

The relationship between components of illness representations

The results showed that a strong illness identity was related to a belief in serious consequences and a more chronic time line (e.g. 'I have lots of symptoms, my illness has serious effects on my life and I believe that it will last for a long time'). A chronic time line was related to more negative beliefs about consequences and a belief that the illness was less controllable and less curable (e.g. 'I believe that my illness will last for a long time, that it has a serious effect on my life and that it cannot be either controlled or cured'). In addition, a belief that CFS was caused by psychological factors (e.g. stress) was related to a greater belief in serious consequences (e.g. 'My illness was caused by stress and has serious effects on my life').

The relationship between illness representations and coping

The results showed a positive relationship between identity (the illness representation) and coping strategies such as planning venting emotions, behavioural disengagement and mental disengagement (e.g. 'I experience lots of symptoms and cope by forming plans of action, venting my feelings, and distracting myself from my symptoms by using substances such as alcohol and by engaging in wishful thinking'). The results also showed a positive relationship between consequences (the illness representation) and coping strategies such as planning, suppression of competing activities, seeking emotional social support, venting emotions, mental disengagement (e.g. 'I believe that my illness has seriously effected my life, and cope by forming plans of action, stopping doing other activities, talking to my friends about my feelings, expressing my emotions and thinking about other things'). In addition, the results showed a positive relationship between internal control/cure (the illness representation) and coping strategies such as active coping, planning, positive reinterpretation and a negative relationship with behavioural disengagement (e.g. 'I believe that I can control/cure my illness and cope actively, form plans, attempt to see my illness in a positive light and do not use substances'). Finally, the results showed a belief that the illness would last a long time (the illness representation) was related to coping by suppressing competing activities, behavioural disengagement (e.g. 'I believe that my illness is chronic and cope by not doing other activities and using substances') and a belief that the illness was caused by psychological factors was related to behavioural disengagement (e.g. 'I believe that stress caused my illness and cope by drinking alcohol').

The relationship between illness representations and level of functioning

The results showed that the illness representation components of illness identity, emotional causes of the illness, controllability/curability and consequences had the strongest overall association with measures of functioning, suggesting that individuals who had the most symptoms, believed that their illness was out of their control, caused by stress and had serious consequences, showed low levels of psychological adjustment and well-being and higher levels of dysfunction.

The relationship between coping and levels of functioning

The results from this analysis showed that psychological dysfunction and low psychological well-being were related to behavioural and mental disengagement and that psychological adjustment was related to positive reinterpretation, seeking emotional support, not using substances and not venting emotions.

Conclusion

The results from this study provide support for the predicted association between cognitive variables (illness representations and coping) and level of functioning (psychological adjustment, well-being and dysfunction) in CFS. In addition, the results provide support for Leventhal's self-regulatory model as illness representations were related to coping and a measure of outcome (level of functioning). However, because of the cross-sectional nature of the design it is not possible to say whether illness representations cause changes in either coping or outcome and as the authors conclude 'only a prospective design can clarify some of these issues'.

pain experience (see Chapter 11 for a discussion of anxiety and pain). In addition, anxiety has been proposed as an explanation for placebo pain reduction as taking any form of medication (even a sugar pill) may reduce the individual's anxiety, increase their sense of control and result in pain reduction (see Chapter 12 for a discussion of anxiety and placebos). An individual's cognitive state may also influence their symptom perception. This is again illustrated by the placebo effect with the individual's expectations of recovery resulting in reduced symptom perception (see Chapter 12). Ruble (1977) carried out a study in which she manipulated women's expectations about when they were due to start menstruating. She gave subjects an 'accurate physiological test' and told women either that their period was due very shortly or that it was at least a week away. The women were then asked to report any premenstrual symptoms. The results showed that believing that they were about to start menstruating (even though they were not) increased the number of reported premenstrual symptoms. This indicates an association between cognitive state and symptom perception. Pennebaker also reported that symptom perception is related to an individual's attentional state and that boredom and the absence of environmental stimuli may result in over-reporting, whereas distraction and attention diversion may lead to under-reporting (Pennebaker, 1983).

A recent study provides support for Pennebaker's theory. Sixty one women who had been hospitalized during pre-term labour were randomized to receive either information, distraction or nothing (van Zuuren 1998). The results showed that distraction had the most beneficial effect on measures of both physical and psychological symptoms suggesting that symptom perception is sensitive to attention. The different factors contributing to symptom perception are illustrated by a condition known as 'medical students' disease', which has been described by Mechanic (1962). A large component of the medical curriculum involves learning about the symptoms associated with a multitude of different illnesses. More than two-thirds of medical students incorrectly report that at some time they have had the symptoms they are being taught about. Perhaps this phenomena can be understood in terms of:

- *Mood*: medical students become quite anxious due to their work load. This anxiety may heighten their awareness of any physiological changes making them more internally focused.
- *Cognition*: medical students are thinking about symptoms as part of their course, which may result in a focus on their own internal states.
- *Social*: once one student starts to perceive symptoms, others may model themselves on this behaviour.

Therefore, symptom perception influences how an individual interprets the problem of illness.

Social messages

Information about illness also comes from other people. This may come in the form of a formal diagnosis from a health professional or a positive test result from a routine health check. Such messages may or may not be a consequence of symptom perception. For example, a formal diagnosis may occur after symptoms have been perceived, the individual has subsequently been motivated to go to the doctor and has been given a diagnosis. However, screening and health checks may detect illness at an asymptomatic stage of development and therefore attendance for such a test may not have been motivated by symptom perception. Information about illness may also come from other lay individuals who are not health professionals. Before (and after) consulting a health professional, people often access their social network, which has been called their 'lay referral system' by Freidson (1970). This can take the form of colleagues, friends or family and involves seeking information and advice from multiple sources. For example, coughing in front of one friend may result in the advice to speak to another friend who had a similar cough, or a suggestion to take a favoured home remedy. Alternatively, it may result in a lay diagnosis or a suggestion to seek professional help from the doctor. In fact, Scambler *et al.* (1981) reported that three-quarters of those taking part in their study of primary care attenders had sought advice from family or friends before seeking professional help. Such social messages will influence how the individual interprets the 'problem' of illness.

Stage 2: Coping

The wide interest in how individuals cope with problems, including the problem of illness, is reflected in the burgeoning literature on the subject and is closely allied with research on coping with pain and stress (see Chapters 10 and 11). This section will examine three approaches to theories of coping: (1) coping with a diagnosis, (2) coping with the crisis of illness and (3) adjustment to physical illness and the theory of cognitive adaptation. These different theoretical approaches have implications for understanding the differences between adaptive and maladaptive coping, and the role of reality and illusions in the coping process. They therefore have different implications for understanding the outcome of the coping process.

Coping with a diagnosis

Shontz (1975) described the following stages of coping that individuals often go through after a diagnosis of a chronic illness:

- *Shock*: initially, according to Shontz most people go into a state of shock following a diagnosis of a serious illness. Being in shock is characterized by being stunned and bewildered, behaving in an automatic fashion and having feelings of detachment from the situation.
- *Encounter reaction*: following shock, Shontz argued that the next stage is an encounter reaction. This is characterized by disorganized thinking and feelings of loss, grief, helplessness and despair.
- *Retreat*: retreat is the third stage in the process of coping with a diagnosis. Shontz argued that this stage is characterized by denial of the problem and its implications and a retreat into the self.

Implications for the outcome of the coping process

Shontz developed these stages from observations of individuals in hospital and suggested that once at the retreat stage, individuals with a diagnosis of a serious illness can gradually deal with the reality of their diagnosis. According to Shontz, retreat is only a temporary stage and denial of reality cannot last forever. Therefore, the retreat stage acts as a launch pad for a gradual reorientation towards the reality of the situation and as reality intrudes the individual begins to face up to their illness. Therefore, this model of coping focuses on the immediate changes following a diagnosis, suggesting that the desired outcome of any coping process is to face up to reality and that reality orientation is an adaptive coping mechanism.

Coping with the crisis of illness

In an alternative approach to coping with illness, Moos and Schaefer (1984) have applied 'crisis theory' to the crisis of physical illness.

What is crisis theory?

Crisis theory has been generally used to examine how people cope with major life crises and transitions and has traditionally provided a framework for understanding the impact of illness or injury. The theory was developed from Lindemann's work on grief and mourning and Erikson's model of developmental crises at transition points in the life-cycle. In general, crisis theory examines the impact of any form of disruption on an individual's established personal and social identity. It suggests that psychological systems are driven towards maintaining homeostasis and equilibrium in the same way as physical systems. Within this framework any crisis is self-limiting as the individual will find a way of returning to a stable state; individuals are therefore regarded as self-regulators.

Physical illness as a crisis

Moos and Schaefer argued that physical illness can be considered a crisis as it represents a turning point in an individual's life. They suggest that physical illness causes the following changes, which can be conceptualized as a crisis:

- *Changes in identity*: illness can create a shift in identity, such as from carer to patient, or from breadwinner to person with an illness.
- *Changes in location*: illness may result in a move to a new environment such as becoming bedridden or hospitalized.
- *Changes in role*: a change from independent adult to passive dependant may occur following illness, resulting in a changed role.
- *Changes in social support*: illness may produce isolation from friends and family effecting changes in social support.
- *Changes in the future*: a future involving children, career or travel can become uncertain.

In addition, the crisis nature of illness may be exacerbated by factors that are often specific to illness such as:

- *Illness is often unpredicted*: if an illness is not expected then the individual will not have had the opportunity to consider possible coping strategies.
- *Information about the illness is unclear*: much of the information about illness is ambiguous and unclear, particularly in terms of causality and outcome.
- *A decision is needed quickly*: illness frequently requires decisions about action to be made quickly (e.g. should we operate, should we take medicines, should we take time off from work, should we tell our friends).
- *Ambiguous meaning*: because of uncertainties about causality and outcome, the meaning of the illness for an individual will often be ambiguous (e.g. is it serious? how long will it effect me?).
- *Limited prior experience*: most individuals are healthy most of the time. Therefore, illness is infrequent and may occur to individuals with limited prior experience. This lack of experience has implications for the development of coping strategies and efficacy based on other similar situations (e.g. 'I've never had cancer before, what should I do next?').

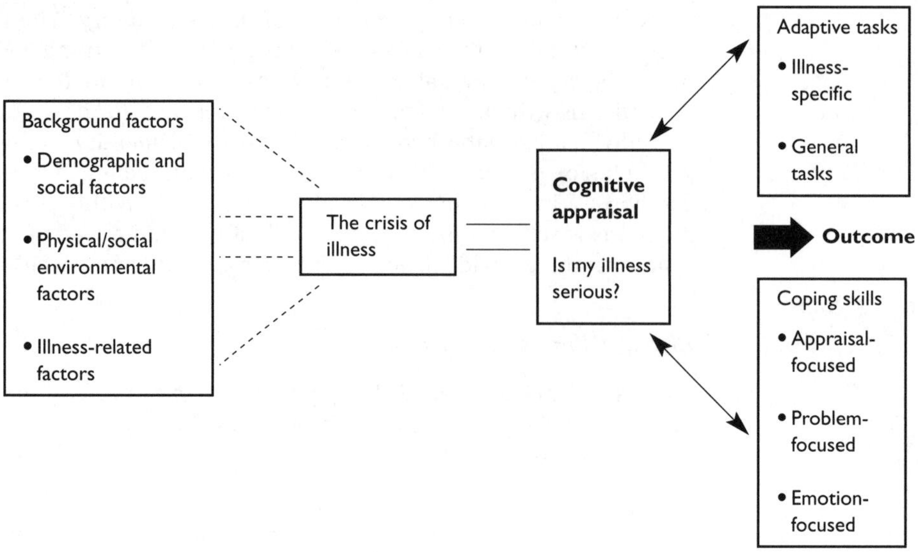

Figure 3.2 Coping with the crisis of illness

Many other crises may be easier to predict, have clearer meanings and occur to individuals with a greater degree of relevant previous experience. Within this framework, Moos and Schaefer considered illness a particular kind of crisis, and applied crisis theory to illness in an attempt to examine how individuals cope with this crisis.

The coping process

Once confronted with the crisis of physical illness, Moos and Schaefer described three processes that constitute the coping process: (1) cognitive appraisal, (2) adaptive tasks and (3) coping skills. These processes are illustrated in Fig. 3.2.

Process 1: Cognitive appraisal

At the stage of disequilibrium triggered by the illness, an individual initially appraises the seriousness and significance of the illness (e.g. Is my cancer serious? How will my cancer influence my life in the long run?). Factors such as knowledge, previous experience and social support may influence this appraisal process. In addition, it is possible to integrate Leventhal's illness cognitions at this stage in the coping process as such illness beliefs are related to how an illness will be appraised.

Process 2: Adaptive tasks

Following cognitive appraisal, Moos and Schaefer describe seven adaptive tasks that are used as part of the coping process. These can be divided into

Table 3.1 Adaptive tasks

Illness-related tasks
- Dealing with pain and other symptoms
- Dealing with the hospital environment and treatment procedures
- Developing and maintaining relationships with health professionals

General tasks
- Preserving an emotional balance
- Preserving self-image, competence and mastery
- Sustaining relationships with family and friends
- Preparing for an uncertain future

three illness specific tasks and four general tasks. These are illustrated in Table 3.1.

The three illness-specific tasks can be described as:

1 *Dealing with pain, incapacitation and other symptoms*. This task involves dealing with symptoms such as pain, dizziness, loss of control and the recognition of changes in the severity of the symptoms.
2 *Dealing with the hospital environment and special treatment procedures*. This task involves dealing with medical interventions such as mastectomy, chemotherapy and any related side-effects.
3 *Developing and maintaining adequate relationships with health care staff*. Becoming ill requires a new set of relationships with a multitude of health professionals. This task describes the development of those relationships.

The four general tasks can be described as:

1 *Preserving a reasonable emotional balance*. This involves compensating for the negative emotions aroused by illness with sufficient positive ones.
2 *Preserving a satisfactory self-image and maintaining a sense of competence and mastery*. This involves dealing with changes in appearance following illness (e.g. disfigurement) and adapting to a reliance on technology (e.g. pacemaker).
3 *Sustaining relationships with family and friends*. This involves maintaining social support networks even when communication can become problematic due to changes in location and mobility.
4 *Preparing for an uncertain future*. Illness can often result in loss (e.g. of sight, lifestyle, mobility, life). This task involves coming to terms with such losses and redefining the future.

Process 3: Coping skills

Following both appraisal and the use of adaptive tasks, Moos and Schaefer described a series of coping skills that are accessed to deal with the crisis of physical illness. These coping skills can be categorized into three forms: (1) appraisal-focused coping; (2) problem-focused coping; and (3) emotion-focused coping (see Table 3.2).

Table 3.2 Coping skills

Appraisal-focused
- Logical analysis and mental preparation
- Cognitive redefinition
- Cognitive avoidance or denial

Problem-focused
- Seeking information and support
- Taking problem-solving action
- Identifying rewards

Emotion-focused
- Affective regulation
- Emotional discharge
- Resigned acceptance

Appraisal focused coping involves attempts to understand the illness and represents a search for meaning. Three sets of appraisal-focused coping skills have been defined:

1. Logical analysis and mental preparation, involving turning an apparently unmanageable event into a series of manageable ones.
2. Cognitive redefinition, involving accepting the reality of the situation and redefining it in a positive and acceptable way.
3. Cognitive avoidance and denial, involving minimizing the seriousness of the illness.

Problem-focused coping involves confronting the problem and reconstructing it as manageable. Three types of problem-focused coping skills have been defined:

1. Seeking information and support, involving building a knowledge base by accessing any available information.
2. Taking problem-solving action, involving learning specific procedures and behaviours (e.g. insulin injections).
3. Identifying alternative rewards, involving the development and planning of events and goals that can provide short-term satisfaction.

Emotion-focused coping involves managing emotions and maintaining emotional equilibrium. Three types of emotion-focused coping skills have been defined:

1. Affective, involving efforts to maintain hope when dealing with a stressful situation.
2. Emotional discharge, involving venting feelings of anger or despair.
3. Resigned acceptance, involving coming to terms with the inevitable outcome of an illness.

Therefore, according to this theory of coping with the crisis of a physical illness, individuals appraise the illness and then use a variety of adaptive tasks and coping skills which in turn determine the outcome.

However, not all individuals respond to illness in the same way and Moos and Schaefer argued that the use of these tasks and skills is determined by three factors:

1 Demographic and personal factors, such as age, sex, class, religion.
2 Physical and social/environmental factors, such as the accessibility of social support networks and the acceptability of the physical environment (e.g. hospitals can be dull and depressing).
3 Illness-related factors, such as any resulting pain, disfigurement, or stigma.

Implications for the outcome of the coping process

Within this model, individuals attempt to deal with the crisis of physical illness via the stages of appraisal, the use of adaptive tasks and the employment of coping skills. The types of tasks and skills used may determine the outcome of this process and such outcome may be psychological adjustment or well-being, or may be related to longevity or quality of life (see Chapter 14). According to crisis theory, individuals are motivated to re-establish a state of equilibrium and normality. This desire can be satisfied by either short-term or long-term solutions. Crisis theory differentiates between two types of new equilibrium: *healthy adaptation*, which can result in maturation and a *maladaptive response* resulting in deterioration. Within this perspective, healthy adaptation involves reality orientation and adaptive tasks and constructive coping skills. Therefore, according to this model of coping the desired outcome of the coping process is reality orientation.

Adjustment to physical illness and the theory of cognitive adaptation

In an alternative model of coping, Taylor and colleagues (e.g. Taylor 1983; Taylor *et al.* 1984) examined ways in which individuals adjust to threatening events. Based on a series of interviews with rape victims and cardiac and cancer patients, they suggested that coping with threatening events (including illness) consists of three processes: (1) a search for meaning, (2) a search for mastery and (3) a process of self-enhancement. They argued that these three processes are central to developing and maintaining illusions and that these illusions constitute a process of cognitive adaptation. Again, this model describes the individual as self-regulatory and as motivated to maintain the *status quo*. In addition, many of the model's components parallel those described earlier in terms of illness cognitions (e.g. the dimensions of cause and consequence). This theoretical perspective will be described in the context of their results from women who had recently had breast cancer (Taylor *et al.* 1984).

A search for meaning

A search for meaning is reflected in questions such as 'Why did it happen?', 'What impact has it had?', 'What does my life mean now?' A search for meaning can be understood in terms of a search for causality and a search to understand the implications.

A search for causality (Why did it happen?)

Attribution theory suggests that individuals need to understand, predict and control their environment (e.g. Weiner 1986). Taylor *et al.* (1984) reported that 95 per cent of the women they interviewed offered an explanation of the cause of their breast cancer. For example, 41 per cent explained their cancer in terms of stress, 32 per cent held carcinogens such as the birth control pill, chemical dumps or nuclear waste as responsible, 26 per cent saw hereditary factors as the cause, 17 per cent blamed diet and 10 per cent considered a blow to the breast to blame. Several women reported multiple causes. Taylor (1983) suggested that no one perception of cause is better than any other, but that what is important for the process of cognitive adaption is the search for any cause.

Understanding the implications (What effect has it had on my life?)

Taylor (1983) also argued that it is important for the women to understand the implications of the cancer for their life now. Accordingly, over 50 per cent of the women stated that the cancer had resulted in them reappraising their life, and others mentioned improved self-knowledge, self-change and a process of reprioritization.

Understanding the cause of the illness and developing an insight into the implications of the illness gives the illness meaning. According to this model of coping, a sense of meaning contributes to the process of coping and cognitive adaptation.

A search for mastery

A search for mastery is reflected in questions such as 'How can I prevent a similar event reoccurring?', 'What can I do to manage the event now?' Taylor *et al.* (1984) reported that a sense of mastery can be achieved by believing that the illness is controllable. In accordance with this, 66 per cent of the women in the study believed that they could influence the course or reoccurrence of the cancer. The remainder of the women believed that the cancer could be controlled by health professionals. Taylor reported that a sense of mastery is achieved either through psychological techniques such as developing a positive attitude, meditation, self-hypnosis or a type of causal attribution, or by behavioural techniques such as changing diet, changing medications, accessing information or controlling any side-effects.

These processes contribute towards a state of mastery, which is central to the progression towards a state of cognitive adaptation.

The process of self-enhancement

Following illness, some individuals may suffer a decrease in their self-esteem. The theory of cognitive adaption suggests that, following illness, individuals attempt to build their self-esteem through a process of self-enhancement. Taylor *et al.* (1984) reported that only 17 per cent of the women in their study reported only negative changes following their illness, whereas 53 per cent reported only positive changes. To explain this result, Taylor *et al.* developed social comparison theory (Festinger 1957). This theory suggests that individuals make sense of their world by comparing themselves with others. Such comparisons may either be downward comparisons (e.g. a comparison with others who are worse off 'At least I've only had cancer once'), or upward (e.g. a comparison with others who are better off 'Why was my lump malignant when hers was only a cyst'). In terms of their study of women with breast cancer, Taylor *et al.* reported that, although many of the women in their study had undergone disfiguring surgery and had been diagnosed as having a life-threatening illness, most of them showed downward comparisons. This indicates that nearly all the women were comparing themselves with others worse off than themselves in order to improve their self-esteem. For example, women who had had a lumpectomy compared themselves with women who had had a mastectomy. Those who had had a mastectomy compared themselves with those who had a possibility of having generalized cancer. Older women compared themselves favourably with younger women, and younger women compared themselves favourably with older women. Taylor and her colleagues suggested that the women selected criteria for comparison that would enable them to improve their self-esteem as part of the process of self-enhancement.

The role of illusions

According to the theory of cognitive adaptation, following a threatening event individuals are motivated to search for meaning, search for mastery and to improve their sense of self-esteem. It is suggested that these processes involve developing illusions. Such illusions are not necessarily in contradiction to reality but are positive interpretations of this reality. For example, although there may be little evidence for the real causes of cancer, or for the ability of individuals to control the course of their illness, those who have suffered cancer wish to hold their own illusions about these factors (e.g. 'I understand what caused my cancer and believe that I can control whether it comes back'). Taylor and her colleagues argued that these illusions are a necessary and essential component of cognitive adaptation and that reality orientation (as suggested by other coping models) may actually be detrimental to adjustment.

The need for illusions raises the problem of disconfirmation of the illusions (what happens when the reoccurrence of cancer cannot be controlled?) Taylor argued that the need for illusions is sufficient to enable individuals to shift the goals and foci of their illusions so that the illusions can be maintained and adjustment persist.

Implications for the outcome of the coping process

According to this model of coping, the individual copes with illness by achieving cognitive adaptation. This involves searching for meaning (I know what caused my illness), mastery (I can control my illness) and developing self-esteem (I am better off than a lot of people). These beliefs may not be accurate but they are essential to maintaining illusions that promote adjustment to the illness. Therefore, within this perspective the desired outcome of the coping process is the developing of illusions, not reality orientation.

Using the self-regulatory model to predict recovery

The self-regulatory model describes a transition from interpretation, through illness cognitions, emotional response and coping to appraisal. This model has primarily been used in research to ask the questions 'How do different people make sense of different illnesses?' and 'How do illness cognitions relate to coping?' Research, however, has also explored the impact of illness cognitions on recovery from illness. Work in this area has mainly focused on recovery from disability following stroke and recovery from myocardial infarction (MI; heart attack).

Predicting recovery from stroke

Partridge and Johnston (1989) addressed the relationship between illness cognitions and recovery. They used a prospective study and reported that individuals' beliefs about their perceived control over their problem predicted recovery from residual disability in stroke patients at follow-up. The results showed that this relationship persisted even when baseline levels of disability were taken into account. In line with this, Johnston *et al.* (1997) also explored the relationship between perceived control and recovery from stroke and followed up 71 stroke patients one and six months after discharge from hospital. In addition, they examined the possible mediating effects of coping, exercise and mood. Therefore, they asked the questions 'Does recovery from stroke relate to illness cognitions?' and 'If so, is this relationship dependent upon other factors?' The results showed no support for the mediating effects of coping, exercise and mood but supported earlier work to indicate a predictive relationship between control beliefs and recovery.

Predicting recovery from MI

Research has also explored the relationship between illness cognitions and recovery from MI. From a broad perspective research suggests that beliefs about factors such as the individual's work capacity (Maeland and Havik 1987), helplessness towards future MIs (called 'cardiac invalidism') (Riegel 1993) and general psychological factors (Diederiks *et al.* 1991) relate to recovery from MI as measured by return to work and general social and occupational functioning. Using a self-regulatory approach, research has also indicated that illness cognitions relate to recovery. In particular, the Heart Attack Recovery Project, which was carried out in New Zealand and followed 143 first time heart attack patients aged 65 or under for 12 months following admission to hospital. All subjects completed follow-up measures at 3, 6 and 12 months after admission. The results showed that those patients who believed that their illness had less serious consequences and would last a shorter time at baseline, were more likely to have returned to work by six weeks (Petrie *et al.* 1996). Furthermore, those with beliefs that the illness could be controlled or cured at baseline predicted attendance at rehabilitation classes (Petrie *et al.* 1996).

Therefore, a self-regulatory approach may not only be useful for describing illness cognitions and for exploring the relationship between such cognitions and coping, but also for understanding and predicting other health outcomes.

To conclude

In the same way that people have beliefs about health they also have beliefs about illness. Such beliefs are often called 'illness cognitions' or 'illness representations'. Beliefs about illness appear to follow a pattern and are made up of: (1) identity (e.g. a diagnosis and symptoms), (2) consequences (e.g. beliefs about seriousness), (3) time line (e.g. how long it will last), (4) cause (e.g. caused by smoking, caused by a virus) and (5) cure/control (e.g. requires medical intervention). This chapter examined these dimensions of illness cognitions and assessed how they relate to the way in which an individual responds to illness via their coping and their appraisal of the illness. Further, it has described the self-regulatory model and its implications for understanding and predicting health outcomes.

Questions

1 How do people make sense of health and illness?

2 Discuss the relationship between illness cognitions and coping.

3 Why is Leventhal's model 'self-regulatory'?

4 Discuss the role of symptom perception in adapting to illness.

5 Illusions are a central component of coping with illness. Discuss.

6 Illness cognitions predict health outcomes. Discuss.

7 Design a research project to evaluate the role of coping in adaptation to illness.

For discussion

Think about the last time you were ill (e.g. headache, flu, broken limb, etc.). Consider the ways in which you made sense of your illness and how they related to your coping strategies.

Assumptions in health psychology

The literature examining illness cognitions highlights some of the assumptions in health psychology:

1 *Humans as information processors.* The literature describing the structure of illness cognitions assumes that individuals deal with their illness by processing the different forms of information. In addition, it assumes that the resulting cognitions are clearly defined and consistent across different people. However, perhaps the information is not always processed rationally and perhaps some cognitions are made up of only some of the components (e.g. just time line and cause), or made up of other components not included in the models.

2 *Methodology as separate to theory.* The literature also assumes that the structure of cognitions exists prior to questions about these cognitions. Therefore, it is assumed that the data collected are separate from the methodology used (i.e. the different components of the illness cognitions pre-date questions about time line, causality, cure, etc.). However, it is possible that the structure of these cognitions is in part an artefact of the types of questions asked. In fact, Leventhal originally argued that interviews should be used to access illness

cognitions as this methodology avoided 'contaminating' the data. However, even interviews involve the interviewer's own preconceived ideas that may be expressed through the structure of their questions, through their responses to the interviewee, or through their analysis of the transcripts.

Further reading

Bird, J.E. and Podmore, V.N. (1990) Children's understanding of health and illness, *Psychology and Health*, 4: 175–85.

This paper examines how children make sense of illnesses and discusses the possible developmental transition from a dichotomous model (ill versus healthy) to one based on a continuum.

de Ridder, D. (1997) What is wrong with coping assessment? A review of conceptual and methodological issues, *Psychology and Health*, 12: 417–31.

This paper explores the complex and ever-growing area of coping and focuses on the issues surrounding the questions 'What is coping?' and 'How should it be measured?'

Leventhal, H., Meyer, D. and Nerenz, D. (1980) The common sense representation of illness danger, in S. Rachman (ed.), *Medical Psychology*, Vol.2, pp. 7–30. New York: Pergamon Press.

This paper outlines the concept of illness cognitions and discusses the implications of how people make sense of their illness for their physical and psychological well-being.

Petrie, K.J. and Weinman, J.A. (1997) *Perceptions of health and illness*. Amsterdam: Harwood Academic Publishers.

This is an edited collection of recent projects using the self-regulatory model as their theoretical framework.

Taylor, S.E. (1983) Adjustment to threatening events: A theory of cognitive adaptation, *American Psychologist*, 38: 1161–73.

This paper describes and analyses the cognitive adaptation theory of coping with illness and emphasizes the central role of illusions in making sense of the imbalance created by the absence of health.

CHAPTER 4

Doctor–patient communication and the role of health professionals' health beliefs

Chapter overview

This chapter first examines the problem of compliance and then describes Ley's cognitive hypothesis model of communication, which emphasizes patient understanding, recall and satisfaction. This educational perspective explains communication in terms of the transfer of knowledge from medical expert to layperson. Such models of the transfer of expert knowledge assume that the health professionals behave according to their education and training, not their subjective beliefs. The chapter then looks at the role of information in terms of determining compliance and also in terms of the effect on recovery, and then reviews the adherence model, which was an attempt to go beyond the traditional model of doctor–patient communication. Next, the chapter focuses on the problem of variability and suggests that variability in health professionals' behaviour is not only related to levels of knowledge but also to the processes involved in clinical decision-making and the health beliefs of the health professional. This suggests that many of the health beliefs described in Chapter 2 are also relevant to health professionals. Finally, the chapter examines doctor–patient communication as an interaction and the role of agreement and shared models.

This chapter covers:

- What is compliance?
- The work of Ley
- How can compliance be improved?
- The role of knowledge in doctor–patient communication
- The problem of doctor variability
- Explaining variability – the role of clinical decision-making
- Explaining variability – the role of health beliefs
- Doctor–patient communication as an interaction

What is compliance?

Haynes *et al.* (1979) defined compliance as 'the extent to which the patient's behaviour (in terms of taking medications, following diets or other lifestyle changes) coincides with medical or health advice'. Compliance has excited an enormous amount of clinical and academic interest over the past few decades and it has been calculated that 3200 articles on compliance in English were listed between 1979 and 1985 (Trostle 1988). Compliance is regarded as important primarily because following the recommendations of health professionals is considered essential to patient recovery. However, studies estimate that about half of the patients with chronic illnesses, such as diabetes and hypertension, are non-compliant with their medication regimens and that even compliance for a behaviour as apparently simple as using an inhaler for asthma is poor (e.g. Dekker *et al.* 1992). Further, compliance also has financial implications: in 1980 between US$396 and US$792 million per year were 'wasted' in the USA because of non-compliance to prescribed drugs (Department of Health and Human Services 1980).

Predicting whether patients are compliant: the work of Ley

Ley (1981, 1989) developed the cognitive hypothesis model of compliance. This claimed that compliance can be predicted by a combination of patient satisfaction with the process of the consultation, understanding of the information given and recall of this information. Several studies have been done to examine each element of the cognitive hypothesis model. This model is illustrated in Fig. 4.1.

Patient satisfaction

Ley (1988) examined the extent of patient satisfaction with the consultation. He reviewed 21 studies of hospital patients and found that 41 per

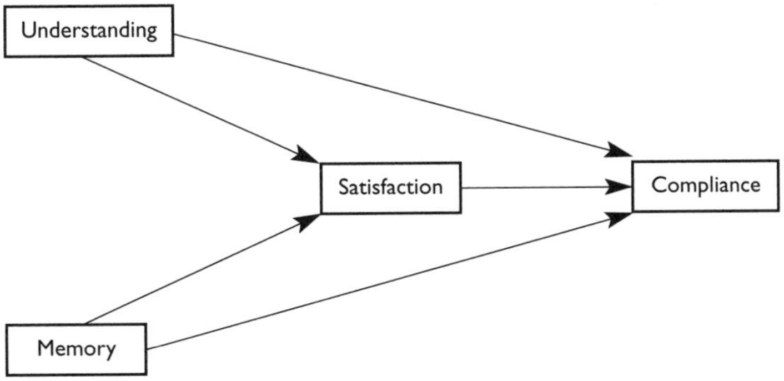

Figure 4.1 Ley's model of compliance

cent of patients were dissatisfied with their treatment and that 28 per cent of general practice patients were dissatisfied. Studies by Haynes *et al.* (1979) and Ley (1988), found that levels of patient satisfaction stem from various components of the consultation, in particular the affective aspects (e.g. emotional support and understanding), the behavioural aspects (e.g. prescribing, adequate explanation) and the competence (e.g. appropriateness of referral, diagnosis) of the health professional. Ley (1989) also reported that satisfaction is determined by the content of the consultation and that patients want to know as much information as possible, even if this is bad news. For example, in studies looking at cancer diagnosis, patients showed improved satisfaction if they were given a diagnosis of cancer rather than if they were protected from this information. Patient satisfaction is increasingly used in health care assessment as an indirect measure of health outcome based on the assumption that a satisfied patient will be a more healthy patient. This has resulted in the development of a multitude of patient satisfaction measures and a lack of agreement as to what patient satisfaction actually is (see Fitzpatrick 1993). However, even though there are problems with patient satisfaction, some studies suggest that aspects of patient satisfaction may correlate with compliance with the advice given during the consultation.

Patient understanding

Several studies have also examined the extent to which patients understand the content of the consultation. Boyle (1970) examined patients' definitions of different illnesses and reported that when given a checklist only 85 per cent correctly defined arthritis, 77 per cent correctly defined jaundice, 52 per cent correctly defined palpitations and 80 per cent correctly defined bronchitis. Boyle further examined patients' perceptions of the location of organs and found that only 42 per cent correctly located the heart, 20 per cent located the stomach and 49 per cent located the liver. This suggests that understanding of the content of the consultation may well be low. Further studies have examined the understanding of illness in terms of causality and seriousness. Roth (1979) asked patients what they thought peptic ulcers were caused by and found a variety of responses, such as problems with teeth and gums, food, digestive problems or excessive stomach acid. He also asked individuals what they thought caused lung cancer, and found that although the understanding of the causality of lung cancer was high in terms of smoking behaviour, 50 per cent of individuals thought that lung cancer caused by smoking had a good prognosis. Roth also reported that 30 per cent of patients believed that hypertension could be cured by treatment.

If the doctor gives advice to the patient or suggests that they follow a particular treatment programme and the patient does not understand the causes of their illness, the correct location of the relevant organ or the processes involved in the treatment, then this lack of understanding is likely to affect their compliance with this advice.

FOCUS ON RESEARCH 4.1

TESTING A THEORY – PATIENT SATISFACTION

A study to examine the effects of a general practitioner's consulting style on patient satisfaction (Savage and Armstrong 1990).

This study examined the effect of an expert, directive consulting style and a sharing patient-centred consulting style on patient satisfaction. This paper is interesting for both methodological and theoretical reasons. Methodologically, it uses a random control design in a naturalistic setting. This means that it is possible to compare the effects of the two types of consulting style without the problem of identifying individual differences (these are controlled for by the design) and without the problem of an artificial experiment (the study took place in a natural environment). Theoretically, the study examines the prediction that the educational model of doctor–patient communication is problematic (i.e. is the expert approach a suitable one?) and examines patient preferences for the method of doctor–patient communication.

Background

A traditional model of doctor–patient communication regards the doctor as an expert who communicates their 'knowledge' to the naïve patient. Within this framework, the doctor is regarded as an authority figure who instructs and directs the patient. However, recent research has suggested that the communication process may be improved if a sharing, patient-centred consulting style is adopted. This approach emphasizes an interaction between the doctor and the patient and suggests this style may result in greater patient commitment to any advice given, potentially higher levels of compliance and greater patient satisfaction. Savage and Armstrong (1990) aimed to examine patients' responses to receiving either a 'directive/doctor-centred consulting style' or a 'sharing/patient-centred consulting style'.

Methodology

Subjects The study was undertaken in a group practice in an inner city area of London. Four patients from each surgery for one doctor, over four months were randomly selected for the study. Patients were selected if they were aged 16–75, did not have a life-threatening condition, if they were not attending for administrative/preventative reasons, and if the GP involved considered that they would not be upset by the project. Overall, 359 patient were invited to take part in the study and a total of 200 patients completed all assessments and were included in the data analysis.

Design The study involved a randomized controlled design with two conditions: (1) sharing consulting style and (2) directive consulting style. Patients were randomly allocated to one condition and received a consultation with the GP involving the appropriate consulting style.

Procedure A set of cards was designed to randomly allocate each patient to a condition. When a patient entered the consulting room they were greeted and asked to describe their problem. When this was completed, the GP turned over a card to determine the appropriate style of consultation. Advice and treatment were then given by the GP in that style. For example, the doctor's judgement on the consultation could have been either 'This is a serious problem/I don't think this is a serious problem' (a directive style) or 'Why do you think this has happened?' (a sharing style). For the diagnosis, the doctor could either say 'You are suffering from . . .' (a directive style) or 'What do you think is wrong?' (a sharing style). For the treatment advice the doctor could either say 'It is essential that you take this medicine' (a directive style) or 'What were you hoping I would be able to do?' (a sharing style). Each consultation was recorded and assessed by an independent assessor to check that the consulting style used was in accordance with that selected.

Measures All subjects were asked to complete a questionnaire immediately after each consultation and one week later. This contained questions about the patient's satisfaction with the consultation in terms of the following factors:

- *The doctor's understanding of the problem.* This was measured by items such as 'I perceived the general practitioner to have a complete understanding'.
- *The adequacy of the explanation of the problem.* This was measured by items such as 'I received an excellent explanation'.
- *Feeling helped.* This was measured by the statements 'I felt greatly helped' and 'I felt much better'.

Results

The results were analysed to evaluate differences in aspects of patient satisfaction between those patients who had received a directive versus a sharing consulting style. In addition, this difference was also examined in relation to patient characteristics (whether the patient had a physical problem, whether they received a prescription, had any tests and were infrequent attenders).

Patient satisfaction

The results showed that although all subjects reported high levels of satisfaction immediately after the consultation in terms of doctor's understanding, explanation and being helped, this was higher in those subjects who had received a directive style in their consultation. In addition, this difference was also found after one week. When the results were analysed to examine the role of patient characteristics on satisfaction, the results indicated that the directive style produced higher levels of satisfaction in those patients who rarely attended the surgery, had a physical problem, did not receive tests and received a prescription.

Conclusion

The results suggest that a directive consulting style was associated with higher levels of patient satisfaction than a sharing consulting style. This provides support for the educational model of doctor–patient communication with the doctor as the 'expert' and the patient as the 'layperson'. In addition, it suggests that patients in the present study preferred an authority figure who offered a formal diagnosis rather than a sharing doctor who asked for the patient's views. Therefore, although recent research has criticized the traditional educational model of doctor–patient communication, the results from this study suggest that some patients may prefer this approach.

Patient's recall

Researchers also examined the process of recall of the information given during the consultation. Bain (1977) examined the recall from a sample of patients who had attended a GP consultation and found that 37 per cent could not recall the name of the drug, 23 per cent could not recall the frequency of the dose and 25 per cent could not recall the duration of the treatment. A further study by Crichton *et al.* (1978), found that 22 per cent of patients had forgotten the treatment regime recommended by their doctors. In a meta-analysis of the research into recall of consultation information, Ley found that recall is influenced by a multitude of factors. For example, Ley argued that anxiety, medical knowledge, intellectual level, the importance of the statement, primacy effect and the number of statements increase recall. However, he concluded that recall is not influenced by the age of the patient, which is contrary to some predictions of the effect of ageing on memory and some of the myths and counter-myths of the ageing process. Recalling information after the consultation may be related to compliance.

How can compliance be improved?

Compliance is considered to be essential to patient well-being. Therefore, studies have been carried out to examine which factors can be used in order to improve compliance.

The role of information

Researchers have examined the role of information and the type of information on improving patient compliance with recommendations made during the consultation by health professionals. Using meta-analysis, Mullen *et al.* (1985) looked at the effects of instructional and educational information on compliance and found that 64 per cent of patients were more compliant when using such information. Haynes (1982) took a baseline of 52 per cent compliance with recommendations made during a consultation, and found that information generally only improved compliance to a level of 66 per cent. However, Haynes reported that behavioural and individualized instruction improved compliance to 75 per cent. Information giving may therefore be a means of improving compliance.

Recommendations for improving compliance

Several recommendations have been made in order to improve communication and therefore improve compliance.

Oral information

Ley (1989) suggested that one way of improving compliance is to improve communication in terms of the content of an oral communication. He believes the following factors are important:

- primacy effect – patients have a tendency to remember the first thing they are told;
- to stress the importance of compliance;
- to simplify the information;
- to use repetition;
- to be specific;
- to follow-up the consultation with additional interviews.

Written information

Researchers also looked at the use of written information in improving compliance. Ley and Morris (1984) examined the effect of written information about medication and found that it increased knowledge in 90 per cent of the studies, increased compliance in 60 per cent of the studies, and improved outcome in 57 per cent of the studies.

Ley's cognitive hypothesis model, and its emphasis on patient satisfaction, understanding and recall, has been influential in terms of promoting research into the communication between health professionals and patients. In addition, the model has prompted the examination of using information to improve the communication process. As a result of this, the role of information has been explored further in terms of its effect on recovery and outcome.

The wider role of information in illness

Information and recovery from surgery

Information may also be related to recovery and outcome following illness and surgery. On the basis that the stress caused by surgery may be related to later recovery, Janis (1958) interviewed patients before and after surgery to examine the effects of pre-operative fear on post-operative recovery. Janis examined the differences between pre-operative extreme fear, moderate fear and little or no fear on outcome. Extreme fear was reflected in patients' constant concern, anxiety and reports of vulnerability, moderate fear was reflected in reality orientation with the individual seeking out information, and little or no fear was reflected by a state of denial. The results were that moderate pre-operative fear (i.e. a reality orientation and information seeking) was related to a decrease in post-operative distress. Janis suggested that moderate fear results in the individual developing a defence mechanism, developing coping strategies, seeking out relevant information, and rehearsing the outcome of the surgery. This approach may lead to increased confidence in the outcome, which is reflected in the decreased post-operative distress. However, there is conflicting evidence regarding this 'U' shaped relationship between anxiety and outcome (see Johnston and Vogele 1993).

Using information to improve recovery

If stress is related to recovery from surgery, then obviously information could be an important way of reducing this stress. There are different types of information that could be used to effect the outcome of recovery from a medical intervention. These have been described as (1) *sensory information*, which can be used to help individuals deal with their feelings or to reflect on these feelings; (2) *procedural information*, which enables individuals to learn how the process or the intervention will actually be done; (3) *coping skills information*, which can educate the individual about possible coping strategies; and (4) *behavioural instructions*, which teach the individual how to behave in terms of factors such as coughing and relaxing.

Researchers have evaluated the relative roles of these different types of information in promoting recovery and reducing distress. Johnson and Leventhal (1974) gave sensory information (i.e. information about feelings) to patients before an endoscopic examination and noted a reduction in the level of distress experienced by these patients. Egbert *et al.* (1964) gave sensory information (i.e. about feelings), and coping skills information (i.e. about what coping skills could be used), to patients in hospital undergoing abdominal surgery. They reported that sensory and coping information reduced the need for pain killers and in addition reduced the hospital stay by three days. Young and Humphrey (1985) gave information to patients going into hospital, and found that information specific to how they could survive hospital reduced the distress and their length of stay in the hospital. Research has also specifically examined the role of pre-operative information. Johnston (1980) found that pre-operative information can influence recovery and reduce anxiety, pain rating, length of hospitalization and analgesic intake. Further, in a detailed meta-analysis of the published and unpublished literature on preparation for surgery, Johnston and Vogele (1993) concluded that preparation for surgery in the form of both procedural information (i.e. what will happen) and behavioural instructions (i.e. how to behave afterwards) resulted in significant benefits on all outcome variables explored, including mood, pain, recovery, physiological indices and satisfaction. Although the reasons why pre-operative information is so successful remain unclear, it is possible that pre-operative information may be beneficial to the individual in terms of the reduction of anxiety by enabling the patient to mentally rehearse their anticipated worries, fears and changes following the operation; thus any changes become predictable. These results therefore suggest that information communicated correctly by the doctor or the health professional may be an important part of reducing the distress following hospitalization or a hospital intervention.

The role of knowledge in doctor–patient communication

Ley's approach to doctor–patient communication can be understood within the framework of an educational model involving the transfer of medical knowledge from expert to layperson (Marteau and Johnston 1990). This traditional approach has motivated research into health professional's medical knowledge, which is seen as a product of their training and education. Accordingly, the communication process is seen as originating from the health professional's knowledge base.

Boyle (1970), although emphasizing patients' knowledge, also provided some insights into doctors' knowledge of the location of organs and the causes of a variety of illnesses. The results showed that although the doctor's knowledge was superior to that of the patient's, some doctors wrongly located organs such as the heart and wrongly defined problems such as 'constipation' and 'diarrhoea'. It has also been found that health professionals show inaccurate knowledge about diabetes (Etzwiler 1967; Scheiderich *et al.* 1983) and asthma (Anderson *et al.* 1983). Over recent years, due to government documents such as *Health for All* and the *Health of the Nation*, primary care team members are spending more time on health promotion practices, which often involve making recommendations about changing behaviours such as smoking, drinking and diet. Research has consequently examined health professionals' knowledge about these practices. Murray *et al.* (1993) examined the dietary knowledge of primary care professionals in Scotland. GPs, community nurses and practice nurses completed a questionnaire consisting of a series of commonly heard statements about diet and were asked to state whether they agreed or disagreed with them. The results showed high levels of correct knowledge for statements such as 'most people should eat less sugar' and 'most people should eat more fibre', and relatively poor accuracy for statements such as 'cholesterol in food is the most important dietary factor in controlling blood lipid levels'. The authors concluded that primary health care professionals show generally good dietary knowledge but that 'there is clearly an urgent need to develop better teaching and training in the dietary aspects of coronary heart disease'.

Problems with the traditional approach to doctor–patient communication

Traditional models of the communication between health professionals and patients have emphasized the transfer of knowledge from expert to layperson. Ley's cognitive hypothesis model of communication includes a role for the patient and emphasizes patient factors in the communication process as well as doctor factors such as the provision of relevant information. This approach has encouraged research into the wider role of information in health and illness. However, there are several problems with this educational approach, which can be summarized as follows:

- It assumes that the communication from the health professional is from an expert whose knowledge base is one of objective knowledge and does not involve the health beliefs of that individual health professional.
- Patient compliance is seen as positive and unproblematic
- Improved knowledge is predicted to improve the communication process.
- It does not include a role for patient health beliefs.

The adherence model of communication

In an attempt to further our understanding of the communication process, Stanton (1987) developed the model of adherence. The shift in terminology from 'compliance' to 'adherence' illustrates the attempt of the model to depart from the traditional view of doctor as an expert who gives advice to a compliant patient. The adherence model suggested that communication from the health professional results in enhanced patient knowledge and patient satisfaction and an adherence to the recommended medical regime. This aspect of the adherence model is similar to Ley's model. In addition, however, it suggested that patients' beliefs are important and the model emphasized the patient's locus of control, perceived social support and the disruption of lifestyle involved in adherence. Therefore, the model progresses from Ley's model, in that it includes aspects of the patients and emphasizes the interaction between the health professionals and the patients.

However, yet again this model of communication assumes that the health professionals' information is based on objective knowledge and is not influenced by their own health beliefs. Patients are regarded as laypeople who have their own varying beliefs and perspectives that need to be dealt with by the doctors and addressed in terms of the language and content of the communication. In contrast, doctors are regarded as objective and holding only professional views.

The problem of doctor variability

Traditionally, doctors are regarded as having an objective knowledge set that comes from their extensive medical education. If this were the case then it could be predicted that doctors with similar levels of knowledge and training would behave in similar ways. In addition, if doctors' behaviour were objective then their behaviour would be consistent. However, considerable variability among doctors in terms of different aspects of their practice has been found. For example, Anderson *et al.* (1983) reported that doctors differ in their diagnosis of asthma. Mapes (1980) suggested that they vary in terms of their prescribing behaviour, with a variation of 15–90 per cent of patients receiving drugs. Bucknall *et al.* (1986) reported variation in the methods used by doctors to measure blood pressure and Marteau and Baum (1984) also reported that doctors vary in their treatment of diabetes.

According to a traditional educational model of doctor–patient communication, this variability could be understood in terms of differing levels of knowledge and expertise. However, this variability can also be understood by examining the other factors involved in the clinical decision-making process.

Explaining variability – clinical decision-making as problem-solving

A model of problem-solving

Clinical decision-making processes are a specialized form of problem-solving and have been studied within the context of problem-solving and

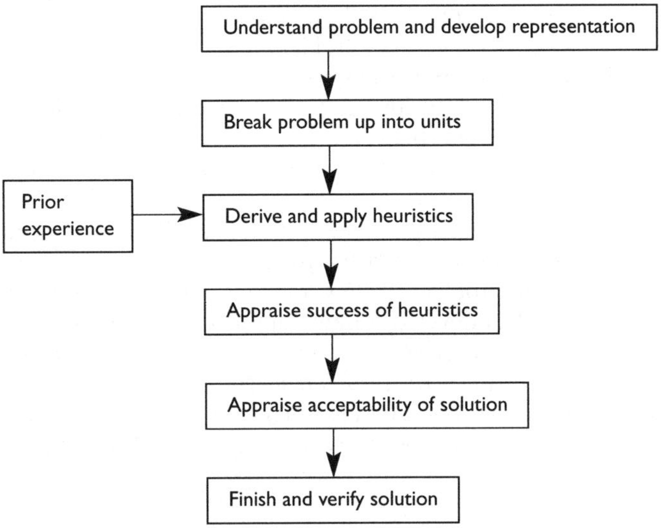

Figure 4.2 A simplified model of problem-solving

theories of information processing. It is often assumed that clinical decisions are made by the process of *inductive reasoning*, which involves collecting evidence and data and using this data to develop a conclusion and a hypothesis. For example, within this framework, a general practitioner would start a consultation with a patient without any prior model of their problem. The GP would then ask the appropriate questions regarding the patient's history and symptoms and develop a hypothesis about the presenting problem. However, doctors' decision-making processes are generally considered within the framework of the *hypothetico-deductive model* of decision-making. This perspective emphasizes the development of hypotheses early on in the consultation and is illustrated by Newell and Simon's (1972) model of problem-solving, which emphasizes hypothesis testing. Newell and Simon suggested that problem-solving involves a number of stages that result in a solution to any given problem. This model has been applied to many different forms of problem-solving and is a useful framework for examining clinical decisions (see Fig. 4.2).

The stages involved are as follows:

1 *Understand the nature of the problem and develop an internal representation.* At this stage, the individual needs to formulate an internal representation of the problem. This process involves understanding the goal of the problem, evaluating any given conditions and assessing the nature of the available data.
2 *Develop a plan of action for solving the problem.* Newell and Simon differentiated between two types of plans: heuristics and algorithms. An algorithm is a set of rules that will provide a correct solution if applied

correctly (e.g. addition, multiplication, etc. involve algorithms). However, most human problem-solving involves heuristics, which are rules of thumb. Heuristics are less definite and specific but provide guidance and direction for the problem solver. Heuristics may involve developing parallels between the present problem and previous similar ones.

3 *Apply heuristics.* Once developed, the plans are then applied to the given situation.
4 *Determine whether heuristics have been fruitful.* The individual then decides whether the heuristics have been successful in the attempt to solve the given problem. If they are considered unsuccessful, the individual may need to develop a new approach to the problem.
5 *Determine whether an acceptable solution has been obtained.*
6 *Finish and verify the solution.* The end-point of the problem-solving process involves the individual deciding that an acceptable solution to the problem has been reached and that this solution provides a suitable outcome.

According to Newell and Simon's model of problem-solving, hypotheses about the causes and solutions to the problem are developed very early on in the process. They regarded this process as dynamic and ever-changing and suggested that at each stage of the process the individual applies a 'means end analysis', whereby they assess the value of the hypothesis, which is either accepted or rejected according to the evidence. This type of model involves information processing whereby the individual develops hypotheses to convert an open problem, which may be unmanageable with no obvious end-point, to one which can be closed and tested by a series of hypotheses.

Clinical decisions as problem-solving

Clinical decisions can be conceptualized as a form of problem-solving and involve the development of hypotheses early on in the consultation process. These hypotheses are subsequently tested by the doctor's selection of questions. Models of problem-solving have been applied to clinical decision-making by several authors (e.g. MacWhinney 1973; Weinman 1987), who have argued that the process of formulating a clinical decision involves the following stages (see Fig. 4.3):

1 *Accessing information about the patient's symptoms.* The initial questions in any consultation from health professional to the patient will enable the health professional to understand the nature of the problem and to form an internal representation of the type of problem.
2 *Developing hypotheses.* Early on in the problem-solving process, the health professional develops hypotheses about the possible causes and solutions to the problem.
3 *Search for attributes.* The health professional then proceeds to test the hypotheses by searching for factors either to confirm or to refute their hypotheses. Research into the hypothesis testing process has

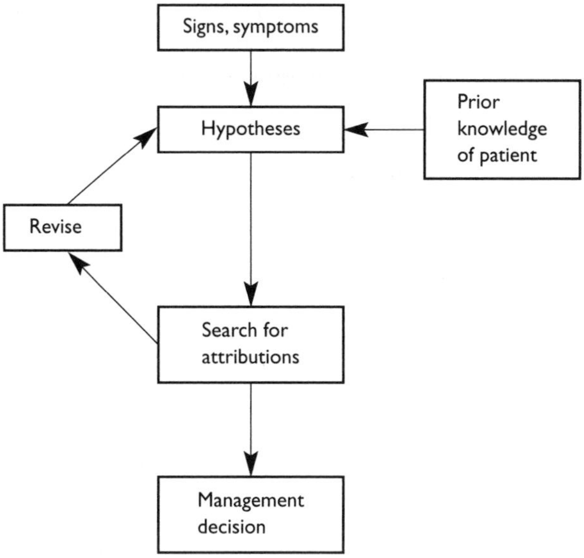

Figure 4.3 Diagnosis as a form of problem-solving

indicated that although doctors aim to either confirm or refute their hypothesis by asking balanced questions, most of their questioning is biased towards confirmation of their original hypothesis. Therefore, an initial hypothesis that a patient has a psychological problem may cause the doctor to focus on the patient's psychological state and ignore the patient's attempt to talk about their physical symptoms. Studies have shown that doctors' clinical information collected subsequent to the development of a hypothesis may be systematically distorted to support the original hypothesis (Wallsten 1978). Furthermore, the type of hypothesis has been shown to bias the collection and interpretation of any information received during the consultation (Wason 1974).

4 *Making a management decision.* The outcome of the clinical decision-making process involves the health professional deciding on the way forward. Weinman (1987) suggested that it is important to realize that the outcome of a consultation and a diagnosis is not an absolute entity, but is itself a hypothesis and an informed guess that will be either confirmed or refuted by future events.

Explaining variability

Variability in the behaviour of health professionals can therefore be understood in terms of the processes involved in clinical decisions. For example, health professionals may:

- access different information about the patient's symptoms;
- develop different hypotheses;

- access different attributes either to confirm or to refute their hypotheses;
- have differing degrees of a bias towards confirmation;
- consequently reach different management decisions.

Explaining variability – the role of health professionals' health beliefs

The hypothesis testing model of clinical decision-making provides some understanding of the possible causes of variability in health professional behaviour. Perhaps the most important stage in the model that may lead to variability is the development of the original hypothesis. Patients are described as having lay beliefs, which are individual and variable. Health professionals are usually described as having professional beliefs, which are often assumed to be consistent and predictable. However, the development of the original hypothesis involves the health professional's own health beliefs, which may vary as much as those of the patient. Components of models such as the health belief model, the protection motivation theory and attribution theory have been developed to examine health professionals' beliefs. The beliefs involved in making the original hypothesis can be categorized as follows:

1 *The health professional's own beliefs about the nature of clinical problems.* Health professionals have their own beliefs about health and illness. This pre-existing factor will influence their choice of hypothesis. For example, if a health professional believes that health and illness are determined by biomedical factors (e.g. lesions, bacteria, viruses) then they will develop a hypothesis about the patient's problem that reflects this perspective (e.g. a patient who reports feeling tired all the time may be anaemic). However, a health professional who views health and illness as relating to psychosocial factors may develop hypotheses reflecting this perspective (e.g. a patient who reports feeling tired all the time may be under stress).
2 *The health professional's estimate of the probability of the hypothesis and disease.* Health professionals will have pre-existing beliefs about the prevalence and incidence of any given health problem that will influence the process of developing a hypothesis. For example, some doctors may regard childhood asthma as a common complaint and hypothesize that a child presenting with a cough has asthma, whereas others may believe that childhood asthma is rare and so will not consider this hypothesis.
3 *The seriousness and treatability of the disease.* Weinman (1987) argued that health professionals are motivated to consider the 'pay-off' involved in reaching a correct diagnosis and that this will influence their choice of hypothesis. He suggested that this pay-off is related to their beliefs about the seriousness and treatability of an illness. For example, a child presenting with abdominal pain may result in an original hypothesis of appendicitis as this is both a serious and treatable condition, and the

benefits of arriving at the correct diagnosis for this condition far outweigh the costs involved (such as time wasting) if this hypothesis is refuted. Marteau and Baum (1984) have argued that health professionals vary in their perceptions of the seriousness of diabetes and that these beliefs will influence their recommendations for treatment. Brewin (1984) carried out a study looking at the relationship between medical students' perceptions of the controllability of a patient's life events and the hypothetical prescription of antidepressants. The results showed that the students reported variability in their beliefs about the controllability of life events; if the patient was seen not to be in control (i.e. the patient was seen as a victim), the students were more likely to prescribe antidepressants than if the patient was seen to be in control. This suggests that not only do health professionals report inconsistency and variability in their beliefs, this variability may be translated into variability in their behaviour

4 *Personal knowledge of the patient.* The original hypothesis will also be related to the health professional's existing knowledge of the patient. Such factors may include the patient's medical history, knowledge about their psychological state, an understanding of their psychosocial environment and a belief about why the patient uses the medical services.
5 *The health professional's stereotypes.* Stereotypes are sometimes seen as problematic and as confounding the decision-making process. However, most meetings between health professionals and patients are time-limited and consequently stereotypes play a central role in developing and testing a hypothesis and reaching a management decision. Stereotypes reflect the process of 'cognitive economy' and may be developed according to a multitude of factors such as how the patient looks/talks/walks or whether they remind the health professional of previous patients. Without stereotypes, consultations between health professionals and patients would be extremely time-consuming.

Other factors which may influence the development of the original hypothesis include:

1 *The health professional's mood.* The health professional's mood may influence the choice of hypotheses and the subsequent process of testing this hypothesis. Isen *et al.* (1991) manipulated mood in a group of medical students and evaluated the effect of induced positive affect on their decision-making processes. Positive affect was induced by informing subjects in this group that they had performed in the top 3 per cent of all graduate students nationwide in an anagram task. All subjects were then given a set of hypothetical patients and asked to decide which one was most likely to have lung cancer. The results showed that those subjects in the positive affect group spent less time to reach the correct decision and showed greater interest in the case histories by going beyond the assigned task. The authors therefore concluded that mood influenced the subjects' decision-making processes.

2 *The profile characteristics of the health professional.* Factors such as age, sex, weight, geographical location, previous experience and the health professional's own behaviour may also effect the decision-making process. For example, smoking doctors have been shown to spend more time counselling about smoking than their non-smoking counterparts (Stokes and Rigotti 1988). Further, thinner practice nurses have been shown to have different beliefs about obesity and offer different advice to obese patients than overweight practice nurses (Hoppe and Ogden 1997).

In summary, variability in health professionals' behaviour can be understood in terms of the factors involved in the decision-making process. In particular, many factors pre-dating the development of the original hypothesis such as the health professional's own beliefs may contribute to this variability.

Communicating beliefs to patients

If health professionals hold their own health-related beliefs, these may be communicated to the patients. A study by McNeil *et al.* (1982) examined the effects of health professionals' language on the patients' choice of hypothetical treatment. They assessed the effect of offering surgery either if it would 'increase the probability of survival' or would 'decrease the probability of death'. The results showed that patients are more likely to choose surgery if they believed it increased the probability of survival rather than if it decreased the probability of death. The phrasing of such a question would very much reflect the individual beliefs of the doctor, which in turn influenced the choices of the patients. In a similar vein, Misselbrook and Armstrong (2000) asked patients whether they would accept treatment to prevent stroke and presented the effectiveness of this treatment in four different ways. The results showed that although all the forms of presentation were actually the same, 92 per cent of the patients said they would accept the treatment if it reduced their chances of stroke by 45 per cent (relative risk); 75 per cent said they would accept the treatment if it reduced their risk from 1 in 400 to 1 in 700 (absolute risk); 71 per cent said they would accept it if the doctor had to treat 35 patients for 25 years to prevent one stroke (number needed to treat); and only 44 per cent said they would accept it if the treatment had a 3 per cent chance of doing them good and a 97 per cent chance of doing no good or not being needed (personal probability of benefit). Therefore, although the actual risk of the treatment was the same in all four conditions, the ways of presenting this risk varied and this resulted in a variation in patient uptake. These results indicate that not only do health professionals hold their own subjective views, but that these views may be communicated to the patient in a way that may then influence the patient's choice of treatment.

Explaining variability – an interaction between health professional and patient

The explanations of variability in health professionals' behaviour presented so far have focused on the health professional in isolation. The educational model emphasizes the knowledge of the health professional and ignores the factors involved in the clinical decision-making process and their health beliefs. This perspective accepts the traditional divide between lay beliefs and professional beliefs. Emphasizing the clinical decision-making processes and health beliefs represents a shift from this perspective and attempts to see the divide between these two types of belief as problematic; health professionals have their own individualized 'lay beliefs' similar to patients. However, this explanation of variability ignores another important factor, namely the patient. Any variability in health professionals' behaviour exists in the context of both the health professional and the patient. Therefore, in order to understand the processes involved in health professional–patient communication, the resulting management decisions and any variability in the outcome of the consultation, both patient and health professional should be considered as a dyad. The consultation involves two individuals and a communication process that exists between these individuals. Research has explored the relationship between health professional and patient with an emphasis not on either the health professional or the patient but on the interaction between the two in the following ways: the level of agreement between health professional and patient and the impact of this agreement on patient outcome.

Agreement between health professional and patient

If health professional–patient communication is seen as an interaction between two individuals then it is important to understand the extent to which these two individuals speak the same language, share the same beliefs and agree as to the desired content and outcome of any consultation. This is of particular relevance to general practice consultations where patient and health professional perspectives are most likely to coincide. For example, Pendleton *et al.* (1984) argued that the central tasks of a general practice consultation involved agreement with the patient about the nature of the problem, the action to be taken and subsequent management. Tuckett *et al.* (1985) likewise argued that the consultation should be conceptualized as a 'meeting between experts' and emphasized the importance of the patient's and doctor's potentially different views of the problem.

Recent research has examined levels of agreement between GPs' and patients' beliefs about different health problems. Ogden *et al.* (1999a) explored GPs' and patients' models of depression in terms of symptoms (mood and somatic), causes (psychological, medical, external), and treatments (medical and non-medical). The results showed that GPs and patients agreed about the importance of mood-related symptoms, psychological causes and non-medical treatments. However, the GPs reported greater support for somatic symptoms, medical causes and medical treatments. Therefore, the results indicated that GPs hold a more medical model of depression than patients. From a similar perspective, Ogden *et al.* (2000) explored GPs' and patients' beliefs about obesity. The results showed that the GPs and patients reported similar beliefs for most psychological, behavioural and social causes of obesity. However, they differed consistently in their beliefs about medical causes. In particular, the patients rated a gland/hormone problem, slow metabolism and overall medical causes more highly than did the GPs. For the treatment of obesity, a similar pattern emerged with the two groups reporting similar beliefs for a range of methods, but showing different beliefs about who was most helpful. Whereas, the patients rated the GP as more helpful, the GPs rated the obese patients themselves more highly. Therefore, although GPs seem to have a more medical model or depression they have a less medical model of obesity. Research has also shown that doctors and patients differ in their beliefs about the role of the doctor (Ogden *et al.* 1997) and in terms of what is important to know about medicines (Berry *et al.* 1997). If the health professional–patient communication is seen as an interaction, then these studies suggest that it may well be an interaction between two individuals with very different perspectives. Do these different perspectives influence patient outcomes?

The role of agreement in patient outcomes

If doctors and patients have different beliefs about illness, different beliefs about the role of the doctor and about medicines, does this lack of agreement relate to patient outcomes? It is possible that such disagreement may result in poor compliance to medication ('why should I take antidepressants if I am not depressed?'), poor compliance to any recommended changes in behaviour ('why should I eat less if obesity is caused by hormones?') or low satisfaction with the consultation ('I wanted emotional support and the GP gave me a prescription'). To date little research has explored these possibilities. One study did, however, examine the extent to which a patient's expectations of a GP consultation were met by the GP and whether this predicted patient satisfaction. Williams *et al.* (1995) asked 504 general practice patients to complete a measure of their expectations of the consultation with their GP prior to it taking place and a measure of whether their expectations were actually met afterwards. The results showed that having more expectations met was related to a higher level of satisfaction with the consultation. However, this study did not explore compliance, nor did it examine whether the GP and patient had a shared belief about the nature of the consultation. Therefore, further research is needed to develop methodological and theoretical approaches to the consultation as an interaction. In addition, research is needed to explore whether the nature of the interaction and the level of the agreement between health professional and patient predicts patient outcomes.

To conclude

Traditional educational models of doctor–patient communication emphasized patient factors and considered non-compliance to be the result of patient variability. The relationship between health professionals and patients was seen as the communication of expert medical knowledge from an objective professional to a subjective layperson. Within this framework, Ley's model explained failures in communication in the context of the failure to comply in terms of patient factors, including patient's satisfaction, lack of understanding, or lack of recall. In addition, methods to improve the communication focused on the health professional's ability to communicate this factual knowledge to the patient. However, recent research has highlighted variability in the behaviours of health professionals that cannot simply be explained in terms of differences in knowledge. This variability can be examined in terms of the processes involved in clinical decision-making by the health professional and in particular the factors that influence the development of hypotheses. This variability has also been examined within the context of health beliefs, and it is argued that the division between professional and lay beliefs may be a simplification, with health professionals holding both professional and lay beliefs; health professionals have beliefs that are individual to them in the way that patients have their own individual beliefs. However, perhaps to further conceptualize the communication process, it is important to understand not only the health professional's preconceived ideas/prejudices/stereotypes/lay beliefs/professional beliefs or the patient's beliefs, but to consider the processes involved in any communication between health professional and patient as an interaction that occurs in the context of these beliefs.

? Questions

1 Health professionals' decisions are based on knowledge. Discuss.

2 What are the problems with the hypothetico-deductive model of decision-making?

3 Discuss the role of health professionals' beliefs in the communication process.

4 To what extent is non-compliance the responsibility of the patient?

5 Shared beliefs are essential for improving patient outcomes. Discuss.

6 Describe a research project designed to evaluate health professionals' beliefs.

▶ For discussion

Consider the last time you had contact with a health professional (e.g. doctor, dentist, nurse, etc.). Discuss the content of the consultation and think about how the health professional's health beliefs may have influenced this.

Assumptions in health psychology

Some of the research cited in this chapter illustrates the kinds of assumptions that underly the study of health professionals and also provides insights into the assumptions of health psychology.

1 *The mind–body split.* Health psychology attempts to challenge the biomedical model of health and illness. This involves challenging biomedical assumptions such as the mind–body split. However, perhaps by emphasizing the mind (attitudes, cognitions, beliefs) as a separate entity, the mind–body split is not challenged but reinforced.

2 *Biomedical outcomes.* Challenging the biomedical model also involves questioning some of the outcomes used by medicine. For example, compliance with recommendations for drug taking, accuracy of recall, changing health behaviours following advice are all established desired outcomes. Health psychology accepts these outcomes by examining ways in which communication can be improved, variability can be understood and reduced and compliance promoted. However, again, accepting these outcomes as legitimate is also a way of supporting biomedicine. Perhaps variability is acceptable. Perhaps inaccuracy of recall sums up what happens in communication (psychologists who study memory would argue that memory is the only process that is defined by its failures – memory is about reconstruction). Even though psychology adds to a biomedical model, by accepting the same outcomes it does not challenge it.

3 *Adding the social context.* Individuals exist within a social world and yet health psychology often misses out this world. An emphasis on the interaction between health professionals and patients represents an attempt to examine the cognitions of both these groups in the context of each other (the relationship context). However, this interaction is still accessed through an individual's beliefs. Is asking someone about the interaction actually examining the interaction or is it examining their cognitions about this interaction?

Further reading

Boyle, C.M. (1970) Differences between patients' and doctors' interpretations of common medical terms, *British Medical Journal*, 2: 286–9.

This is a classic paper illustrating differences between doctors' and patients' knowledge and interpretation. At the time it was written it was central to the contemporary emphasis on a need to acknowledge how uninformed patients were. However, it also illustrates variability in doctors' knowledge.

Marteau, T.M. and Johnston, M. (1990) Health professionals: a source of variance in health outcomes, *Psychology and Health*, 5: 47–58.

This paper examines the different models of health professional's behaviour and emphasizes the role of health professional's health beliefs.

Trostle, J.A. (1988) Medical compliance as an ideology, *Social Science and Medicine*, 27: 1299–308.

This theoretical paper examines the background to the recent interest in compliance and discusses the relationship between compliance and physician control.

CHAPTER 5

Smoking and alcohol use

Chapter overview

This chapter examines the prevalence of smoking and alcohol consumption and evaluates the health consequences of these behaviours. The history of theories of addictive behaviours and the shift from a disease model of addictions to the social learning theory perspective is then described. The chapter also examines the four stages of substance use from initiation and maintenance to cessation and relapse, and discusses these stages in the context of the different models of addictive behaviours. The chapter concludes with an examination of a cross-behavioural perspective on addictive behaviours and an assessment of the similarities and differences between smoking and drinking and their relationship to other behaviours.

This chapter covers:

- What is an addiction?
- What is the 2nd disease concept?
- What is the social learning perspective?
- The stages of substance use
- Initiating and maintaining an addictive behaviour
- The cessation of an addictive behaviour
- Relapse in smoking and drinking
- A cross-addictive behaviour perspective

Who smokes?

Data from the 1992 General Household Survey in the UK showed that 28 per cent of people aged 16 and over were smokers compared with 30 per cent in 1990. This decrease in smoking behaviour follows a trend for an overall decline and is shown in Fig. 5.1. However, the data also showed that, although women smoke fewer cigarettes than men, fewer women than men are giving up.

Smokers can also be categorized in terms of whether they are 'ex-smokers', 'current smokers' or whether they have 'never smoked'. The trends in smoking behaviour according to these categories are shown in Fig. 5.2. Again, sex differences can be seen for these types of smoking behaviour with men showing an increase in the numbers of 'never smoked' and 'ex-smokers', and a decrease in 'current smokers', whilst women show the same profile of change for both 'current smokers' and 'ex-smokers' but show a consistently high level of individuals who have 'never smoked'.

In general, data about smoking behaviour (General Household Survey 1994) suggests the following about smokers:

- Smoking behaviour is on the decline, but this decrease is greater in men than in women.
- Smokers tend to be in the unskilled manual group.
- There has been a dramatic reduction in the number of smokers smoking middle-tar cigarettes.

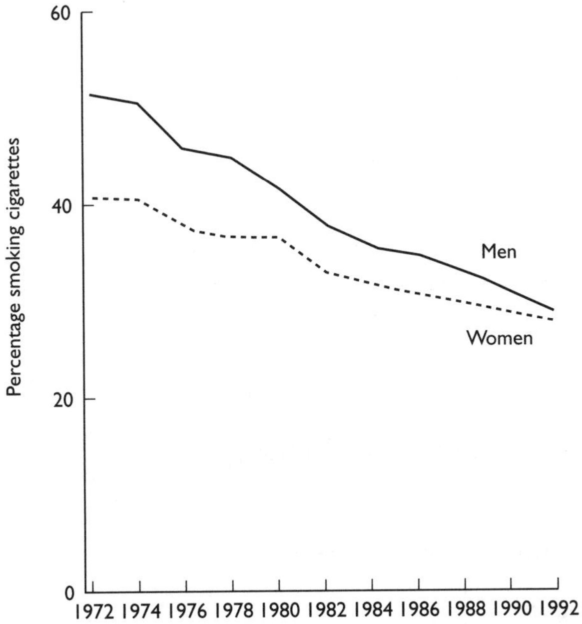

Figure 5.1 Changes in smoking, 1972–92

- Two-thirds of smokers report wanting to give up smoking.
- The majority of smokers (58 per cent) say that it would be fairly/very difficult to go without smoking for a whole day.

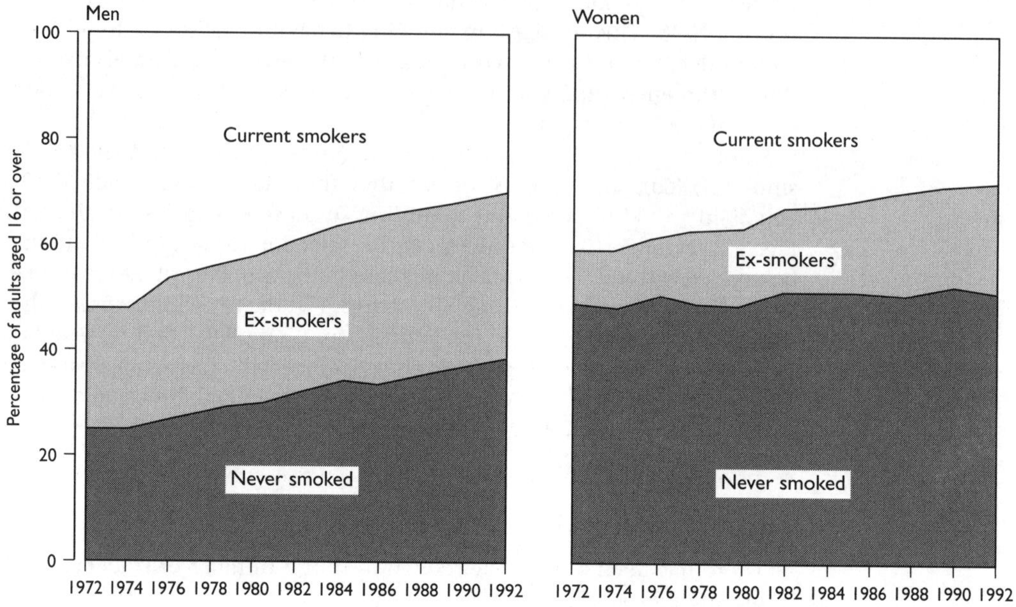

Figure 5.2 Current smokers, ex-smokers and non-smokers by sex, 1972–92

Who drinks?

According to the General Household Survey(1992), men on average drank 15.9 units a week (about eight pints of beer) and women drank about 5.4 units (about two and a half pints of beer). About 27 per cent of men and 11 per cent of women were drinking more than the recommended sensible amounts of alcohol which at this time were 21 units for men and 14 units for women. These limits have now been increased to 28 for men and 21 for women. Sex differences in drinking behaviour are shown in Fig. 5.3.

Health implications of smoking and alcohol use

Is smoking bad for health?

Negative effects

Doll and Hill (1954) reported that smoking cigarettes was related to lung cancer. Since then, smoking has also been implicated in coronary heart

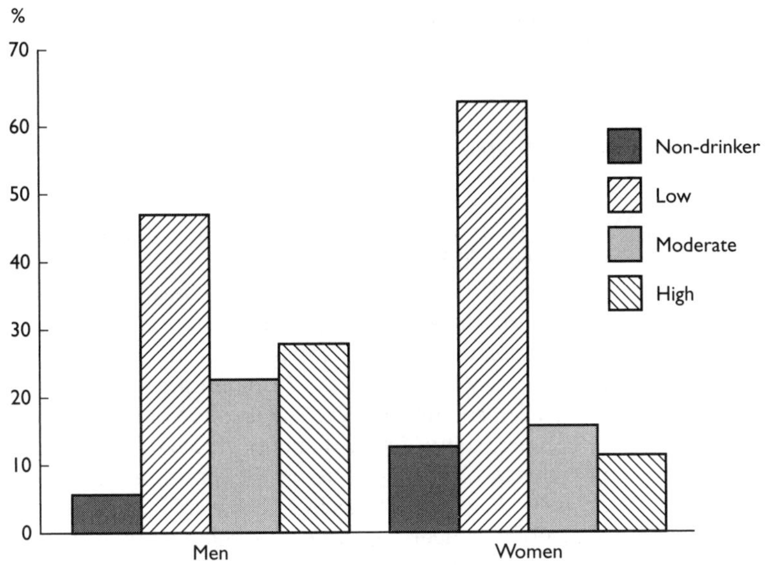

Figure 5.3 Alcohol consumption levels by sex, 1992

disease and a multitude of other cancers such as throat, stomach and bowel. In addition, the increase in life expectancy over the past 150 years is considerably less for smokers than for non-smokers (see Chapter 2). The risks of smoking were made explicit in a book by Peto *et al.*(1994), who stated that of 1000 20-year-olds in the UK who smoke cigarettes regularly about one will be murdered, six will die from traffic accidents, 250 will die from cigarettes in middle age (35–69) and another 250 will die from smoking in old age (70 and over). Recently, there has also been an interest in passive smoking and research suggests an association between passive smoking and lung cancer in adults and respiratory ill health in children (US Environmental Protection Agency 1992).

Positive effects

There are very few positive health effects of cigarette smoking. It has been suggested that smokers report positive mood effects from smoking and that smoking can help individuals to cope with difficult circumstances (Graham 1987).

Is alcohol consumption bad for health?

Negative effects

Alcohol consumption has several negative effects on health. For example, alcoholism increases the chance of disorders such as liver cirrhosis, cancers (e.g. pancreas and liver), hypertension and memory deficits (Smith and Kraus 1988). Alcohol also increases the chances of self-harm through accidents.

Positive effects

Alcohol may also have a positive effect on health. In a longitudinal study, Friedman and Kimball (1986) reported that light and moderate drinkers had lower morbidity and mortality rates than both non-drinkers and heavy drinkers. They argued that alcohol consumption reduces coronary heart disease via the following mechanisms: (1) a reduction in the production of catecholamines when stressed; (2) the protection of blood vessels from cholesterol; (3) a reduction in blood pressure; (4) self-therapy and (5) a short-term coping strategy. The results from the General Household Survey (1992) also showed some benefits of alcohol consumption with the reported prevalence of ill-health being higher amongst non-drinkers than among drinkers. However, it has been suggested that the apparent positive effects of alcohol on health may be an artefact of poor health in the non-drinkers who have stopped drinking due to health problems.

In an attempt to understand why people smoke and drink it is first necessary to examine the theories that have been developed to explain addictions.

What is an addiction?

Many theories have been developed to explain addictions and addictive behaviours, including moral models, which regard an addiction as the result of weakness and a lack of moral fibre; biomedical models, which see an addiction as a disease; and social learning theories, which regard addictive behaviours as behaviours that are learned according to the rules of learning theory. The multitude of terms that exist and are used with respect to behaviours such as smoking and alcohol are indicative of these different theoretical perspectives and in addition illustrate the tautological nature of the definitions. For example:

- *An addict*: someone who 'has no control over their behaviour', 'lacks moral fibre', 'uses a maladaptive coping mechanism', 'has an addictive behaviour'.
- *An addiction*: 'a need for a drug', 'the use of a substance that is psychologically and physiologically addictive', 'showing tolerance and withdrawal'.
- *Dependency*: 'showing psychological and physiological withdrawal'.
- *Drug*: 'an addictive substance', 'a substance that causes dependency', 'any medical substance'.

These different definitions indicate the relationship between terminology and theory. For example, concepts of 'control', 'withdrawal', 'tolerance' are indicative of a biomedical view of addictions. Concepts such as 'lacking moral fibre' suggest a moral model of addictions, and 'maladaptive coping mechanism' suggests a social learning perspective. In addition, the terms illustrate how difficult it is to define one term without using another with the risk that the definitions become tautologies.

Many questions have been asked about different addictive behaviours, including:

- What causes someone to start smoking?
- What causes drinking behaviour to become a problem?
- Why can some people just smoke socially whilst others need to smoke first thing in the morning?
- Is it possible for an alcoholic to return to normal drinking?
- Do addictions run in families?

Questions about the causes of an addiction can be answered according to the different theoretical perspectives that have been developed over the past 300 years to explain and predict addictions, including the moral model, the 1st disease concept, the 2nd disease concept and the social learning theory. These different theories and how they relate to attitudes to different substances will now be examined.

Historical changes in attitude and theoretical approach

Theory is often viewed as independent of changes in social attitudes. However, parallels can be seen between changes in theoretical perspective over the past 300 years and contemporary attitudes. These parallels will be discussed in terms of alcohol use.

The seventeenth century and the moral model of addictions

During the seventeenth century, alcohol was generally held in high esteem by society. It was regarded as safer than water, nutritious and the inn keeper was valued as a central figure in the community. In addition, at this time humans were considered to be separate from Nature, in terms of possessing a soul and a will and being responsible for their own behaviour. Animals' behaviour was seen as resulting from biological drives, whereas the behaviour of humans was seen to be a result of their own free choice. Accordingly, alcohol consumption was considered an acceptable behaviour, but excessive alcohol use was regarded as a result of free choice and personal responsibility. Alcoholism was therefore seen as a behaviour that deserved punishment, not treatment; alcoholics were regarded as choosing to behave excessively. This model of addiction was called the *moral model*. This perspective is similar to the arguments espoused by Thomas Szasz in the 1960s concerning the treatment versus punishment of mentally ill individuals and his distinction between being 'mad' or 'bad'. Szasz suggested that to label someone 'mad' and to treat them, removed the central facet of humanity, namely personal responsibility. He suggested that holding individuals responsible for their behaviour gave them back their sense of responsibility even if this resulted in them being seen as 'bad'. Similarly, the moral model of addictions considered alcoholics to have chosen to behave excessively and therefore deserving of punishment (acknowledging their responsibility) not treatment (denying them their responsibility). In effect, contemporary social attitudes were reflected in contemporary theory.

The nineteenth century and the 1st disease concept

During the nineteenth century, attitudes towards addictions and, in particular alcohol, changed. The temperance movement was developed and spread the word about the evils of drink. Alcohol was regarded as a powerful and destructive substance and alcoholics were regarded as its victims. This perspective is also reflected in prohibition and the banning of alcohol consumption in the USA. During this time, the *1st disease concept* of addiction was developed. This was the earliest form of a biomedical approach to addiction and regarded alcoholism as an illness. Within this model, the focus for the illness was the substance. Alcohol was seen as an addictive substance, and alcoholics were viewed as passively succumbing to its influence. The 1st disease concept regarded the substance as the problem and called for the treatment of excessive drinkers. Again, social attitudes to addiction were reflected in the development of theory.

The twentieth century and the 2nd disease concept

Attitudes towards addiction changed again at the beginning of the twentieth century. The USA learned quickly that banning alcohol consumption was more problematic than expected, and governments across the Western world realized that they could financially benefit from alcohol sales. In parallel, attitudes towards human behaviour were changing and a more liberal *laissez faire* attitude became dominant. Likewise, theories of addiction reflected these shifts. The *2nd disease model* of addiction was developed, which no longer saw the substance as the problem but pointed the finger at those individuals who became addicted. Within this perspective, the small minority of those who consumed alcohol to excess were seen as having a problem, but for the rest of society alcohol consumption returned to a position of an acceptable social habit. This perspective legitimized the sale of alcohol, recognized the resulting government benefits and emphasized the treatment of addicted individuals. Alcoholism was regarded as an illness developed by certain individuals who therefore needed support and treatment.

The 1970s and onwards – social learning theory

Over the past few years attitudes towards addictions have changed again. With the development of behaviourism, learning theory and a belief that behaviour was shaped by an interaction with both the environment and other individuals, the belief that excessive behaviour and addictions were illnesses began to be challenged. Since the 1970s, behaviours such as smoking, drinking and drug taking have been increasingly described within the context of all other behaviours. In the same way that theories of aggression shifted from a biological cause (aggression as an instinct) to social causes (aggression as a response to the environment/upbringing), addictions were also seen as learned behaviours. Within this perspective, the term addictive behaviour replaced addictions and such behaviours were regarded as a consequence of learning processes. This shift challenged the concepts of addictions, addict, illness and disease, however the theories still emphasized treatment.

Therefore, over the past 300 years there have been shifts in attitudes towards addictions and addictive behaviours that are reflected by the changing theoretical perspectives. Although the development of social learning theory highlighted some of the problems with the 2nd disease concept of addictions, both these perspectives still remain, and will now be examined in greater detail.

What is the 2nd disease concept?

The three perspectives in this category represent (1) pre-existing physical abnormalities, (2) pre-existing psychological abnormalities and (3) acquired dependency theory. All of these have a similar model of addiction in that they:

- regard addictions as discrete entities (you are either an addict or not);
- regard an addiction as an illness;
- focus on the individual as the problem;
- regard the addiction as irreversible;
- emphasize treatment;
- emphasize treatment through total abstinence.

A pre-existing physical abnormality

There are a number of perspectives which suggest that an addiction is the result of a pre-existing physical abnormality. For example, Alcoholics Anonymous argue that some individuals may have an allergy to alcohol and therefore become addicted once exposed to the substance. From this perspective comes the belief 'one drink – a drunk', 'once a drunk always a drunk' and stories of abstaining alcoholics relapsing after drinking sherry in a sherry trifle. In terms of smoking, this perspective would suggest that certain individuals are more sensitive to the effects of nicotine.

Nutritional/endocrinological theories suggest that some individuals may metabolize alcohol differently to others, that they become drunk quicker and may not experience any of the early symptoms of drunkenness. Similarly, this perspective would suggest that some individuals may process nicotine differently to others.

Genetic theories suggest that there may be a genetic predisposition to becoming an alcoholic or a smoker. To examine the influences of genetics, researchers have examined either identical twins reared apart or the relationship between adoptees and their biological parents. These methodologies tease apart the separate effects of environment and genetics. In an early study on genetics and smoking, Sheilds (1962) reported that out of 42 twins reared apart only 9 were discordant (showed different smoking behaviour). He reported that 18 pairs were both non-smokers and 15 pairs were both smokers. This is a much higher rate of concordance than predicted by chance. Evidence for a genetic factor in smoking has also been reported by Eysenck (1990) and in an Australian study examining the role of genetics in both the uptake of smoking (initiation) and committed smoking (maintenance) (Hannah *et al.* 1985). Research into the role of genetics in alcoholism has been more extensive and reviews of this literature can be found elsewhere (Peele 1984; Schuckit 1985). However, it has been estimated that a male child may be up to four times more likely to develop alcoholism if they have a biological parent who is an alcoholic.

A pre-existing psychological abnormality

Some theories suggest that certain individuals may become addicts due to a pre-existing psychological problem. For example, Freud argued that an addiction may be the result of either latent homosexuality, or a need for oral gratification. It has also been suggested that alcoholism may be related to a self-destructive personality or a need for power (e.g. McClelland *et al.* 1972). This perspective emphasizes a psychological abnormality that is irreversible and pre-dates the onset of the addictive behaviour.

Acquired dependency

Models within the 2nd disease perspective have also viewed addiction as the result of excess. For example, Jellinek in the 1960s developed a theory of species of alcoholism and phases of alcoholism (Jellinek 1960). This suggested that there were different types of addiction (alpha, gamma, delta) and that increased consumption of alcohol caused the individual to progress through different stages of the illness. He suggested that addiction resulted from exposure to the addictive substance and resulted in

(1) acquired tissue tolerance, (2) adaptive cell metabolism, (3) withdrawal and craving and (4) loss of control. In a similar vein, Edwards and Gross's (1976) theory of alcohol dependence syndrome argued that consistent alcohol use resulted in cell changes and subsequent dependency. Applied to smoking, this perspective suggests that nicotine causes addiction through its constant use. Although this perspective is classified as a 2nd disease concept, it is reminiscent of the 1st disease concept as the emphasis is on the substance rather than on the individual.

Problems with a disease model of addiction

Although many researchers still emphasize a disease model of addictions, there are several problems with this perspective:

- The disease model encourages treatment through lifelong abstinence. However, lifelong abstinence is very rare and may be difficult to achieve.
- The disease model does not incorporate relapse into its model of treatment. However, this 'all or nothing' perspective may actually promote relapse through encouraging individuals to set unreasonable targets of abstinence and by establishing the self-fulfilling prophecy of 'once a drunk always a drunk'.
- The description of controlled drinking, which suggested that alcoholics can return to 'normal drinking' patterns (Davies 1962; Sobel and Sobel 1976, 1978) challenged the central ideas of the disease model. The phenomenon of controlled drinking indicated that perhaps an addiction was not irreversible and that abstinence may not be the only treatment goal.

What is the social learning perspective?

The social learning perspective differs from the disease model of addiction in several ways:

- Addictive behaviours are seen as acquired habits, which are learned according to the rules of social learning theory.
- Addictive behaviours can be unlearned; they are not irreversible.
- Addictive behaviours lie along a continuum; they are not discrete entities.
- Addictive behaviours are no different from other behaviours.
- Treatment approaches involve either total abstinence or relearning 'normal' behaviour patterns.

The processes involved in learning an addictive behaviour

To a social learning perspective, addictive behaviours are learned according to the following processes: (1) classical conditioning, (2) operant conditioning, (3) observational learning and (4) cognitive processes.

Classical conditioning

The rules of classical conditioning state that behaviours are acquired through the processes of associative learning. For example, an unconditioned stimulus (US, e.g. going to the pub) may elicit an unconditioned response (UR, e.g. feeling relaxed). If the unconditioned stimulus is associated with a conditioned stimulus (CS, e.g. a drink) then eventually, this will elicit the conditioned response (CR, e.g. feeling relaxed). This will happen as follows:

The unconditioned stimulus and the unconditioned response:
going to the pub ⇒ feeling relaxed
(US) ⇒ (UR)

Pairing the unconditioned stimulus and the conditioned stimulus:
going to the pub + a drink
(US) + (CS)

The conditioned stimulus and the conditioned response:
a drink ⇒ feeling relaxed
(CS) ⇒ (CR)

Therefore, the conditioned stimulus now elicits the conditioned response.

What factors can pair with the conditioned stimulus?

Two types of factor can pair with the conditioned stimulus: *external* (e.g. the pub) and *internal* (e.g. mood) cues. In terms of a potentially addictive behaviour, smoking cigarettes may be associated with external cues (e.g. seeing someone else smoking, being with particular friends), or with internal cues (e.g. anxiety, depression or happiness). It has been argued that a pairing with an internal cue is more problematic because these cues cannot be avoided. In addition, internal cues also raise the problem of *generalization*. Generalization occurs when the withdrawal symptoms from a period of abstinence from an addictive behaviour act as cues for further behaviour. For example, if an individual has paired feeling anxious with smoking, their withdrawal symptoms may be interpreted as anxiety and therefore elicit further smoking behaviour; the behaviour provides relief from its own withdrawal symptoms.

Operant conditioning

The rules of operant conditioning state that the probability of behaviour occurring is increased if it is either *positively reinforced* by the presence of a positive event, or *negatively reinforced* by the absence or removal of a negative event. In terms of an addictive behaviour such as smoking, the probability of smoking will be increased by feelings of social acceptance, confidence and control (the positive reinforcer) and removal of withdrawal symptoms (the negative reinforcer).

Observational learning/modelling

Behaviours are also learned by observing significant others carrying them out. For example, parental smoking, an association between smoking and attractiveness/thinness, and the observation of alcohol consumption as a risk-taking behaviour may contribute to the acquisition of the behaviour.

Cognitive factors

Factors such as self-image, problem-solving behaviour, coping mechanisms and attributions also contribute to the acquisition of an addictive behaviour.

The stages of substance use

Research into addictive behaviours has defined four stages of substance use: (1) initiation, (2) maintenance, (3) cessation and (4) relapse. These four stages will now be examined in detail for smoking and alcohol use and are illustrated in Fig. 5.4.

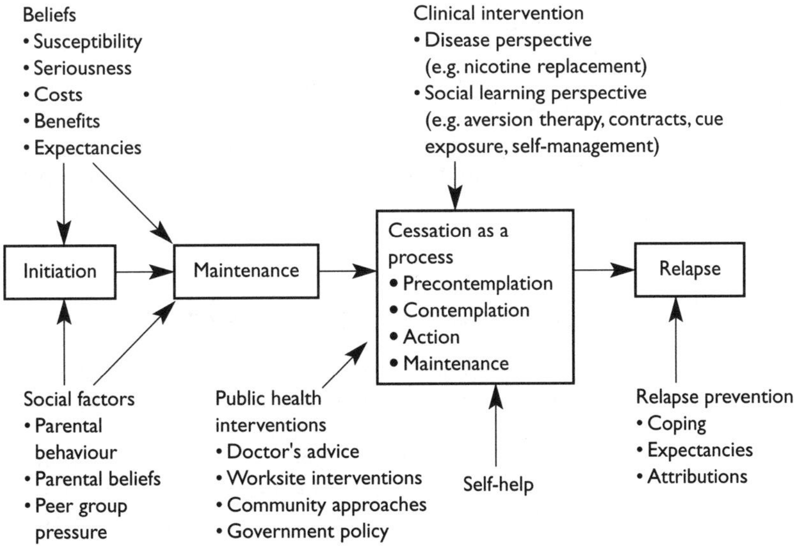

Figure 5.4 The stages of substance use

Stages 1 and 2: Initiating and maintaining an addictive behaviour

Smoking initiation and maintenance

In 1954, Doll and Hill indicated that smoking was predictive of lung cancer. Nearly fifty years later, approximately 30 per cent of the adult population still smoke even though most of them are aware of the related health risks. In fact, research exploring whether smokers appreciate the risks of smoking in comparison with the risks of murder and traffic accidents (see page 93) showed that smokers were accurate in their perception of the risks of smoking and showed similar ratings of risk to both ex-smokers and never smokers (Sutton 1998b). The early health promotion campaigns focused mainly on the determinants of smoking in adult men, but over recent years there has been an increasing interest in smoking in children. Most children/adolescents try a puff of a cigarette. It is therefore difficult to distinguish between actual initiation and maintenance of smoking behaviour. Accordingly, these stages will be considered together.

Smoking in children

Doll and Peto (1981) reported that people whose smoking is initiated in childhood have an increased chance of lung cancer compared with those who start smoking later on in life. This is particularly significant as most adult smokers start the habit in childhood and very few people start smoking regularly after the age of 19 or 20 (Charlton 1992). Lader and Matheson (1991) reviewed the data from national surveys between 1982 and 1990 and indicated that smoking behaviour in 11- to 15-year-old school boys – including those boys who have just tried a cigarette – had fallen from 55 per cent to 44 per cent and that smoking in school girls of a comparable age had fallen from 51 per cent to 42 per cent. Although this showed a decrease, it was less than the decrease shown in adult smoking, and the data showed that in 1990 nearly a half of the school children had at least tried one cigarette. In fact, many children try their first cigarette whilst at primary school (Murray *et al.* 1984; Swan *et al.* 1991).

Psychological predictors of smoking initiation

In an attempt to understand smoking initiation and maintenance, researchers have searched for the psychological and social processes that may promote smoking behaviour. Models of health behaviour such as the health belief model, the protection motivation theory, the theory of reasoned action and the health action process approach (see Chapter 2) have been used to examine the cognitive factors that contribute to smoking initiation (e.g. Sherman *et al.* 1982; Sutton 1982). Additional cognitions that predict smoking behaviour include associating smoking with fun and pleasure, smoking as a means of calming nerves and smoking as being sociable and building confidence, all of which have been reported by young smokers (Charlton 1984; Charlton and Blair 1989; see also Chapter 10 for a discussion of smoking and stress reduction).

Social predictors of smoking initiation and maintenance

Much research focuses on the individual and takes the individual out of their social context. Individual cognitions may predict smoking behaviour but they are a product of the individual's socialization. Interactions within the individual's social world help to create and develop a child's beliefs and behaviour. In Britain, there have been five longitudinal studies that have identified elements of the child's social world that are predictive of smoking behaviour (Murray *et al.* 1984; McNeil *et al.* 1988; Charlton and Blair 1989; Gillies and Galt 1990; Goddard 1990). The main factor that predicts smoking is parental smoking, with reports that children are twice as likely to smoke if their parents smoke (Lader and Matheson 1991). In addition, parents' attitudes to smoking also influence their offsprings' behaviour. For example, if a child perceives the parents as being strongly against smoking, he or she is up to seven times less likely to be a smoker (Murray *et al.* 1984). The next most important influence on smoking is peer group pressure. Studies in the USA have examined the relationship between peer group identity and tobacco use. The results showed that individuals who are identified by themselves and others as being problem-prone, doing poorly at school, rarely involved in school sports, high in risk-taking behaviour such as alcohol and drug use, and with low self-esteem were more likely to have smoked (Mosbach and Leventhal 1988; Sussman *et al.* 1990). On the other hand, research has also found that high rates of smoking can also be found in children who are seen as leaders of academic and social activities, have high self-esteem and are regarded as popular by their peers (Mosbach and Leventhal 1988). Another factor that influences whether children smoke is the attitude of their school to smoking behaviour. A Cancer Research Campaign study (1991) found that smoking prevalence was lower in schools that had a 'no smoking' policy, particularly if this policy included staff as well students. In summary, social factors such as the behaviour and beliefs of parents, peers and schools influence the beliefs and behaviours of children.

Alcohol initiation and maintenance

Most people try alcohol at some time in their lives. However, in a recent survey, about a quarter of those questioned (men and women) described themselves as lifelong abstainers (GHS 1994). The most common reasons for never drinking alcohol were religion and not liking it. Therefore, rather than examining predictors of drinking 'ever' or 'occasionally', this section examines what factors predict developing a problem with drinking.

Psychological predictors of alcohol initiation and maintenance

The tension-reduction hypothesis (Cappell and Greeley 1987) suggests that individuals may develop a drink problem because alcohol reduces tension and anxiety. Tension creates a heightened state of arousal and alcohol reduces this state, which perpetuates further drinking behaviour. However, it has been suggested that it is not the actual effects of alcohol use that promote drinking but the expected effects (George and Marlatt 1983). Therefore, because a small amount of alcohol may have positive effects people assume that these positive effects will continue with increased use. This perspective is in line with the social learning model of addictive behaviours and emphasizes the role of reinforcement and cognitions.

Social predictors of alcohol initiation and maintenance

Many of the social factors that relate to smoking behaviour are also predictive of alcohol consumption. For example, parental drinking is predictive of problem drinking in children. According to a disease model of addictions it could be argued that this reflects the genetic predisposition to develop an addictive behaviour. However, parental drinking may be influential through 'social hereditary factors', with children being exposed to drinking behaviour and learning this behaviour from their parents (Orford and Velleman 1991). In addition, peer group alcohol use and abuse also predicts drinking behaviour as does being someone who is sensation seeking, with a tendency to be aggressive and having a history of getting into trouble with authority.

Stage 3: The cessation of an addictive behaviour

Because of the potential health consequences of both smoking and alcohol consumption, research has examined different means to help smokers and drinkers quit their behaviour. Cessation of an additive behaviour can be examined in terms of the *processes* involved in cessation and the *interventions* designed to motivate individuals to quit their behaviour.

The process of cessation

Traditionally, smoking cessation was viewed as a dichotomy: an individual either smoked or did not. Individuals were categorized as either smokers, ex-smokers or non-smokers. This perspective was in line with a biomedical model of addictions and emphasized the 'all or nothing nature' of smoking behaviour. In addition, alcoholics were encouraged to abstain and to become non-drinkers. However, early attempts at promoting total abstinence were relatively unsuccessful and research now often emphasizes cessation as a process. In particular, Prochaska and DiClemente

(1984; see Chapter 2) adapted their stages of change model to examine cessation of addictive behaviours. This model highlighted the processes involved in the transition from a smoker to a non-smoker and from a drinker to a non-drinker. They argued that cessation involves a shift across four basic stages:

1 *precontemplation*: defined as not seriously considering quitting;
2 *contemplation*: having some thoughts about quitting;
3 *action*: initial behaviour change;
4 *maintenance*: maintaining behaviour change for a period of time.

Prochaska and DiClemente maintain that individuals do not progress through these stages in a straightforward and linear fashion but may switch backwards and forwards (e.g. from precontemplation to contemplation and back to precontemplation again). They call this 'the revolving door' schema and emphasize the dynamic nature of cessation. This model of change has been tested to provide evidence for the different stages for smokers and outpatient alcoholics (DiClemente and Prochaska 1982; 1985; DiClemente and Hughes 1990), and for the relationship between stage of change for smoking cessation and self-efficacy (DiClemente 1986). In addition, DiClemente *et al.* (1991) examined the relationship between stage of change and attempts to quit smoking and actual cessation at one- and six-month follow-ups. The authors categorized smokers into either precontemplators or contemplators and examined their smoking behaviour at follow-up. They further classified the contemplators into either contemplators (those who were smoking, seriously considering quitting within the next 6 months, but not within the next 30 days) or those in the preparation stage (those who were seriously considering quitting smoking within the next 6 months and within the next 30 days). The results showed that those in the preparation stage of change were more likely to have made a quit attempt at both one and six months, that they had made more quit attempts, and were more likely to be not smoking at the follow-ups. This study is described in detail in **Focus on research 5.1**.

Research has also used the health beliefs and structured models outlined in Chapter 2 to examine the predictors of both intentions to stop smoking and successful smoking cessation. For example, individual cognitions such as perceptions of susceptibility, past cessation attempts and perceived behavioural control have been shown to relate to reductions in smoking behaviour (Giannetti *et al.* 1985; Cummings *et al.* 1988; Godin *et al.* 1992). In addition, the theory of planned behaviour (TPB) has been used as a framework to explore smoking cessation in a range of populations, including those following a worksite ban (Borland *et al.* 1991), pregnant women and the general population (Godin *et al.* 1992).

Along these lines, a recent study examined the usefulness of the TPB at predicting intention to quit smoking and making a quit attempt in a group of smokers attending health promotion clinics in primary care (Norman *et al.* 1999). The results showed that the best predictors of intentions to quit were perceived behavioural control (i.e. 'How much control do you feel you have over not smoking over the next 6 months?')

FOCUS ON RESEARCH 5.1

TESTING A THEORY – STAGES OF SMOKING CESSATION

A study to examine the stages of change in predicting smoking cessation (DiClemente *et al.* 1991).

Traditionally addictive behaviours were viewed as 'either/or' behaviours. Therefore, smokers were considered either smokers, ex-smokers or non-smokers. However, DiClemente and Prochaska, 1982 developed their transtheoretical model of change to examine the stages of change in addictive behaviours. This study examined the validity of the stages of change model and assessed the relationship between stage of change and smoking cessation.

Background

The stages of change model describes the following stages:

- *Precontemplation*: not seriously considering quitting in the next 6 months.
- *Contemplation*: considering quitting in the next 6 months.
- *Action*: making behavioural changes.
- *Maintenance*: maintaining these changes.

The model is described as dynamic, not linear with individuals moving backwards and forwards across the stages. In this study, the authors categorized those in the contemplation stage as either contemplators (not considering quitting in the next 30 days) and those in the preparation stage (planning to quit in the next 30 days).

Methodology

Subjects 1466 subjects were recruited for a minimum intervention smoking cessation programme from Texas and Rhode Island. The majority of the subjects were white, female, had started smoking at about 16 and smoked on average 29 cigarettes a day.
Design The subjects completed a set of measures at baseline and were followed up at 1 and 6 months.
Measures The subjects completed the following set of measures:

- *Smoking abstinence self-efficacy* (DiClemente *et al.* 1985), which measures the smokers' confidence that they would not smoke in 20 challenging situations.

- *Perceived stress scale* (Cohen *et al.* 1985), which measures how much perceived stress the individual has experienced in the last month.
- *Fagerstrom Tolerance Questionnaire* which measures physical tolerance to nicotine.
- *Smoking decisional balance scale* (Velicer *et al.* 1985), which measures the perceived pros and cons of smoking.
- *Smoking processes of change scale* (DiClemente and Prochaska 1985), which measures the individual's stage of change. According to this scale, subjects were defined as precontemplators (n = 166), contemplators (n = 794) and those in the preparation stage (n = 506).
- *Demographic data,* including age, gender, education and smoking history.

Results

The results were first analysed to examine baseline difference between the three subject groups. The results showed that those in the preparation stage smoked less, were less addicted, had higher self-efficacy, rated the pros of smoking as less and the costs of smoking as more, had made more prior quitting attempts than the other two groups. The results were then analysed to examine the relationship between stage of change and smoking cessation. At both 1 and 6 months, the subjects in the preparation stage had made more quit attempts and were more likely to not be smoking.

Conclusion

The results provide support for the stages of change model of smoking cessation and suggest that it is a useful tool for predicting successful outcome of any smoking cessation intervention.

and perceived susceptibility (i.e. 'How likely do you think it might be that you will develop any of the following problems in the future if you continue to smoke?'). At follow-up, the best predictors of making a quit attempt were intentions at baseline (i.e. 'How likely is it that you will not smoke during the next 6 months?') and the number of previous quit attempts. Therefore, the process of smoking cessation can be explored using either a stages of change perspective, individual cognitions or structured models such as the TPB.

Interventions to promote cessation

Interventions to promote cessation can be described as either (1) clinical interventions, which are aimed at the individual, (2) self-help movements, or (3) public health interventions, which are aimed at populations.

Clinical interventions: promoting individual change

Clinical interventions often take the form of group or individual treatment programmes based in hospitals or universities requiring regular attendance over a 6- or 12-week period. These interventions use a combination of approaches that reflect the different disease and social learning theory models of addiction and are provided for those individuals who seek help.

Disease perspectives on cessation

Within the most recent disease models of addiction, nicotine and alcohol are seen as addictive and the individual who is addicted is seen as having acquired tolerance and dependency to the substance. Accordingly, cessation programmes offer ways for the individual to reduce this dependency. For example, *nicotine fading* procedures encourage smokers to gradually switch to brands of low nicotine cigarettes and gradually to smoke fewer cigarettes. It is believed that when the smoker is ready to completely quit, their addiction to nicotine will be small enough to minimize any withdrawal symptoms. Although there is no evidence to support the effectiveness of nicotine fading on its own, it has been shown to be useful alongside other methods such as relapse prevention (e.g. Brown *et al.* 1984).

Nicotine replacement procedures also emphasize an individual's addiction and dependency on nicotine. For example, nicotine chewing gum is available over the counter and is used as a way of reducing the withdrawal symptoms experienced following sudden cessation. The chewing gum has been shown to be a useful addition to other behavioural methods, particularly in preventing short-term relapse (Killen *et al.* 1990). However, it tastes unpleasant and takes time to be absorbed into the bloodstream. More recently, nicotine patches have become available, which only need to be applied once a day in order to provide a steady supply of nicotine into the bloodstream. They do not need to be tasted, although it could be argued that chewing gum satisfies the oral component of smoking. However, whether nicotine replacement procedures are actually compensating for a physiological addiction or whether they are offering a placebo effect via expecting not to need cigarettes is unclear. Treating excessive drinking from a disease perspective involves aiming for total abstinence as there is no suitable substitute for alcohol.

Social learning perspectives on cessation

Social learning theory emphasizes learning an addictive behaviour through processes such as operant conditioning (rewards and punishments), classical conditioning (associations with internal/external cues), observational learning and cognitions. Therefore, cessation procedures emphasize these processes in attempts to help smokers and excessive drinkers stop their behaviour. These cessation procedures include: aversion therapies, contingency contracting, cue exposure, self-management techniques and multi-perspective cessation clinics:

1 *Aversion therapies* aim to punish smoking and drinking rather than rewarding it. Early methodologies used crude techniques such as electric shocks whereby each time the individual smoked a puff of a cigarette or drank some alcohol they would receive a mild electric shock. However, this approach was found to be ineffective for both smoking and drinking (e.g. Wilson 1978), the main reason being that it is difficult to transfer behaviours that have been learnt in the laboratory to the real world. In an attempt to transfer this approach to the real world alcoholics are sometimes given a drug called Antabuse, which induces vomiting whenever alcohol is consumed. This therefore encourages the alcoholic to associate drinking with being sick. This has been shown to be more effective than electric shocks (Lang and Marlatt 1982), but requires the individual to take the drug and also ignores the multitude of reasons behind their drink problem. Imaginal aversion techniques have been used for smokers and encourage the smoker to imagine the negative consequence of smoking, such as being sick (rather than actually experiencing them). However, imaginal techniques seem to add nothing to other behavioural treatments (Lichtenstein and Brown 1983). Rapid smoking is a more successful form of aversion therapy (Danaher 1977) and aims to make the actual process of smoking unpleasant. Smokers are required to sit in a closed room and take a puff every 6 seconds until it becomes so unpleasant they cannot smoke any more. Although there is some evidence to support rapid smoking as a smoking cessation technique, it has obvious side-effects, including increased blood carbon monoxide levels and heart rates. Other aversion therapies include focused smoking, which involves smokers concentrating on all the negative experiences of smoking and smoke holding, which involves smokers holding smoke in their mouths for a period of time and again thinking about the unpleasant sensations. Smoke holding has been shown to be more successful at promoting cessation than focused smoking and it does not have the side-effects of rapid smoking (Walker and Franzini 1985).
2 *Contingency contracting* procedures also aim to punish smoking and drinking and to reward abstinence. Smokers and drinkers are asked to make a contract with either a therapist, a friend or partner and to establish a set of rewards/punishments, which are contingent on their smoking/drinking cessation. For example, money may be deposited with the therapist and only returned when they have stopped smoking/drinking for a given period of time. They are therefore rewarding abstinence. Schwartz (1987) analysed a series of contingency contracting studies for smoking cessation from 1967 to 1985 and concluded

that this procedure seems to be successful in promoting initial cessation, but once the contract was finished, or the money returned, relapse was high. In a study of alcoholics, 20 severe alcoholics who had been arrested for drunkenness were offered employment, health care, counselling, food and clothing if they remained sober (Miller 1975). The results showed that those with the contracts were arrested less, employed more, and were more often sober according to unannounced blood alcohol checks than those who were given these 'rewards' non-contingently. However, whether such changes in behaviour would persist over time is unclear. In addition, this perspective is reminiscent of a more punitive moral model of addictions.

3 *Cue exposure procedures* focus on the environmental factors that have become associated with smoking and drinking. For example, if an individual always smokes when they drink alcohol, alcohol will become a strong external cue to smoke and vice versa. Cue exposure techniques gradually expose the individual to different cues and encourage them to develop coping strategies to deal with them. This procedure aims to extinguish the response to the cues over time and is opposite to cue avoidance procedures, which encourage individuals not to go to the places where they may feel the urge to smoke or drink. Cue exposure highlights some of the problem with in-patient detoxification approaches to alcoholism whereby the alcoholic is hospitalized for a length of time until they have reduced the alcohol from their system. Such an approach aims to reduce the alcoholic's physiological need for alcohol by keeping them away from alcohol during their withdrawal symptoms. However, being in hospital does not teach the alcoholic how to deal with the cues to drink. It means that they avoid these cues, rather than being exposed to them.
4 *Self-management procedures* use a variety of behavioural techniques to promote smoking and drinking cessation in individuals and may be carried out under professional guidance. Such procedures involve self-monitoring (keeping a record of own smoking/drinking behaviour), becoming aware of the causes of smoking/drinking (What makes me smoke? Where do I smoke? Where do I drink?), and becoming aware of the consequences of smoking/drinking (Does it make me feel better? What do I expect from smoking/drinking?). However, used on their own, self-management techniques do not appear to be more successful than other interventions (Hall *et al.* 1990).
5 *Multi-perspective cessation clinics* represent an integration of all the above clinical approaches to smoking and drinking cessation and use a combination of aversion therapies, contingency contracting, cue exposure and self-management. In addition, for smoking cessation this multi-perspective approach often incorporates disease model based interventions such as nicotine replacement. Lando (1977) developed an integrated model of smoking cessation, which has served as a model for subsequent clinics. His approach included the following procedures:
   - 6 sessions of rapid smoking for 25 minutes for 1 week;
   - doubled daily smoking rate outside the clinic for 1 week;

- onset of smoking cessation;
- identifying problems encountered when attempting to stop smoking;
- developing ways to deal with these problems;
- self-reward contracts for cessation success (e.g. buying something new);
- self-punishment contracts for smoking (e.g. give money to a friend/therapist).

Lando's model has been evaluated and research suggested a 76 per cent abstinence rate at 6 months (Lando 1977) and 46 per cent at 12 months (Lando and McGovern 1982), which was higher than the control group's abstinence rates. Killen *et al.* (1984) developed Lando's approach but used smoke holding rather than rapid smoking, and added nicotine chewing gum into the programme. Their results showed similarly high abstinence rates to the study by Lando.

Multi-perspective approaches have also been developed for the treatment of alcohol use. These include an integration of the above approaches and also an emphasis on drinking as a coping strategy. Drinking is therefore not simply seen as an unwanted behaviour that should stop but as a behaviour which serves a function in the alcoholic's life. Such approaches include:

- Assessing the drinking behaviour both in terms of the degree of the problem (e.g. frequency and amount drank) and the factors that determine the drinking (e.g. What function does the drinking serve? When does the urge to drink increase/decrease? What is the motivation to change? Do the individual's family/friends support their desire to change?).
- Self-monitoring (e.g. When do I drink?).
- Developing new coping strategies (e.g. relaxation, stress management).
- Cue exposure (e.g. learning to cope with high-risk situations).

Multi-perspective approaches are often regarded as skills training approaches as they encourage individuals to develop the relevant skills needed to change their behaviour.

Self-help movements

Although clinical and public health interventions have proliferated over the past few decades, up to 90 per cent of ex-smokers report having stopped without any formal help (Fiore *et al.* 1990). Lichtenstein and Glasgow (1992) reviewed the literature on self-help quitting and reported that success rates tend to be about 10–20 per cent at 1-year follow-up and 3–5 per cent for continued cessation. The literature suggests that lighter smokers are more likely to be successful at self-quitting than heavy smokers and that minimal interventions, such as follow-up telephone calls, can improve this success. Research also suggests that smokers are more likely to quit if they receive support from their partners and if their partners also stop smoking (Cohen and Lichtenstein 1990) and that partner support is particularly relevant for women trying to give up smoking during pregnancy (e.g. Appleton and Pharoah 1998). However, although many ex-smokers report that 'I did it on my own', it is important not to discount their exposure to the multitude of health education messages received via television, radio or leaflets.

Public health interventions: promoting cessation in populations

Public health interventions aim to promote behaviour change in populations and have become increasingly popular over recent years. Such interventions are aimed at all individuals, not just those who seek help. For smoking cessation, they take the form of doctor's advice, worksite interventions, community-wide approaches, government interventions. For drinking behaviour, most public health interventions take the form of government interventions.

1 *Doctor's advice.* Approximately 70 per cent of smokers will visit a doctor at some time each year. Research suggests that the recommendation from a doctor, who is considered a credible source of information, can be quite successful in promoting smoking cessation. In a classic study carried out in five general practices in London (Russell *et al.* 1979), smokers visiting their GP over a four-week period were allocated to one of four groups: (1) follow-up only, (2) questionnaire about their smoking behaviour and follow-up, (3) doctor's advice to stop smoking, questionnaire about their smoking behaviour and follow-up, and (4) doctor's advice to stop smoking, leaflet giving tips on how to stop and follow-up. All subjects were followed up at 1 and 12 months. The results showed at 1-year follow-up, 3.3 per cent of those who had simply been told to stop smoking were still abstinent, and 5.1 per cent of those who were told to stop and had received a leaflet showed successful cessation. This was in comparison to 0.3 per cent in the group that had received follow-up only and 1.6 per cent in the group that had received the questionnaire and follow-up. Although these changes are quite small, if all GPs recommended that their smokers stopped smoking, this would produce half a million ex-smokers within a year in the UK. Research also suggests that the effectiveness of doctor's advice may be increased if they are trained in patient-centred counselling techniques (Wilson *et al.* 1988). Minimum interventions for smoking cessation by health professionals are also illustrated by the results of the OXCHECK and Family Heart Study results (Muir *et al.* 1994; Wood *et al.* 1994), which are described in Chapter 9.
2 *Worksite interventions.* Over the past decade there has been an increasing interest in developing worksite-based smoking cessation interventions. These take the form of either a company adopting a no-smoking policy and/or establishing work-based health promotion programmes. Worksite interventions have the benefit of reaching many individuals who would not consider attending a hospital or a university-based clinic. In addition, the large number of people involved presents the opportunity for group motivation and social support. Furthermore, they may have implications for reducing passive smoking at work, which may be a risk factor for coronary heart disease (He *et al.* 1994). Research

into the effectiveness of no-smoking policies has produced conflicting results with some studies reporting an overall reduction in the number of cigarettes smoked for up to 12 months (e.g. Biener *et al.* 1989) and others suggesting that smoking outside work hours compensates for any reduced smoking at the workplace (e.g. Gomell *et al.* 1993) (see **Focus on research 5.2**). In two Australian studies, public service workers were surveyed following smoking bans in 44 government office buildings about their attitudes to the ban immediately after the ban and after 6 months. The results suggested that although immediately after the ban many smokers felt inconvenienced, these attitudes improved at 6 months with both smokers and non-smokers recognizing the benefits of the ban. However, only 2 per cent stopped smoking during this period (Borland *et al.* 1990). Although worksite interventions may be a successful means to access many smokers, this potential does not yet appear to have been fully realized.

3 *Community-based programmes*. Large community-based programmes have been established as a means of promoting smoking cessation within large groups of individuals. Such programmes aim to reach those who would not attend clinics and to use the group motivation and social support in a similar way to worksite interventions. Early community-based programmes were part of the drive to reduce coronary heart disease. In the Stanford Five City Project, the experimental groups received intensive face-to-face instruction on how to stop smoking and in addition were exposed to media information regarding smoking cessation. The results showed a 13 per cent reduction in smoking rates compared with the control group (Farquhar *et al.* 1990). In the North Karelia Project, individuals in the target community received an intensive educational campaign and were compared with those in a neighbouring community who were not exposed to the campaign. The results from this programme showed a 10 per cent reduction in smoking in men in North Karelia compared with men in the control region. In addition, the results also showed a 24 per cent decline in cardiovascular deaths, a rate twice that of the rest of the country (Puska *et al.* 1985). Other community-based programmes include the Australia North Coast Study, which resulted in a 15 per cent reduction in smoking over 3 years, and the Swiss National Research Programme, which resulted in an 8 per cent reduction over 3 years (Egger *et al.* 1983; Autorengruppe Nationales Forschungsprogramm 1984).

4 *Government interventions*. An additional means to promote both smoking cessation and healthy drinking is to encourage governments to intervene. Such interventions can take several forms:

- *Restricting/banning advertising*. According to social learning theory, we learn to smoke and drink by associating smoking and drinking with attractive characteristics, such as 'It will help me relax', 'It makes me look sophisticated', 'It makes me look sexy', 'It is risky'. Advertising aims to access and promote these beliefs in order to encourage smoking and drinking. Implementing a ban/restriction on advertising would remove this source of beliefs.

FOCUS ON RESEARCH 5.2

PUTTING THEORY INTO PRACTICE – WORKSITE SMOKING BAN

A pilot study to examine the effects of a workplace smoking ban on smoking, craving, stress and other behaviours (Gomel *et al.* 1993).

Over the past few years many organizations have set up workplace bans. These offer an opportunity to examine the effects of policy of behaviour change and to assess the effectiveness of public health interventions in promoting smoking cessation.

Background

Workplace bans provide an opportunity to use group motivation and group social support to promote smoking cessation. In addition, they can access individuals who would not be interested in attending clinics based in hospitals or universities. The present study examined the effect of worksite ban on smoking behaviour (both at work and outside) and also examined the interrelationship between smoking and other behaviours. The ban was introduced on 1 August 1989 at the New South Wales Ambulance Service in Australia. This study is interesting because it included physiological measures of smoking to identify any compensatory smoking.

Methodology

Subjects A screening question showed that 60 per cent of the employees were current smokers ($n = 47$). Twenty-four subjects (15 males and 9 females) completed all measures. They had an average age of 34 years, had smoked on average for 11 years and smoked an average of 26 cigarettes a day.

Design The subjects completed a set of measures 1 week before the ban (time 1) and 1 (time 2) and 6 weeks (time 3) after.

Measures At times 1, 2 and 3, the subjects were evaluated for cigarette and alcohol consumption, demographic information (e.g. age), exhaled carbon monoxide and blood cotinine. The subjects also completed daily record cards for 5 working days and 2 non-working days, including measures of smoking, alcohol consumption, snack intake and ratings of subjective discomfort.

Results

The results showed a reduction in self-reports of smoking in terms of number of cigarettes smoked during a working day and the number smoked during working hours at both 1-week and 6-week follow-up compared with baseline, indicating that the smokers were smoking less following the ban. However, the cotinine levels suggested that although there was an initial decrease at week 1, by 6 weeks blood cotinine was almost back to baseline levels suggesting that the smokers may have been compensating for the ban by smoking more outside of work. The results also showed increases in craving and stress following the ban; these lower levels of stress were maintained, whereas craving gradually returned to baseline (supporting compensatory smoking). The results showed no increases in snack intake or alcohol consumption.

Conclusion

The self-report data from the study suggest that worksite bans may be an effective form of public health intervention for decreasing smoking behaviour. However, the physiological data suggests that simply introducing a no-smoking policy may not be sufficient as smokers may show compensatory smoking.

- *Increasing the cost.* Research indicates a relationship between the cost of cigarettes and alcohol and their consumption. Increasing the price of cigarettes and alcohol could promote smoking and drinking cessation and deter the initiation of these behaviours, particularly among children. According to models of health beliefs, this would contribute to the perceived costs of the behaviours and the perceived benefits of behaviour change.
- *Banning smoking in public places.* Smoking is already restricted to specific places in many countries (e.g. in the UK most public transport is no smoking). A wider ban on smoking may promote smoking cessation. According to social learning theory, this would result in the cues to smoking (e.g. restaurants, bars) becoming eventually disassociated from smoking. However, it is possible that this would simply result in compensatory smoking in other places as illustrated by some of the research on worksite no-smoking policies.
- *Banning cigarette smoking and alcohol drinking.* Governments could opt to ban cigarettes and alcohol completely (although they would forego the large revenues they currently receive from advertising and sales). Such a move might result in a reduction in these behaviours. However, other drugs such as cannabis are illegal in most countries,

and this is still smoked by large percentages of the population. In addition, prohibition in the USA was remarkably unsuccessful.

Methodological problems evaluating clinical and public health interventions

Although researchers and health educators are motivated to find the best means of promoting smoking cessation and healthy drinking, evaluating the effectiveness of any intervention is fraught with methodological problems. For smoking cessation these problems include:

- *Who has become a non-smoker?* Someone who has not smoked in the last month/week/day? Someone who regards themselves as a non-smoker? (Smokers are notorious for under-reporting their smoking.) Does a puff of a cigarette count as smoking? Do cigars count as smoking? These questions need to be answered to assess success rates.
- *Who is still counted as a smoker?* Someone who has attended all clinic sessions and still smokes? Someone who dropped out of the sessions half-way through and has not been seen since? Someone who was asked to attend but never turned up? These questions need to be answered to derive a baseline number for the success rate.
- *Should the non-smokers be believed when they say they have not smoked?* Methods other than self-report exist to assess smoking behaviour, such as carbon monoxide in the breath, cotinine in the saliva. These are more accurate, but time-consuming and expensive.
- *How should smokers be assigned to different interventions?* In order for success rates to be calculated, comparisons need to be made between different types of intervention (e.g. aversion therapy versus cue exposure). These groups should obviously be matched for age, gender, ethnicity and smoking behaviour. What about stage of change (contemplation versus precontemplation versus preparation)? What about other health beliefs such as self-efficacy, costs and benefits of smoking? The list could be endless.

For interventions aimed at changing drinking behaviour, these problems include:

- *What is the desired outcome of any intervention?* Being totally abstinent (for the last month/week)? Drinking a normal amount? (What is normal?) Coping with life? (What constitutes acceptable coping?) Drinking that is not detrimental to work? (Should work be a priority?) Drinking that is no longer detrimental to family life? (Should family life be a priority?) In his autobiography, John Healy describes his transition from an alcoholic living on the 'Grass Arena' in London to becoming addicted to chess. Is this success? Should the experts impose their view of success on a drinker, or should success be determined by them?

◆ *How should drinking behaviour be measured?* Should intrusive measures such as blood taking be used? Should self-reports be relied on?

Stage 4: Relapse in smoking and drinking

Although, many people are successful at initially stopping smoking and changing their drinking behaviour, relapse rates are high. Interestingly, the pattern for relapse is consistent across a number of different addictive behaviours, with high rates initially tapering off over a year. This relapse pattern is shown in Fig. 5.5.

Marlatt and Gordon (1985) developed a relapse prevention model of addictions, which specifically examined the processes involved in successful and unsuccessful cessation attempts. The relapse prevention model was based on the following concept of addictive behaviours:

◆ Addictive behaviours are learned and therefore can be unlearned; they are reversible.
◆ Addictions are not 'all or nothing' but exist on a continuum.
◆ Lapses from abstinence are likely and acceptable.
◆ Believing that 'one drink – a drunk' is a self-fulfilling prophecy.

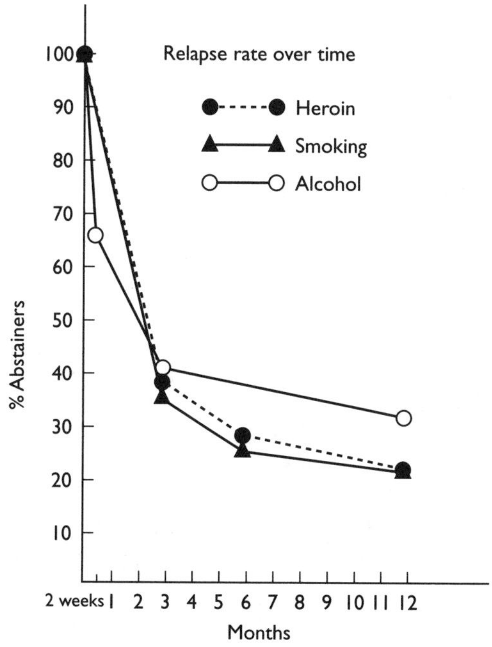

Figure 5.5 Relapse curves for individuals treated for heroin, smoking and alcohol addiction

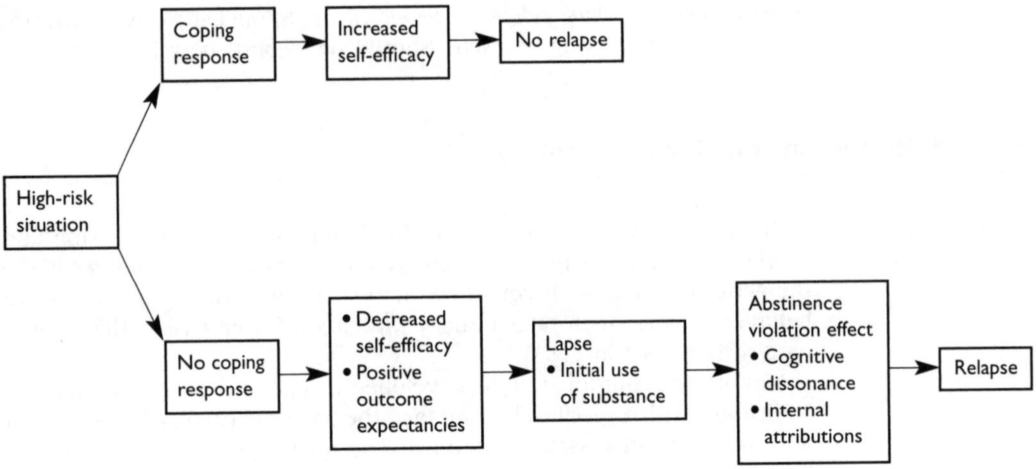

Figure 5.6 The relapse process

They distinguished between a lapse, which entails a minor slip (e.g. a cigarette, a couple of drinks) and a relapse, which entails a return to former behaviour (e.g. smoking 20 cigarettes, getting drunk). Marlatt and Gordon examined the processes involved in the progression from abstinence to relapse and in particular assessed the mechanisms that may explain the transition from lapse to relapse (see Fig. 5.6). These processes are described below.

Baseline state

Abstinence. If an individual sets total abstinence as the goal, then this stage represents the target behaviour and indicates a state of behavioural control.

Pre-lapse state

High-risk situation. A high-risk situation is any situation that may motivate the individual to carry out the behaviour. Such situations may be either external cues, such as someone else smoking or the availability of alcohol, or internal cues, such as anxiety. Research indicates that the most commonly reported high-risk situations are negative emotions, interpersonal conflict and social pressure. This is in line with social learning theories, which predict that internal cues are more problematic than external cues.

Coping behaviour. Once exposed to a high-risk situation the individual engages the coping strategies. Such strategies may be behavioural, such as avoiding the situation or using a substitute behaviour (e.g. eating), or cognitive, such as remembering why they are attempting to abstain.

Positive outcome expectancies. According to previous experience the individual will either have positive outcome expectancies if the behaviour is carried out (e.g. smoking will make me feel less anxious) or negative outcome expectancies (e.g. getting drunk will make me feel sick).

No lapse or lapse?

Marlatt and Gordon argue that when exposed to a high-risk situation, if an individual can engage good coping mechanisms and also develop negative outcome expectancies, the chances of a lapse will be reduced and the individual's self-efficacy will be increased. However, if the individual engages poor coping strategies and has positive outcome expectancies, the chances of a lapse will be high and the individual's self-efficacy will be reduced.

- *No lapse*: good coping strategies and negative outcome expectancies will raise self-efficacy, causing the period of abstinence to be maintained.
- *Lapse*: poor or no coping strategies and positive outcome expectancies will lower self-efficacy, causing an initial use of the substance (the cigarette, a drink). This lapse will either remain an isolated event and the individual will return to abstinence, or will become a full-blown relapse. Marlatt and Gordon describe this transition as the abstinence violation effect (AVE).

The abstinence violation effect

The transition from initial lapse to full blown relapse is determined by dissonance conflict and self-attribution. Dissonance is created by a conflict between a self-image as someone who no longer smokes/drinks and the current behaviour (e.g. smoking/drinking). This conflict is exacerbated by a disease model of addictions, which emphasizes 'all or nothing', and minimized by a social learning model, which acknowledges the likelihood of lapses.

Having lapsed, the individual is motivated to understand the cause of the lapse. If this lapse is attributed to the self (e.g. 'I am useless, it's my fault'), this may create guilt and self-blame. This internal attribution may lower self-efficacy, thereby increasing the chances of a full-blown relapse. However, if the lapse is attributed to the external world (e.g. the situation, the presence of others), guilt and self-blame will be reduced and the chances of the lapse remaining a lapse will be increased.

Marlatt and Gordon developed a relapse prevention programme based on cognitive behavioural techniques to help prevent lapses turning into full-blown relapses. This programme involved the following procedures:

- self-monitoring (What do I do in high-risk situations?)
- relapse fantasies (What would it be like to relapse?)
- relaxation training/stress management

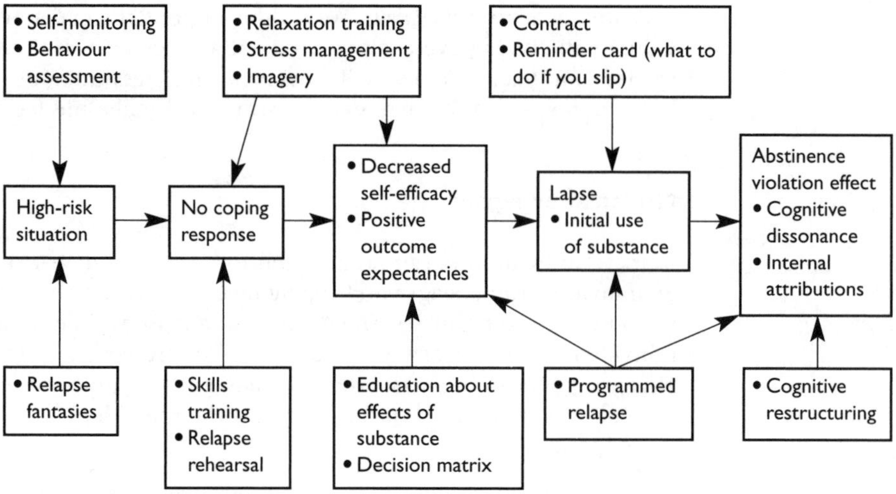

Figure 5.7 Relapse prevention intervention strategies

- skills training
- contingency contracts
- cognitive restructuring (learning not to make internal attributions for lapses)

How these procedures relate to the different stages of relapse is illustrated in Fig. 5.7.

A cross-addictive behaviour perspective

According to the disease models of addiction, each behaviour is examined separately. Therefore, an addiction to cigarettes is seen as separate and different to an addiction to alcohol. However, from a social learning perspective, it is possible to examine similarities between behaviours and to apply similar processes to the initiation, maintenance, cessation and relapse of behaviours such as exercise, sex, gambling and eating (e.g. Orford 1985). Research has examined these behaviours independently of each other and, in addition, has also assessed the associations between them. In particular, recent research has examined the interrelationship between smoking and eating behaviour.

Smoking and eating behaviour

Research into the interrelationship between smoking and eating has examined (1) gender differences in smoking, (2) smoking cessation and changes in food intake, and (3) substitution between substances.

Gender differences in smoking

Research has highlighted gender differences in tobacco use (Grunberg *et al.* 1991) with the suggestion being that whilst male smoking has remained stable, or even declined over the past 20 years in the USA and UK, female smoking has increased. This increase is reflected by reports of gender differences in cancer with lung cancer now being the leading cause of death in American women. To explain increases in female smoking, research has focused on the perceived benefits of smoking, suggesting that smokers of both genders continue to smoke for fear of weight gain. Consequently, the present cultural obsession with thinness in women may account for increased female smoking. Smokers generally weigh about 7 lbs less than comparably-aged non-smokers, and abstinent smokers tend to show weight gains of about 6 lbs (US Department of Health and Human Services 1990). As a result, research suggests that female dieters may use cigarette smoking as a weight loss/maintenance strategy (Klesges and Klesges 1988; Ogden and Fox 1994). For example, in a recent study dieters showed greater agreement with statements relating to smoking initiation and smoking maintenance for weight control, the role of weight gain in previous experiences of smoking relapse, intentions to quit following weight loss and intentions to quit in 5 years (Ogden and Fox 1994).

Smoking and changes in food intake

How cigarette smoking influences weight is unclear with different possible mechanisms predicting either a change or no change in food intake. For example, it has been proposed that weight gain could be a result of decreased energy use due to withdrawal or fatigue, or that nicotine may increase metabolic rate; both mechanisms suggest no post-cessation changes in eating behaviour. However, Grunberg (1986) suggests that nicotine may increase blood sugar levels and that post-cessation weight gain could be explained by an increase in sweet food consumption, which has been supported by both animal and human research. Further research suggests that smoking cessation may result in increases in consumption of calories, increases in sucrose, fats and carbohydrate intake (see Ogden 1994 for an overview). Theories to explain the changes in food intake following smoking cessation have focused on physiological factors such as a release of brain serotonin following nicotine withdrawal (Benwell *et al.* 1988), which may be compensated for by carbohydrates. However, an alternative explanation of the relationship focuses on the subjective experience of craving for a substance.

The subjective experience of craving

The desire to eat and the response to food deprivation is characterized by the experience of 'emptiness', 'tension', 'agitation', 'light-headedness' as well as more specific feelings such as a 'rumbling stomach'. Smoking abstainers also describe their desire for a cigarette in similar ways, again using language such as 'emptiness', 'agitation' and 'light-headedness'. A possible explanation of the interaction between smoking and eating is that sensations of deprivation may be interchangeable. Alcohol research suggests that craving for alcohol may be a form of misattribution of internal states, with the alcoholic labelling internal states as a desire for alcohol (Ludwig and Stark 1974; Marlatt 1978). With reference to eating and smoking, the desire to smoke may be labelled as hunger and therefore satiated by food intake. In a recent experimental study, smokers were asked either to abstain for 24 hours or to continue smoking as usual, and their craving for food and cigarettes and food intake was compared with each other and with a group of non-smokers (Ogden 1994). The results showed that smoking abstinence resulted in an increased craving for food and increased food intake. In addition, the results showed that an increased craving for cigarettes resulted in increased food intake. Furthermore, the results showed that this association between craving for cigarettes and food was greater in women than men, and particularly apparent in dieting women.

These studies support a cross-behavioural perspective of addictions and suggest an interrelationship between different behaviours. It is possible that because women dieters may use smoking as a means to reduce their eating they develop an association between these behaviours. It is also possible that the substitution between addictive behaviours may also exist between other behaviours such as alcohol and smoking (stopping smoking increases drinking), or gambling and eating (stopping gambling increases eating).

To conclude

Smoking and alcohol consumption both have negative effects on health and yet are common behaviours. There are many different theories to explain why people smoke or drink and how they can be encouraged to adopt healthy behaviours. This chapter examined the different models of addiction, including the moral model, the disease models and the social learning perspective. It then examined the stages of substance use from initiation and maintenance (involving psychological factors, such as beliefs and expectancies, and social factors, such as parental and peer group behaviour), to cessation (involving clinical perspectives, self-help methods and public health interventions) or relapse. Finally, this chapter examined the interrelationship between different behaviours, in particular smoking and eating, to examine the validity of a cross-behavioural perspective.

? Questions

1 Is alcoholism a disease?

2 Discuss the role of conditioning in the acquisition of an addictive behaviour.

3 Smoking is an addiction to nicotine. Discuss.

4 Discuss the role of health beliefs in the initiation of smoking behaviour.
5 Discuss the role of clinical and public health interventions in promoting smoking cessation.
6 To what extent are addictions governed by similar processes?
7 Outline a research project designed to evaluate the effect of role models on smoking.

▶ For discussion

Have you ever tried a puff of a cigarette? If so, consider the reasons why you did or did not become a smoker. If you have never even tried a cigarette, discuss the possible reasons for this.

Assumptions in health psychology

The research on smoking and alcohol highlights some of the assumptions in health psychology:

1 *Mind–body dualism.* Theories of addictions and addictive behaviour emphasize either the psychological or physiological processes. This separation is reflected in the differences between the disease models and the social learning perspectives. Therefore, although some of the treatment perspectives emphasize both mind (e.g. cue exposure) and body (e.g. nicotine replacement), they are still seen as distinct components of the individual.

2 *Changes in theory represents improvement.* It is often assumed that the most recent theoretical perspective is an improvement of previous theories. In terms of addictive behaviours, the moral model is seen as more naïve than the disease model, which is more naïve than a social learning theory perspective. However, perhaps these different models also illustrate different (and not necessarily better) ways of explaining behaviour and of describing the individual. Therefore, to see an individual who drinks a great deal as to blame and as being responsible for his or her behaviour (the moral model) reflects a different model of the individual than an explanation which describes a physiological predisposition (the 2nd disease model) or learning the behaviour via reinforcement.

Further reading

Heather, N. and Robertson, D. (1989) *Problem Drinking*. Oxford: Oxford University Press.

This book examines the different theories of addictive behaviours and in particular outlines the contribution of social learning theory.

Marlatt, G.A. and Gordon, J.R. (1985) *Relapse Prevention*. New York: Guilford Press.

This book provides a detailed analysis and background to relapse prevention and applies this approach to a variety of addictive behaviours. Chapter 1 is a particularly useful overview.

Orford, J. (1985) *Excessive Appetites: A Psychological View of Addictions*. Chichester: John Wiley.

This book illustrates the extent to which different addictive behaviours share common variables in both their initiation and maintenance and discusses the interrelationship between physiological and psychological factors.

CHAPTER 6

Obesity and eating behaviour

Chapter overview

This chapter is arranged into three main sections: obesity, dieting and the implications of the dieting literature for obesity treatment. The chapter first examines the definitions of obesity, its prevalence, potential consequences and the beliefs people hold about obesity. It then examines the causes of obesity in terms of physiological theories (e.g. genetic theory, metabolic rate theory, fat cell theory and appetite control) and behavioural theories (e.g. physical activity and eating behaviour). Some of the problems with this research are then highlighted. The chapter next describes the role of body dissatisfaction in dieting and explores restraint theory as an alternative approach to examining eating behaviour. In particular, it examines the relationship between restrained eating and under- and overeating. Finally, the chapter discusses the implications of restraint theory for obesity treatment raising the question 'should obesity be treated at all?'

This chapter covers:

- What is obesity?
- What causes obesity?
- Why do so many women diet?
- Restraint theory: an alternative approach to overeating.
- The implications of restraint theory for obesity treatment.
- Should obesity be treated at all?

What is obesity?

Obesity can be defined in a number of ways, including the use of population means and in terms of body mass index. Using population means involves exploring mean weights given a specific population and deciding whether someone is below average weight, average or above average in terms of percentage overweight. Stunkard (1984) suggested that obesity should be categorized as either mild (20–40 per cent overweight), moderate (41–100 per cent overweight) or severe (100 per cent overweight) obesity. This approach is problematic as it depends on which population is being considered – someone could be obese in India but not in the USA.

Body mass index (BMI) is calculated using the equation weight (kg)/ height (m^2). This produces a figure which has been categorized as normal weight (20–24.9), overweight (grade 1; 25–29.9), clinical obesity (grade 2; 30–39.9), and severe obesity (grade 3; 40+) (see Fig. 6.1). This is the most frequently used definition of obesity. However, it does not allow for

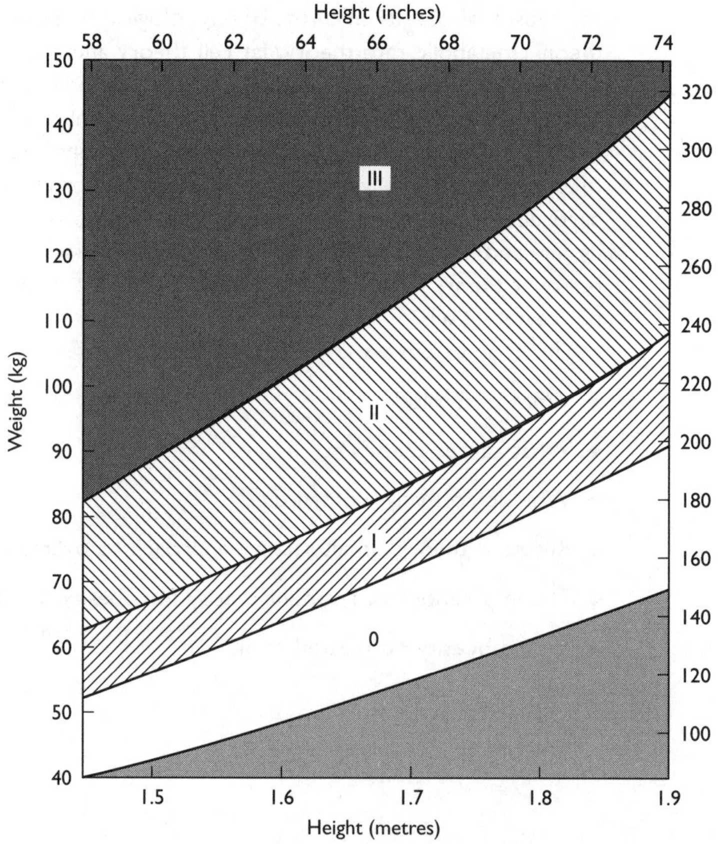

Figure 6.1 Grades of obesity by height and weight

differences in weight between muscle and fat – a bodybuilder would be defined as obese.

How common is obesity?

In the UK the rates of obesity are on the increase. If obesity is defined as a BMI greater than 30, reports show that in 1980, 6 per cent of men and 8 per cent of women were obese and that this had increased to 13 per cent and 16 per cent in 1994; by the year 2005 it is predicted that the figures will have risen to 18 per cent and 24 per cent respectively (Department of Health 1995). Estimates for the USA suggest that 24 per cent of men and 27 per cent of women are at least mildly obese (Kuczmarski 1992) and that women have grown particularly heavier in recent years (Flegal *et al.* 1988). Across the world, the highest rates of obesity are found in Tunisia, the USA, Saudi Arabia and Canada, and the lowest are found in China, Mali, Japan, Sweden and Brazil; the UK, Australia and New Zealand are all placed in the middle of the range. Across Europe the highest rates are in Lithuania, Malta, Russia and Serbia and the lowest are in Sweden, Ireland, Denmark and the UK. Overall, people in Northern and Western Europe are thinner than Eastern and Southern Europe and women are more likely to be obese than men.

What are the problems with obesity?

Physical problems

Obesity has been associated with cardiovascular disease, diabetes, joint trauma, back pain, cancer, hypertension and mortality (e.g. Bray 1986; Chan *et al.* 1994). The effects of obesity are related to where the excess weight is carried; weight stored in the upper body, particularly in the abdomen, is more detrimental to health than weight carried on the lower body. It is interesting to note that although men are more likely than women to store fat on their upper bodies, and are therefore more at risk if obese, women are more concerned about weight than men and most treatment studies examine women. The relationship between BMI and mortality is shown in Fig. 6.2. It has been suggested that most problems seem to be associated with severe obesity and weights in the top 10 per cent (Wooley and Wooley 1984).

Psychological problems

Research has examined the relationship between psychological problems and obesity. The contemporary cultural obsession with thinness, the

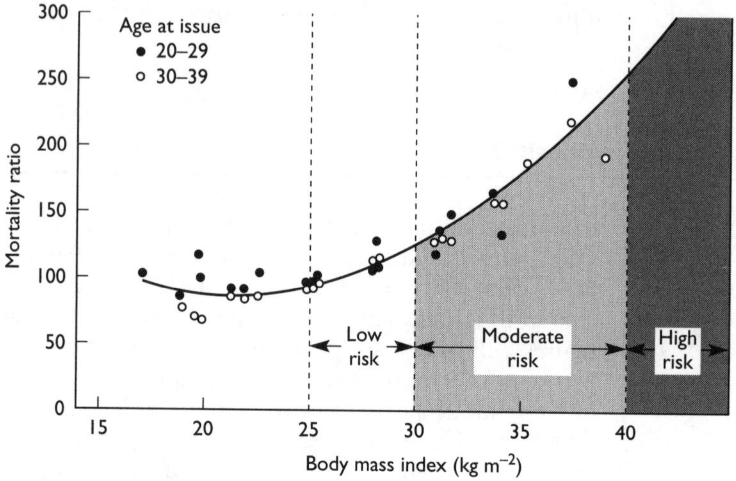

Figure 6.2 Relationship between BMI and mortality

aversion to fat found in both adults and children and the attribution of blame to the obese may promote low self-esteem and poor self-image in those individuals who do not conform to the stereotypically attractive thin image. In line with this, Bull *et al.* (1983) reported that both obese patients waiting for a gastric bypass operation and normal obese patients rated themselves as more depressed than normal weight subjects, although the levels of depression did not reach clinical proportions. Furthermore, Hopkinson and Bland (1982) reported that one-fifth of their sample of obese subjects, also waiting for surgical treatment, reported having at least one period of clinical depression requiring treatment. In addition, Rand and MacGregor (1991) reported that individuals who had lost weight following gastric bypass surgery stated that they would rather be deaf, dyslexic, diabetic, have heart disease or acne than return to their former weight. These studies suggest a relationship between body size and depression. However, it is possible that depressed obese individuals are more likely to seek treatment for their obesity than those who are not depressed and that there may be many obese individuals who are quite happy and therefore do not come into contact with health professionals.

In contrast to the above studies, Halmi *et al.* (1980) reported that although just over 28 per cent of a group of 80 patients waiting to have a gastric bypass operation were (or had been) clinically depressed, they argued that this is compatible with the prevalence of depression in the general population. Therefore, although some obese people may be depressed there is no consistent support for a simple relationship between body size and psychological problems.

Beliefs about obesity

A number of studies in the 1960s and 1970s were carried out to evaluate the beliefs about obesity. In 1969, Maddox and Liederman asked a group of physicians and medical students to rate their overweight patients for a set of personal characteristics. They found that 97 per cent judged them stupid, 90 per cent unsuccessful, 90 per cent weak, 86 per cent lazy, 69 per cent not nice, 65 per cent unhappy, 60 per cent weak-willed, 54 per cent ugly and 55 per cent awkward. In a further study in 1979, Larkin and Pines found that overweight men and women were less likely to be recommended for employment by college students who watched them performing tasks in an identical fashion to their thinner counterparts.

Research has also evaluated how young we are when we learn these beliefs. In 1969, Lerner and Gellert showed groups of 5- and 10-year-old children drawings of different sized adults. The adults were either thin, medium or overweight. The children were then asked to describe what kind of person each adult was. The children associated the medium-sized adults with all positive qualities and the thin and fat adults with all the negative qualities. In a further experiment, the researchers presented the children with five drawings of children: a handicapped child, a child with facial disfigurement, a child with crutches and a leg brace, a child whose left forearm had been amputated and an obese child. The children were then asked, 'Tell me which boy [girl] you like the best'. All the children rated the obese child as the one they liked least. The researchers concluded that this was because obesity was seen as the fault of the child and not something with which to sympathize. The children saw obesity as resulting from being greedy, weak and lazy. Negative beliefs about obesity are strong in both adults and children.

What causes obesity?

The theories relating to the causes of obesity include both physiological theories and behavioural theories.

Physiological theories

Several physiological theories describe the possible causes of obesity.

Genetic theories

Size appears to run in families and the probability that a child will be overweight is related to the parents' weight. For example, having one obese parent results in a 40 per cent chance of producing an obese child and having two obese parents results in an 80 per cent chance. In contrast, the probability that thin parents will produce overweight children is very small, about 7 per cent (Garn *et al.* 1981). However, parents and children share both environment and genetic constitution, so this likeness could be due to either factor. To address this problem research has examined twins and adoptees.

Twin studies

Twin studies have examined the weight of identical twins reared apart, who have identical genes but different environments. Studies have also examined the weights of non-identical twins reared together, who have different genes but similar environments. The results show that the identical twins reared apart are more similar in weight than non-identical twins reared together. For example, Stunkard *et al.* (1990) examined the BMI in 93 identical twins reared apart and reported that genetic factors accounted for 66–70 per cent in the variance in their body weight, suggesting a strong genetic component in determining obesity. However, the role of genetics appears to be greater in lighter twin pairs than in heavier pairs.

Adoptee studies

Research has also examined the role of genetics in obesity using adoptees. Such studies compare the adoptees' weight with both their adoptive parents and their biological parents. Stunkard *et al.* (1986b) gathered information about 540 adult adoptees in Denmark, their adopted parents and their biological parents. The results showed a strong relationship between the weight class of the adoptee (thin, median weight, overweight, obese) and their biological parents' weight class but no relationship with their adoptee parents' weight class. This relationship suggests a major role for genetics and was also found across the whole range of body weight. Interestingly, the relationship to biological mother's weight was greater than the relationship with the biological father's weight.

Research therefore suggests a strong role for genetics in predicting obesity. Research also suggests that the primary distribution of this weight (upper *vs* lower body) is also inherited (Bouchard *et al.* 1990). However, how this genetic predisposition expresses itself is unclear. *Metabolic rate,* the *number of fat cells* and *appetite regulation* may be three factors influenced by genetics.

Metabolic rate theory

The body uses energy for exercise and physical activity and to carry out all the chemical and biological processes that are essential to being alive (e.g. respiration, heart rate, blood pressure). The rate of this energy use is called the 'resting metabolic rate', which has been found to be highly heritable (Bouchard *et al.* 1990). It has been argued that lower metabolic rates may be associated with obesity as people with lower metabolic rates burn up less calories when they are resting and therefore require less food intake to carry on living.

Research in the USA has evaluated the relationship between metabolic rate and weight gain. A group in Phoenix assessed the metabolic rates of 126 Pima Indians by monitoring their breathing for a 40-minute period. The study was carried out using Pima Indians because they have an abnormally high rate of obesity (about 80–85 per cent) and were considered an interesting population. The subjects remained still and the levels of oxygen consumed and carbon dioxide produced was measured. The researchers then followed any changes in weight and metabolic rate for a 4-year period and found that the people who gained a substantial amount of weight were the ones with the lowest metabolic rates at the beginning of the study. In a further study, 95 subjects spent 24 hours in a respiratory chamber and the amount of energy used was measured. The subjects were followed up 2 years later and the researchers found that those who had originally shown a low level of energy use were four times more likely to also show a substantial weight increase (cited in Brownell 1989).

These results suggest a relationship between metabolic rate and the tendency for weight gain. If this is the case, then it is possible that the some individuals are predisposed to become obese because they require fewer calories to survive than thinner individuals. Therefore, a genetic tendency to be obese may express itself in lowered metabolic rates. However, in apparent contrast to this prediction, there is no evidence to suggest that obese people generally have lower metabolic rates than thin people. In fact, research suggests that overweight people tend to have slightly higher metabolic rates than thin people of similar height. To explain these apparently contradictory findings it has been suggested that obese people may have lower metabolic rates to start with, which results in weight gain and this weight gain itself results in an increase in metabolic rate (Ravussin and Bogardus 1989).

Fat cell theory

A genetic tendency to be obese may also express itself in terms of the number of fat cells. People of average weight usually have about 25–35 billion fat cells, which are designed for the storage of fat in periods of energy surplus and the mobilization of fat in periods of energy deficit. Mildly obese individuals usually have the same number of fat cells but they are enlarged in size and weight. Severely obese individuals, however, have more fat cells – up to 100–125 billion (Sjostrom 1980). Cell number is mainly determined by genetics; however, when the existing number of cells have been used up, new fat cells are formed from preexisting preadipocytes. Most of this growth in the number of cells occurs during gestation and early childhood and remains stable once adulthood has been reached. Although the results from studies in this area are unclear, it would seem that if an individual is born with more fat cells then there are more cells immediately available to fill up. In addition, research suggests that once fat cells have been made they can never be lost (Sjostrom

1980). An obese person with a large number of fat cells, may be able to empty these cells but will never be able to get rid of them.

Appetite regulation

A genetic predisposition may also be related to appetite control. Over recent years researchers have attempted to identify the gene, or collection of genes, responsible for obesity. Although some work using small animals has identified a single gene that is associated with profound obesity, for humans the work is still unclear. Two children have, however, been identified with a defect in the 'ob gene', which produces leptin which is responsible for telling the brain to stop eating (Montague *et al.* 1997). It has been argued that the obese may not produce leptin and therefore overeat. To support this, researchers have given these two children daily injections of leptin, which has resulted in a decrease in food intake and weight loss at a rate of 1–2 kg per month (Farooqi *et al.* 1999). Despite this, the research exploring the role of genetics on appetite control is still in the very early stages.

Behavioural theories

Behavioural theories of obesity have examined both physical activity and eating behaviour.

Physical activity

Increases in the prevalence of obesity coincide with decreases in daily energy expenditure due to improvements in transport systems, and a shift from an agricultural society to an industrial and increasingly information-based society. As a simple example, a telephone company in the USA has suggested that in the course of one year an extension phone saves an individual approximately one mile of walking, which could be the equivalent of 2–3 lb of fat or up to 10,500 kcal (Stern 1984). Further, at present only 20 per cent of men and 10 pet cent of women are employed in active occupations (Allied Dunbar National Fitness Survey 1992) and for many people leisure times are dominated by inactivity (Central Statistical Office 1994). Although data on changes in activity levels are problematic, there exists a useful database on television viewing which shows that whereas the average viewer in the 1960s watched 13 hours of television per week, in England this has now doubled to 26 hours per week (General Household Survey 1994). This is further exacerbated by the increased use of videos and computer games by both children and adults. It has therefore been suggested that obesity may be caused by inactivity. In a survey of adolescent boys in Glasgow in 1964 and 1971, whereas daily food diaries indicated a decrease in daily energy intake from 2795 kcals to 2610 kcals, the boys in 1971 showed an increase in body fat from 16.3 per cent to 18.4 per cent. This suggests that decreased physical activity was

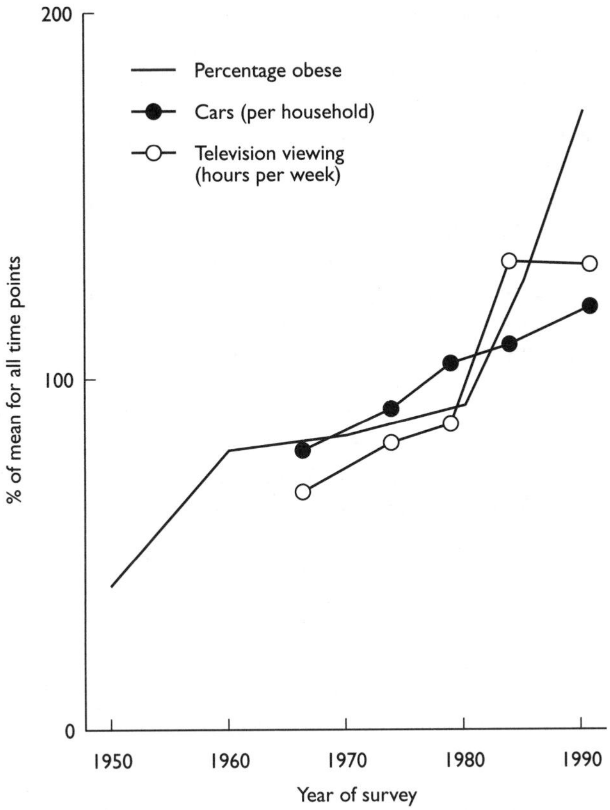

Figure 6.3 Changes in physical activity and obesity

related to increased body fat (Durnin *et al.* 1974). To examine the role of physical activity in obesity, research has asked 'Are changes in obesity related to changes in activity?', 'Do the obese exercise less?', 'What effect does exercise have on food intake?' and 'What effect does exercise have on energy expenditure?' These questions will now be examined.

Are changes in obesity related to changes in activity?

This question can be answered in two ways: first using epidemiological data on a population and second using prospective data on individuals.

In 1995, Prentice and Jebb presented epidemiological data on changes in physical activity from 1950 to 1990, as measured by car ownership and television viewing, and compared these with changes in the prevalence of obesity. The results from this study suggested a strong association between an increase in both car ownership and television viewing and an increase in obesity (see Fig. 6.3). They commented that 'it seems reasonable to conclude that the low levels of physical inactivity now prevalent in Britain must play an important, perhaps dominant role in the development of obesity by greatly reducing energy needs' (Prentice and Jebb 1995). However, their data was only correlational. Therefore, it remains unclear whether obesity and physical activity are related (the third factor problem – some other variable may be determining both obesity and activity) and whether decreases in activity cause increases in obesity or whether, in fact, increases in obesity actually cause decreases in activity. In addition, the data is at the population level and therefore could miss important individual differences (i.e. some people who become obese could be active and those who are thin could be inactive).

In an alternative approach to assessing the relationship between activity and obesity a large Finnish study of 12,000 adults examined the association between levels of physical activity and excess weight gain over a 5-year follow-up period (Rissanen *et al.* 1991). The results showed that lower levels of activity were a greater risk factor for weight gain than any other baseline measures. However, although this data was prospective it is still possible that a third factor may explain the relationship (i.e. those with lower levels of activity at baseline were women, the women had children and therefore put on more weight). Unless experimental data is collected, conclusions about causality remain problematic.

Do the obese exercise less?

Research has also examined the relationship between activity and obesity using a cross-sectional design to examine differences between the obese and non-obese. In particular, several studies in the 1960s and 1970s examined whether the obese exercised less than the non-obese. Using time-lapse photography, Bullen *et al.* (1964) observed girls considered obese and those of normal weight on a summer camp. They reported that during swimming the obese girls spent less time swimming and more time floating, and while playing tennis the obese girls were inactive for 77 per cent of the time compared with the girls of normal weight, who were inactive for only 56 per cent of the time. In addition, research indicates that the obese walk less on a daily basis than the non-obese and are less likely to use stairs or walk up escalators. However, whether reduced exercise is a cause or a consequence of obesity is unclear. It is possible that the obese take less exercise due to factors such as embarrassment and stigma and that exercise plays a part in the maintenance of obesity but not in its cause.

What effect does exercise have on food intake?

The relationship between exercise and food intake is complex, with research suggesting that exercise may increase, decrease or have no effect on eating behaviour. For example, a study of middle-aged male joggers who ran approximately 65 km per week, suggested that increased calorie intake was related to increased exercise with the joggers eating more than the sedentary control group (Blair *et al.* 1981). However, another study of military cadets reported that decreased food intake was related to increased exercise (Edholm *et al.* 1955). Much research has also been carried out on rats, which shows a more consistent relationship between increased exercise and decreased food intake. However, the extent to which such results can be generalized to humans is questionable.

What effect does exercise have on energy expenditure?

Exercise burns up calories. For example, 10 minutes of sleeping uses up to 16 kcals, standing uses 19 kcals, running uses 142 kcals, walking downstairs uses 88 kcals and walking upstairs uses 229 kcals (Brownell 1989). In addition, the amount of calories used increases with the individual's body weight. Therefore, exercise has long been recommended as a weight loss method. However, the number of calories exercise burns up is relatively few compared with those in an average meal. In addition, exercise is recommended as a means to increase metabolic rate. However, only intense and prolonged exercise appears to have an effect on metabolic rate.

Therefore, the role of exercise in obesity is still unclear. There appears to be an association between population decreases in activity and increases in obesity. In addition, prospective data support this association and highlight lower levels of activity as an important risk factor. Further, cross-sectional data indicate that the obese appear to exercise less than the non-obese. However, whether inactivity is a cause or consequence of obesity is questionable. It is possible that an unidentified third factor may be creating this association, and it is also debatable whether exercise has a role in reducing food intake and promoting energy expenditure. However, exercise may have psychological effects, which could benefit the obese either in terms of promoting weight loss or simply by making them feel better about themselves (see Chapter 7 for the effects of exercise on mood).

Eating behaviour

In an alternative approach to understanding the causes of obesity, research has examined eating behaviour. Research has asked 'Are changes in food intake associated with changes in obesity?', 'Do the obese eat for different reasons than the non-obese?' and 'Do the obese eat more than the non-obese?' These questions will now be examined.

Are changes in food intake associated with changes in obesity?

The UK National Food Survey collects data on food intake in the home, which can be analysed to assess changes in food intake over the past 50 years. The results from this database illustrate that, although overall calorie consumption increased between 1950 and 1970, since 1970 there has been a distinct decrease in the amount we eat (see Fig. 6.4).

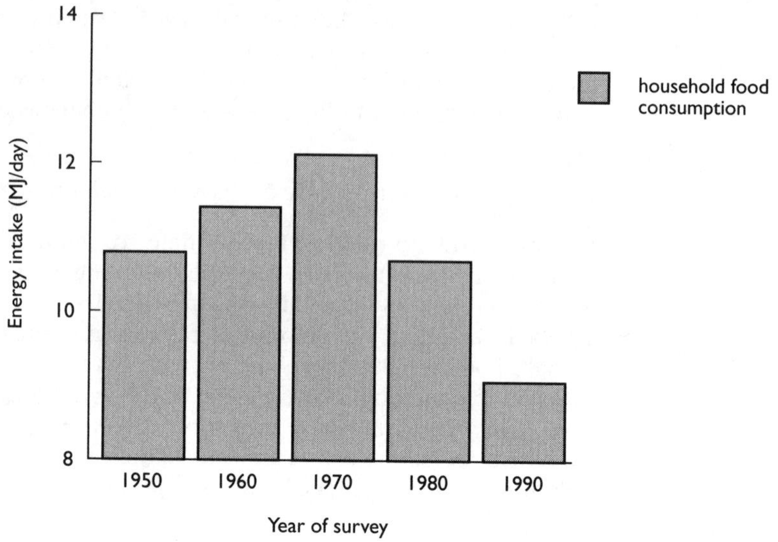

Figure 6.4 Changes in food intake over the past 50 years

Prentice and Jebb (1995) examined the association between changes in food intake in terms of energy intake and fat intake and changes in obesity. Their results indicated no obvious association between the increase in obesity and the changes in food intake (see Fig. 6.5).

Therefore, using population data there appears to be no relationship between changes in food intake and changes in obesity.

Do the obese eat for different reasons than the non-obese?

Throughout the 1960s and 1970s theories of eating behaviour emphasized the role of food intake in predicting weight. Original studies of obesity were based on the assumption that the obese ate for different reasons than people of normal weight (Ferster *et al.* 1962). Schachter's externality theory suggested that, although all people were responsive to environmental stimuli such as the sight, taste and smell of food, and that such stimuli might cause overeating, the obese were highly and sometimes uncontrollably responsive to external cues. It was argued that normal weight individuals mainly ate as a response to internal cues (e.g. hunger, satiety) and obese individuals tended to be under-responsive to their internal cues and over-responsive to external cues. Within this perspective, research examined the eating behaviour and eating style of the obese and non-obese in response to external cues such as the time of day, the sight of food, the taste of food and the number and salience of food cues (e.g. Schachter 1968; Schachter and Gross 1968; Schachter and Rodin 1974). The results from these studies produced fairly inconsistent results. Therefore, research also examined whether the obese ate more than the non-obese.

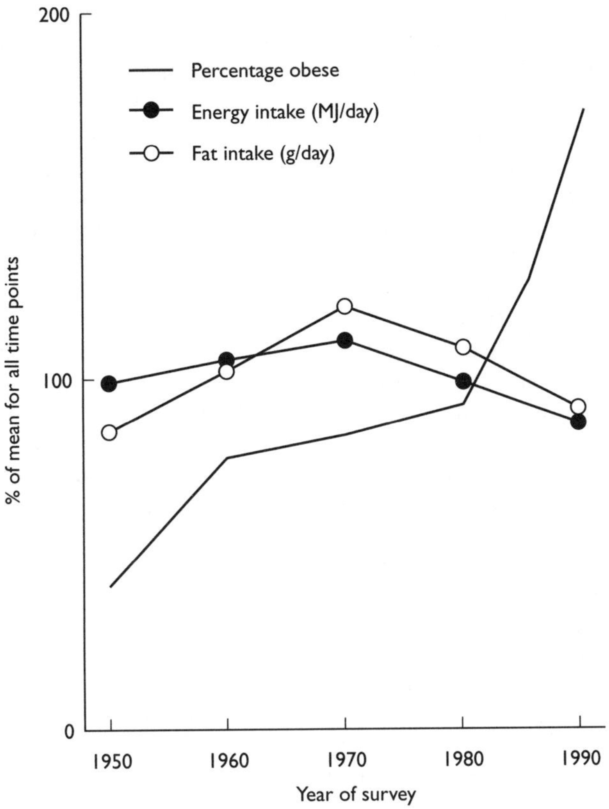

Figure 6.5 Changes in calorie consumption and obesity

Do the obese eat more than the non-obese?

Research exploring the amount eaten by the obese has either focused on the amount consumed *per se* or on the type of food consumed.

Because it was believed that the obese ate for different reasons than the non-obese it was also believed that they ate more. Research therefore explored the food intake of the obese in restaurants, at home, and examined what food they bought. For example, Coates *et al.* (1978) suggested that perhaps the obese were overeating at home and went into the homes of 60 middle-class families to examine what was stored in their cupboards. They weighed all members of the families and found no relationship between body size and the mass and type of food they consumed at home. In an attempt to clarify the problem of whether the obese eat more than the non-obese, Spitzer and Rodin (1981) examined the research into eating behaviour and suggested that 'of twenty nine studies examining the effects of body weight on amount eaten in laboratory studies . . . only nine reported that overweight subjects ate significantly more than their lean counterparts'. Therefore, the answer to the question 'do the obese eat more/differently to the non-obese?' appears to be 'no'; the obese do not necessarily overeat (compared with others). If overeating is defined as 'compared with what the body needs', it could be argued that the obese overeat because they have excess body fat. Over recent years, research has focused on the eating behaviour of the obese not in terms of calories consumed, or in terms of amount eaten, but more specifically in terms of the type of food eaten.

Population data indicates that calorie consumption has decreased since the 1970s and that this decrease is unrelated to the increase in obesity (see Figs 6.4 and 6.5). However, this data also shows that the ratio between carbohydrate consumption and fat consumption has changed; whereas we now eat less carbohydrate, we eat proportionally more fat (Prentice and Jebb 1995). One theory that has been developed is that, although the obese may not eat more than the non-obese overall, they may eat proportionally more fat. Further, it has been argued that not all calories are equal (Prentice 1995) and that calories from fat may lead to greater weight gain than calories from carbohydrates. To support this theory, one study of 11,500 people in Scotland showed that men consuming the lowest proportion of carbohydrate in their diets were four times more likely to be obese than those consuming the highest proportion of carbohydrate. A similar relationship was also found for women, although the difference was only two- to threefold. Therefore, it was concluded that relatively lower carbohydrate consumption is related to lower levels of obesity (Bolton-Smith and Woodward 1994). A similar study in Leeds also provided support for the fat proportion theory of obesity (Blundell and Macdiarmid 1997). This study reported that high fat eaters who derived more than 45 per cent of their energy from fat were 19 times more likely to be obese than those who derived less than 35 per cent of their energy from fat. Therefore, these studies suggest that the obese do not eat more overall than the non-obese, nor do they eat more calories, carbohydrate or fat *per se* than the non-obese. But they do eat more fat compared with the amount of carbohydrate; the proportion of fat in their diet is higher. So how might a relative increase in fat consumption relate to obesity?

As a possible explanation of these results, research has examined the role of fat and carbohydrates in appetite regulation. Three possible mechanisms have been proposed (Blundell *et al.* 1996; Blundell and Macdiarmid 1997):

1 *The benefits of complex carbohydrates to energy use*. First, it has been suggested that it takes more energy to burn carbohydrates than fat. Further, as the body prefers to burn carbohydrates than fat, carbohydrate intake is accompanied by an increase of carbohydrate oxidation. In contrast, increased fat intake is not accompanied by an increase in fat oxidation. Therefore, carbohydrates are burned, fat is stored.
2 *The benefits of complex carbohydrates to hunger*. Second it has been suggested that complex carbohydrates (such as bread, potatoes, pasta, rice) reduce hunger and cause reduced food intake due to their bulk and the

amount of fibre they contain. In addition, they switch off the desire to eat. Therefore, carbohydrates make you feel fuller faster.

3 *The costs of fat to hunger*. Third it has been suggested that fat does not switch off the desire to eat, making it easier to eat more and more fat without feeling full.

What does all this research mean?

The evidence for the causes of obesity is therefore complex and can be summarized as follows:

- There is good evidence for a genetic basis to obesity. The evidence for how this is expressed is weak.
- The prevalence of obesity has increased at a similar rate to decreases in physical activity.
- There is some evidence that the obese exercise less than the non-obese.
- The prevalence of obesity has increased at a rate unrelated to the overall decrease in calorie consumption.
- There is no evidence that the obese eat more calories than the non-obese.
- The relative increase in fat is parallel to the increase in obesity.
- The obese may eat proportionally more fat than the non-obese.

Therefore, the following points would seem likely.

- Some individuals have a genetic tendency to be obese.
- Obesity is related to under-exercise.
- Obesity is related to consuming relatively more fat and relatively less carbohydrate.

Problems with obesity research

There are several problems with the research into obesity and these can be considered in terms of the following stages of research:

The problem being studied

Obesity has been described as having a dynamic phase (becoming obese) and a static phase (maintaining a level of obesity) (Garrow 1984). Research indicates that it may take fewer calories to maintain a level of obesity than it does to become obese in the first place. Therefore, obese individuals may overeat (compared with the non-obese) in the dynamic phase and under-eat (compared with the non-obese) in the static phase.

Data collection

Measuring food intake is extremely problematic; laboratory studies, diary studies and observation studies may actually change what people eat. Observational studies do not involve people in controlled conditions and self-report studies are open to problems of forgetting and social desirability.

Data analysis

Much of the data is purely correlational (e.g. associations between changes in obesity and changes in activity/food intake). This does not enable conclusions about causality to be drawn (i.e. does inactivity cause obesity or obesity cause inactivity?). Further, it is possible that a third factor (as yet unknown) is responsible for the associations reported. In addition, much of the data is cross-sectional (e.g. obese *vs* non-obese) and this also does not allow conclusions about causality to be made (i.e. how someone eats when they are obese may not reflect how they ate to become obese).

Some data is measured at the population level; for example, changes in activity levels, calorie intakes and fat intakes are all based on measures of populations. Some data is measured at the level of the individual; for example, differences between the obese and non-obese.

Finally, comparing population data and individual data is open to the 'ecological fallacy' – population data can hide a multitude of individual differences; that is, the data at the population level may show one pattern, which is completely different to the pattern at the individual level.

Data interpretation

If the obese do eat proportionally more fat than the non-obese, and this causes obesity via appetite control, why do the obese not eat more overall than the non-obese (i.e. the fat they consume makes them want to eat more in absolute terms)? Similarly, if relative increases in fat effect appetite control, why are the population increases in relative fat not reflected in overall population increases in food intake (i.e. the more fat we eat relatively, the more we eat overall)? Finally, if relative increases in fat effect appetite control, which causes eating more overall, why isn't eating more overall associated with an increase in obesity (i.e. as the population eats relatively more fat, it eats more overall and gets more obese)?

The values of the researchers

'Overeating' assumes that this behaviour is 'wrong' because it may lead to weight gain. This judgement is only accepted within a culture where food is freely available and weight gain is regarded as unacceptable. In other cultures, eating to maintain weight could be seen as 'under-eating'.

Therefore, the causes of obesity remain complex and unclear. Perhaps an integration of all theories is needed before proper conclusions can be drawn.

Restraint theory: an alternative approach to overeating

Behavioural theories of obesity, which focus on food intake, suggest a relationship between body weight and eating behaviour. In the late 1970s, however, a new theory of eating behaviour emerged, which shifted the emphasis from weight (a biological construct) as a predictor of food intake to restrained eating (a psychological construct). Attempts to understand the causes of obesity continue but examinations of eating behaviour suggest that restrained eating (attempting to eat less) might be a better predictor of food intake than weight *per se* (Hibscher and Herman 1977).

Attempting to eat less: the problem of dieting

Restrained eating has become increasingly synonymous with dieting and research suggests that between 61 and 89 per cent of the female population attempt to restrain their food intake at some time in their life. In addition, dieting is also found in adolescents and girls as young as 9 years of age (Wardle and Beales 1986; Hill *et al.* 1994). These studies illustrate the central role that dieting behaviour plays in the lives of many women. So why do so many women diet? The main answer to this is that they are dissatisfied with their body shape.

What is body dissatisfaction?

Body dissatisfaction comes in many forms. Some research has conceptualized body dissatisfaction in terms of a *distorted body size estimation* and a perception that the body is larger than it really is. For example, Slade and Russell (1973) asked anorexics to adjust the distance between two lights on a beam in a darkened room until the lights represented the width of aspects of their body such as their hips, waist and shoulders. The results showed that anorexics consistently overestimated their size compared with control subjects. Other studies coming from the same perspective have asked subjects to mark either two ends of a life-size piece of paper (Gleghorn *et al.* 1987), to adjust the horizontal dimensions on either a television or video image of themselves (Freeman *et al.* 1984; Gardner *et al.* 1987), or to change the dimensions on a distorting mirror (Brodie *et al.* 1989). This research has consistently shown that individuals with clinically defined eating disorders show greater perceptual distortion than non-clinical subjects. However, the research has also shown that the vast majority of women, with or without an eating disorder, think that they are fatter than they actually are.

Some research has emphasized a discrepancy between *perceptions of reality versus those of an ideal* without a comparison to the individual's actual size as objectively measured by the researcher. This research has tended to use whole-body silhouette pictures of varying sizes whereby the subject is asked to state which one is closest to how they look now and which one best illustrates how they would like to look. For example, Stunkard *et al.* (1983) used this approach with normal male and female students; Counts and Adams (1985) used it with bulimics, dieters and ex-obese females; and Collins (1991) used it with pre-adolescent children. It has consistently been shown that most girls and women would like to be thinner than they are and most males would like to be either the same or larger.

The final and most frequent way in which body dissatisfaction is understood is simply in terms of *negative feelings* and cognitions towards the body. This has been assessed using questionnaires such as the body shape questionnaire (Cooper *et al.* 1987), the body areas satisfaction scale (Brown *et al.* 1990) and the body dissatisfaction subscale of the eating disorders inventory (Garner 1991). These questionnaires ask questions such as 'Do you worry about parts of your body being too big?', 'Do you worry about your thighs spreading out when you sit down?' and 'Does being with thin women make you feel conscious of your weight?' The research has shown that, although those individuals with eating disorders show greater body dissatisfaction than those without, dieters show greater body dissatisfaction than non-dieters and women in general show greater body dissatisfaction than men.

Therefore, body dissatisfaction can be conceptualized as either a discrepancy between individuals' perception of their body size and their real body size, a discrepancy between their perception of their actual size as compared with their ideal size, or simply as feelings of discontent with the body's size and shape. However, whichever conceptualization is used and whichever measurement tool is chosen to operationalize body dissatisfaction it seems clear that it is a common phenomenon and certainly not one that is limited to those few individuals with clinically defined eating disorders. So what causes this problem?

Where does body dissatisfaction come from?

Much research has looked at the role of social factors in causing body dissatisfaction in terms of the media, ethnicity, social class and the family environment. In addition, research has explored the role of psychological factors that may translate the social factors into actual body dissatisfaction.

Social factors

The role of the media

The most commonly held belief in both the lay and academic communities is probably that body dissatisfaction is a response to representations of thin women in the media. Magazines, newspapers, television, films and even novels predominantly use images of thin women. These women may be advertising body size related items such as food and clothes or neutral items, such as vacuum cleaners and wall paper, but they are always thin. Alternatively, they may be characters in a story or simply passers-by who illustrate the real world, but this real world is always represented by thinness. Whatever their role and wherever their existence women used by the media are generally thin and we are therefore led to believe that thinness is not only the desired norm but also the actual norm. When, on those rare occasions a fatter woman appears she is usually there making a statement about being fat (fat comedians make jokes about chocolate cake and fat actresses are either evil or unhappy) not simply as a normal woman. Do these representations then make women dissatisfied with their bodies? Some research suggests that this is the case. For example, Ogden and Mundray (1996) asked men and women to rate their body dissatisfaction both before and after studying pictures of either fat or thin men or women (the pictures were matched in gender to the participant). The results showed that all participants, regardless of sex, felt more body satisfied after studying the fatter pictures and more body dissatisfied after studying the thinner pictures. It was also shown that this response was greater in the women than the men. Similar results have been found for anorexics, bulimics and pregnant women (Waller *et al.* 1992; Hamilton and Waller 1993; Sumner *et al.* 1993). If such changes in body dissatisfaction can occur after only acute exposure to these images then it is possible that longer term exposure might be more serious. However, is the media the only explanation of body dissatisfaction? Are women (and sometimes men) simply passive victims of the whims of the media? Perhaps body dissatisfaction also comes from a range of additional sources.

Ethnicity

Although body dissatisfaction has predominantly been seen as a problem for white women, the literature examining the relationship between body dissatisfaction and ethnic group is contradictory. For example, higher rates of a range of behaviours associated with body dissatisfaction have been found in white women when compared with black and/or Asian women in terms of bulimic behaviours (Gray *et al.* 1987), generalized disordered eating (Abrams *et al.* 1992; Akan and Grilo 1995) and body dissatisfaction and eating concerns (Rucker and Cash 1992; Powell and Khan 1995).

However, in direct contrast, other studies report the reverse relationship between ethnicity and weight concern. For example, Mumford *et al.* (1991) reported results from a school in the north of England that indicated that the prevalence of bulimia nervosa was higher amongst Asian schoolgirls than their white counterparts. In parallel, Striegal-Moore *et al.* (1995) reported higher levels of drive for thinness in black girls, and Hill and Bhatti (1995) reported higher levels of dietary restraint in 9-year-old Asian girls when both these samples were compared with white girls. Furthermore, additional studies have suggested that equally high levels of weight concern can be found in women and girls regardless of their ethnicity (Dolan *et al.* 1990; Ahmed *et al.* 1994). Therefore, some research indicates that whites are more body dissatisfied than Asians and blacks, other research shows that whites are less dissatisfied and some research even shows that there is no difference by ethnic group.

Social class

Body dissatisfaction is also generally believed to be a problem for the higher classes. However, the literature on social class is also contradictory. Several studies in this area indicate that factors ranging from body dissatisfaction, body distortion, dieting behaviour to eating disorders are more prevalent in higher class individuals. For example, Dornbusch *et al.* (1984) examined social class and the desire to be thin in a representative sample of 7000 American adolescents and concluded that higher class females wanted to be thinner when compared with their lower class counterparts. In parallel, Drenowski *et al.* (1994) reported that the higher class subjects in their sample showed increased prevalence of dieting, binging and vigorous exercise for weight loss and Wardle and Marsland (1990) reported that, although their higher class school children were thinner, they showed greater levels of weight concern. Similar results have also been reported for the prevalence of anorexia nervosa (Crisp *et al.* 1976).

However, research also suggests that the relationship between social class and weight concern is not straightforward. For example, in direct contrast to the above studies, Story *et al.* (1995) reported the results from a sample of 36,320 American students and suggested that higher social class was related to greater weight satisfaction and lower rates of pathological weight control behaviours such as vomiting. Similar results were reported by Eisler and Szmukler (1985), who examined abnormal eating attitudes. Furthermore, additional studies report that social class is unrelated to factors such as body dissatisfaction, the desire for thinness, the desire for weight loss and symptoms indicative of eating disorders (Cole and Edelmann 1988; Whitaker *et al.* 1989). Therefore, although social class is believed to be a cause of body dissatisfaction, the results remain unclear.

The family

Research has also focused on the impact of the family on predicting body dissatisfaction. In particular, it has highlighted a role for the mother and suggested that mothers who are dissatisfied with their own bodies communicate this to their daughters which results in the daughters' own body dissatisfaction. For example, Hall and Brown (1982) reported that mothers of girls with anorexia show greater body dissatisfaction than mothers of non-disordered girls. Likewise, Steiger *et al.* (1994) found a direct correspondence between mothers' and daughters' levels of weight concern, and Hill *et al.* (1990) reported a link between mothers' and daughters' degree of dietary restraint. However, research examining concordance between mothers and daughters has not always produced consistent results. For example, Attie and Brooks-Gunn (1989) reported that mothers' levels of compulsive eating and body image could not predict these factors in their daughters. Likewise, Ogden and Elder (1998) reported discordance between mothers' and daughters' weight concern in both Asian and white families.

Therefore, research exploring the role of social factors has highlighted a role for the media, ethnicity, social class and the mother's own body dissatisfaction. However, there are problems with the literature. First much of the evidence is contradictory and therefore straightforward conclusions are problematic. Secondly, even if there was a relationship between social factors and body dissatisfaction, simply looking for group differences (i.e. white *vs* Asian, lower class *vs* higher class, mother *vs* daughter) does not explain how body dissatisfaction may come about. Therefore research has also looked for psychological explanations.

Psychological factors

The research suggests that body dissatisfaction may be related to class, ethnicity and the family environment but that this relationship is not a consistent one. Perhaps, simply looking for group differences hides the effect of other psychological causes. From this perspective, ethnicity may relate to body dissatisfaction, but only when ethnicity is also accompanied by a particular set of beliefs. Similarly, it may not be class *per se* that is important but whether class reflects the way an individual thinks. Further, a mother's body dissatisfaction may only be important if it occurs within a particular kind of relationship. So what might these psychological factors be? Research has explored the role of beliefs, the mother–daughter relationship and the central role of control.

Beliefs

Some research has examined the beliefs held by the individuals themselves and their family members. For example, when attempting to understand ethnicity, studies have highlighted a role for beliefs about competitiveness, the value of achievement, material success and a parental belief that the child is their future (Ogden and Chanana 1998). In addition, the literature has also emphasized beliefs about a woman's role within society. For example, Mumford *et al.* (1991) concluded that eating disorders in Asian girls may be related to a family background that believes in a traditional role for women. Such conclusions were also made by Hill and Bhatti (1995).

In a similar vein, when attempting to explain the role of social class research has highlighted a role for beliefs about achievement and it has been suggested that eating disorders may be a response to such pressures (Bruch 1974; Kalucy *et al.* 1977; Selvini 1988). Lower class individuals, in contrast, may aspire more in terms of family life and having children, which may be protective against weight concern. Cole and Edelmann

(1988) empirically tested this possibility and assessed the relationship between the need to achieve and eating behaviour. However, although the need to achieve was associated with class, it was not predictive of weight concern. It has also been suggested that class may be associated with a greater value placed on physical appearance and attitudes towards obesity (Wardle *et al.* 1995). Further, Dornbusch *et al.* (1984) commented that 'there are higher standards for thinness in higher social classes', which may contribute to higher levels of weight concern. In addition, Striegel-Moore *et al.* (1986) argued that higher class women are more likely to emulate trend setters of beauty and fashion, again predisposing them to feelings of dissatisfaction with their appearance.

Therefore, beliefs about competitiveness, achievement, material success, the role of women, stereotypes of beauty and the child–parent relationship have been highlighted as the kinds of beliefs that may predict body dissatisfaction. Ogden and Chanana (1998) explored the role of these beliefs in Asian and white teenage girls and Ogden and Thomas (1999) focused on lower and higher class individuals; both studies concluding that, although social factors such as class and ethnicity may be related to body dissatisfaction, it is likely that their influence is mediated through the role of such beliefs held by both the individual who is dissatisfied with their body and their family members.

Mother–daughter relationship

Some research has also explored the nature of the mother–daughter relationship. For example, Crisp *et al.* (1980) argued that undefined boundaries within the family and the existence of an enmeshed relationship between mother and daughter may be important factors. Likewise, Smith *et al.* (1995) suggested that a close relationship between mother and daughter may result in an enmeshed relationship and problems with separation in adolescence. Further, Minuchin *et al.* (1978) argued that although optimum autonomy does not mean breaking all bonds between mother and daughter, mother–daughter relationships that permit poor autonomy for both parties may be predictive of future psychopathology. Further, Bruch (1974) argued that anorexia may be a result of a child's struggle to develop her own self-identity within a mother–daughter dynamic that limits the daughter's autonomy. Some authors have also examined the relationship between autonomy, enmeshment and intimacy. For example, Smith *et al.* (1995) argued that an increased recognition of autonomy within the mother–daughter relationship corresponds with a decrease in enmeshment and a resulting increase in intimacy. Further, it is suggested that such intimacy may be reflected in a reduction in conflict and subsequent psychological problems (Smith *et al.* 1995). A recent study directly explored whether the mother–daughter relationship was important in terms of a 'modelling hypothesis' (i.e. the mother is body dissatisfied and therefore is the daughter) or an 'interactive hypothesis' (i.e. it is the relationship itself between mother and daughter that is important). Therefore, it examined both the mothers' and the daughters' own levels of body dissatisfaction and the nature of the relationship between mother and daughter (Ogden and Steward in press). The results showed no support for the modelling hypothesis but suggested that a relationship in which mothers did not believe in either their own or their daughter's autonomy and rated projection as important was more likely to result in daughters who were dissatisfied with their bodies.

Therefore, it would seem that body dissatisfaction may come from the media. Further, it may be related to social factors such as ethnicity, social class and the mother's own body dissatisfaction. In addition, it is possible that the impact of such social factors is mediated through psychological factors such as beliefs and the nature of relationships. Research has suggested that all these factors illustrate a central role for the need for control.

The role of control

Beliefs relating to materialism, competitiveness, achievement, autonomy, the role of women and a projected relationship between mother and daughter all have one thing in common. They are based on the assumption that the object of these beliefs (i.e. the daughter) has control over her destiny. It is being assumed that she can achieve, she can compete and she can fulfil the desires of others if only she were to put her mind to it; anything can be achieved if the effort is right. This is quite a lot of pressure to place on anyone. It is particularly a lot of pressure to place upon a woman who may well feel that the world is still designed for men. And it is even more pressure to place upon a young woman who may feel that the world is designed for adults. Such expectations may result in feelings of being out of control: 'how can I achieve all these things?', 'what do I have to do?', 'I can never fulfil everyone's demands', 'my world is simply not that open to change', 'things are not that controllable'. However, the one thing that we are led to believe can be changed is our body. A family's beliefs may make us want to control and change a whole range of factors. But the only factor which may seem controllable may simply be the way we look. In fact the media constantly tells us that this is so. Therefore, feelings of being out of control need to be expressed. Body dissatisfaction may well be an expression of this lack of control (Orbach 1978; Ogden 1999).

Body dissatisfaction and dieting

Body dissatisfaction is consistently related to dieting and attempting to eat less. Restraint theory (e.g. Herman and Mack 1975; Herman and Polivy 1984) was developed to evaluate the causes and consequences of dieting (referred to as restrained eating) and suggests that dieters show both under- and overeating.

The role of restrained eating in under- and overeating

Successful dieting

Restrained eating aims to reduce food intake and several studies have found that at times this aim is successful. Thompson *et al.* (1988) used a preload/taste test methodology to examine restrained eaters' eating behaviour. This experimental method involves giving subjects either a high-calorie preload (e.g. a high-calorie milk shake, a chocolate bar) or a low-calorie preload (e.g. a cracker). After eating/drinking the preload, subjects are asked to take part in a taste test. This involves asking subjects to rate a series of different foods (e.g. biscuits, snacks, ice cream) for a variety of different qualities, including saltiness, preference and sweetness. The subjects are left alone for a set amount of time to rate the foods and then the amount they have eaten is weighed (the subjects do not know that this will happen). The aim of the preload/taste test method is to measure food intake in a controlled environment (the laboratory) and to examine the effect of preloading on their eating behaviour. Thompson *et al.* (1988) reported that in this experimental situation the restrained eaters consumed fewer calories than the unrestrained eaters after both the low and high preloads. This suggests that their attempts at eating less were successful. Kirkley *et al.* (1988) assessed the eating style of 50 women using 4-day dietary self-monitoring forms and also reported that the restrained eaters consumed fewer calories than the unrestrained eaters. Laessle *et al.* (1989) also used food diaries and found that the restrained eaters consumed around 400 kcal less than the unrestrained eaters, with the restrained eaters specifically avoiding food items of high carbohydrate and fat content. Therefore, restrained eaters aim to eat less and are sometimes successful.

Unsuccessful dieting

In opposition to these findings, several studies have suggested that higher levels of restrained eating are related to increased food intake. For example, Ruderman and Wilson (1979) used a preload/taste test procedure and reported that restrained eaters consumed significantly more food than the unrestrained eaters, irrespective of preload size. In particular, restraint theory has identified the disinhibition of restraint as characteristic of overeating in restrained eaters (Herman and Mack 1975; Spencer and Fremouw 1979; Herman *et al.* 1987). The original study illustrating disinhibition (Herman and Mack 1975) used a preload/taste test paradigm, and involved giving groups of dieters and non-dieters either a high-calorie preload or a low-calorie preload. The results are illustrated in Fig. 6.6 and indicated that whereas the non-dieters showed compensatory regulatory behaviour, and ate less at the taste test after the high-calorie preload, the dieters consumed more in the taste test if they had had the high-calorie preload than the low-calorie preload.

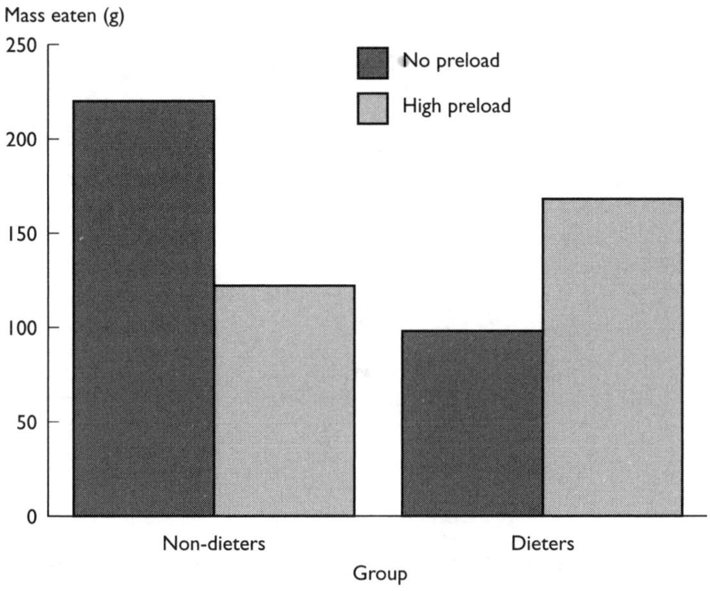

Figure 6.6 Overeating in dieters in the laboratory

This form of disinhibition or 'the what the hell effect' illustrates overeating in response to a high-calorie preload. Disinhibition in general has been defined as 'eating more as a result of the loosening restraints in response to emotional distress, intoxication or preloading' (Herman and Polivy 1989: 342), and its definition paved the way for a wealth of research examining the role of restraint in predicting overeating behaviour. Research into restraint and overeating has examined (1) the causal model of overeating, (2) the boundary model of overeating, (3) the relationship between restraint and weight, (4) the effect of restrained eating on mood and (5) overeating as relapse.

The causal analysis of overeating

The causal analysis of eating behaviour (e.g. Wardle 1980) argued that 'restraint not only precedes overeating but contributes to it causally' (Herman and Polivy 1989: 33). This suggests that attempting not to eat, paradoxically increases the probability of overeating, the specific behaviour that dieters are attempting to avoid. The causal analysis represented a new approach to the eating behaviour of restrained eaters and the prediction that restraint actually caused overeating was an interesting reappraisal of the situation. Wardle and Beales (1988) experimentally tested the causal analysis of overeating and randomly assigned 27 obese women to one of three groups for 7 weeks: a diet group, an exercise group, or a no-treatment control group. At 4 and 6 weeks all subjects took part in a laboratory session designed to assess their food intake. The results showed

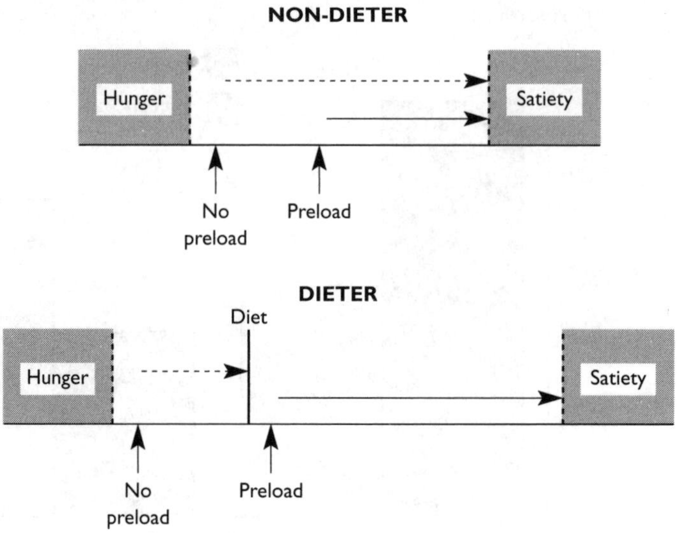

Figure 6.7 A boundary model explanation of overeating in dieters

that subjects in the diet condition ate more than both the exercise and the control groups, supporting a causal link between dieting and overeating.

The boundary model of overeating

In an attempt to explain how dieting causes overeating, Herman and Polivy (1984) developed the 'boundary model' (see Fig. 6.7), which represented an integration of physiological and cognitive perspectives on food intake. According to the model, food intake is motivated by a physiologically determined hunger boundary and deterred by a physiologically determined satiety boundary. In addition, the boundary model suggests that the food intake of restrained eaters is regulated by a cognitively determined 'diet boundary'. It suggests that dieters attempt to replace physiological control with cognitive control, which represents 'the dieters selected imposed quota for consumption on a given occasion' (Herman and Polivy 1984: 149). Herman and Polivy described how, after a low-calorie preload, dieters can maintain their diet goal for the immediate future since food intake remains within the limits set by the 'diet boundary'. However, after the dieters have crossed the diet boundary (i.e. eaten something 'not allowed'), they will consume food ad lib until the pressures of the satiety boundary are activated. The boundary model proposes a form of dual regulation, with food intake limited either by the diet boundary or the satiety boundary.

Research suggests that crossing the diet boundary and subsequent overeating may be triggered by lowered mood, high-calorie preloads, preloads believed to be high in calorie, a need to escape from self-awareness and smoking abstinence (e.g. Herman and Mack 1975; Spencer and

FOCUS ON RESEARCH 6.1

TESTING A THEORY – OVEREATING AS A REBELLION

A study to examine the cognitive changes to preloading using self-report and the Stroop task (Ogden and Greville 1993).

The aim of this study was to examine changes in cognitive state in dieters and non-dieters following the consumption of a 'forbidden food'. The study used both self-report measures and the Stroop task to examine these changes. Self-report measures provide some insights into an individual's state of mind, but are open to factors such as denial and expectancy effects. The Stroop task, however, also aims to access an individual's cognitions but without these problems.

Background

Dieters have been shown to overeat following a high-calorie preload. This behaviour has been called disinhibition or 'the what the hell' effect. The boundary model of overeating suggests that the preload forces the dieters to cross their diet boundary and consequently overeat. It has been suggested that this overeating may be related to lowered mood (either as a result of the preload, or independently) and/or changes in their cognitive state. This study aimed to examine shifts in cognitive state following the consumption of a 'forbidden food' using self-report measures and the Stroop task.

Methodology

Subjects A total of 56 female subjects from a London university took part in the study and were categorized as either restrained eaters or unrestrained eaters according to their scores on the restrained eating section of the Dutch Eating Behaviour Questionnaire (DEBQ) (van Strien *et al.* 1986). They ranged in age from 19 to 25 years and were of average weight.

Design The subjects were randomly allocated to one of two conditions (low-calorie preload *vs* high-calorie preload) and completed a set of rating scales and the Stroop tasks before and after the preload.

Procedure After completing the rating scales and the Stroop tasks, the subjects were given either a high-calorie preload (a chocolate bar) or a low-calorie preload (a cream cracker). Subjects then completed the ratings scales and Stroop tasks again.

Measures The following measures were completed before and after the preload:

1 *Stroop tasks*. The original Stroop task (Stroop 1935) involved a repeated set of colour names (e.g. 'green', 'red', 'blue', 'black') written on a card in different colour inks (e.g. green, red, blue, black). Subjects were asked to name the colour of the ink (not the word itself). For example, if the word 'green' was written in blue ink, the subject should say 'blue'. The time to complete the task was recorded and it was argued that a longer time indicated greater interference of the meaning of the word. Research has used the Stroop task to examine anxiety, phobias and post-traumatic stress disorder using words such as 'fear', 'anxiety' and 'panic' instead of names of colours. Subjects are still asked to name the colour of the ink and it has been suggested that longer times infer that the words are more relevant to the individual's concerns. For example, an anxious subject would take longer to colour name anxiety-related words than a non-anxious one. The present study used an adaptation of the Stroop task to examine (1) 'food' words, (2) 'body shape' words and words relating to the individual and (3) cognitive state, in order to assess the effect of preloading on the subjects' processing of these words.

- Food Stroop: the subjects were asked to colour name a set of food-related words (e.g. dinner, cake, sugar), which were compared with a set of neutral words matched for word length and frequency (e.g. record, powder, boot).
- Body shape Stroop: the subjects colour named body shape words (e.g. chest, fat, thigh) and matched neutral words (e.g. crowd, grass, rust).
- Cognitive state: items were included to examine two types of cognitive state, which were hypothesized to trigger overeating. These were a 'passive cognitive state' (e.g. submit, quit, abandon) representing 'giving in to the overpowering drive to eat' and an 'active cognitive state' (e.g. rebellious, defiant, challenge) representing overeating as an active decision to rebel against self-imposed restraint.

2 *Rating scales*. The subjects also completed the following set of rating scales:

- Motivational state: the subjects completed ratings of their hunger and fullness using visual analogue scales ('not at all hungry/full' to 'as hungry/full as I've ever been').
- Mood: anxiety and depression were measured using the Profile of Mood State checklist (McNair *et al.* 1971).
- Cognitive state: The active and passive cognitive states were measured using a checklist of relevant items.

Results

The results for the Stroop tasks were analysed by creating a pure reaction time (experimental words – matched control words) and then by assessing the effect of condition (low preload *vs* high preload) on the change in the reaction time from before the preload to after the preload. The results showed that the dieters responded to the high-calorie preload with increases in 'rebelliousness', as measured by the active cognitive state Stroop, increases in preoccupation with body shape and increases in the preoccupation food, as indicated by retarded reaction times on these tasks compared with the non-dieters, and the dieters responses to the low-calorie preload. The results also suggested that the dieters showed an increase in rebelliousness as measured by the rating scales.

Conclusion

The results suggest that overeating in dieters in response to preloading may be related to increased feelings of rebelliousness ('what the hell, I'm going to eat whatever I want'), increased concern with body shape and increased preoccupation with food. These results indicate that diet-breaking behaviour shown by normal-weight dieters, the obese on weight-reduction programmes and bulimics may relate to an active decision to overeat and suggest that perhaps self-imposed limits ('I'm going to eat less') may activate a desire to rebel against these limits.

Fremouw 1979; Heatherton and Baumeister 1991; Ogden 1994). In addition, research suggests that dieters may respond to high-calorie 'forbidden foods' with anxiety and feelings of 'rebelliousness' and 'defiance', which may cause overeating (Ogden and Wardle 1991; Ogden and Greville 1993; see **Focus on research 6.1**). The boundary model has also been used to examine differences between dieters, binge eaters, anorexics and normal eaters. This comparison is shown in Fig. 6.8.

Restrained eating and weight loss

Results from the study of restrained eating suggest that although restrained eaters aim to lose weight by attempting to restrict their food intake, this aim is only sometimes achieved. Heatherton *et al.* (1991) reported that restrained eaters show both under- and overeating and that this behaviour results in weight fluctuations but not actual weight loss. Thus, actual weight loss is limited by compensatory overeating. Heatherton *et al.* (1988: 20) argued that 'the restrained eater who is exclusively

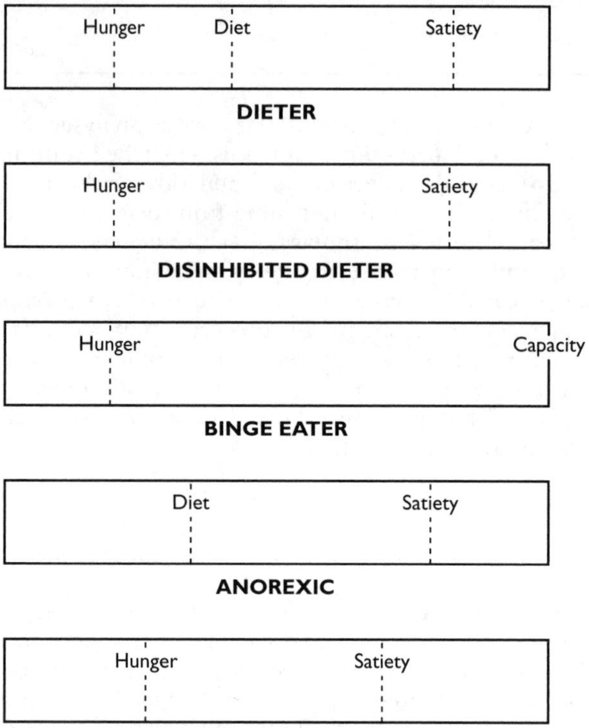

Figure 6.8 A comparison of the boundaries for different types of eaters

restrained . . . is not representative of restrained eaters in general, whereas the restrained eater who occasionally splurges is'. Ogden (1993) examined the concept of restraint as assessed by a variety of measures and found that high scorers on measures of restraint were characterized by both successful and failed restriction, suggesting that restrained eating is best characterized as an intention which is only sporadically realized. Therefore, 'to diet' is probably best understood as 'attempting to lose weight but not doing so' and 'attempting to eat less which often results in eating more'.

The role of dieting in mood and cognitive changes

A classic study by Keys *et al.* (1950) suggested that overeating is not the only possible consequence of restricting food intake. The study involved 36 healthy non-dieting men who were conscientious objectors from the Korean War. They received a carefully controlled daily food intake of approximately half their normal intake for a period of 12 weeks, and consequently lost 25 per cent of their original body weight. Keys stated that they developed a preoccupation with food, often resulting in hoarding or stealing it. They showed an inability to concentrate and mood

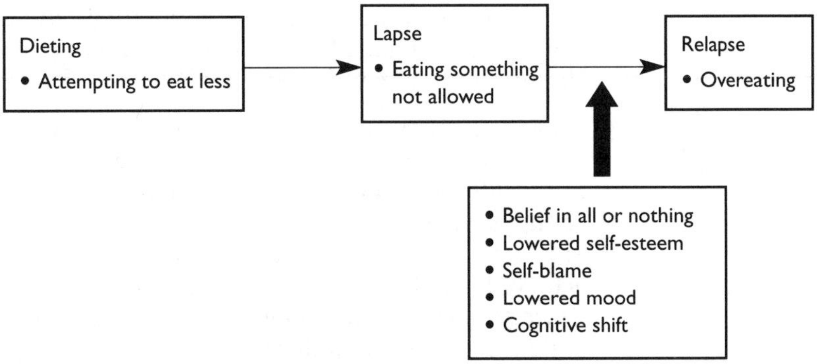

Figure 6.9 The 'what the hell effect' as a form of relapse

changes, with depression and apathy being common. At the end of the period of dieting, the men were allowed to eat freely. They often ate continuously and reported loss of control over their eating behaviour sometimes resulting in binge eating. The authors concluded that these effects were probably due to the restriction of their diet. To examine the effects of dieting without extreme weight loss, Warren and Cooper (1988) carried out a controlled study for a 2-week period and found that food restriction resulted in increased preoccupation with food. In a further study, Ogden (1995a) monitored the effects of self-imposed dieting over a 6-week period and reported increased depression and preoccupation with food. These results suggest that dieting can have several negative consequences and that these changes are possibly involved in causing overeating.

Overeating as a relapse

Parallels exist between the under- and overeating of the restrained eater and the behaviour of the relapsing smoker or alcoholic (see Chapter 5). The traditional biomedical perspective of addictive behaviours views addictions as being irreversible, out of the individual's control and discrete. It has been argued that this perspective encourages the belief that the behaviour is either 'all or nothing', and that this belief is responsible for the high relapse rate shown by both alcoholics and smokers (Marlatt and Gordon 1985). Thus, abstaining alcoholics believe in either total abstention or relapse, which itself may promote the progression from lapse to full-blown relapse. In the case of restrained eaters, it is possible that they too believe in the 'all or nothing' theory of excess, which promotes the shift from a high calorie lapse to the 'what the hell' relapse characterized by disinhibition. This transition from lapse to relapse and the associated changes in mood and cognitions is illustrated in Fig. 6.9.

These parallels have been supported by research suggesting that both excessive eating and alcohol use can be triggered by low mood and situational pressures (Brownell *et al.* 1986a; Grilo *et al.* 1989). In addition, the transition from lapse to relapse in both alcohol and eating behaviour has been found to be related to the internal attributions (e.g. 'I am to blame') for the original lapse (e.g. Ogden and Wardle 1990).

The research therefore suggests that:

- Dieting may have many negative consequences.
- Increasing or promoting dieting can result in an increased preoccupation with food, increased depression and, paradoxically, increased eating behaviour.
- The dieter's aim to eat less and consequently to lose weight is rarely achieved, and this failure may be a product of changes which occur as a direct response to imposing a cognitive structure on eating behaviour.
- If a dieter believes that dieting is an 'all or nothing' condition, and that they are denying themselves pleasure, this may itself be responsible for the disinhibitory behaviour characteristic of the restrained eater.

Problems with restraint theory

Although restraint theory has generated a wealth of research and provides an insight into overeating behaviour, there are several problems with this theory:

- Central to the boundary model is the traditional dualistic division between mind and body. The concept of separate biological and psychological boundaries suggests that the physical and psychological are separate entities which interact.
- Restraint theory relies on a belief in the association between food restriction and overeating. However, although dieters, bulimics and binging anorexics report episodes of overeating, restricting anorexics cannot be accounted for by restraint theory. If attempting not to eat results in overeating how do anorexics manage to starve themselves?
- If attempting not to eat something results in eating it, how do vegetarians manage never to eat meat?

The implications of restraint theory for obesity treatment

If dieting is related to overeating, what are the implications for obesity treatment? The rest of this chapter will examine traditional and multidimensional treatment approaches to obesity and will assess these approaches in the context of restraint theory.

Traditional treatment approaches

The traditional treatment approach to obesity was a corrective one, the assumption being that obesity was a product of overeating and underactivity. Treatment approaches therefore focused on encouraging the obese to eat 'normally' and this consistently involved putting them on a diet. Stuart (1967) and Stuart and Davis (1972) developed a behavioural programme for obesity involving monitoring food intake, modifying cues for inappropriate eating and encouraging self-reward for appropriate behaviour, which was widely adopted by hospitals and clinics. The programme aimed to encourage eating in response to physiological hunger and not in response to mood cues such as boredom or depression, or in response to external cues such as the sight and smell of food or other people eating. In 1958, Stunkard concluded his review of the past 30 years' attempts to promote weight loss in the obese with the statement, 'Most obese persons will not stay in treatment for obesity. Of those who stay in treatment, most will not lose weight, and of those who do lose weight, most will regain it' (Stunkard 1958). More recent evaluations of their effectiveness indicate that although traditional behavioural therapies may lead to initial weight losses of on average 0.5 kg per week (Brownell and Wadden 1992), 'weight losses achieved by behavioural treatments for obesity are not well maintained'.

However, it is now generally accepted that obesity is not simply a behavioural problem and as Brownell and Steen said somewhat optimistically in 1987 'psychological problems are no longer inferred simply because an individual is overweight'. Therefore, traditional behavioural programmes make some unsubstantiated assumptions about the causes of obesity by encouraging the obese to eat 'normally' like individuals of normal weight.

Multidimensional behavioural programmes

The failure of traditional treatment packages for obesity resulted in longer periods of treatment, an emphasis on follow-up and the introduction of a multidimensional perspective to obesity treatment. Recent comprehensive, multidimensional cognitive–behavioural packages aim to broaden the perspective for obesity treatment and combine traditional self-monitoring methods with information, exercise, cognitive restructuring, attitude change and relapse prevention (e.g. Brownell 1990). Brownell and Wadden (1991) emphasized the need for a multidimensional approach, the importance of screening patients for entry onto a treatment programme and the need to match the individual with the most appropriate package. State-of-the-art behavioural treatment programmes aim to encourage the obese to eat less than they do usually rather than encouraging them to eat less than the non-obese. Analysis of the effectiveness of this treatment approach suggests that average weight loss during the treatment programme is 0.5 kg per week, that approximately 60–70 per cent of the weight loss is maintained during the first year but that follow-up at 3 and 5 years tends to show weight gains back to baseline weight (Brownell and Wadden 1992). In a comprehensive review of the treatment interventions for obesity, Wilson (1994) suggested that although there has been an improvement in the effectiveness of obesity treatment since the 1970s, success rates are still poor.

Wadden examined both the short- and long-term effectiveness of both moderate and severe caloric restriction on weight loss. He reviewed all the studies involving randomized control trials in four behavioural journals and compared his findings with those of Stunkard (Stunkard 1958). Wadden concluded that 'Investigators have made significant progress in inducing weight loss in the 35 years since Stunkard's review'. He states that 80 per cent of patients will now stay in treatment for 20 weeks and that 50 per cent will achieve a weight loss of 20 lbs or more. Therefore, modern methods of weight loss produce improved results in the short term. However, Wadden also concludes that 'most obese patients treated in research trials still regain their lost weight'. This conclusion has been further supported by a recent systematic review of interventions for the treatment and prevention of obesity, which identified 92 studies that fitted the authors' inclusion criteria (NHS Centre for Reviews and Dissemination 1997). The review examined the effectiveness of dietary, exercise, behavioural, pharmacological and surgical interventions for obesity and concluded that 'the majority of the studies included in the present review demonstrate weight regain either during treatment or post intervention'. Accordingly, the picture for long-term weight loss is as pessimistic as it ever was.

The role of restraint in treating obesity

With the exception of the multitude of surgical interventions now available, all obesity treatment programmes involve recommending dieting in one form or another. Traditional treatment programmes aimed to correct the obese individual's abnormal behaviour, and recent packages suggest that the obese need to readjust their energy balance by eating less than they usually do. But both styles of treatment suggest that to lose weight the individual must impose cognitive restraint upon their eating behaviour. They recommend that the obese deny food and set cognitive limits to override physiological limits of satiety. And this brings with it all the problematic consequences of restrained eating.

Psychological problems and obesity treatment

Wadden *et al.* (1986) reported that dieting resulted in increased depression in a group of obese patients, and McReynolds (1982) reported an association between ongoing obesity treatment and psychological disturbance. In addition, results from a study by Loro and Orleans (1981) indicated that obese dieters report episodes of binging precipitated by 'anxiety, frustration, depression and other unpleasant emotions'. This suggests that the obese respond to dieting in the same way as the non-obese, with lowered mood and episodes of overeating, both of which are detrimental to attempts at weight loss. The obese are encouraged to impose a cognitive limit on their food intake, which introduces a sense of denial, guilt and the inevitable response of overeating. Consequently, any weight loss is precluded by episodes of overeating, which are a response to the many cognitive and emotional changes that occur during dieting.

Physiological problems and obesity treatment

In addition to the psychological consequences of imposing a dieting structure on the obese, there are physiological changes which accompany attempts at food restriction. Heatherton *et al.* (1991) reported that restraint in the non-obese predicts weight fluctuation, which parallels the process of weight cycling or 'yo-yo' dieting in the obese. Research on rats suggests that repeated attempts at weight loss followed by weight regain result in further weight loss becoming increasingly difficult due to a decreased metabolic rate and an increase in the percentage of body fat (Brownell *et al.* 1986b). Human research has found similar results in dieters and athletes who show yo-yo dieting (Brownell *et al.* 1989). Research has also found that weight fluctuation may have negative effects on health, with reports suggesting an association between weight fluctuation and mortality and morbidity from coronary heart disease (Hamm *et al.* 1989) and all-cause mortality (Lissner *et al.* 1991). Repeated failed attempts at dieting, therefore, may be more detrimental to physical health than remaining statically obese.

Restraint, obesity and health

Restraint theory suggests that dieting has negative consequences, and yet the treatment of obesity recommends dieting as a solution. This paradox can be summarized as follows:

- Obesity is a physical health risk, but restrained eating may promote weight cycling, which is also detrimental to health.
- Obesity treatment aims to reduce food intake, but restrained eating can promote overeating.
- The obese may suffer psychologically from the social pressures to be thin (although evidence of psychological problems in the non-dieting obese is scarce), but failed attempts to diet may leave them depressed, feeling a failure and out of control. For those few who do succeed in their attempts at weight loss, Wooley and Wooley (1984: 187) suggest that they 'are in fact condemned to a life of weight obsession, semi starvation and all the symptoms produced by chronic hunger . . . and seem precariously close to developing a frank eating disorder'.

If restraint theory is applied to obesity, the obese should not be encouraged to restrain their food intake. Obesity may not be caused by overeating but overeating may be a consequence of obesity if restrained eating is recommended as a cure.

Should obesity be treated at all?

The problems with treating obesity raise the question of whether it should be treated at all. In order to answer this it is necessary to examine the benefits of treatment, the treatment alternatives and the role of individual responsibility.

The benefits of treatment

Although failed obesity treatment may be related to negative mood, actual weight loss has been found to be associated with positive changes such as elation, self-confidence and increased feelings of well-being (Stunkard 1984). This suggests that whereas failed dieting attempts are detrimental, successful treatment may bring with it psychological rewards. The physical effects of obesity treatment also show a similar pattern of results. Yo-yo dieting and weight fluctuation may increase chances of coronary heart disease and death, but actual weight loss of only 10 per cent may result in improved blood pressure and benefits for type II diabetes (Blackburn and Kanders 1987; Wing *et al.* 1987). These results again suggest actual weight loss can be beneficial. Halmi *et al.* (1980) reported significant psychological and physical benefits of weight loss in the severely obese. They compared a group of severely obese subjects who received surgery with a comparison group who received a behavioural diet programme. The results indicated that the surgery group showed higher rates of both weight loss and weight maintenance. In addition, the diet group reported significantly higher changes in psychological characteristics, such as preoccupation with food and depression, than the surgery group (Halmi *et al.* 1980). Thus, permanent weight loss through surgery brought both physical and psychological benefits. Weight loss, therefore, can be beneficial in the obese, but only if treatment is successful and the results are permanent. Therefore, dieting may be rejected as a treatment but weight loss may still be seen as beneficial.

An argument for treating severe obesity can be made, but only if a positive outcome can be guaranteed, as failed treatment may be more detrimental than no treatment attempts at all.

The treatment alternatives

The problems with dieting

The implications of restraint theory suggest that the obese should avoid restrained eating. Dieting offers a small chance of weight loss and a high chance of both negative physical and psychological consequences.

Surgical treatments of obesity

Taking dieting out of the treatment equation leaves us primarily with surgery. Although there are 21 different surgical procedures for obesity (Kral 1983), the two most popular are the gastric bypass and the vertical banded gastroplasty (e.g. Mason 1987). Halmi *et al.* (1980) reported high levels of weight loss and maintenance following surgery, with accompanying changes in satiety, body image and eating behaviour. Stunkard *et al.* (1986a) suggested that after one year weight losses average at 50 per cent of excess weight. In fact, Stunkard (1984: 171) stated that 'Severe obesity . . . is most effectively treated by surgical measures, particularly ones that reduce the size of the stomach and of its opening into the large gastrointestinal tract'. However, in parallel to the problems with dieting, individuals who have surgery may show complete weight regain or no initial weight loss. In addition, they are subjected to the dangers of any operation and the accompanying problems of anaesthetics (Mason 1987).

Obesity and the role of personal responsibility

If obesity is understood as a product of a physiological predisposition (e.g. genetics) and not an illustration of psychological pathology (e.g. underactivity, overeating), then maybe it should not be treated by corrective psychological interventions but as a medical problem. Psychological interventions put the responsibility for change with the individual. This may well be empowering for disorders that are controllable by the individual, but results in frustration and self-blame if this perception of control is illusory. If the responsibility for the cause of obesity lies purely within an individual's uncontrollable genes, then taken to its logical conclusion, the responsibility for a cure – if a cure is needed at all – should rest in the hands of the surgeon. Therefore, surgery provides the chance for permanent change without suggesting that the individual is to blame for their size and that they are inadequate for not being able to change it themselves. However, this conclusion is based on the assumption that surgery is always successful, results in permanent weight loss and presents no physical risks to the individual. Both dieting and surgery have high failure rates and the research suggests that failed attempts at weight loss may be more detrimental to the individual than remaining statically obese. Rejecting dieting and surgery as solutions does not reject the need for a solution, but rejects solutions that may cause more problems than they solve.

In summary, perhaps, to answer the question 'Should obesity be treated at all?', it is necessary to consider the following points:

- Obesity is a health risk, but most risks come with severe obesity.
- Obesity is caused by a combination of physiological and behavioural factors – it is not simply a product of overeating.
- Treating obesity with dieting emphasizes the behavioural causes and

personal responsibility ('you can make yourself well'), but may result in overeating, which could exacerbate the weight problem.

- Treating obesity with surgery emphasizes the physiological causes and places the obese in the hands of the medical profession ('we can make you well'), but may result in medical complications and weight regain.
- Any treatment intervention should therefore weigh up the potential benefits of any weight loss (e.g. improved self-esteem, reduced risk of CHD, etc.) against the potential costs of intervention (e.g. overeating, weight fluctuations).

To conclude

Obesity is related to several health problems and a number of theories have been developed in an attempt to understand its aetiology. These have ranged from physiological theories focusing on genetics, metabolic rates, fat cells and appetite control to behavioural theories focusing on physical activity and food intake. In particular, research has suggested that there may be a strong genetic predisposition to obesity, which is reflected in underactivity and the relative over-consumption of fat. However, the research examining the causes of obesity is often contradictory, suggesting that the story is not yet complete. Over recent years, there has been a shift from examining eating behaviour in the context of obesity, to eating behaviour in its own right. Many women diet due to body dissatisfaction and restraint theory was developed in an attempt to examine the psychological predictors of under- and overeating. Restraint theory suggests that attempting to eat less may contribute causally to overeating. This chapter has examined these different theories and has highlighted the implications of restraint theory for obesity treatment.

? Questions

1. To what extent can obesity be explained by physiological factors?
2. Obesity is an eating disorder. Discuss.
3. Discuss the methodological problems with the research examining the causes of obesity.
4. Why are so many women dissatisfied with their body shape?
5. Restrained eating causes overeating. Discuss.
6. What factors contribute to the shift from under- to overeating?
7. Treating obesity causes more problems than it solves. Discuss.
8. Design a research study to examine the consequences of dieting.

For discussion

Have you ever tried to change your diet (eat less fat/stop eating meat)? If so, consider the extent to which this was successful and the possible cognitions that may relate to your behaviour.

Assumptions in health psychology

The research into obesity and eating behaviour highlights some of the assumptions in health psychology:

1 *The role of behaviour in illness.* Throughout the twentieth century there has been an increasing emphasis on behavioural factors in health and illness. Research has examined the problem of obesity from the same perspective and has evaluated the role of overeating as a causal factor. However, perhaps not all problems are products of behaviour.

2 *Treatment as beneficial.* Drug and surgical interventions are stopped if they are found to be either ineffective or to have negative consequences. However, behavioural interventions to promote behaviour change, such as smoking cessation, exercise and weight loss programmes, are developed and promoted even when the evidence for their success is poor. Within health psychology, behavioural programmes are considered neutral enough to be better than nothing. However, obesity treatment using dieting is an example of the potential negative side-effects of encouraging individual responsibility for health and attempting to change behaviour. Perhaps behavioural interventions can have as many negative consequences as other medical treatments.

3 *The mind–body problem.* Research into obesity also raises the problem of the relationship between the mind and the body. Theories are considered either physiological or psychological and treatment perspectives are divided in a similar fashion, therefore maintaining a dualistic model of individuals. In addition, restraint theory examines the effects of cognitions (the mind) on the physiological process of eating (the body). Although these separate systems interact, they are still regarded as distinct.

Further reading

Brownell, K.D. (1991) Personal responsibility and control over our health: When expectation exceeds reality, *Health Psychology*, 10: 303–10.

This paper discusses the recent emphasis on patient responsibility for health and suggests that encouraging the obese to diet may be an example of attempting to control the uncontrollable.

Brownell, K.D. and Wadden, T.A. (1992) Etiology and treatment of obesity: Understanding a serious, prevalent and refractory disorder, *Journal of Consulting and Clinical Psychology*, 60.

This is a good overview of the obesity literature and provides an insight into contemporary views on obesity treatment.

Wooley, S.C. and Wooley, O.W. (1984) Should obesity be treated at all? in A.J. Stunkard and E. Stellar (eds), *Eating and Its Disorders*. New York: Raven Press.

This chapter examines the potential costs and benefits of obesity treatment and argues that perhaps only severe obesity should be treated in order to avoid causing more problems than the treatment solves.

CHAPTER 7

Exercise

Chapter overview

Over the past few decades, there has been an increasing interest in the role of exercise in promoting health. This chapter examines the development of the contemporary interest in exercise and describes definitions of exercise and fitness. The chapter then examines the physical and psychological benefits of exercise, describes programmes designed to increase exercise uptake and evaluates social/political and individual predictors of exercise behaviour.

This chapter covers:

- What is exercise?
- Why exercise?
- What factors predict exercise?
- Exercise relapse

Developing the contemporary concern with exercise behaviour

Until the 1960s exercise was done by the young and talented and the emphasis was on excellence. The Olympics, Wimbledon tennis and football leagues were for those individuals who were the best at their game and who strove to win. At this time, the focus was on high levels of physical fitness for the élite. However, at the beginning of the 1960s there was shift in perspective. The 'Sport for All' initiative developed by the Council of Europe, the creation of a Minister for Sport and the launching of the Sports Council suggested a shift towards exercise for everyone. Local councils were encouraged to build swimming pools, sports centres and golf courses. However, although these initiatives included everyone, the emphasis was still on high levels of fitness and the recommended levels of exercise were intensive. The 'no pain no gain' philosophy abounded. More recently, however, there has been an additional shift. Exercise is no longer for the élite, nor does it have to be at intensive, and often impossible levels. Government initiatives such as 'Look after yourself', 'Feeling Great' and 'Fun Runs' encourage everyone to be involved at a manageable level. In addition, the emphasis is no longer on fitness, but on both physical and psychological health. Contemporary messages about exercise promote moderate exercise for everyone to improve general (physical and psychological) well-being. This shifting perspective is illustrated by contemporary research on the benefits of exercise.

What is exercise?

Aspects of exercise have been defined in different ways according to intention, outcome and location.

1 *Intention*. Some researchers have differentiated between different types of behaviours in terms of the individual's intentions. For example, Caspersen *et al.* (1985) distinguished between physical activity and exercise. *Physical activity* has been defined as 'any bodily movement produced by skeletal muscles that results in energy expenditure'. This perspective emphasizes the physical and biological changes that happen both automatically and through intention. *Exercise* has been defined as 'planned, structured and repetitive bodily movement done to improve or maintain one or more components of physical fitness'. This perspective emphasizes the physical and biological changes that happen as a result of intentional movements.
2 *Outcome*. Distinctions have also been made in terms of the outcome of the behaviour. For example, Blair *et al.* (1992) differentiated between physical exercise that improves fitness and physical exercise that improves health. This distinction illustrates a shift in emphasis from intensive exercise resulting in cardiovascular fitness to moderate

exercise resulting in mild changes in health status. It also illustrates a shift towards using a definition of health that includes both biological and psychological changes.

3 *Location*. Distinctions have also been made in terms of location. For example, Paffenbarger and Hale (1975) differentiated between *occupational activity*, which was performed as part of an individual's daily work, and *leisure activity*, which was carried out in the individual's leisure time.

These definitions are not mutually exclusive and illustrate the different ways exercise has been conceptualized.

Who exercises?

The results of a survey, in which men and women were asked about their exercise behaviour, are shown in Fig. 7.1. They suggest that the four most common forms of exercise are walking, swimming, snooker/pool/billiards and keep fit/yoga.

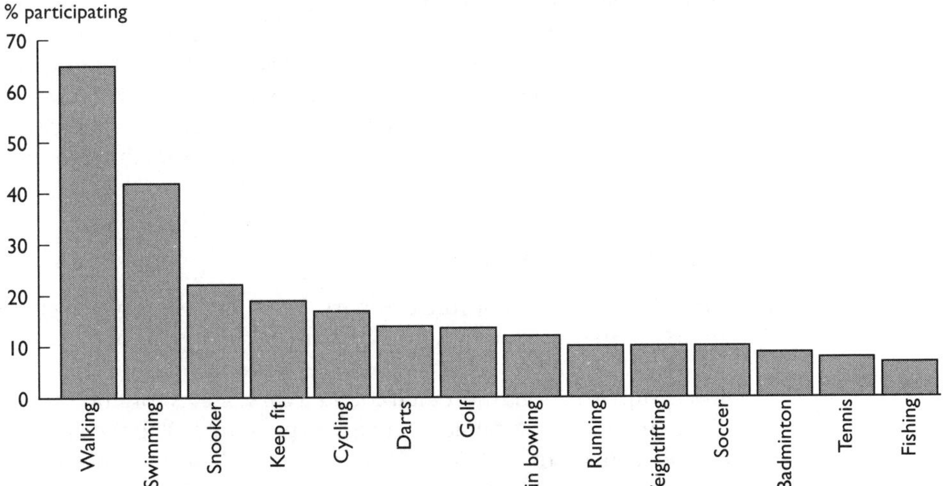

Figure 7.1 Participation in sport, 1990

Why exercise?

Research has examined the possible physical and psychological benefits of exercise.

The physical benefits of exercise

Longevity

Paffenbarger *et al.* (1986) examined the relationship between weekly energy expenditure and longevity for a group of 16,936 Harvard alumni aged 35 to 70. They reported the results from a longitudinal study which suggested that individuals with a weekly energy expenditure of more than 2000 kcals on exercise reported as walking, stair climbing and sports, lived for $2^1/2$ years longer on average than those with an energy expenditure of less than 500 kcal per week on these activities.

The possible reasons for the effects of exercise on longevity are as follows:

1 *Reduction in blood pressure*: physical activity has an inverse relationship to both diastolic and systolic blood pressure. Therefore, increased exercise decreases blood pressure. This effect is particularly apparent in those who have mild or moderately raised blood pressure.
2 *Reduction in weight and obesity*: overweight and obesity are related to certain cancers, hypertension, and coronary heart disease. Exercise may help promote weight loss/maintenance (see Chapter 6 for details of exercise and obesity).
3 *Reduction in diabetes*: exercise may be related to improved glucose control, resulting in a reduction in the possible effects of diabetes.
4 *Protection against osteoporosis and thinning bones*: exercise may be protective against osteoporosis, which is common among older women.
5 *Reduction in coronary heart disease*: the main effect of exercise is on the occurrence of coronary heart disease and rehabilitation following a heart attack.

Coronary heart disease

The effects of exercise on coronary heart disease have been examined by assessing the consequences of both occupational activity and leisure activity. Regarding *occupational activity*, Paffenbarger and Hale (1975) followed up 3975 longshoremen for 22 years. Longshoremen have occupations that involve a range of energy expenditure. The results showed that at the end of this period, 11 per cent had died from coronary heart disease and that those longshoremen who expended more than 8500 kcal per week had a significantly lower risk of coronary heart disease than those in jobs requiring less energy. This difference remained when other risk factors such as smoking and blood pressure were controlled. This relationship between occupational activity and coronary heart disease has also been shown in samples of both men and women (Salonen *et al.* 1982).

Research has also evaluated the relationship between *leisure-time activity* and coronary heart disease. Morris *et al.* (1980) followed up a group of middle-aged sedentary office workers over $8^1/2$ years and compared those who engaged in sport with those who reported no leisure-time activity.

The results showed that those who attempted to keep fit showed less than half the incidence of coronary heart disease at follow-up compared with the other subjects. This association has also been reported in students in the USA (Paffenbarger *et al.* 1978, 1983, 1986).

Regardless of the location of the activity, research indicates an association between physical fitness and health status. Blair *et al.* (1989) examined the role of generalized physical fitness and health status in 10,224 men and 3120 women for 8 years and reported that physical fitness was related to a decrease in both mortality rates (all cause) and coronary heart disease.

Exercise may influence coronary heart disease in the following ways:

1 Increased muscular activity may protect the cardiovascular system by stimulating the muscles that support the heart.
2 Increased exercise may increase the electrical activity of the heart.
3 Increased exercise may increase an individual's resistance to ventricular fibrillation.
4 Exercise may be protective against other risk factors for coronary heart disease (e.g. obesity, hypertension).

The physical benefits of exercise have been summarized by Smith and Jacobson (1989) as: (1) improved cardiovascular function; (2) increased muscle size and strength and ligament strength for maintaining posture, preventing joint instability and decreasing back pain; (3) improved work effort; and (4) changing body composition.

The psychological benefits of exercise

Research also indicates that exercise may improve psychological well-being. These effects are outlined below:

Depression

Research using correlational designs suggests an association between the amount of exercise carried out by an individual and their level of depression. Much of the reviews into this association have stressed the correlational nature of the research and the inherent problems in determining causality (e.g. Morgan and O'Connor 1988). However, McDonald and Hodgdon (1991) carried out a meta-analysis of both the correlational and experimental research into the association between depression and exercise. They concluded that aerobic exercise was related to a decrease in depression and that this effect was greatest in those with higher levels of initial depressive symptoms. In an attempt to clarify the problem of causality, McCann and Holmes (1984) carried out an experimental study to evaluate the effect of manipulating exercise levels on depression. Forty-three female students who scored higher than the cut-off point on the Beck Depression Inventory (BDI) were randomly allocated to one of three groups: (1) aerobic exercise group (one hour of exercise, twice a week for 10 weeks); (2) placebo group (relaxation); (3) no treatment. After 5 weeks, the results showed a significant reduction in depressive symptomatology in the exercise group compared with the other two subject groups supporting the relationship between exercise and depression and suggesting a causal link between these two variables; that is, increased exercise resulted in a reduction in depression. However, the authors report that subsequent exercise had no further effects.

Anxiety

Research has also indicated that exercise may be linked to a reduction in anxiety. Again, there are problems with determining the direction of causality in this relationship, but it has been suggested that exercise may decrease anxiety by diverting the individual's attention away from the source of anxiety.

Response to stress

Exercise has been presented as a mediating factor for the stress response. Exercise may influence stress either by changing an individual's appraisal of a potentially stressful event by distraction or diversion (e.g. 'This situation could be stressful but if I exercise I will not have to think about it') or may act as a potential coping strategy to be activated once an event has been appraised as stressful (e.g. 'Although the situation is stressful, I shall now exercise to take my mind off things').

Self-esteem and self-confidence

It has also been suggested that exercise may enhance an individual's psychological well-being by improving self-esteem and self-confidence. King *et al.* (1992) report that the psychological consequences of exercise may be related to improved body satisfaction, which may corelate to general self-esteem and confidence. In addition, exercise may result in an improved sense of achievement and self-efficacy.

How does exercise influence psychological well-being?

Many theories have been developed to explain the factors that mediate the link between exercise and psychological state. These reflect both the *physiological* and *psychological* approaches to the study of exercise. For example, it has been argued that exercise results in the release of endorphins, the brain's natural opioids (Steinberg and Sykes 1985), and increases in the levels of brain norepinephrine, which have been hypothesized to be a cause of depression. It has also been suggested that improved psychological state is related to the social activity often associated with exercise and the resulting increased confidence and self-esteem. Any reduction in levels of depression may be related to greater social contact, improved social support and increased self-efficacy.

FOCUS ON RESEARCH 7.1

TESTING A THEORY – EXERCISE AND MOOD

A study to examine the effects of exercise on mood (Steptoe *et al.* 1993).

This study examined the relationship between exercise and mood. Because of the experimental design, the results allow some conclusions to be made about the direction of causality.

Background

Exercise is believed to be important for a healthy life. However, as with many health-related behaviours, adherence to health promotion recommendations may be more motivated by short-term immediate effects (e.g. feeling good) than the potential changes in the long term (e.g. living longer). Therefore, understanding the immediate effects of exercise on mood has obvious implications for encouraging individuals to take regular exercise. Steptoe *et al.* (1993) examined changes in mood, mental vigour and exhilaration in sportsmen and inactive men following maximal, moderate and minimal exercise.

Methodology

Subjects The subjects were 36 male amateur athletes who were regularly involved in a variety of sports and exercised for more than 30 minutes at least three times per week, and 36 inactive men who exercised for less than 30 minutes per week.

Design All subjects took part in two exercise sessions and completed measures of mood before and after each exercise session. This study was therefore experimental in design and involved repeated measures.

Procedure At session one, all subjects completed a set of profile questionnaires (background physical and psychological measures) and took part in a maximal exercise session on a cycle ergonometer. Maximal exercise was determined by oxygen uptake. At session two, subjects were randomly allocated to 20 minutes of either maximal, moderate or minimal exercise. All subjects completed ratings of mood before exercise, 2 minutes after exercise and after 30 minutes of recovery.

Measures The subjects rated items relating to tension/anxiety, mental vigour, depression/dejection, exhilaration and perceived exertion before and after each exercise session. In addition, all subjects completed measures of (1) personality and (2) trait anxiety once only at the beginning of the first session.

Results

The results were analysed to examine the effect of the differing degrees of exercise on changes in mood in the sportsmen and the inactive men. The results showed that only the sportsmen reported decreases in tension/anxiety after the maximal exercise. However, *all* subjects reported increased exhilaration and increased mental vigour 2 minutes after both the maximal and moderate exercise compared with the minimal condition, and in addition, the increase in exhilaration was maintained after the 30 minutes of recovery.

Conclusion

The authors conclude that both maximal and moderate exercise results in beneficial changes in both mental vigour and exhilaration in both sportsmen and inactive men and suggest that 'exercise leads to positive mood changes even among people who are unaccustomed to physical exertion'. They also suggest that greater attention to the immediate effects of exercise may improve adherence to exercise programmes.

What factors predict exercise?

Because of the potential benefits of exercise, research has evaluated which factors are related to exercise behaviour. The determinants of exercise can be categorized as either social/political or individual.

Social/political predictors of exercise

An increased reliance on technology and reduced daily activity in paid and domestic work may have resulted in an increase in the number of people having relatively sedentary lifestyles. In addition, a shift towards a belief that exercise is good for an individual's well-being and is relevant for everyone has set the scene for social and political changes in terms of emphasizing exercise. Therefore, since the late 1960s many government initiatives have aimed to promote sport and exercise. Factors such as the availability of facilities and cultural attitudes towards exercise may be related to individual participation. Consequently, the Sports Council launched an official campaign in 1972 in an attempt to create a suitable climate for increasing exercise behaviour. Initiatives such as 'Sport for All', 'Fun Runs' and targets for council facilities, such as swimming pools and sports centres, were part of this initiative. In collaboration with the

Sports Council, McIntosh and Charlton (1985) reported that the provision of council services had exceeded the Sports Council's targets by 100 per cent. This evaluation concluded that:

- Central government funding for sport and specific local authority allocations have helped participation in sport.
- Despite small improvements, the Sport for All objective is far from being realized and inequalities persist.
- Inequalities in the provision of sport facilities have diminished – especially for indoor sport.
- The recognition of the Sports Council's earlier emphasis on élite sports has been slow and disproportionately large amounts of the Council's funds are still being spent on élite sport.

One recent approach to increasing exercise uptake is the exercise prescription scheme whereby GPs refer targeted patients for exercise. Therefore, in the same way that an overweight or depressed patient would be referred to see a counsellor, or a patient with a suspected skin cancer would be referred to a hospital specialist, a GP can now also refer a patient for exercise. This could take the form of vouchers for free access to the local leisure centre, an exercise routine with a health and fitness advisor at the leisure centre, or recommendations from the health and fitness advisor to follow a home-based exercise programme, such as walking.

Therefore, these initiatives have aimed to develop a suitable climate for promoting exercise. In addition, as a result of government emphasis on exercise, specific exercise programmes have been established in an attempt to assess the best means of encouraging participation. In particular it is possible to differentiate between individual and supervised exercise programmes.

Individual vs *supervised exercise programmes*

King *et al.* (1991) carried out a study in the USA to examine the relative value of individual *vs* supervised exercise programmes. Using random telephone numbers they identified 357 adults, aged 50–65, who led relatively sedentary lifestyles. These subjects were then randomly allocated to one of four groups:

- Group 1: the subjects were encouraged to attend a 1-hour vigorous exercise session at a local community centre at least three times a week.
- Group 2: the subjects were instructed to do some intensive exercise on their own and were encouraged and monitored with periodic phone calls.
- Group 3: the subjects were instructed to do lower intensity exercise on their own.
- Group 4: the control subjects were not instructed to do any exercise.

The results showed greater adherence in the unsupervised home-based programmes, than in the supervised programme. However, all subjects who had been instructed to do some exercise showed an increase in cardiovascular fitness compared with the control group. The authors suggested that the results from this study provide insights into the development of successful national campaigns to promote exercise behaviour that involve a minimal and cheap intervention and argued for an emphasis on unsupervised individual exercising.

Other factors that appear to play a role in developing successful exercise programmes are the use of behavioural contracts, whereby the individual signs a contract with an instructor agreeing to participate in a programme for a set period of time (e.g. Oldridge and Jones 1983) and the use of instructor praise and feedback and flexible goal-setting by the subject (e.g. Martin *et al.* 1984). These factors involve supervised exercise and suggest that individualized exercise programmes may not be the only form of intervention.

The social/political climate therefore has implications for predicting and promoting exercise. However, even if councils provide the facilities and government programmes are established, individuals have to make decisions about whether or not to participate. Research has, therefore, also examined the individual predictors of exercise behaviour.

Individual predictors of exercise

Dishman and colleagues carried out a series of studies to examine the best individual predictors of exercise and suggested that these factors can be defined as either non-modifiable or modifiable.

Non-modifiable predictors of exercise

Dishman (1982) reported that non-modifiable factors such as age, education, smoking, ease of access to facilities, body fat/weight and self-motivation were good predictors of exercise. The results of a prospective study indicated that the best predictors of exercise behaviour were low body fat, low weight and high self-motivation (Dishman and Gettman 1980). However, whether factors such as access to facilities and self-motivation should be regarded as non-modifiable is problematic. King *et al.* (1992) reported the results of a study that evaluated the factors predicting being active in leisure time. They described the profile of an active individual as younger, better educated, more affluent and more likely to be male. However, it is possible that other individuals (less affluent/less educated) may be more active at work. Research has also examined ethnic differences in predicting exercise behaviour. Several studies indicate that blacks are less active than whites, that black women are especially less active and that these differences persist even when income and education are controlled (e.g. Shea *et al.* 1992).

Modifiable predictors of exercise

Dishman *et al.* (1985) summarized the following variables as modifiable predictors:

- *Childhood exercise*: individuals who exercise as children are more likely to exercise as adults.
- *Positive self-image*: research also indicates that a positive self-image and confidence in one's ability influences future activity levels.
- *No role for knowledge*: interestingly the research suggests that good knowledge about the benefits of exercise does not predict exercise behaviour.

The role of attitudes and beliefs

Research has examined the role of attitudes and beliefs in predicting exercise. Research into beliefs has used either a cross-sectional or a prospective design. Cross-sectional research examines the relationships between variables that co-occur, whereas prospective research attempts to predict future behaviour.

Cross-sectional research

This type of research indicates a role for the following beliefs and attitudes:

- *Perceived social benefits of exercise.* Research examining the predictors of exercise behaviour consistently suggests that the main factors motivating exercise are the beliefs that it is enjoyable and provides social contact. In a cross-sectional study examining the differences in attitude between joggers and non-joggers, the non-joggers reported beliefs that exercise required too much discipline, too much time, they did not believe in the positive effects of jogging and reported a lower belief that significant others valued regular jogging (Riddle 1980).
- *Value on health.* Although many individuals exercise for reasons other than health, a MORI poll in 1984 suggested that the second main correlate of exercising is a belief that health and fitness are important (MORI 1984). In support of this, the non-joggers in the study by Riddle (1980) also reported a lower value on good health than the joggers.
- *Benefits of exercise.* Exercisers have also been shown to differ from non-exercisers in their beliefs about the benefits of exercise. For example, a study of older women (aged 60–89 years) indicated that exercisers reported a higher rating for the health value of exercise, reported greater enjoyment of exercise, rated their discomfort from exercise as lower and perceived exercise programmes to be more easily available than non-exercisers (Paxton *et al.* 1997).

Prospective research

This has examined which factors predict the uptake of exercise. It has often been carried out in the context of the development of exercise programmes and studies of adherence to these programmes. Sallis *et al.* (1986) examined which factors predicted initiation and maintenance of vigorous/moderate exercise for one year. The results indicated that exercise self-efficacy, attitudes to exercise and health knowledge were the best predictors. In a further study, Jonas *et al.* (1993) followed up 100 men and women and reported the best predictors of intentions to participate in the exercise programmes and actual participation were attitudes to continued participation, perceived social norms and perceived behavioural control. Jones *et al.* (1998) also examined the predictors of uptake and adherence, and used repertory grids to explore the personal constructs of those individuals who had been referred to exercise as part of an exercise prescription scheme. They concluded that having realistic aims and an understanding of the possible outcomes of a brief exercise programme were predictive of adherence to the programme.

To further understand the predictors of exercise adherence, social cognition models have been used. Riddle (1980) examined predictors of exercise using the theory of reasoned action (Fishbein and Ajzen 1975; see Chapter 2) and reported that attitudes to exercise and the normative components of the model predicted intentions to exercise and that these intentions were related to self-reports of behaviour. The theory of planned behaviour (TPB) has also been developed to assess exercise behaviour. Valois *et al.* (1988) incorporated a measure of past exercising behaviour (a central variable in the TPB) and reported that attitudes, intentions and past behaviour were the best predictors of exercise. The use of TPB to predict exercise is discussed further in **Focus on research 7.2**. Research has also used the health belief model (Sonstroem 1988) and models emphasizing exercise self-efficacy (e.g. Schwarzer 1992). Furthermore, research has applied the stages of change model to exercise behaviour (see Chapters 2 and 5). This model describes behaviour change in four stages: precontemplation, contemplation, action and maintenance (e.g. DiClemente and Prochaska 1982). Marcus *et al.* (1992) examined the relationship between the pros and cons of exercise and stage of change in 778 men and women. They concluded that pros and cons and decisional balance (pros *vs* cons) was related to exercise adoption and that higher ratings of pros were found in those individuals closer to the maintenance stage of behaviour. This suggests that encouraging individuals to focus on the pros of exercise may increase the transition from thinking about exercising to actually doing it.

Exercise relapse

Research has also examined which variables predict relapse and drop out rates from exercise programmes. Dishman *et al.* (1985) examined factors

FOCUS ON RESEARCH 7.2

TESTING A THEORY – PREDICTING EXERCISE

A study using the theory of planned behaviour to predict exercise (Norman and Smith 1995).

This study was an attempt to test directly the role of two social cognition models in predicting exercise behaviour.

Background

Social cognition models such as the theory of reasoned action and the health belief model have been used to predict and examine health behaviours such as smoking (see Chapter 5), screening (see Chapter 9) and contraception use (see Chapter 8). Norman and Smith (1995) used the theory of planned behaviour (Ajzen 1988) to predict exercise behaviour over a 6-month period.

Methodology

Subjects Eighteen people were asked to complete open-ended questions in order to identify beliefs about exercise that could then be incorporated into a questionnaire. The questionnaire was distributed to 250 subjects and returned by 182 (a response rate of 72.8 per cent). Because the study used a prospective design, a second questionnaire was sent out after 6 months; 83 individuals returned it completed.
Design The study involved a repeated-measures design with questionnaires completed at baseline (time 1) and after 6 months (time 2).
Measures The questionnaire at time 1 asked for the subject's age and sex and contained questions about the following aspects of the theory of planned behaviour, which were rated on a 7-point Likert scale.

- *Prior behaviour*: subjects were asked to rate how frequently they took exercise ('include activities such as aerobics, badminton, jogging, etc., but not activities which form part of your everyday life, such as walking to the bus stop, dancing at discos, etc.').
- *Desires and self-predictions*: subjects were asked to rate (1) their desire to take regular exercise ('I want to take regular exercise') and (2) their self-prediction of exercise behaviour ('I will take exercise during the next 6 months').

- *Attitude*: subjects were asked to rate their attitude towards taking regular exercise on a set of scales: worrying–reassuring, unpleasant–pleasant, punishing–rewarding, unenjoyable–enjoyable, useless–useful, unattractive–attractive.
- *Attitude variability*: subjects were asked to rate their variability in attitude to exercise by stating how they agreed/disagreed with the following statements: 'At times, my feelings about taking exercise are more favourable than at others', 'I have conflicting feelings about taking exercise'. In addition they were asked to rate 'My feelings about taking exercise . . . do not vary at all/vary a great deal' on a 7-point Likert scale.
- *Subjective norm*: subjects rated the statement 'Most people who are important to me think I should take regular exercise'.
- *Perceived behavioural control*: subjects rated the following statements: (1) 'For me to take regular exercise is . . . extremely difficult/extremely easy'; (2) 'How much control do you have over taking regular exercise'; and (3) 'If I wanted to I could easily take regular exercise'.
- *Behavioural beliefs*: subjects were asked to rate beliefs about exercise such as 'Taking regular exercise increases agility and suppleness', and to place a value on these beliefs such as 'Increasing agility and suppleness is . . . extremely bad/good'.
- *Normative beliefs*: subjects were asked to rate whether 'members of my family', 'my friends', 'the media', and 'people I know who exercise regularly' would think that they should take regular exercise, and to what extent they would comply with what these people thought.
- *Control beliefs*: subjects were asked to rate whether factors such as 'a lack of time', 'other commitments', 'laziness', 'not being near to facilities' would prevent them from taking regular exercise.

At time 2, the subjects were asked about their frequency of exercising (as in *prior behaviour*). This variable was included in order to examine which variables at time 1 predicted *future behaviour* at time 2.

Results

The data were analysed using correlation analysis, which examines associations between the different variables (e.g. an increase in a positive attitude towards exercise is related to an increase in the frequency of exercise) and regression analysis, which examines which variables are the best predictor of the dependent variable (e.g. age and frequency of current behaviour are the best predictors of future behaviour). The results of the correlation analysis showed that all the time 1 variables (apart from normative belief) were significantly correlated with future exercise behaviour (at time 2). Therefore, frequent exercisers at time 2 were more likely at time 1 to believe that they would take regular exercise, to hold a strong desire to exercise, to have a positive attitude towards exercise, to perceive pressure from others to exercise, to believe that taking exercise was under their control, and to have exercised frequently in the past. The results from the regression analysis showed that the strongest predictor of future behaviour after 6 months was prior behaviour.

Conclusions

The authors concluded that although most of the variables of the theory of planned behaviour were related to future behaviour, the best predictor of future behaviour was prior behaviour. This suggests that exercise may be under a strong habitual influence, perhaps because its mood-enhancing effects promote further exercise, and/or perhaps because exercise is based on habit and not cognition.

that predicted relapse rates and indicated that relapse was highest among blue-collar workers, smokers, those who believed that exercise was an effort, and lowest in those who reported a history of past participation, those with high self-motivation, those who had the support of a spouse, those who reported having the available time, those who had access to exercise facilities, and those who reported a belief in the value of good health. Further, using a stages of change approach, Ingledew *et al.* (1998) explored which factors were important for the transition between the earlier stages of adoption and the later stages of continued behaviour and concluded that continued exercise was predicted by intrinsic motives, specifically enjoyment. These factors are very similar to those that relate to both the initiation and maintenance of exercise behaviour and reflect the role of both non-modifiable and modifiable factors.

To conclude

Exercise is regarded as central to promoting good health both in terms of physical and psychological well-being. Research has therefore examined factors that correlate and predict exercise behaviour. Such factors include the social and political climate and the individual's beliefs. Although interventions aimed to promote exercise do so because of the health benefits, an interest in these benefits does not appear to be the best predictor of initiation or maintenance of exercise behaviour. The recognition of this is reflected in recent recommendations for exercise, which emphasize the encouragement of small changes in lifestyle, not major increases in exercise through vigorous and intensive exercise campaigns.

? Questions

1 Exercise has both psychological and physical benefits. Discuss.

2 To what extent can we predict exercise behaviour?

3 How does the exercise research contribute to our understanding of the mind–body problem?

4 How can psychological models be used to promote exercise behaviour?

5 Exercise behaviour occurs within a social context. Discuss.

6 Describe a possible research project designed to predict attendance at an exercise class.

▶ For discussion

Consider your own exercise behaviour and discuss the extent to which your health beliefs are contributing factors.

Assumptions in health psychology

The exercise literature illustrates some of the assumptions central to health psychology:

1 *The mind–body problem.* Research into exercise maintains the mind–body split. This is illustrated in the discussion of the benefits of exercise (physical and psychological) and the reasons for exercising (e.g. health and fitness *vs* enjoyment).

2 *Data exist independently of the methodology used.* If different sets of cognitions are measured according to the different models, do these beliefs exist prior to the subject being asked about them (e.g. do you think health is important, primes the subject to think about health as having a value)? Methodology is seen as objective, and not interacting with the 'data'.

Further reading

Dishman, R.K. (1982) Compliance/adherence in health-related exercise, *Health Psychology*, 1: 237–67.

This paper examines the literature on factors predicting exercise behaviour.

Marcus, B.H., Rakowski, W. and Rossi, J.S. (1992) Assessing motivational readiness and decision-making for exercise, *Health Psychology*, 22: 3–16.

This paper applies the transtheoretical approach to exercise behaviour and illustrates the extent to which research can be used to change behaviour.

CHAPTER 8

Sex

Chapter overview

This chapter first examines the literature on sex, including early discussions of reproduction and the debate about sexual pleasure. It then focuses on the more recent literature, which has examined the risks of sexual behaviour initially in the context of pregnancy avoidance and subsequently in the light of sexually transmitted diseases (STDs)/HIV and AIDS. This literature includes a variety of psychological perspectives from the use of social cognition models, which highlight the role of individual cognitions, to an emphasis on an interaction between individuals in terms of the relationship context. Finally the chapter outlines recent literature on sex, which examines the broader social context in terms of educational influences, the gay community, gendered power relations and theories about sex, HIV and illness.

This chapter covers:

- Developing the contemporary perspectives on sex
- Sex as a risk and pregnancy avoidance
- Sex as a risk in the context of STDs/HIV and AIDS
- Sex as an interaction between individuals – adding the relationship context
- The broader social context

Developing the contemporary research perspectives on sex

Sex as biological, for reproduction

Prior to the nineteenth century, sexual behaviour was regarded as a religious or spiritual concern. However, from the beginning of the 1800s sexuality and sexual behaviour became a focus for scientific study. Doctors and scientists took over the responsibility for teaching about sex and sex was subsequently studied within medicine and biological sciences. Sex was viewed as a biological function alongside eating and drinking.

During the nineteenth century, much was written about sexual behaviour. Attempts were made to develop criteria to describe sexual normality and abnormality. Generally behaviours linked to reproduction were seen as normal and those such as masturbation and homosexuality as abnormal. This is illustrated by the Victorian concern with sexual morality, movements proclaiming sexual puritanism and attempts to control prostitution. Sex was seen as a biological drive that needed to be expressed but which should be expressed within the limitations of its function, reproduction.

Sex as biological, for pleasure

Since the beginning of the twentieth century, there has been a shift in perspective. Although sex is still seen as biological, the emphasis is now on sexual behaviour rather than on outcome (reproduction). This involves a study of sexual desire, sexual pleasure and orgasms. It has resulted in a burgeoning literature on sex therapy and manuals on how to develop a good sex life. This emphasis is illustrated by the classic survey carried out by Kinsey in the 1940s and 1950s, the research programmes developed by Masters and Johnson in the 1960s and the Hite reports on sexuality in the 1970s and 1980s.

The Kinsey Report

Kinsey interviewed and analysed data from 12,000 white Americans and his attempts to challenge some of the contemporary concerns with deviance were credited with causing 'a wave of sexual hysteria' (e.g. Kinsey *et al.* 1948). He developed his analysis of sexual behaviour within models of biological reductionism and argued that sex was natural and therefore healthy. Kinsey argued that the sexual drive was a biological force and the expression of this drive to attain pleasure was not only acceptable but desirable. He challenged some of the contemporary concerns with premarital sex and argued that as animals do not get married, there could be no difference between marital and premarital sex. He emphasized similarities between the sexual behaviour of men and women and argued that if scientific study could promote healthy sex lives then this could improve the quality of marriages and reduce the divorce rates. His research suggested that a variety of sexual outlets were acceptable and emphasized the role of sexual pleasure involving both sexual intercourse and masturbation for men and women.

Masters and Johnson

This emphasis on the activity of sex is also illustrated by the work of Masters and Johnson in the 1960s. Masters and Johnson used a variety of experimental laboratory techniques to examine over 10,000 male and female orgasms in 694 white middle-class heterosexuals (e.g. Masters and Johnson 1966). They recorded bodily contractions, secretions, pulse rates and tissue colour changes and described the sexual response cycle in terms of the following phases: (1) excitement, (2) plateau, (3) orgasm and (4) resolution. They emphasized similarities between men and women (although it has been argued that their data suggests more difference than they acknowledged; Segal 1994) and emphasized that stable marriages depended on satisfactory sex. According to Masters and Johnson, sexual pleasure could be improved by education and sex therapy and again their research suggested that masturbation was an essential component of sexuality – sex was for pleasure, not for reproduction.

The Hite Reports

Shere Hite (1976, 1981, 1987) published the results from her 20 years of research in her reports on female and male sexuality. Her research also illustrates the shift from the outcome of sex to sex as an activity. Hite's main claim is that 'most women (70 per cent) do not orgasm as a result of intercourse' but she suggests that they can learn to increase clitoral stimulation during intercourse to improve their sexual enjoyment. She describes her data in terms of women's dislike of penetrative sex ('Perhaps it could be said that many women might be rather indifferent to intercourse if it were not for feelings towards a particular man') and discusses sex within the context of pleasure, not reproduction. Segal (1994) has criticized Hite's interpretation of the data and argues that the women in Hite's studies appear to enjoy penetration (with or without orgasm). Although this is in contradiction to Hite's own conclusion, the emphasis is still on sex as an activity.

In summary

Throughout the twentieth century, therefore, sex is no longer described as a biological means to an end (reproduction) but as an activity in itself. Discussions of 'good sex', orgasms and sexual pleasure emphasize sex as action, however, even as an activity sex remains predominantly biological. Kinsey regarded sex as a drive that was natural and healthy, Masters and Johnson developed means to measure and improve the sexual experience by examining physiological changes and Hite explains pleasure with descriptions of physical stimulation.

Sex as a risk to health

Recently, there has been an additional shift in the literature on sex. Although research still emphasizes sex as an activity, this activity has been viewed as increasingly risky and dangerous. As a consequence, sex is discussed in terms of health promotion, health education and self-protection. This shift has resulted in a psychological literature on sex as a risk both in terms of pregnancy avoidance and in the context of STDs/HIV preventive behaviour. However, studying sexual behaviour is not straightforward from a psychological perspective as it presents a problem for psychologists – a problem of interaction.

Sex as interaction

Social psychologists have spent decades emphasizing the context within which behaviour occurs. This is reflected in the extensive literature on areas such as conformity to majority and minority influence, group behaviour and decision-making, and obedience to authority. Such a perspective emphasizes that an individual's behaviour occurs as an interaction both with other individuals and with the broader social context. Sex highlights this interaction as it is inherently an interactive behaviour. However, health psychology draws on many other areas of psychology (e.g. physiological, cognitive, behavioural), which have tended to examine individuals on their own. In addition, psychological methodologies such as questionnaires and interviews involve an individual's experience (e.g. I felt, I believe, I think, I did). Even if individuals discuss their interactions with other individuals (e.g. we felt, we believe, we think, we did), or place their experiences in the context of others (e.g. I felt happy because she made me feel relaxed), only their own individual experiences are accessed using the psychological tools available. Therefore, sex provides an interesting problem for psychologists. Sex is intrinsically an interaction between individuals, yet many areas of psychology traditionally study individuals on their own. Furthermore, the recent emphasis on sex as a risk to health and resulting attempts to examine individuals' competence at protecting themselves from danger, may have resulted in a more individualistic model of behaviour. This problem of interaction is exacerbated by the psychological methodologies available (unless the researcher simply observes two people having sex!). The following theories of sexual behaviour both in the context of pregnancy avoidance and STD/HIV preventive behaviour illustrate the different ways in which psychologists have attempted to deal with the problem of the interaction. They highlight the problem with adding both the relationship context (e.g. the interaction between individuals) and the wider social context (e.g. social meanings, social norms) onto the individual (e.g. their beliefs and knowledge). They also raise the question of how much can and should psychologists be concerned with the context of individual behaviour?

Sex as a risk and pregnancy avoidance

A focus on sex for pleasure and an emphasis on sex as a risk has resulted in a literature on contraception use and pregnancy avoidance. Psychologists have developed models in order to describe and predict this behaviour.

What is contraceptive use?

Researchers have used several different classifications of contraception in an attempt to predict contraceptive use. For example, contraception has been characterized as:

- coitus-independent (the pill) or coitus-dependent (the condom);
- reliable (the pill, condom) or unreliable (rhythm method);
- female-controlled (the pill, IUD) or male-controlled (the condom);
- prescription-based (the pill, IUD) or prescription-independent (the condom).

In addition, different measures of actual behaviour have been used when predicting contraception use:

- at first ever intercourse;
- at most recent intercourse;
- at last serious intercourse;
- at last casual intercourse.

Who uses contraception?

The National Survey of Sexual Attitudes and Lifestyles (Wellings *et al.* 1994) examined the sexual behaviour of nearly 20,000 men and women across Britain. This produced a wealth of data about factors such as age of first intercourse, homosexuality, attitudes to sexual behaviours and contraception use. For example, Fig. 8.1 shows the proportion of respondents who used no contraception at first intercourse. These results suggest that the younger someone is when they first have sex (either male or female), the less likely they are to use contraception.

The results from this survey also show what kinds of contraception people use at first intercourse. The data for men and women aged 16–24 years are shown in Fig. 8.2 and suggest that the condom is the most popular form of contraception; however, many respondents in this age group reported using no contraception, or unreliable methods, such as withdrawal or the safe period.

The different measures of contraception use have implications for interpreting findings on contraception. Sheeran *et al.* (1991) discussed these problems and analysed the literature on contraceptive use in 'never married' individuals aged 13–25 years, and suggested that models used to

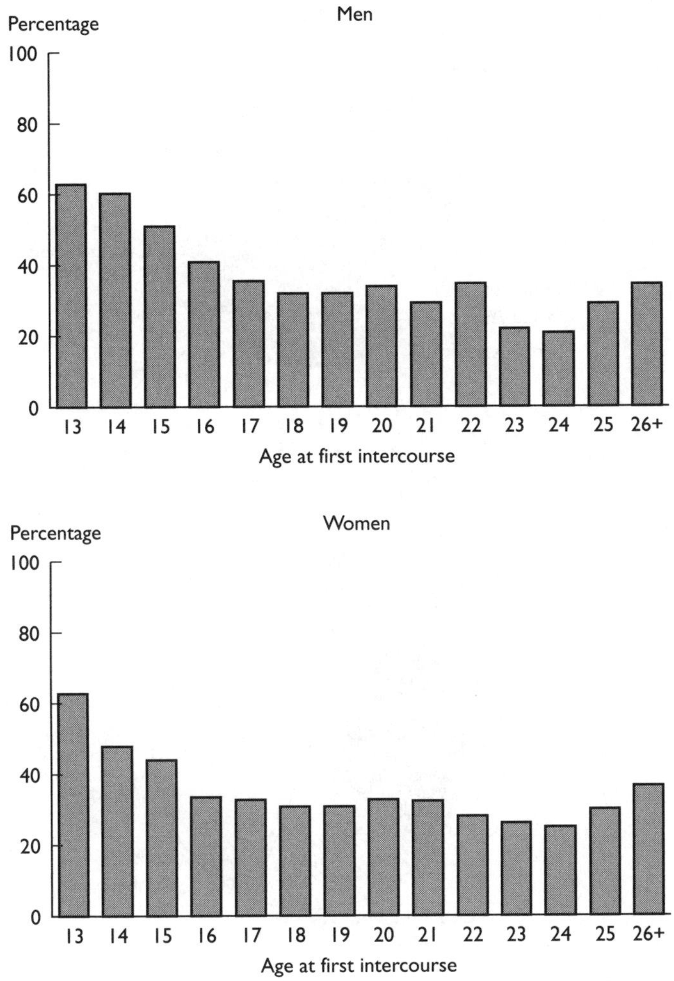

Figure 8.1 Percentage using no contraception at first intercourse, by age at first intercourse

examine contraceptive use for pregnancy avoidance can be described as either *developmental models* or *decision-making models*. The focus on sex as risky resulted in a need to understand risk-taking behaviour. Developmental models are more descriptive, whereas decision-making models examine the predictors and precursors to this behaviour.

Developmental models

Developmental models emphasize contraception use as involving a series of stages. They suggest that the progress through these stages is related to

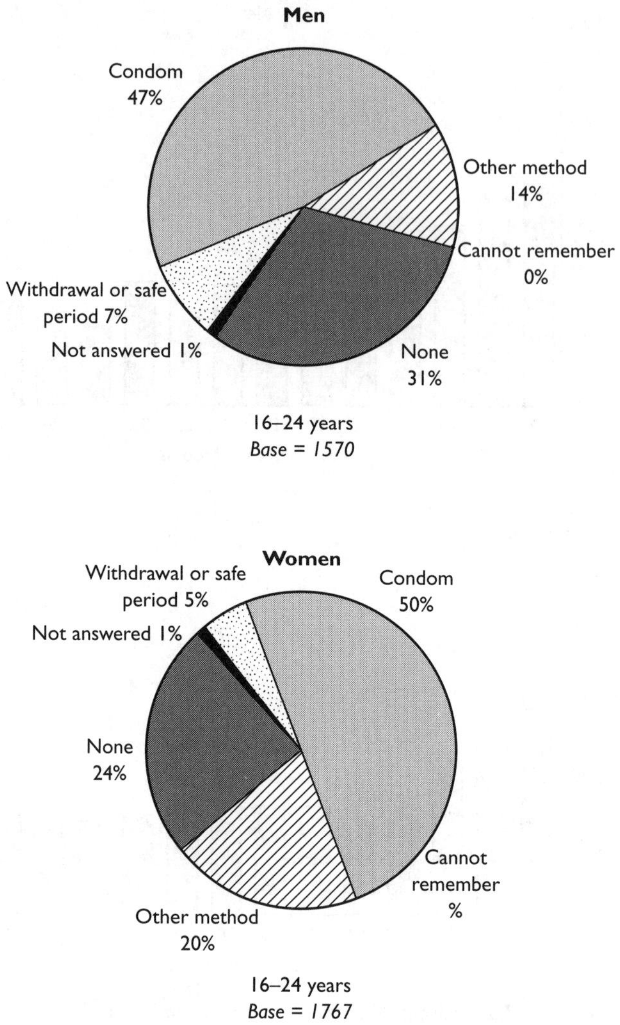

Figure 8.2 Contraception use at first intercourse in those aged 16–24

sexual experience and an increasing role for sexuality in the individual's self-concept. Therefore, they describe the transition through the different stages but do not attempt to analyse the cognitions that may promote this transition.

Lindemann's three-stage theory

Lindemann (1977) developed the three-stage theory of contraception use, which suggests that the likelihood of an individual using contraception increases as they progress through the three stages:

1 *Natural stage*: at this stage intercourse is relatively unplanned, and the individual does not regard themselves as sexual. Therefore, contraception use is unlikely.
2 *Peer prescription stage*: at this stage the individual seeks contraceptive advice from friends, sexual intercourse is more frequent and most contraception involves less effective methods.
3 *Expert stage*: at this stage, the individual has incorporated sexuality into their self-concept and will seek professional advice and plan contraceptive use.

Rain's model

This model was developed by Rains (1971) and again places contraception use within the context of sexuality and self-concept. It suggests that contraception use is more likely to occur at a stage when the individual believes that sexual activity is 'right for them'. This process involves the following four stages:

1 Falling in love: this provides a rationale for sex.
2 Having an exclusive, long-term relationship.
3 Sexual intercourse becomes an acceptable behaviour.
4 Individuals accept themselves as sexual and plan sex for the future.

According to this model, reaching stage 4 predicts reliable contraception use.

Decision-making models

Decision-making models examine the psychological factors that predict and are the precursors to contraception use. There are several different decision-making models and they vary in their emphasis on individual cognitions (e.g. costs and benefits of contraception use) and the extent to which they place these cognitions within the specific context of the relationship (e.g. the interaction, seriousness of relationship, frequency of sexual intercourse in the relationship) and the broader social context (e.g. peer norms, social attitudes).

Subjective expected utility theory

Most decision-making models of behaviour are based on the subjective expected utility theory (SEU) (Edwards 1954). The SEU predicts that individuals make subjective estimates of the possible costs and benefits of any particular behaviour and, based on this assessment, make a decision as to which behaviour results in the least costs and the most benefits (material, social and psychological). It therefore characterizes behaviour as rational. Luker (1975) examined the SEU in the context of contraceptive use and argued that individuals weigh up the costs and benefits of pregnancy against the costs and benefits of contraception. Sheeran *et al.* (1991) argued that this approach was important as it undermined the belief that contraception has no costs for women and pregnancy had no benefits. The SEU is predominantly individualistic and the role of both the relationship and social context is minimal.

The five-component model

This model was developed by Reiss *et al.* (1975) and, although it still regards contraceptive use as resulting from a rational appraisal of the situation, it includes measures of more general attitudes. The components of the model are: (1) endorsement of sexual choices (e.g. permissiveness, religiosity), (2) self-assurance, (3) early information on sex and contraception and (4) congruity between premarital sexual standards and behaviour and commitment. Reiss *et al.* tested the model and reported support for the first three of the variables as predictive of contraception use. This model is still predominantly concerned with individual cognitions.

The health belief model

This model was developed by Rosenstock and colleagues and is described in detail in Chapter 2. The original HBM emphasized individual cognitions and ignores the problem of interaction. Lowe and Radius (1982) developed the HBM specifically to predict contraception and aimed to examine individual cognitions within both the context of the relationship and broader social norms. They added the following variables:

- self-esteem,
- interpersonal skills,
- knowledge about sex and contraception,
- attitudes to sex and contraception,
- previous sexual, contraceptive and pregnancy experiences,
- peer norms,
- relationship status,
- substance use prior to sex.

Therefore, although this model still examines cognitions, it includes measures of the individuals' cognitions about their social world.

The theory of reasoned action

This theory was developed by Fishbein and Ajzen (1975) and is described in detail in Chapter 2. The TRA was the first cognition model to include measures of individuals' cognitions about their social world in the form of subjective norms. It therefore represents an attempt to add the social context to individual cognitive variables and consequently addresses the problem of interaction. The TRA has been used to predict contraceptive use and research has indicated a correlation between the components of the model and intentions to use the oral contraceptive (Cohen *et al.* 1978). In addition, research by Werner and Middlestadt (1979) reported correlations between attitudes to contraception and subjective norms and actual use of oral contraception.

Sexual behaviour sequence model

This model was developed by Byrne *et al.* (1977) and adds sexual arousal and emotional responses to sex to the factors included in the TRA. Sexual arousal refers to how aroused an individual is at the time of making a decision about contraception. Emotional responses to sex describes a personality trait that Byrne *et al.* defined as either erotophilia (finding sexual cues pleasurable) or erotophobia (finding sexual cues aversive). According to the sexual behaviour sequence model, decisions about contraception are made in the context of both rational information processing and emotions. This model attempts to add a degree of emotions and social norms (from the TRA) to the individual's cognitions.

Herold and McNamee's (1982) model

This model is made up of the following variables: (1) parental and peer group norms for acceptance of premarital intercourse; (2) number of lifetime sexual partners; (3) guilt about intercourse and attitudes to contraception; (4) involvement with current partner; (5) partner's influence to use contraception; and (6) frequency of intercourse. This model differs from other models of contraception use as it includes details of the relationship. It places contraception use both within the general context of social norms and also within the context of the relationship.

In summary

These decision-making models regard contraceptive use as resulting from an analysis of the relevant variables. However, they vary in the extent to which they attempt to place the individual's cognitive state within a broader context, both of the relationship and the social world.

Integrating developmental and decision-making approaches to contraception use

Developmental models emphasize behaviour and describe reliable contraception use as the end product of a transition through a series of stages. These models do not examine the psychological factors, which may speed up or delay this transition. In contrast, decision-making models emphasize an individual's cognitions and, to a varying degree, place these cognitions within the context of the relationship and social norms. Perhaps these cognitions could be used to explain the behavioural stages described by the developmental models. Sheeran *et al.* (1991) argued that these perspectives could be combined and that the best means to examine contraceptive use is as a product of (1) background, (2) intrapersonal, (3) interpersonal and (4) situational factors. They defined these factors as follows:

Background factors

1 *Age*: evidence suggests that young women's contraceptive use increases with age (e.g. Herold 1981).
2 *Gender*: women appear to be more likely to use contraception than men (e.g. Whitely and Schofield 1986).
3 *Race*: some evidence suggests that whites are more likely to use contraception than blacks (e.g. Whitely and Schofield 1986).
4 *Socio-economic status*: there is conflicting evidence concerning the relationship between SES and contraceptive use with some research indicating a relationship (e.g. Hornick *et al.* 1979) and others indicating no relationship (e.g. Herold 1981).
5 *Education*: evidence indicates that higher school performance and higher educational aspirations may be linked with contraception use (e.g. Herold and Samson 1980; Furstenburg *et al.* 1983).

Although these background factors may influence contraceptive use, whether this effect is direct or through the effect of other factors such as knowledge and attitudes is unclear.

Intrapersonal factors

1 *Knowledge*: Whitely and Schofield (1986) analysed the results of 25 studies of contraceptive use and reported a correlation of 0.17 between objective knowledge and contraceptive use in both men and women, suggesting that knowledge is poorly linked to behaviour. Ignorance about contraception has also been shown by several studies. For example, Cvetkovich and Grote (1981) reported that of their sample 10 per cent did not believe that they could become pregnant the first time they had sex, and 52 per cent of men and 37 per cent of women could not identify the periods of highest risk in the menstrual cycle. In addition, Lowe and Radius (1982) reported that 40 per cent of their sample did not know how long sperm remained viable.
2 *Attitudes*: Fisher (1984) reported that positive attitudes towards contraception parallel actual use. Negative attitudes included beliefs that 'it kills spontaneity', 'it's too much trouble to use' and that there are possible side-effects. In addition, carrying contraceptives around is often believed to be associated with being promiscuous (e.g. Lowe and Radius 1982).
3 *Personality*: Many different personality types have been related to contraceptive use. This research assumes that certain aspects of individuals are consistent over time and research has reported associations between the following types of personality:
   - *conservatism and sex role* have been shown to be negatively related to contraceptive use (e.g. Geis and Gerard 1984; McCormick *et al.* 1985).
   - *an internal locus of control* appears to correlate with contraceptive use but not with choice of type of contraception (Morrison 1985).
   - *sex guilt and sex anxiety* positively relate to use and consistency of use of contraception (Herold and McNamee 1982).

Interpersonal factors

Research highlights a role for characteristics of the following significant others:

1 *Partner*: facets of the relationship may influence contraception use including duration of relationship, intimacy, type of relationship (e.g. casual *vs* steady), exclusivity, and ability to have overt discussions about contraception (e.g. DeLamater and MacCorquodale 1978; 1979).
2 *Parents*: there is some evidence to suggest that increased parental permissiveness and explicit communication between mothers and daughters about contraception is related to contraception use (e.g. Herold and McNamee 1982).
3 *Peers*: increased contraceptive use relates to peer permissiveness and peer's own contraceptive behaviour (e.g. Herold 1981).

Situational factors

Sheeran *et al.* (1991) have also argued that situational factors contribute to contraceptive use, including:

1 *The spontaneity of sex*: spontaneity is often given as a reason for not using contraception (e.g. Holland *et al.* 1990b).
2 *Substance use prior to sex*: taking substances such as drugs or alcohol prior to sex may relate to risky sex.
3 *The accessibility of contraception*: research has also examined whether easy access to contraception both in general (i.e. the provision of condom machines in pubs) and at the time of contemplating sex predicts contraception use (e.g. Gold *et al.* 1991).

Sheeran *et al.* (1991) argued that these different variables interact in order to predict contraception use. They included interpersonal and situational factors as a means to place the individual's cognitions within the context of the relationship and the broader social world. These variables can be applied individually or alternatively incorporated into models. In particular, social cognition models emphasize cognitions about the individual's social world, particularly their normative beliefs. However, whether asking an individual about the relationship really accesses the interaction between two people is questionable. For example, is the belief that 'I decided to go on the pill because I had talked it over with my partner' a statement describing the interaction between two individuals, or is it one individual's cognitions about that interaction?

Since the beginnings of the HIV/AIDS epidemic, sex as a risk has taken on a new dimension – the dimension of chronic illness and death. Research into HIV and AIDS preventive behaviour also illustrates the different ways of dealing with sex as an interaction. Although sometimes ignored, this research is also relevant to other sexually transmitted diseases.

Sex as a risk in the context of STDs/HIV and AIDS

The HIV virus was identified in 1982 (see Chapter 13 for a discussion of HIV and AIDS). Since then, health education programmes have changed in their approach to preventing the spread of the virus. For example, early campaigns emphasized monogamy or at least cutting down on the number of sexual partners. Campaigns also promoted non-penetrative sex and suggested alternative ways to enjoy a sexual relationship. However, more recent campaigns emphasize safe sex and using a condom. In fact, Reiss and Leik (1989) argued that increased condom use and not abstinence or non-penetrative sex or a reduction in the number of partners is likely to be the best approach to HIV. As a result, research has examined the prerequisites to safer sex and condom use in an attempt to develop successful health promotion campaigns.

Do people use condoms?

Young people

Some researchers have suggested that the mass media campaigns have not changed teenagers' sexual behaviour (Sherr 1987) and that there has even been a recent increase in sexually transmitted diseases (STDs) among this age group in the USA (Boyer and Kegles 1991). In the UK, data indicate that there has been an increase in Chlamydia and that the dramatic reduction in gonorrhoea seen in the older population is not evident among younger people. Richard and van der Pligt (1991) examined condom use among a group of Dutch teenagers and report that 50 per cent of those with multiple partners were consistent condom users. In an American study, 30 per cent of adolescent women were judged to be at risk from STDs, of whom 16 per cent used condoms consistently (Weisman *et al.* 1991). The Women, Risk and AIDS Project (WRAP) (e.g. Holland *et al.* 1990b) interviewed and collected questionnaires from heterosexual women aged 16–19 years. It reported that 16 per cent of these used condoms on their own, 13 per cent had used condoms while on the pill, 2 per cent had used condoms in combination with spermicide and 3 per cent had used condoms together with a diaphragm. Overall only 30 per cent of their sample had ever used condoms, while 70 per cent had not. Fife-Schaw and Breakwell (1992) undertook an overview of the literature on condom use among young people and found that between 24 per cent and 58 per cent of 16- to 24-year-olds had used a condom during their most recent sexual encounter.

Homosexuals

Research has also examined condom use among homosexually active men. Weatherburn *et al.* (1991) interviewed 930 homosexually active men in England and Wales and reported that 270 of them had had insertive anal intercourse in the preceding month, with 38.9 per cent reporting always using a condom, 49.6 per cent never using a condom and 11.5 per cent sometimes using a condom. Of the 254 who reported having receptive anal sex in the preceding month, 42.5 per cent had always used a condom, 45.7 per cent had never used a condom and 11.8 per cent had sometimes used a condom. Weatherburn *et al.* reported that condom use was associated with casual not regular sexual partners and was more common in open and not monogamous relationships. Therefore, within this high-risk group, condom use is low.

Bisexuals

In a recent study, Boulton *et al.* (1991) asked 60 bisexual men about their sexual behaviour and their condom use. Over the previous 12 months, 80 per cent had had male partners, 73 per cent had had female partners and 60 per cent had had at least one male and one female partner. In terms of their condom use with their current partner, 25 per cent reported always using a condom with their current male partner, 12 per cent reported always using a condom with their current female partner, 27 per cent reported sometimes/never using a condom with their male partner and 38 per cent reported sometimes/never using a condom with their female partner. In terms of their non-current partner, 30 per cent had had unprotected sex with a man and 34 per cent had had unprotected sex with a woman. Bisexuals are believed to present a bridge between the homosexual and heterosexual populations and these data suggest that their frequency of condom use is low. This highlights a need to identify possible reasons for this behaviour.

Changes in condom use

In an attempt to examine the effects of HIV prevention educational campaigns in The Netherlands, Hooykaas *et al.* (1991) examined changes in sexual behaviour in 340 heterosexual men and women and prostitutes. They reported that over the one-year follow-up, condom use during vaginal intercourse with prostitutes/clients was high and remained high, condom use with private partners was low and remained low, but that both men and women reduced their number of sexual partners by 50 per cent.

The results from the General Household Survey (1993) provided some further insights into changes in condom use in Britain from 1983 to 1991 (see Fig. 8.3). These data indicate an overall increase in condom use as the usual form of contraception, which is particularly apparent in the younger age groups.

Condom use is recommended as the main means to prevent the spread of the HIV virus. These data suggest that many individuals do report using condoms, although not always on a regular basis. In addition, many individuals say that they do not use condoms. Therefore, although

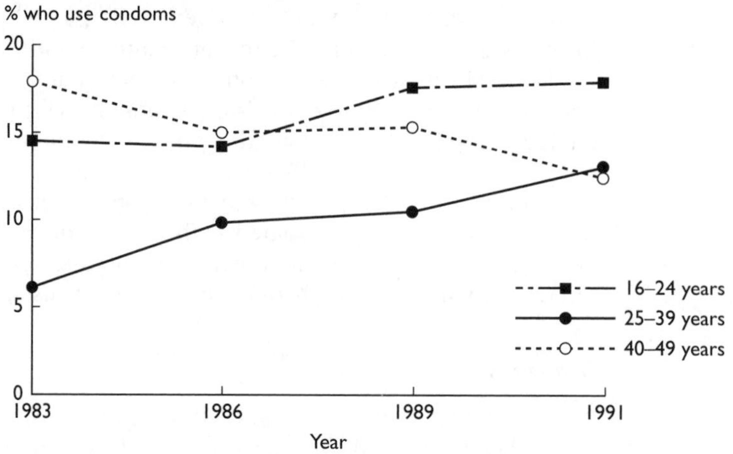

Figure 8.3 Changes in the use of condoms as the usual method of contraception by age, 1983–91

the health promotion messages may be reaching many individuals, many others are not complying with their recommendations.

Predicting condom use

Simple models using knowledge only have been used to examine condom use. However, these models ignore the individual's beliefs and assume that simply increasing knowledge about HIV will promote safe sex. In order to incorporate an individual's cognitive state, social cognition models have been applied to condom use in the context of HIV and AIDS (see Chapter 2 for a discussion of these models). These models are similar to those used to predict other health-related behaviours, including contraceptive use for pregnancy avoidance, and illustrate varying attempts to understand cognitions in the context of the relationship and the broader social context.

Social cognition models

The health belief model (HBM)

The HBM was developed by Rosenstock and colleagues (see Chapter 2) and has been used to predict condom use. McCusker *et al.* (1989) adapted the HBM to predict condom use in homosexual men over a 12-month period. They reported that the components of the model were not good predictors and only perceived susceptibility was related to condom use. In addition, they reported that the best predictor was previous risk behaviour. This suggests that condom use is a habitual behaviour and that placing current condom use into the context of time and habits may be the way to assess this behaviour.

The reasons why the HBM fails to predict condom use have been examined by Abraham and Sheeran (1994). They suggest the following explanations:

- *Consensus of severity*: everyone knows that HIV is a very serious disease. This presents the problem of a ceiling effect with only small differences in ratings of this variable.
- *Failure to acknowledge personal susceptibility*: although people appear to know about HIV, its causes and how it is transmitted, feelings of immunity and low susceptibility ('it won't happen to me') are extremely common. This presents the problem of a floor effect with little individual variability. Therefore, these two central components of the HBM are unlikely to distinguish between condom users and non-users.
- *Safer sex requires long-term maintenance of behaviour*: the HBM may be a good predictor of short-term changes in behaviour (e.g. taking up an exercise class, stopping smoking in the short term), but safer sex is an ongoing behaviour, which requires an ongoing determination to adopt condom use as a habit.
- *Sex is emotional and involves a level of high arousal*: these factors may make the rational information processing approach of the HBM redundant.
- *Sex is interactive and involves negotiation*: condom use takes place between two people, it involves a process of negotiation and occurs within the context of a relationship. Assessing individual cognitions does not access this negotiation process. Abraham and Sheeran (1993) suggest that social skills may be better predictors of safe sex.
- *From beliefs to behaviour*: the HBM does not clarify how beliefs (e.g. 'I feel at risk') are translated into behaviour (e.g. 'I am using a condom').

The theory of reasoned action (TRA) and the theory of planned behaviour (TPB)

In an attempt to resolve some of the problems with the HBM, the TRA and TPB have been used to predict condom use. These models address the problem of how beliefs are turned into action using the 'behavioural intentions' component. In addition, they attempt to address the problem of placing beliefs within a context by an emphasis on social cognitions (the normative beliefs component). Research suggests that the TRA has had some degree of success at predicting condom use with behavioural intentions predicting condom use at 1, 3, and 4 months (Fisher 1984; Boyd and Wandersman 1991; van der Velde *et al.* 1992). In addition, attitudes to condoms predict behavioural intentions (Boldero *et al.* 1992), and perceived partner support (partner norms) appears to be a good predictor of condom use by women (Weisman *et al.* 1991).

Research has also explored the relative usefulness of the TRA compared with the TPB at predicting intentions to use condoms (Sutton *et al.* 1999). The results from this study indicated that the TPB was not more effective than the TRA (in contrast to the authors' predictions) and that past behaviour was the most powerful predictor. In a recent study of condom use, the best predictors appeared to be a combination of normative beliefs involving peers, friends, siblings, previous partners, parents and the general public. This suggests that although cognitions may play a role in predicting condom use, this essentially interactive behaviour is probably best understood within the context of both the relationship and the broader social world, highlighting the important role of social cognitions in the form of normative beliefs. Therefore, although TRA and TPB, address some of the problems with the HBM, they still do not address some of the others.

The role of self-efficacy

The concept of self-efficacy (Bandura 1977) has been incorporated into many models of behaviour. In terms of condom use, self-efficacy can refer to factors such as confidence in buying condoms, confidence in using condoms or confidence in suggesting that condoms are used. Research has highlighted an association between perceived self-efficacy and reported condom use (Richard and van der Pligt 1991), and a denial of HIV risk during the contemplation of sex (Abraham *et al.* 1994). Schwarzer (1992) developed the health action process approach (HAPA, see Chapter 2), which places self-efficacy in a central role for predicting behaviour. In addition, this model may be particularly relevant to condom use as it emphasizes time and habit.

Problems with social cognition models

Many of the problems highlighted by the HBM are also characteristic of other social cognition models. These problems can be summarized as follows:

1 *Inconsistent findings*. The research examining condom use has not produced consistent results. For example, whereas Fisher (1984) reported an association between intentions and actual behaviour, Abraham *et al.* (1991) did not. Joseph *et al.* (1987) suggested that condom use is predicted by peer norms, whereas Catania *et al.* (1989) found that it is not. Furthermore, Catania *et al.* (1989) reported that condom use relates to perceived severity and self-efficacy, but Hingson *et al.* (1990) said that it does not relate to these factors. However, such studies have used very different populations (homosexual, heterosexual, adolescents, adults). Perhaps models of condom use should be constructed to fit the cognitive sets of different populations; attempts to develop one model for everyone may ignore the multitude of different cognitions held by different individuals within different groups.
2 *Sex as a result of individual cognitions*. Models that emphasize cognitions and information processing intrinsically regard behaviour as the result of information processing – an individualistic approach to behaviour. In particular, early models tended to focus on representations of an individual's risks without taking into account their interactions with

the outside world. Furthermore, models such as the HBM emphasized this process as rational. However, recent social cognition models have attempted to remedy this situation by emphasizing cognitions about the individual's social world (the normative beliefs) and by including elements of emotion (the behaviour becomes less rational).

3 *Perception of susceptibility*. In addition, these models predict that because people appear to know that HIV is an extremely serious disease, and they know how it is transmitted, they will feel vulnerable (e.g. 'HIV is transmitted by unprotected sex, I have unprotected sex, therefore I am at risk from HIV'). This does not appear to be the case. Furthermore, the models predict that high levels of susceptibility will relate to less risk-taking behaviour (e.g. 'I am at risk, therefore I will use condoms'). Again this association is problematic.
4 *Sex as an interaction between individuals – the relationship context*. Models of condom use focus on cognitions. In attempts to include an analysis of the place of this behaviour (the relationship), variables such as peer norms, partner norms and partner support have been added. However, these variables are still accessed by asking one individual about their beliefs about the relationship. Perhaps this is still only accessing a cognition not the interaction.
5 *Sex in a social context*. Sex also takes place within a broader social context, involving norms about sexual practices, gender roles and stereotypes, the role of illness and theories of sexual behaviour. Cognitive models cannot address this broader context.

Perceptions of susceptibility, sex as an interaction between individuals and the broader social context will now be dealt with in more detail.

Perceptions of susceptibility – are you at risk?

Having a sexual career today involves a relationship to risk that is different to that seen previously. However, one of the most consistent findings to emerge from the research is the perception of personal invulnerability in heterosexual and homosexual populations. These feelings of invulnerability to HIV are shown by quantitative studies that have examined ratings of perceived susceptibility and unrealistic optimism (see Chapters 2 and 13). For example, Abrams *et al.* (1990: 49) concluded from their survey in 1988 that young people 'have a strong sense of AIDS invulnerability which seems to involve a perception that they have control over the risk at which they place themselves'. In a study of beliefs in a population of young people in Scotland from 1988 to 1989, the authors reported an increased sense of complacency and invulnerability over this time period.

In addition, qualitative methods have been used to further examine whether individuals feel that they are at risk from HIV. Woodcock *et al.* (1992) interviewed 125 young people aged 16–25 years about their sexual behaviour and examined how these individuals evaluated their own risk factors. The authors reported that many of the interviewees endorsed risky behaviour and gave reasons both acknowledging their own risk and denying that they had put themselves at risk. These ways of coping with risk were as follows:

1 *Acknowledging risk.* One subject acknowledged that their behaviour had been risky saying 'I'm a chancer and I know I'm a chancer . . . with this AIDS thing, I know that I should use a condom'. However, most subjects even though they acknowledged some degree of risk managed to dismiss it in terms of 'it would show by now', 'it was in the past' or 'AIDS wasn't around in those days' (from a 21-year-old interviewee).
2 *Denying risk.* Most commonly, people denied that they had ever put themselves at risk and the complex ways in which their sexual behaviour was rationalized illustrates how complicated the concept of susceptibility and 'being at risk' is. Woodcock *et al.* (1992) presented many ways of rationalizing risky behaviour. These include believing 'it's been blown out of proportion', that 'AIDS is a risk you take in living' and the authors report that 'the theme of being run over, particularly by buses' was common and believing that 'it doesn't effect me' was also apparent. In addition, the interviewees evaluated their own risk in the context of the kinds of people with whom they had sex. For example, 'I don't go with people who go around a lot', 'He said I've only slept with you in the last six months', and 'I do not have sex in risky geographical areas' – one interviewee said 'London is the capital: has to be more AIDS'.

Most cognitive models emphasizing rational information processing suggest that condom use is related to feelings of susceptibility and being at risk from HIV. However, many people do not appear to believe that they themselves are at risk, which is perhaps why they do not engage in self-protective behaviour, and even when some acknowledgment of risk is made, this is often dismissed and does not appear to relate to behaviour change.

Sex as an interaction between individuals

Because sex is intrinsically an interactive behaviour, psychologists have attempted to add an interactive component to the understanding of condom use. In an attempt to access the interaction between individuals, Abraham and Sheeran (1993) argued that social cognition models should be expanded to include the interpersonal and situational variables described by the literature on contraception use. In particular, they have argued that relationship factors such as duration, intimacy, quality of communication, status (casual *vs* steady) should be added to intrapersonal factors such as knowledge and beliefs and situational factors such as substance use and spontaneity.

To further the understanding of the process of interaction, qualitative methods have been used, particularly in terms of negotiation of condom

FOCUS ON RESEARCH 8.1

TESTING A THEORY – THE SITUATION AND CONDOM USE

A study to examine situational factors and cognitions associated with condom use in gay men (Gold *et al.* 1991).

Background

Homosexual men are at greatest risk from HIV in the western world. Therefore, understanding safer sex in this group has obvious implications for health promotion. The aim of this study was to examine which situational factors (e.g. physical location, type of partner) and cognitions (e.g. desires, intentions to use drugs/alcohol) and mood are related to either protected or unprotected sex. This study by Gold *et al.* (1991) illustrates an attempt to place individual cognitions within both the relationship context and the broader social context. In addition, the mood measurements reflect an attempt to examine the less rational aspects of sex.

Methodology

Subjects A total of 219 Australian gay men completed a questionnaire containing questions about two sexual encounters in the preceding year. They were recruited from a range of gay venues (e.g. gay bar/disco, sex on premises venue, established gay group, AIDS council premises, a medical practice known to have a large gay clientele).
Design The study involved a cross-sectional design with all subjects completing a self-administered questionnaire.
Questionnaire The subjects were asked to think about two sexual encounters in the preceding year, one involving safe sex and one involving unsafe sex. They were asked to complete the following ratings/questions about each of these encounters:

1 *Details of the encounters.* The subjects were asked questions about their encounters, including (i) how long ago it had taken place, (ii) whether the respondent had known about AIDS at the time of the encounter and (iii) what form of sexual activity had occurred (e.g. intercourse, ejaculation into the rectum). The encounter was then divided into four temporal stages: (i) start of the 'evening', (ii) time of meeting the potential partner, (iii) start of sex and (iv) during sex. The subjects were then asked to answer questions about each stage of the encounter for both the safe and unsafe encounter.

2 *Start of the evening.* The subjects were asked to rate (i) the type of desires that had been in their mind (e.g. to have sex without intercourse, to have intercourse without a condom, to have exciting sex, to have a drink or get mildly stoned), and (ii) to rate their mood at this time (e.g. happy, relaxed, under stress) and how intoxicated they were.
3 *Meeting the partner.* The subjects were asked (i) where they met their partner (e.g. at my place, at his place), (ii) which of the above various desires had been on his mind, (iii) how sexually attracted he was to his partner, and (iv) how intoxicated he was.
4 *Start of sex.* The subjects were asked (i) how much time there was between meeting the partner and the start of sex, (ii) details of the sex (e.g. place, time of day), (iii) kinds of desires, (iv) how sexually aroused he was, (v) how intoxicated he was, and (iv) whether he/his partner had communicated a desire for safe sex.
5 *During sex.* The subject was asked (i) how intoxicated he was and (ii) whether he/his partner communicated about safe sex.
6 *Additional questions for unsafe encounter.* Subjects were also asked to rate a series of statements for the unsafe encounter. They related to (i) ways in which the subjects may have engaged in unsafe sex without really wanting to (e.g. physically forced, tricked), and (ii) self-justifications for not using a condom (e.g. 'I thought to myself something like . . . condoms are such horrible things and to put one on destroys the magic of sex. Here we are on cloud nine: how can we suddenly interrupt everything just to get a bit of rubber out and roll it on', 'Other guys fuck without a condom much more often than I do. I'm less at risk than most guys').

Results

The results were analysed to examine the characteristics of both the safe and unsafe encounter and to evaluate any differences. The results showed that type of partner, desires, sexual attraction, mood, knowledge of condom availability and communication about safe sex differentiated between the two encounters. For example, unsafe sex was more likely to occur if the partner was a regular lover, if the subject reported a greater desire to have sex without a condom, to be more interested in having exciting sex, to be more attracted to their partner, to be in a better mood, to have less communication about safe sex, and to be less knowledgable about the availability of a condom. However, level of intoxication was not related to the type of resulting encounter. The results were also analysed to examine the frequency of self-justifications used. The most common justification was a belief that they could have sex without ejaculation ('It'll be safe to fuck without a condom, so long as we don't cum up the arse. So we'll just fuck without cumming'), followed by beliefs about faithfulness.

Conclusion

This study is interesting because it integrates cognitions with situational factors. Therefore, it attempts to place safe and unsafe sex in a context. The authors discuss the results in terms of developing educational interventions to promote safe sex. In addition, the authors emphasize that it is the thoughts and beliefs that occur during sexual encounters which are perhaps more relevant than those described in the cold light of day.

use. The Women's Risk and AIDS Project (WRAP) interviewed 150 women from London and Manchester about their sexual histories and sexual behaviour and described the factors that related to the negotiation of condom use. Holland *et al.* (1990b: 4) stated that during sex 'words are likely to be the most difficult things to exchange' and suggest that the negotiation of condom use is far more complex than 'a simple, practical question about dealing rationally with risk, it is the outcome of negotiation between potentially unequal partners'. They suggested that although the process of negotiation may be hindered by embarrassment as suggested by some of the health promotion campaigns, this 'embarrassment over using condoms is not simply a question of bad timing but indicates a very complex process of negotiation'. Therefore, they place condom use within the context of the relationship and rather than see the interaction between individuals as only one component of the process of condom use, they place this interaction centrally.

The results from the WRAP study provide some insights into the process of negotiation and the interaction between individuals. Some of the interviewees reported no difficulties in demanding safe sex, with one woman saying 'if they don't want to wear a condom, then tough, you know, go and find someone else'. Another woman said 'he really hates using them, so I used to say to him, look, right, look, I have no intention of getting pregnant again and you have no intention to become a father so you put one of these on'. However, other women described how difficult it was to suggest safe sex to their partner with reasons for this relating to not wanting to hurt their boyfriend's feelings, not wanting to 'ruin the whole thing', and not being able to approach the subject. One woman said 'When I got pregnant I thought to myself, "I'm not using a condom here, I'm not using anything" but I just couldn't say, just couldn't force myself to say, "look you know".' Holland *et al.* (1990b) argued that safe sex campaigns present condoms as neutral objects, which can be easily negotiated prior to sex and that this did not appear to be the case with the women they interviewed. The qualitative data from the WRAP study provides some insights into the process of negotiation; it also emphasizes sex as an interaction. In addition, it provides a relationship context for individual beliefs and cognitions. Indeed, several of the findings from recent research examining negotiation have been taken on board by Health Education Campaigns with recent advertisements highlighting the problem of raising the issue of safer sex (e.g. When would you mention condoms?). However, do interviews really access the interaction? Can the interaction be accessed using the available (and ethical) methodologies? (It would obviously be problematic to observe the interaction!) Are qualitative methods actually accessing something different from quantitative methods? Are interviews simply another method of finding out about people's cognitions and beliefs? Debates about methodology (quantitative *vs* qualitative) and the problem of behaviour as an interaction are relevant to all forms of behaviour but are particularly apparent when discussing sex.

The broader social context

Beliefs, attitudes and cognitions about sex, risk and condom use do not just exist within individuals, or within the context of an interaction between two individuals, they exist within a much broader social context. This social context takes many forms such as the form and influence of sex education, the social meanings, expectations and social norms developed and presented through the multiple forms of media, and created and perpetuated by individual communities and the wider world of gender and inequality. Psychological theory predominantly studies the individual. However, it is important to have some acknowledgment and understanding of this broader world. The final part of this chapter will examine this context in terms of sex education, power relations between men and women, social norms of the gay community and discourses about sex, HIV and illness.

Sex education

Education about sex, pregnancy, HIV and contraception comes from a variety of different sources, including government health education campaigns, school sex education programmes and from an individual's social world. These three sources of information will now be examined further.

Government health education campaigns

Ingham *et al.* (1991) examined UK campaigns that promoted safe sex and suggested that slogans such as 'Unless you're completely sure about your partner, always use a condom', 'Nowadays is it really wise to have sex with a stranger?', and 'Sex with a lot of partners, especially with people you don't know can be dangerous' emphasize knowing your partner. They interviewed a group of young people in the South of England to examine how they interpreted 'knowing their partners'. The results suggest that 27 per cent of the interviewees had had sex within 24 hours of becoming a couple, that 10 per cent of the sample reported having sex on the first ever occasion on which they met their partner, and that over 50 per cent reported having sex within two weeks of beginning a relationship. In terms of 'knowing their partner', 31 per cent of males and 35 per cent of females reported knowing nothing of their partner's sexual history, and knowing was often explained in terms of 'she came from a nice family and stuff', and having 'seen them around'. The results from this study indicate that promoting 'knowing your partner' may not be the best way to promote safe sex as knowledge can be interpreted in a multitude of different ways. In addition, safer sex campaigns emphasize personal responsibility and choice in the use of condoms and condoms are presented as a simple way to prevent contraction of the HIV virus. This presentation is epitomized by government health advertisement slogans such as 'You know the risks: the decision is yours'. This view of sex and condom use is in contradiction with the research suggesting that people believe that they are not at risk from HIV and that condom use involves a complex process of negotiation.

School sex education programmes

Information about sex also comes from sex education programmes at school. Holland *et al.* (1990a) interviewed young women about their experiences of sex education and concluded that sex education in schools is impersonal, mechanistic and concerned with biology. The women in their study made comments such as 'It was all from the book. It wasn't really personal' and 'Nobody ever talks to you about the problems and the entanglements, and what it means to a relationship when you start having sex'. It has been argued that this impersonal and objective approach to sex education is counter-productive (Aggleton 1989) and several alternatives have been suggested. Aggleton and Homans (1988) argued for a 'socially transformatory model' for AIDS education, which would involve discussions of (1) ideas about sex, (2) social relations, (3) political processes involved and (4) the problem of resource allocation. This approach would attempt to shift the emphasis from didactic teachings of facts and knowledge to a discussion of sex within a context of relationships and the broader social context. An additional solution to the problem of sex education is a skills training approach recommended by Abraham and Sheeran (1993). They argued that individuals could be taught a variety of skills, including buying condoms, negotiation of condom use and using condoms. These skills could be taught using tuition, role-play, feedback, modelling and practice. They are aimed at changing cognitions, preparing individuals for action and encouraging people to practise different aspects of the sequences involved in translating beliefs into behaviour. These problems with school sex education, reflect the debates about using psychological models to examine sexual behaviour and emphasize a need to place an individual's beliefs with the context of an interaction between individuals. In addition, the discussions about sex education in schools highlights the social context in which sex occurs.

An individual's social world

Information about sex also comes from an individual's social world in terms of one's peers, parents and siblings. Holland *et al.* (1990a) argued that sex education and the process of learning about sex occurs in the context of a multitude of different sources of information. They redefined the 'problem of sex education' as something that is broader than acquiring facts. They also argued that the resulting knowledge not only influences an individual's own knowledge and beliefs but also creates their sexuality. They identified the following five sources: school, peers, parents, magazines, and partners and relationships. Holland *et al.* argued that through these different sources, individuals learn about sex and their sexuality and suggested that 'the constructions which are presented are of women as passive, as potential victims of male sexuality or at best reproductive' (p. 43). However, they also argued that women do not simply passively accept this version of sexuality but are in a 'constant process of negotiating and re-negotiating the meaning which others give to their behaviour' (p. 43). Therefore, perhaps any understanding of sexual behaviour should take place within an understanding of the social context of sex education in the broadest sense.

Power relations between men and women

Sex has also been studied within the context of power relations between men and women. Holland *et al.* (1990b) argued that condom use 'must be understood in the context of the contradictions and tensions of heterosexual relationships' and the 'gendered power relations which construct and constrain choices and decisions'. They presented examples of power inequalities between men and women and the range of ways in which this can express itself, from coercion to rape. For example, one woman in their study said 'I wasn't forced to do it but I didn't want to do it' and another explained her ambivalence to sex as 'like do you want a coffee? Okay, fine you drink the coffee, because you don't really like drinking coffee but you drink it anyway'. In fact, empirical research suggests that men's intentions to use condoms may be more likely to correlate with actual behaviour than women's, perhaps because women's intentions may be inhibited by the sexual context (Abraham *et al.* 1996). Sex should also be understood within the context of gender and power.

Social norms of the gay community

Sex also occurs between two individuals of the same gender and within gay communities, which have their own sets of norms and values. A recent study by Flowers *et al.* (1997; 1998: 411) explored 'the transformation of men who come to find themselves within a specific gay culture, one in which there are clear values which structure their new social world, shaping their relationships and their sexual behaviour'. Therefore, Flowers *et al.* asked the question 'How do the social norms and values of the gay community influence gay men's sexual practices?' They interviewed 20 gay men from a small town in Northern England about their experiences of becoming gay within a gay community. The results provided some interesting insights into the norms of gay culture and the impact of this social context on an individual's behaviour. First, the study describes how men gain access to the gay community: 'through sex and socialising they come to recognise the presence of other gay men where once . . . they only felt isolation' (p. 415); second, the study illustrates how simply having a gay identity is not enough to prepare them for their new community and that they have 'to learn a gay specific knowledge and a gay language'; and third the study describes how this new culture influences their sexual behaviour. For example, the interviewees described how feelings of romance, trust, love, commitment, inequality within the relationship, lack of experience and desperation resulted in having anal sex without a condom even though they had the knowledge that their behaviour was risky (Flowers *et al.* 1997; 1998). Therefore, sexual behaviour also occurs within the context of specific communities with their own sets of norms and values.

Discourses about sex, HIV and illness

Sex also takes place within the broader context of theories and discussions about sex, HIV and illness. This literature is beyond the scope of this book, but includes discussions about HIV as a metaphor for concerns about sexuality and death in the late twentieth century (Sontag 1988), the social response to HIV as a moral panic (Weeks 1985) and the social construction of sex through theory and practice (Foucault 1979). Many of these discussions about sex challenge the traditional biological reductionist approach to sex and argue for an understanding of sex within a context of social meanings and discourses.

To conclude

Since the beginning of the twentieth century sex has been studied as an activity rather than in terms of its biological outcome. Recently, sex has also been examined in terms of it being a risk to health. Psychologists have contributed to this literature in terms of an examination of sexual behaviour both in the context of pregnancy avoidance and HIV/AIDS. These behaviours have been predominantly understood using cognitive models, which emphasize individual differences and individual cognitions. However, sex presents a problem for psychologists as it is intrinsically an interactive behaviour involving more than one person. Therefore, cognitive models have been expanded in an attempt to emphasize cognitions about the individual's social world, particularly in terms of the relationship. To further the understanding of sex as an interaction, qualitative methods have been used to examine the process of negotiation. However, sex also occurs within a broader social context. Social cognition models have also been developed in an attempt to address individuals' representations of this world – their normative beliefs. However, perhaps an understanding of sexual behaviour can only take place within the wider context of educational influences, power relations, community norms and theories about sexuality.

? Questions

1 To what extent do decision-making models predict contraceptive use?

2 Is contraceptive use a rational process?

3 Can social cognition models be expanded to understand contraceptive use as an interaction?

4 Why do people use condoms?

5 How can qualitative research contribute to an understanding of condom use?

6 To what extent can psychology incorporate the context of a behaviour?

7 To what extent do the problems highlighted by the sex literature relate to other health behaviours?

8 Describe a possible research study aimed at predicting condom use in adolescents.

▶ For discussion

Health education campaigns frequently use billboards and magazines to promote safe sex. Consider a recent advertisement and discuss whether or not this would encourage you to use condoms.

Assumptions in health psychology

The research into sex and contraceptive use highlights some of the assumptions that are central to psychology as follows:

1 *Methodology accesses information, it does not create it.* It is believed that questionnaires/interviews provide us with insights into what people think and believe. However, does the method of asking questions influence the results? For example, do people have beliefs about risk until they are asked about risk? Do people have behavioural

intentions prior to being asked whether they intend to behave in a particular way?

2 *Individuals can be studied separately from their social context.* Social psychologists have studied processes such as conformity, group dynamics, obedience to authority and diffusion of responsibility, all of which suggest that individuals behave differently when on their own than when in the presence of others and also indicate the extent to which an individual's behaviour is determined by their context. However, much psychological research continues to examine behaviour and beliefs out of context. To what extent can psychological research incorporate the context? To what extent should it attempt to incorporate the environment?

3 *Theories are derived from data.* Theories are not data themselves. It is assumed that eventually we will develop the best way to study sex, which will enable us to understand and predict sexual behaviour. However, perhaps the different approaches to sex can tell us something about the way we see individuals. For example, attempting to incorporate interactions between individuals into an understanding of sex may be a better way of understanding sex, and it may also suggest that we now see individuals as being interactive. In addition, examining the social context may also suggest that our model of individuals is changing and we see individuals as being social products.

Further reading

Abraham, C., Sheeran, P., Abrams, D., Spears, R. and Marks, D. (1991) Young people learning about AIDS: a study of beliefs and information sources, *Health Education Research: Theory and Practice*, 6: 19–29.
This paper examines the multitude of information sources used by young people in the context of current school health education.

Gallois, C., Terry, D., Timmins, P., Kashima, Y. and McCamish, M. (1994) Safe sex intentions and behaviour among heterosexuals and homosexual men: testing the theory of reasoned action, *Psychology and Health*, 10: 1–16.
This study uses the TRA to examine condom use and in particular focuses on the relationship between intentions and actual behaviour.

Holland, J., Ramazanoglu, C. and Scott, S. (1990) Managing risk and experiencing danger: Tensions between government AIDS health education policy and young women's sexuality, *Gender and Education*, 2: 125–46.
This paper presents some of the results from the WRAP studies and examines how young women feel about their sexuality in the context of HIV.

CHAPTER 9

Screening

Chapter overview

This chapter examines definitions of screening and describes the history of the screening of populations both in general practice and in hospital-based medical centres. It then outlines the guidelines for developing screening programmes and assesses the psychological predictors of the uptake of screening. The chapter then examines recent research which has emphasized the negative consequences of screening in terms of ethical principles, the cost effectiveness and the possible psychological consequences.

This chapter covers:

- What is screening?
- Guidelines for screening
- Psychological predictors of screening uptake
- Screening as problematic
- Is screening ethical?
- Is screening cost-effective?
- What are the psychological consequences of screening?

What is screening?

There are three forms of prevention aimed at improving a nation's health:

1 *Primary prevention* refers to the modification of risk factors (such as smoking, diet, alcohol intake) before illness onset. The recently developed health promotion campaigns are a form of primary prevention.
2 *Secondary prevention* refers to interventions aimed at detecting illness at an asymptomatic stage of development so that its progression can be halted or retarded. *Screening* is a form of secondary prevention.
3 *Tertiary prevention* refers to the rehabilitation of patients or treatment interventions once an illness has manifested itself.

Screening programmes (secondary prevention) take the form of health checks, such as measuring weight, blood pressure, height (particularly in children), urine and carrying out cervical smears and mammograms. There are two types of screening: *opportunistic screening,* which involves using the time when a patient is involved with the medical services to measure aspects of their health, and *population screening,* which involves setting up services specifically aimed at identifying problems.

The history of the screening ethos

Early screening programmes

Screening has increasingly become an important facet of biomedicine throughout the twentieth century. The drive to detect an illness at an asymptomatic stage of its development (secondary prevention) can be seen throughout both secondary and primary care across the western world. In 1900, Gould introduced the regular health examination in the USA, which stimulated interest in the concept of population screening. In Britain, the inter-war years saw the development of the Pioneer Health Centre in Peckham, South London, which provided both a social and health nucleus for the community and enabled the health of the local community to be surveyed and monitored with ease (Williamson and Pearse 1938; Pearse and Crocker 1943). The ethos of screening received impetus from multiphasic screening, which became popular in the USA in the late 1940s, and in 1951 the Kaiser Permanente organization incorporated screening methods into its health examinations. Sweden mounted a large-scale multiphasic screening programme that was completed in 1969 and similar programmes were set up in the former West Germany and Japan in 1970. In London, in 1973, the Medical Centre at King's Cross organized a computerized automated unit that could screen 15,000 individuals a year. General practice also promoted the use of screening to evaluate what

Last (1963) called the 'iceberg of disease'. In the 1960s and 1970s, primary care developed screening programmes for disorders such as anaemia (Ashworth 1963), diabetes (Redhead 1960), bronchitis (Gregg 1966), cervical cancer (Freeling 1965) and breast cancer (Holleb *et al.* 1960).

Recent screening programmes

Enthusiasm for screening has continued into the last two decades of the twentieth century. Forrest chaired a working party in 1985 to consider the validity of a breast screening programme in the UK. The report (Forrest 1986) concluded that the evidence of the efficacy of screening was sufficient to establish a screening programme with 3-year intervals. Furthermore, in the late 1980s, Family Practitioner Committees began computer-assisted calls of patients for cervical screening, and in 1993 a report from the Professional Advisory Committee for the British Diabetic Association suggested implementing a national screening programme for non-insulin-dependent diabetes for individuals aged 40–75 years (Patterson 1993). In addition, the new contracts for GPs include mandatory tasks such as assessments of patients over 75, and financial incentives for achieving set levels of immunizations, cervical screening and health checks for pre-school children (Department of Health and Welsh Office 1989). Likewise, practice nurses routinely measure weight and blood pressure to screen for obesity and hypertension. Recent screening programmes have also focused on genetic risks for illness in the form of preconceptual screening, screening during pregnancy and antenatal care. Such programmes aim to identify those individuals at risk from disorders such as cystic fibrosis, Down's syndrome, Alzheimer's disease and forms of muscular dystrophy, though many of these programmes are still in the early stages of development.

Screening as a useful tool

The proliferation of screening programmes was at first welcomed as an invaluable and productive means of improving the health of a country's population. It was seen as a cost-effective method of preventing disease as well as providing statistics on the prevalence and incidence of a wide variety of disorders and illnesses. Morris (1964), in his book *Uses of Epidemiology*, stressed the importance of penetrating to the 'early minor stages', then back to the precursors of disease and then back to its predispositions. In 1968, Butterfield, in a Rock Carling Lecture on priorities in medicine, advocated a new emphasis on screening in health-care delivery. This enthusiasm is reflected in a statement by Edward VII that is often repeated: 'If preventable, why not prevented?'

Guidelines for screening

As a result of the enthusiasm for screening, sets of criteria have been established. Wilson (1965) outlined the following set of screening criteria:

- **The disease**
  An important problem
  Recognizable at the latent or early symptomatic stage
  Natural history must be understood (including development from latent to symptomatic stage)
- **The screen**
  Suitable test or examination (of reasonable sensitivity and specificity)
  Test should be acceptable by the population being screened
  Screening must be a continuous process
- **Follow-up**
  Facilities must exist for assessment and treatment
  Accepted form of effective treatment
  Agreed policy on whom to treat
- **Economy**
  Cost must be economically balanced in relation to possible expenditure on medical care as a whole.

More recently, the criteria have been developed as follows:

- The disease must be sufficiently prevalent and/or sufficiently serious to make early detection appropriate.
- The disease must be sufficiently well defined to permit accurate diagnosis.
- There must be a possibility (or probability) that the disease exists undiagnosed in many cases (i.e. that the disease is not so manifest by symptoms as to make rapid diagnosis almost inevitable).
- There must be a beneficial outcome from early diagnosis in terms of disease treatment or prevention of complications.
- There must be a screening test that has good sensitivity and specificity and a reasonably positive predictive value in the population to be screened.

Psychological predictors of the uptake of screening

The numbers of individuals who attend different screening programmes vary enormously according to factors such as the country, the illness being screened and time of the screening programme. For example, uptake for neonatal screening for phenylketonuria is almost 100 per cent. However, whereas up to 99 per cent of pregnant women in Sweden and France undertake HIV testing (Larsson *et al.* 1990; Moatti *et al.* 1990), in the UK and North America only a small minority elect to take the test. Marteau

(1993) suggested that there are three main factors that influence uptake of screening: patient factors, health professional factors and organizational factors.

Patient factors

Several studies have been carried out to examine which factors predict the uptake of screening. MacLean *et al.* (1984) reported that women who attended for breast screening were more likely to be of high socio-economic status, more sympathetic to screening and to have suffered less anxiety following the invitation to attend. Age and gender have also been suggested as factors with Owens *et al.* (1987) reporting that older women were more likely to attend for breast screening than younger women and Simpson *et al.* (1997) concluding that older women were more likely to attend a worksite screening programme for cardiovascular disease than either younger women or men. In addition, Waller *et al.* (1990) suggested that those individuals who are the most healthy are more likely to attend for an HIV test. Other patient factors that may influence uptake are their health beliefs, which can be measured using the different models, a desire for medical intervention and a determination to avoid feelings of regret. For example, Simpson *et al.* (1997) indicated that attenders at a worksite screening programme perceived fewer barriers to attending than non-attenders, including fear of the results and not wanting anyone to tell them how to live their lives, and perceived themselves to be less at risk from serious diseases such as heart disease, stroke and cancer. Further, Shiloh *et al.* (1997) examined the predictors of uptake for four screening programmes (a dental check-up, blood pressure measurement and cholesterol testing, a cervical smear, mammography) and suggested that both the cognitions derived from a range of models and emotional factors such as reassurance predicted uptake. However, they also argued that although beliefs and emotions predict screening uptake, the nature of these beliefs and emotions is very much dependent upon the screening programme being considered.

Health professional factors

Marteau and Johnston (1990) argued that it is important to assess health professionals' beliefs and behaviour alongside those of the patients. In a study of general practitioners' attitudes and screening behaviour, a belief in the effectiveness of screening was associated with an organized approach to screening and time spent on screening (Havelock *et al.* 1988). Such factors may influence patient uptake. In addition, the means of presenting a test may also influence patient uptake. For example, uptake rates for HIV testing at antenatal clinics are reported to vary from 3 to 82 per cent (Meadows *et al.* 1990). These rates may well be related to the way in which these tests were offered by the health professional, which in turn may reflect the health professional's own beliefs about the test.

FOCUS ON RESEARCH 9.1

TESTING A THEORY – PREDICTING SCREENING

A study to examine the role of the health belief model, health locus of control and emotional control in predicting women's cancer screening behaviour (Murray and McMillan 1993).

This study examines the role of three social psychological models in predicting breast self-examination and cervical screening behaviour. The study illustrates how theories can be empirically tested and how research results can be used to develop interventions to promote screening behaviour.

Background

It is generally believed that early detection of both breast and cervical cancer may reduce mortality from these illnesses. Therefore, screening programmes aim to help the detection of these diseases at the earliest possible stages. However, even when invited to attend for cervical screening, or when encouraged to practise breast self-examination many women still do not carry out these health protective behaviours. Social psychology models have been used to predict cancer screening behaviour. This study examined the health belief model and health locus of control (see Chapter 2) in the context of cancer screening. In addition, the authors included a measure of emotional control (sometimes described as expressed emotion, repression and defensiveness). Individuals with high emotional control are sometimes described as having a cancer prone personality (see Chapter 13), which has been linked to cancer onset.

Methodology

Subjects A letter informing residents about a regional health survey was sent to 1530 randomly selected addresses in Northern Ireland. An interviewer then visited each address and contacted a 'responsible adult' in order to record details of all of those in the household aged over 16. One person from each household was then randomly selected and left a questionnaire. After follow-up letters and visits to the household, 65.1 per cent of the eligible sample completed the questionnaire. This paper reports the results from 391 women who completed questions about breast and cervical screening behaviour.

Design The study involved a cross-sectional design with subjects completing a questionnaire once.
Measures The questionnaire consisted of the following measures:

1 *Screening behaviour (the dependent variables).* The subjects were asked about their breast and cervical screening behaviour.

- *Breast screening behaviour*: the subjects were asked 'If you examine your breasts for lumps how often do you do this?' (rated from 'once a month' to less than 'once every 6 months').
- *Cervical screening behaviour*: the subjects were asked (i) 'have you had a cervical smear test' (rated 'once', 'several times', 'never'), (ii) 'Did you have a smear test because . . . (a) you asked for it, (b) your doctor suggested it, (c) it was taken routinely at a post-natal check-up, (d) because of some other reason. From these responses the women were classified as non-attenders, passive attenders (following advice from someone else) or active attenders (asked for the test).

2 *Health beliefs (the independent variables).* The subjects rated 22 items for how much they agreed with them. These items reflected the dimensions of the health belief model as follows:

- *Susceptibility*: the subjects rated items such as 'my chances of getting cancer are great' and 'my physical health makes it more likely that I will get cancer'.
- *Seriousness*: the subjects rated items such as 'the thought of cancer scares me' and 'I am afraid to even think about cancer'.
- *Benefits*: the subjects rated items such as 'if cancer is detected early it can be successfully treated' and 'there has been much progress in the treatment of cancer in the past 10 years'.
- *Barriers*: the subjects rated items such as 'I just don't like doctors or hospitals' and 'I would be afraid that I might need to have an operation'.
- *Costs*: the subjects rated items such as 'I would have trouble because of the distance or time to get to the doctor or clinic' and 'I would have to wait a long time at the doctor's office or clinic'.

In addition, the questionnaire included measures of the following health beliefs:

- *Health motivation*: the subjects were asked whether they engaged in a list of five health-related activities (e.g. take physical exercise, reduce alcohol consumption).
- *Cancer knowledge*: the subjects were asked open-ended questions about their knowledge of the early warning signs of breast and cervical cancer.
- *Confidence*: the subjects were asked to rate their confidence in performing breast self-examination as a measure of their self-efficacy.
- *Contact with cancer*: the subjects were asked whether or not a member of their family had ever had cancer.

3 *Health locus of control (the independent variables).* The subjects completed the 18-item Multidimensional Health Locus of Control Scale (MHLC) (Wallston *et al.* 1978). The questionnaire was used to provide a measure of internal control (e.g. 'If I get sick it is my own behaviour which determines how soon I get well again'), external control/powerful others (e.g. 'Whenever I don't feel well I should consult my doctor') and external control/chance (e.g. 'Good health is largely a matter of good luck').
4 *Emotional control (the independent variables).* The subjects completed the 21-item Courtauld Emotional Control scale developed by Watson and Greer (1983). This consists of three subscales to measure the extent to which someone expresses or controls (i) anger, (ii) depressed mood and (iii) anxiety.

Demographic characteristics In addition, subjects completed questions about their age, social class, marital status and religion.

Results

The results were analysed to assess the role of the different social psychological models in predicting screening behaviour for both breast and cervical cancer. Originally, individual correlations were evaluated between the dependent variables (breast cancer and cervical cancer screening behaviour) and the subjects' demographic characteristics, their health beliefs, health locus of control and their emotional control.

Breast self-examination

The results showed that breast self-examination was more frequent amongst those who attended for smear tests; negatively related to age and social class, a high belief in the costs of attendance for treatment, a high belief in the role of powerful others; and positively related to marital status, benefits of treatment, health motivation, knowledge of breast and cervical cancer.

Cervical screening behaviour

The results indicated that attending for cervical smears was positively related to religion, marital status, perceived benefits of treatment, health motivation, knowledge of breast and cervical cancer; and negatively associated with social class, perceived barriers and costs and a belief in the role of chance.

The results were then analysed to assess the overall best predictors of screening behaviour using multiple-regression analysis. This type of analysis puts a multitude of variables into the equation to see which combination of the independent variables is the best predictor of the dependent variable. The results suggest that the best predictor of breast self-examination was confidence in carrying out the examination (self-efficacy) and the best predictor of attending for cervical smears was having a lower fear of the consequences of the investigation (barriers).

Conclusion

The results from this study provide some support for the individual components of the health belief model and health locus of control in predicting screening behaviour for both cervical and breast cancer. In particular, the results suggest that self-efficacy (added to the recent version of the HBM, see Chapter 2) and barriers are the most powerful predictors of behaviour. However, the results provide no support for a role of emotional control in screening behaviour. The authors conclude that health promotion aimed at increasing breast self-examination 'must consider how to improve women's confidence in how to practise it' and education aimed at promoting attendance for cervical smears should 'reduce the anxiety felt among many women about the possible consequences of the investigation'. This paper therefore illustrates how a theory can be tested, and how the results from such a study could be turned into practice.

Organizational factors

Many organizational factors may also influence the uptake of screening. Research has examined the effects of the means of invitation on the uptake rate and indicates that if the invitation is issued in person, and if the individual is expected to opt out, not in, the rates of uptake are higher (Mann *et al.* 1988; Smith *et al.* 1990). The place of the screening programme may also be influential with more accessible settings promoting high uptake. In addition, making attendance at a screening programme mandatory rather than voluntary will also obviously have an effect (Marteau 1993).

Screening as problematic

Over the past decade, however, a new dimension has emerged in the screening literature, namely, the negative elements of screening. There are now debates about the following aspects of screening: (1) *ethics*, in terms of the relevance of the four main ethical principles (beneficence, non-maleficence, autonomy and justice); (2) *the cost effectiveness* of screening programmes; and (3) the possible *psychological side-effects* of screening on the individual. These criticisms constitute what can be seen as a backlash against the screening of populations.

Is screening ethical?

Debates about the ethical issues surrounding screening have traditionally been polarized between what Sackett and Holland (1975) referred to as 'the evangelists and snails' (1975). These debates are best understood within the context of the four major ethical principles relating to decision-making principles in medicine: beneficence, non-maleficence, autonomy and justice.

Beneficence – screening as beneficial to the patient

Beneficence refers to the likelihood that any benefits to the patient will outweigh any burdens. Screening should therefore bring about benefits to the patient in terms of detecting a treatable disease or abnormality and enabling the individual's life to be prolonged or enhanced. There is evidence both in favour and against screening as a benefit to the patient.

Evidence for beneficence

In terms of screening for hypertension, Hart (1987) has argued 'we are surely under a moral if not legal obligation to record blood pressure at least once in every 5 year span for every registered adult in our practice'. In terms of cervical screening it has been estimated that for every 40,000 smears one life has been saved (*Lancet* 1985). In terms of breast cancer, reports from the Health Insurance Plan Study (Shapiro *et al.* 1972) suggested that early detection of breast cancer through screening reduced mortality in the study group compared with the control group by 30 per cent. Results at follow-up indicated that the study group were still benefiting after 12 years (Shapiro *et al.* 1982). Further results concerning the benefits of breast screening have been reported following a large random controlled trial in Sweden (Lundgren 1981). Hinton (1992: 231) concluded from his review of the literature that 'lives may be saved by annual mammographic screening'. Jones (1992) argued that screening for colorectal cancer may also be beneficial. He suggested that the 'evidence and arguments . . . are becoming compelling' and noted that the death rate due to colorectal cancer was ten times that due to cervical cancer, for which there is an existing screening programme. In addition, the identification of the absence of illness through screening may also benefit the patient in that a negative result may 'give health back to the patient' (Grimes 1988). Therefore, according to the ethical principle of beneficence, screening may have some positive effects on those individuals being screened.

Evidence against beneficence

Electronic fetal monitoring was introduced as a way of improving obstetric outcomes. However, the results from two well-controlled trials indicated that such monitoring may increase the rate of Caesarean section without any benefit to the babies both immediately after birth (MacDonald *et al.* 1985) and at 4 years of age (Grant and Elbourne 1989). In addition, electronic fetal monitoring appeared to increase the rate of cerebral palsy measured at 18 months of age (Shy *et al.* 1990). In a recent review of the effects of antenatal blood pressure screening on the incidence of pre-eclampsia (high blood pressure in pregnancy, which threatens the mother's life), the authors concluded that the introduction of antenatal screening has had no significant effect on pre-eclampsia, suggesting that this screening process does not benefit the individual. Recent papers have also questioned the efficacy of screening for congenital dislocation of the hip in neonates (Leck 1986), hypertension, breast cancer and cervical cancer in terms of the relative effectiveness of early (rather than later) medical interventions and the effects of simply increasing the lead time (the period of time between detection and symptoms).

Non-maleficence – screening must do no harm

Skrabanek (1988) suggested that screening should be subjected to the same rigours as any experimental procedure, that the possible risks should be evaluated and that the precept of 'first do no harm' should be remembered. Therefore, for screening to be ethical, it must not only benefit the patient, but it must also have no negative consequences either to the individual or to society as a whole. The psychological and financial consequences of screening will be dealt with under later headings. However, screening may cause personal harm in terms of biological consequences and false-negative (receiving a negative result when the problem is actually present) or false-positive (receiving a positive result when the problem is actually absent) results; it may also cause social harm in terms of the medicalization of populations and the exacerbation of the existing stigmatization of certain groups of individuals.

Personal harm

Some of the techniques used to monitor an individual's health may have a detrimental effect on their biological state. This is of particular concern for the frequent use of mammography for the detection of breast cancer. Evidence for the harmful effects of the irradiation of breast tissue and the links to cancer can be found in reports of breast cancer in women who have been treated for benign conditions using radiation therapy (Metler *et al.* 1969; Simon 1977), in survivors of the bombings of Hiroshima and Nagasaki (Wanebo *et al.* 1968) and in women who have been given fluoroscopy for tuberculosis (MacKenzie 1965). It has been argued that there is a threshold, below which radiation could be considered totally safe, and that the above examples of an association between irradiation and breast cancer are due to the unusually high levels of radiation (Perquin *et al.* 1976). However, there is some disagreement with this view. In particular, Upton *et al.* (1977) suggested that exposure to 1 rad would increase the risk of breast cancer by 1 per cent. Furthermore, Strax (1978) suggested that if 40 million women were screened for 20 years, 120 would die from radiation-induced breast cancer. However, since these concerns were raised, the dose of radiation used in mammography has been reduced, although some concerns still remain.

All tests are fallible and none can promise 100 per cent accuracy. Therefore, there is always the chance of false positives and false negatives. A false-positive result may lead to unnecessary treatment interventions and the associated anxiety and uncertainty. A false-negative result may lead to an illness remaining undetected, untreated and consequently progressing without medical intervention. In addition, a false-negative result may lead to subsequent signs of illness (e.g. a breast lump, vaginal discharge) being ignored by the patient.

Social harm

Zola (1972) has argued that medicine is a means of social control and suggested that there is a danger if individuals become too reliant on experts. In terms of screening, monitoring and surveillance of populations could be seen as a forum for not only examining individuals but controlling them. This argument is also made by Illich (1974) in his book *Medical Nemesis,* where he argued that medicine is taking over the responsibility for people's health and creating a society of medical addicts. Screening epitomizes this shift towards social control in that not only are the ill seen by the medical profession but also the healthy as all individuals are now 'at risk' from illness (Armstrong 1995). Skrabanek (1988: 1155) argued that screening and the medicalization of health 'serves as a justification for State intrusion into people's private lives, and for stigmatising those who do not conform'.

The possibility that screening may exacerbate existing stigma of particular social groups is particularly relevant to the screening for genetic disorders. At present, society is constituted of a variety of individuals, some of whom have genetic deficits such as Down's syndrome, cystic fibrosis and sickle cell anaemia. Although these individuals may be subjected to stereotyping and stigma, society provides treatment and support and attempts to integrate them into the rest of the population. It is possible, however, that screening for such disorders would lead to terminations of pregnancy and a reduction in this stigmatized population. Although this would lead to fewer individuals with these disorders (this may be a positive consequence, as no one wants to suffer from sickle cell anaemia) the individuals who are born with these problems may face increased stigma as they would be part of a greatly reduced minority existing in a world with reduced social provisions for support and treatment.

Autonomy – the patient has a right to choose

The third ethical principle is that of autonomy. This is based on the view that 'mentally competent and mature individuals should make decisions about their own future, subject to the constraints required to ensure social order' (Burke 1992). Proponents of screening argue that screening is central to promoting autonomy in that the individual has a right to have access to information about their health status. According to this model of screening, the doctor is the patient's gatekeeper to relevant information. However, screening may also undermine an individual's autonomy if it is construed as a form of social control and doctors are seen as 'lifestyle police'.

Justice – the equal distribution of resources

The fourth ethical principle of justice refers to the need for an equal distribution of resources. This principle is relevant because screening programmes may be costly and involve shifting funds from other services. In addition, the 'inverse care law' (Hart 1971), which suggests that those who seek out tests most frequently are often those who need them the least, when applied to screening, highlights a shifting of finances to the most healthy individuals in society.

Is screening cost-effective?

The second problem with screening concerns its cost-effectiveness. A cost-effectiveness analysis involves assessing either how to achieve a set objective at minimum cost or how to use a fixed resource to produce the best output. In terms of screening, this raises issues about the objectives of screening (to detect asymptomatic illness, which can be treated) and the degree of resources required to achieve these objectives (minimum interventions such as opportunistic weighing *vs* expensive interventions such as breast screening clinics). The economic considerations of screening have been analysed for different policies for cervical screening (Smith and Chamberlain 1987). The different policies include: (1) opportunistic screening (offer a smear test when an individual presents at the surgery), (2) offer a smear every 5 years, (3) offer a smear every 3 years and (4) offer a smear annually. The results from this analysis are shown in Fig. 9.1. These different policies have been offered as possible solutions to the problem of screening for cervical cancer. The results suggest that annual screening in England and Wales would cost £165 million and would potentially prevent 4300 cancers, whereas smears every 5 years would cost £34 million and would potentially prevent 3900 cancers.

The problem of cost-effectiveness is also highlighted by a discussion of the OXCHECK and Family Heart Study results (Muir *et al.* 1994; Wood *et al.* 1994). Both studies indicated that intensive screening, counselling and health checks have only a moderate effect on risk factors and the

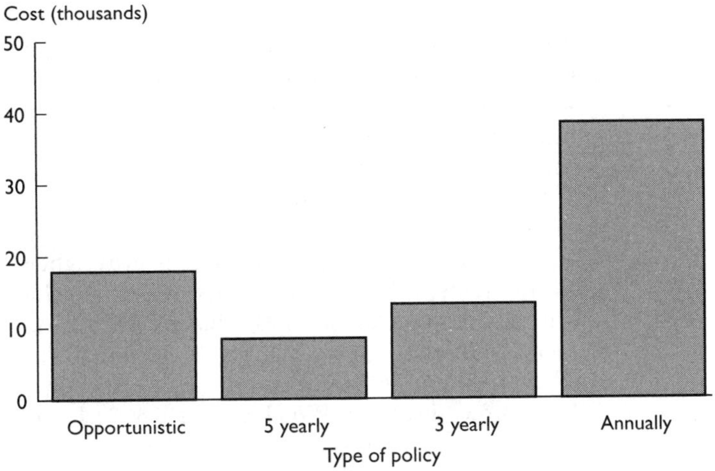

Figure 9.1 Costs per potential cancer prevented for different screening policies

authors discuss these results in terms of the implications for government policies for health promotion through doctor-based interventions.

The Family Heart Study

The Family Heart Study (Wood *et al.* 1994) examined the effects of screening and lifestyle interventions on cardiovascular risk factors in families over a one-year period. The study involved 26 general practices in 13 towns in Britain and recruited 12,472 individuals aged 40–59 years. The total sample consisted of 7460 men and 5012 women. The practices within each town were paired according to socio-demographic characteristics and were randomly designated as either the intervention or the comparison practice. Intervention practices were then randomly allocated either to a further comparison group or to an intervention group. This provided both an internal and external comparison with the subjects receiving the intervention. All intervention practices received screening, but only the intervention group of these practices received lifestyle counselling and follow-up within the one-year period. All subjects from all practices were followed up at one year. The screening process involved an appointment with a trained research nurse, who asked about demographic, lifestyle and medical factors and measured height, weight, carbon monoxide, blood pressure, blood glucose and blood cholesterol. The subjects in the intervention group also received lifestyle counselling and repeated follow-up. The counselling used a client-centred family approach and involved an assessment of the patients' risk status, educational input and a booklet for the subject to document their personally negotiated lifestyle changes. All subjects were then offered follow-up every 1, 2, 3, 4, 6 or 12 months, depending on their risk status. Outcome was measured at the follow-up in terms of changes in the main risk factors for coronary heart disease and the Dundee risk score, which is dependent on serum cholesterol concentration, systolic blood pressure, and previous and current smoking behaviour. Outcome was compared within the intervention practices, between the intervention practice and the internal comparison practice, and between the intervention practice and practices in the external comparison group. The results showed a 16 per cent reduction in overall risk score in the intervention practices at one year, a 4 per cent reduction in smoking, a small reduction in systolic (7 mmHg) and diastolic (3 mmHg) blood pressure and marginal reductions in weight (1 kg) and cholesterol concentrations (0.1 mM). The results showed no changes in blood glucose levels. In addition, the greatest changes in risk status were reported in subjects with the highest risk levels. Although this intensive screening and intervention did result in changes in risk for coronary heart disease in the correct direction, Wood *et al.* (1994: 319) concluded that 'whether these small reductions can be sustained long term is not known, but even if they were they would correspond only to a 12 per cent lower risk of coronary heart disease events'. The authors also concluded that the government sponsored health promotion clinics 'would probably have achieved considerably less and possibly no change at all' (p. 319) and that 'the government's screening policy cannot be justified by these results' (p. 313).

The OXCHECK study

The results from the OXCHECK study also produced similarly pessimistic conclusions (Muir *et al.* 1994). This study involved 6124 patients recruited from five urban practices in Bedfordshire and aimed to evaluate the effectiveness of health checks by nurses in general practice in reducing risk factors for cardiovascular disease. All subjects received an initial health check and the intervention group received an additional follow-up health check after one year (further results were also collected for subjects over a 4-year period). The health checks involved the nurse recording information about personal and family history of heart disease, stroke, hypertension, diabetes and cancer. Information about smoking history, alcohol consumption and habitual diet, height, weight, serum cholesterol concentration and blood pressure was also recorded. The nurses were also instructed to counsel patients about risk factors and to negotiate priorities and targets for risk reduction. The re-examination was briefer than the original health check but it involved re-measurement of the same profile and lifestyle factors. The results showed a lower cholesterol level (by 2.3 per cent) in the intervention group than the control group, lower systolic (2.5 per cent) and diastolic (2.4 per cent) blood pressure, and no differences in body mass index, or smoking prevalence or quit rates. The authors concluded that using health checks to reduce smoking may be ineffective as the effectiveness of health information may be diluted if the health check attempts to change too many risk factors at once. They suggested that the reduction in blood pressure was probably due to an accommodation effect, suggesting that the health checks were ineffective. Muir *et al.* (1994: 312) also concluded that, although the health checks did appear to reduce serum cholesterol concentration, 'it is disappointing that the difference . . . was smaller in men than in women in view of the greater effect of cholesterol concentration on absolute risk in men' and they questioned whether such a shift in concentration could be sustained in the long term in the light of a previous trial in Oxfordshire. Therefore, although the results of the OXCHECK study suggested some reduction in risk factors for cardiovascular disease, the authors were fairly pessimistic in their presentation of these reductions.

Both of the above studies suggested that screening and minimal interventions are not cost-effective, as the possible benefits are not worthy of the amount of time and money needed to implement the programmes.

The effects of screening on the psychological state of the individual

The third problem with screening concerns its impact on the individuals psychological state.

The debates

Early evaluations of screening included an assessment of screening outcome in terms of the patients' understanding and recall of their diagnosis, not in terms of possible negative consequences (Sibinga and Friedman 1971; Reynolds *et al.* 1974). Recent discussions of the effects of screening, however, have increasingly emphasized negative consequences. McCormick (1989) in a discussion of the consequences of screening, suggested that 'false positive smears in healthy women cause distress and anxiety that may never be fully allayed' (p. 208). Grimes (1988) stated that 'Promotion of health inevitably results in the awareness of sickness' and suggested that screening results in introspection. Skrabanek (1988) specifically expressed an awareness of the negative consequences of screening in his statement that 'the hazards of screening are undisputed: they include false positives leading to unnecessary investigations and treatments, with resulting iatrogenic morbidity both physical and psychological' (p. 1156). He was supported by Marteau (1989), who commented that 'a positive result in any screening test is invariably received with negative feelings'.

The research: the psychological impact of screening

The negative sequelae of screening have been described as 'the intangible costs' (Kinlay 1988) but research suggests that they are indeed experienced by the individuals involved. These psychological sequelae can be a result of the various different stages of the screening process:

1 The receipt of a screening invitation.
2 The receipt of a negative result.
3 The receipt of a positive result.
4 The effect of any subsequent interventions.
5 The existence of a screening programme.

1 *The receipt of a screening invitation.* Research indicates that sending out invitations to enter into a screening programme may not only influence an individual's behaviour, but also their psychological state. Fallowfield *et al.* (1990) carried out a retrospective study of women's responses to receiving a request to attend a breast screening session. Their results showed that 55 per cent reported feeling worried although 93 per cent were pleased. Dean *et al.* (1984) sent a measure of psychological morbidity to women awaiting breast screening and then followed them up 6 months later. The results showed no significant increases in psychological morbidity. However, when asked in retrospect 30 per cent said that they had become anxious after receiving the letter of invitation. Therefore, receiving a screening invitation may increase anxiety. However, some research suggests that this is not always the case (Cockburn *et al.* 1994).
2 *The receipt of a negative result.* It may be assumed that receiving a negative result would only decrease an individual's anxiety. Most research suggests that this is the case and that a negative result may create a sense of reassurance (Orton *et al.* 1991) or no change in anxiety (Dean *et al.* 1984; Sutton *et al.* 1995). Further, Sutton (1999) in his review of the literature on receiving a negative result following breast cancer screening concluded 'anxiety is not a significant problem among women who receive a negative screening result'. However, some research points towards a relationship between a negative result and an increased level of anxiety (Stoate 1989). Perhaps receiving any result is a reminder of the possibility of illness even if that illness is not yet present.
3 *The receipt of a positive result.* As expected, the receipt of a positive result can be associated with a variety of negative emotions ranging from worry to anxiety and shock. In 1978, Haynes *et al.* pointed to increased absenteeism following a diagnosis of hypertension and suggested that the diagnosis may have caused distress. Moreover, an abnormal cervical smear may generate anxiety, morbidity and even terror (Campion *et al.* 1988; Nathoo 1988; Wilkinson *et al.* 1990). Psychological costs have also been reported after screening for coronary heart disease (Stoate 1989), breast cancer (Fallowfield *et al.* 1990) and genetic diseases (Marteau *et al.* 1992). In addition, levels of depression have been found to be higher in those labelled as hypertensive (Bloom and Monterossa 1981). However, some research suggests that these psychological changes may only be maintained in the short term (Reelick *et al.* 1984). This decay in the psychological consequences has been particularly shown with the termination of pregnancy following the detection of fetal abnormalities (Black 1989).
4 *The psychological effects of subsequent interventions.* Although screening is aimed at detecting illness at an asymptomatic stage of development and subsequently delaying or averting its development, not all individuals identified as being 'at risk' receive treatment. In addition, not all of those identified as being 'at risk' will develop the illness. The recent literature concerning cervical cancer has debated the efficacy

of treating those individuals identified by cervical screening as 'at risk' and has addressed the possible consequence of this treatment. Duncan (1992) produced a report on NHS guidelines concerning the management of positive cervical smears. This suggested that all women with more severe cytological abnormalities should be referred for colposcopy, whilst others with milder abnormalities should be monitored by repeat cervical smears. Shafi (1994) suggests that it is important to consider the psychological impact of referral and treatment and that this impact may be greater than the risk of serious disease. However, Soutter and Fletcher (1994) suggest that there is evidence of a progression from mild abnormalities to invasive cervical cancer and that these women should also be directly referred for a colposcopy. This suggestion has been further supported by the results of a prospective study of 902 women presenting with mild or moderate abnormalities for the first time (Flannelly *et al.* 1994). A study carried out in 1993 examined the effects of a diagnosis of pre-cancerous changes of the cervix on the psychological state of a group of women and further assessed the additional impact of treatment (Palmer *et al.* 1993). The results showed that following the diagnosis, the women experienced high levels of intrusive thoughts, avoidance and high levels of anger. In addition, the diagnosis influenced their body image and sexuality. However, the authors reported that there was no additional impact of treatment on their psychological state. Perhaps, the diagnosis following screening is the factor that creates distress and the subsequent treatment is regarded as a constructive and useful intervention. Further research is needed to assess this aspect of screening.

5 *The existence of a screening programme.* Marteau (1993) suggested that the existence of screening programmes may influence social beliefs about what is healthy and may change society's attitude towards a screened condition. In a study by Marteau and Riordan (1992), health professionals were asked to rate their attitudes towards two hypothetical patients, one of whom had attended a screening programme and one had not. Both patients were described as having developed cervical cancer. The results showed that the health professionals held more negative attitudes towards the patient who had not attended. In a further study, community nurses were given descriptions of either a heart attack patient who had changed their health-related behaviour following a routine health check (healthy behaviour condition) or a patient who had not (unhealthy behaviour condition) (Ogden and Knight 1995). The results indicated that the nurses rated the patient in the unhealthy behaviour condition as less likely to follow advice, more responsible for their condition and rated the heart attack as more preventable. In terms of the wider effects of screening programmes, it is possible that the existence of such programmes encourages society to see illnesses as preventable and the responsibility of the individual, which may lead to victim blaming of those individuals who still develop these illnesses. This may be relevant to illnesses such as coronary heart disease, cervical cancer and breast cancer, which have established

screening programmes. In the future, it may also be relevant to genetic disorders, which could have been eradicated by terminations.

Why has this backlash happened?

Screening in the form of secondary prevention involves the professional in both detection and intervention and places the responsibility for change with the doctor. The backlash against screening could, therefore, be analysed as a protest against professional power and paternalistic intervention. Recent emphasis on the psychological consequences of screening could be seen as ammunition for this movement, and the negative consequences of population surveillance as a useful tool to burst the 'screening bubble'. Within this framework, the backlash is a statement of individualism and personal power.

The backlash may reflect, however, a shift in medical perspective – a shift from 'doctor help' to 'self-help'. In 1991, the British Government published the *Health of the Nation* document, which set targets for the reduction of preventable causes of mortality and morbidity (DoH 1991). This document no longer emphasized the process of secondary prevention – and therefore implicitly that of professional intervention – but illustrated a shift towards primary prevention, health promotion and 'self-help'. General practitioners are still encouraged to promote good health, but no longer by identifying diseases at an asymptomatic stage, but by encouraging patients to change their behaviour. During recent years there has been a shift towards self-help and health promotion, reflected by the preoccupation with diet, smoking, exercise and self-examination. Prevention and cure are no longer the result of professional intervention but come from the individual – patients are becoming their own doctors.

To conclude

Screening (secondary prevention) has been developed throughout the twentieth century as an important means to detect illness at an asymptomatic stage. Specific criteria have been developed to facilitate the screening process and research has been carried out to evaluate means to increase patient uptake of screening programmes. Recently, however, there have been debates about the problems with screening. These have concerned the ethics of screening, its cost-effectiveness and its possible psychological consequences. Although screening programmes are still being developed and regarded as an important facet of health, there has been a recent shift from a system of 'doctor help' to 'self-help', which is reflected in the growing interest in health beliefs and health behaviour and the process of health promotion.

Questions

1 Screening is an essential aspect of promoting health. Discuss.
2 Discuss the factors effecting the uptake of a screening programme.
3 Screening is unethical. Discuss.
4 What are the possible psychological side-effects of screening for illness?
5 Develop a research protocol designed to improve attendance for cervical screening.

For discussion

Consider which factors (e.g. beliefs, environmental) relate to whether you do or do not practise breast self-examination (for women) or testicular self-examination (for men).

Assumptions in health psychology

The literature on screening highlights some of the assumptions in health psychology:

1 *Challenging the biomedical model.* Health psychology aims to challenge the biomedical model. However, it often does not challenge some of the biomedical approaches to 'a successful outcome'. For example, although by examining the psychological consequences of screening it is suggested that screening for its own sake is not necessarily a good idea, there is still an emphasis on methods to improve uptake of screening. Perhaps promoting uptake implicitly accepts the biomedical belief that screening is beneficial.

2 *Changes in theory reflect progression.* It is often assumed that changes in theoretical perspective reflect greater knowledge about how individuals work and an improved understanding of health and illness. Therefore, within this perspective, a shift in focus towards an examination of the potential negative consequences of screening can be understood as a better understanding of ways to promote health. However, perhaps the 'backlash' against screening also reflects a different (not necessarily better) way of seeing individuals – a shift from individuals who require expert help from professionals towards a belief that individuals should help themselves.

Further reading

Norman, P. (1993) Predicting uptake of health checks in General Practice: Invitation methods and patients' health beliefs, *Social Science and Medicine*, 37: 53–9.

This paper illustrates how to use the HBM and how theory can be translated into practice.

Orbell, S. and Sheeran, P. (1993) Health psychology and uptake of preventive health services: A review of 30 years' research on cervical screening, *Psychology and Health*, 8: 417–33.

This paper provides a comprehensive overview of the literature on screening and examines the contribution of psychological, service provision and demographic factors.

Shaw, C., Abrams, K. and Marteau, T.M. (1999) Psychological impact of predicting individuals' risk of illness: A systematic review, *Social Science and Medicine*, 49: 1571–98.

This comprehensive review examines the research to date on the impact of receiving either a positive or negative test result in terms of cognitive, emotional and behavioural outcomes.

CHAPTER 10

Stress

Chapter overview

This chapter examines definitions of stress and looks at the early models of stress in terms of the fight/flight response, the general adaptation syndrome and life events theory. It then describes the introduction of the concept of appraisal, which included a role for psychological factors in eliciting stress, and outlines the psychophysiological model of stress. The chapter then assesses the relationship between stress and illness in terms of behavioural and physiological pathways and outlines the approach of psychoneuroimmunology (PNI). Finally, after examining the mediating factors that may influence the association between stress and illness, it highlights the role of social support and control on the stress–illness link.

This chapter covers:

- What is stress?
- The development of stress theories
- The role of psychological factors in stress
- Does stress cause illness?
- Which factors mediate the stress/illness link?

What is stress?

The term 'stress' means many things to many different people. A layperson may define stress in terms of pressure, tension, unpleasant external forces or an emotional response. Psychologists have defined stress in a variety of different ways. Contemporary definitions of stress regard the external environmental stress as a stressor (e.g. problems at work), the response to the stressor as stress or distress (e.g. the feeling of tension), and the concept of stress as something that involves biochemical, physiological, behavioural and psychological changes. Researchers have also differentiated between stress that is harmful and damaging (distress) and stress that is positive and beneficial (eustress). The most commonly used definition of stress was developed by Lazarus and Launier (1978), who regarded stress as a transaction between people and the environment. Within this definition, stress involves an interaction between the stressor and distress.

The development of stress models

Throughout the twentieth century, models of stress have varied in terms of their definition of stress, their differing emphasis on physiological and psychological factors, and their description of the relationship between individuals and their environment.

Cannon's fight or flight model

One of the earliest models of stress was developed by Cannon (1932). This was called the fight or flight model of stress, which suggested that external threats elicited the fight or flight response involving an increased activity rate and increased arousal. He suggested that these physiological changes enabled the individual to either escape from the source of stress or fight. Within Cannon's model, stress was defined as a response to external stressors, which was predominantly seen as physiological.

Selye's general adaptation syndrome

Selye's general adaptation syndrome (GAS) was developed in 1956 and described three stages in the stress process (Selye 1956). The initial stage was called the 'alarm' stage, which described an increase in activity, and occurred immediately the individual was exposed to a stressful situation. The second stage was called 'resistance', which involved coping and attempts to reverse the effects of the alarm stage. The third stage was called 'exhaustion', which was reached when the individual had been repeatedly exposed to the stressful situation and was incapable of showing further resistance. This model is shown in Fig. 10.1.

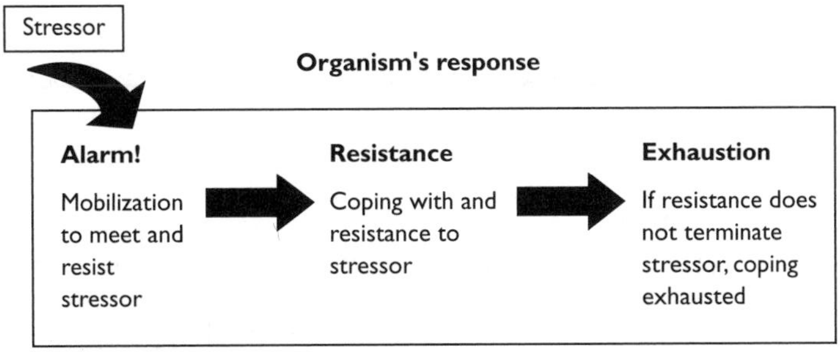

Figure 10.1 Selye's three-stage general adaptation syndrome

Both Cannon's early fight/flight model and Selye's GAS regarded the individual as automatically responding to an external stressor and described stress within a straightforward stimulus–response framework. They suggested a consistent response towards stressors and included only a minor role for psychological factors. Therefore, these two models described individuals as passive and as responding automatically to their external world.

Life events theory

In an attempt to depart from both Selye's and Cannon's models of stress, which emphasized physiological changes, the life events theory was developed to examine stress and stress-related changes as a response to life experiences. Holmes and Rahe (1967) developed the schedule of recent experiences (SRE), which provided respondents with an extensive list of possible life changes or life events. These ranged in supposed objective severity from events such as 'death of a spouse', 'death of a close family member' and 'jail term' to more moderate events such as 'son or daughter leaving home' and 'pregnancy' to minor events such as 'vacation', 'change in eating habits', 'change in sleeping habits' and 'change in number of family get-togethers'. Originally, the SRE was scored by simply counting the number of actual recent experiences. For example, someone who had experienced both the death of a spouse and the death of a close family member would receive the same score as someone who had recently had two holidays. It was assumed that this score reflected an indication of their level of stress. Early research using the SRE in this way showed some links between individuals' SRE score and their health status. However, this obviously crude method of measurement was later replaced by a variety of others, including a weighting system whereby each potential life event was weighted by a panel creating a degree of differentiation between the different life experiences.

The use of the SRE and similar measures of life experiences have been criticized for the following reasons.

The individual's own rating of the event is important

It has been argued by many researchers that life experiences should not be seen as either objectively stressful or benign, but that this interpretation of the event should be left to the individual. For example, a divorce for one individual may be regarded as extremely upsetting, whereas for another it may be a relief from an unpleasant situation. Pilkonis *et al.* (1985) gave checklists of life events to a group of subjects to complete and also interviewed them about these experiences. They reported that a useful means of assessing the potential impact of life events is to evaluate the individual's own ratings of the life experience in terms of (1) the desirability of the event (was the event regarded as positive or negative), (2) how much control they had over the event (was the outcome of the event determined by the individual or others), and (3) the degree of required adjustment following the event. This methodology would enable the individual's own evaluation of the events to be taken into consideration.

The problem of retrospective assessment

Most ratings of life experiences or life events are completed retrospectively, at the time when the individual has become ill or has come into contact with the health profession. This has obvious implications for understanding the causal link between life events and subsequent stress and stress-related illnesses. For example, if an individual has developed cancer and is asked to rate their life experiences over the last year, their present state of mind will influence their recollection of that year. This effect may result in the individual over-reporting negative events and under-reporting positive events if they are searching for a psychosocial cause of their illness ('I have developed cancer because my husband divorced me and I was sacked at work'). Alternatively, if they are searching for a more medical cause of their illness they may under-report negative life events ('I developed cancer because it is a family weakness; my lifestyle and experiences are unrelated as I have had an uneventful year'). The relationship between self-reports of life events and causal models of illness is an interesting area of research. Research projects could select to use this problem of selective recall as a focus for analysis. However, this influence of an individual's present state of health on their retrospective ratings undermines attempts at causally relating life events to illness onset.

Life experiences may interact with each other

When individuals are asked to complete a checklist of their recent life experiences, these experiences are regarded as independent of each other. For example, a divorce, a change of jobs and a marriage would be regarded as an accumulation of life events that together would contribute to a stressful period of time. However, one event may counter the effects of another and cancel out any negative stressful consequences. Evaluating the potential effects of life experiences should include an assessment of any interactions between events.

What is the outcome of a series of life experiences?

Originally, the SRE was developed to assess the relationship between stressful life experiences and health status. Accordingly, it was assumed that if the life experiences were indeed stressful then the appropriate outcome measure was one of health status. The most straightforward measure of health status would be a diagnosis of illness such as cancer, heart attack or hypertension. Within this framework, a simple correlational analysis could be carried out to evaluate whether a greater number of life experiences correlated with a medical diagnosis. Apart from the problems with retrospective recall, etc., this would allow some measure of causality – subjects with higher numbers of life events would be more likely to get a medical diagnosis. However, such an outcome measure is restrictive, as it ignores lesser 'illnesses' and relies on an intervention by the medical profession to provide the diagnosis. In addition, it also ignores the role of the diagnosis as a life event in itself. An alternative outcome measure would be to evaluate symptoms. Therefore, the individual could be asked to rate not only their life experiences but also their health-related symptoms (e.g. pain, tiredness, loss of appetite, etc.). Within this framework, correlational analysis could examine the relationship between life events and symptoms. However, this outcome measure has its own problems: Is 'a change in eating habits' a life event or a symptom of a life event? Is 'a change in sleeping habits' a stressor or a consequence of stress? Choosing the appropriate outcome measure for assessing the effects of life events on health is therefore problematic.

Stressors may be short-term or ongoing

Traditionally, assessments of life experiences have conceptualized such life events as short-term experiences. However, many events may be ongoing and chronic. Moos and Swindle (1990) identified domains of ongoing stressors, which they suggested reflect chronic forms of life experiences:

- physical health stressors (e.g. medical conditions);
- home and neighbourhood stressors (e.g. safety, cleanliness);
- financial stressors;
- work stressors (e.g. interpersonal problems, high pressure);
- spouse/partner stressors (e.g. emotional problems with partner);
- child stressors;
- extended family stressors;
- friend stressors.

They incorporated these factors into their measure (the Life Stressors and Social Resources Inventory, LISRES), which represented an attempt to emphasize the chronic nature of life experiences and to place them within the context of the individual's coping resources. Moos and Swindle (1990) argued that life events should not be evaluated in isolation but should be integrated into two facets of an individual's life: their ongoing social resources (e.g. social support networks, financial resources) and their ongoing stressors.

A role for psychological factors in stress

Both Cannon's and Selye's early models of stress conceptualized stress as an automatic response to an external stressor. This perspective is also reflected in versions of life events theory, which suggests that individuals respond to life experiences with a stress response that is therefore related to their health status. However, the above criticisms of the life events theory suggest a different approach to stress, an approach that includes an individual who no longer simply passively responds to stressors but actively interacts with them. This approach to stress provides a role for an individual's psychological state and is epitomized by Lazarus's transactional model of stress and his theory of appraisal.

The transactional model of stress

The role of appraisal

In the 1970s, Lazarus's work on stress introduced psychology to understanding the stress response (Lazarus and Cohen 1973, 1977; Lazarus 1975). This role for psychology took the form of his concept of appraisal. Lazarus argued that stress involved a transaction between the individual and their external world, and that a stress response was elicited if the individual appraised a potentially stressful event as actually being stressful. Lazarus's model of appraisal therefore described individuals as psychological beings who appraised the outside world, not simply passively responding to it. Lazarus defined two forms of appraisal, primary and secondary. According to Lazarus, the individual initially appraises the event itself – defined as *primary appraisal*. There are three possible ways that the event can be appraised: (1) irrelevant, (2) benign and positive, (3) harmful and negative. Lazarus then described *secondary appraisal*, which involves the individual evaluating the pros and cons of their different coping strategies. Therefore, primary appraisal involves an appraisal of the outside world and secondary appraisal involves an appraisal of the individual themselves. This model is shown in Fig. 10.2.

Lazarus's model of appraisal and the transaction between the individual and the environment indicated a novel way of looking at the stress response – the individual no longer passively responded to their external world, but interacted with it.

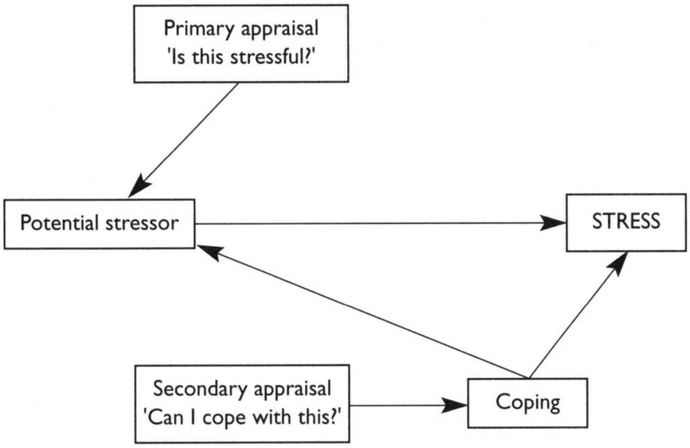

Figure 10.2 The role of appraisal in stress

Does appraisal influence the stress response?

The form of the primary and secondary appraisals determines whether the individual shows a stress response or not. According to Lazarus's model this stress response can take different forms: (1) direct action, (2) seeking information, (3) doing nothing, or (4) developing a means of coping with the stress in terms of relaxation or defence mechanisms.

Several studies have examined the effect of appraisal on stress and have evaluated the role of the psychological state of the individual on their stress response. In an early study by Speisman *et al.* (1964), subjects were shown a film depicting an initiation ceremony involving unpleasant genital surgery. The film was shown with three different sounds tracks. In condition one, the trauma condition, the sound track emphasized the pain and the mutilation. In condition two, the denial condition, the sound track showed the participants as being willing and happy. In condition three, the intellectualization condition, the sound track gave an anthropological interpretation of the ceremony. The study therefore manipulated the subjects' appraisal of the situation and evaluated the effect of the type of appraisal on their stress response. The results showed that subjects reported that the trauma condition was most stressful. This indicates that it is not the events themselves that elicit stress, but the individuals' interpretation or appraisal of those events.

Mason (1975) argued that the stress response needed a degree of awareness of the stressful situation and reported that dying patients who were unconscious showed less signs of physiological stress than those who were conscious. He suggested that the conscious patients were able to appraise their situation whereas the unconscious ones were not. These studies therefore suggest that appraisal is related to the stress response.

Stress as psychophysiological changes

Once elicited, stress has been examined in terms of psychophysiological changes. If an event is appraised as being a stressor, physiological changes may be elicited, which include the following:

- sympathetic arousal and increases in the release of stress hormones, such as catecholamines (e.g. noradrenalin) and corticosteroids (e.g. cortisol);
- increases in physical factors such as heart rate, blood pressure and muscle potential;
- changes in psychological factors, such as increases in fear, anxiety and anger, and decreases in cognitive ability and sensitivity to others.

Some of the psychophysiological effects of stress can be seen as adaptive, in that they prepare the individual to respond, or non-adaptive, in that they may be damaging to health.

Self-control and stress

Recently, theories of stress have emphasized forms of self-control as important in understanding stress. This is illustrated in theories of self-efficacy, hardiness and feelings of mastery.

1 *Self-efficacy*. In 1987, Lazarus and Folkman suggested that self-efficacy was a powerful factor for mediating the stress response. Self-efficacy refers to an individual's feeling of confidence that they can perform a desired action. Research indicates that self-efficacy may have a role in mediating stress-induced immunosuppression and physiological changes such as blood pressure, heart rate and stress hormones (e.g. Bandura *et al.* 1982, 1988; Wiedenfeld *et al.* 1990). For example, the belief 'I am confident that I can succeed in this exam' may result in physiological changes that reduce the stress response. Therefore, a belief in the ability to control one's behaviour may relate to whether or not a potentially stressful event results in a stress response.

2 *Hardiness*. This shift towards emphasizing self-control is also illustrated by Kobasa's concept of 'hardiness' (Kobasa *et al.* 1982; Maddi and Kobasa 1984). Hardiness was described as reflecting (a) personal feelings of control, (b) a desire to accept challenges and (c) commitment. It has been argued that the degree of hardiness influences an individual's appraisal of potential stressors and the resulting stress response. Accordingly, a feeling of being in control may contribute to the process of primary appraisal.

3 *Mastery*. Karasek and Theorell (1990) defined the term 'feelings of mastery', which reflected an individual's control over their stress response. They argued that the degree of mastery may be related to the stress response.

According to these recent developments, stress is conceptualized as a product of the individual's capacity for self-control. Successful coping and self-management eradicates stress, failed self-regulation results in a stress response and stress-related illness is considered a consequence of prolonged failed self-management.

Does stress cause illness?

One of the reasons why stress has been studied so consistently is because of its potential effect on the health of the individual. Stress can effect health via two pathways: via *behavioural* or *physiological* changes.

Stress and changes in behaviour

Most of the research into the stress–illness link has studied the physiological effects of stress. However, in support of the suggested behavioural pathway (Krantz *et al.* 1981) some recent research has examined the effect of stress both on specific health-related behaviours and more general behavioural change.

Smoking

Research suggests a link between stress and smoking behaviour in terms of smoking initiation, relapse and the amount smoked. Wills (1985) argued that smoking initiation in adolescents was related to the amount of stress in their lives. In addition, there has been some support for the prediction that children who experience the stressor of changing schools may be more likely to start smoking than those who stay at the same school throughout their secondary education (Santi *et al.* 1991). In terms of relapse, Lichtenstein *et al.* (1986) and Carey *et al.* (1993) reported that people who experience high levels of stress are more likely to start smoking again after a period of abstinence than those who experience less stress. Research also indicates that increased smoking may be effective at reducing stress. In an experimental study, Perkins *et al.* (1992) exposed smokers to either a stressful or a non-stressful computer task and asked the subjects to smoke a cigarette or sham smoke an unlit cigarette. The results showed that regardless of whether the smokers smoked or not, all subjects reported an increased desire to smoke in the stressful condition. However, this desire was less in those smokers who were actually allowed to smoke. This suggests that stress causes an increased urge for a cigarette, which can be modified by smoking. In a more naturalistic study, smokers were asked to attend a stressful social situation and were instructed either to smoke or not to smoke. Those who could not smoke reported the occasion as more socially stressful than those who could smoke (Gilbert and Spielberger 1987).

Alcohol

Research has also examined the relationship between stress and alcohol consumption. Many authors have suggested that work stress in particular, may promote alcohol use (e.g. Herold and Conlon 1981; Gupta and Jenkins 1984). The tension reduction theory suggests that people drink alcohol for its tension-reducing properties (Cappell and Greeley 1987). Tension refers to states such as fear, anxiety, depression and distress. Therefore according to this model, negative moods are the internal stressors, or the consequence of an external stressor, which cause alcohol consumption due to the expected outcome of the alcohol. For example, if an individual feels tense or anxious (their internal state) as a result of an exam (the external stressor) and believes that alcohol will reduce this tension (the expected outcome), they may drink alcohol to improve their mood. This theory has been supported by some evidence of the relationship between negative mood and drinking behaviour (Violanti *et al.* 1983) suggesting that people are more likely to drink when they are feeling depressed or anxious.

Eating

Greeno and Wing (1994) proposed two hypotheses concerning the link between stress and eating: (1) the general effect model, which predicts that stress changes food intake generally, and (2) the individual difference model, which predicts that stress only causes changes in eating in vulnerable groups of individuals. Most research has focused on the individual difference model and has examined whether either naturally occurring stress or laboratory-induced stress causes changes in eating in specific individuals. For example, Michaud *et al.* (1990) reported that exam stress was related to an increase in eating in girls but not in boys, Baucom and Aiken (1981) reported that stress increased eating in both the overweight and dieters, and Cools *et al.* (1992) reported that stress was related to eating in dieters only. Therefore, gender, weight and levels of dieting (see Chapter 6) seem to be important predictors of a link between stress and eating. However, the research is not always consistent with this suggestion. For example, Conner *et al.* (1999) examined the link between daily hassles and snacking in 60 students who completed diaries of their snacking and hassles for seven consecutive days. Their results showed a direct association between increased daily hassles and increased snacking but showed no differences according to either gender or dieting. Such inconsistencies in the literature have been described by Stone and Brownell (1994) as the 'stress eating paradox' to describe how at times stress causes overeating and in others it causes under-eating without any clear pattern emerging.

General behaviour change

Research has also examined the effects of stress on behaviour changes generally. Correlational research suggests that individuals who experience high levels of stress show a greater tendency to perform behaviours that increase their chances of becoming ill or injured (Wiebe and McCallum 1986). In particular, it has been suggested that stress increases the types of behaviour that increase the likelihood of the individual being harmed. For example, stress may result in increases not only in the consumption of alcohol, cigarettes and coffee, a reduction in the amount of exercise taken and may have detrimental effects on diet. All such behavioural changes are linked to the development of various illnesses (Conway *et al.* 1981; Baer *et al.* 1987). Johnson (1986) has also suggested that stress increases accidents at home, work and in the car.

Furthermore, it has been suggested that medical students' lifestyle and the occurrence of problem drinking may be related to the stress they experience (Wolf and Kissling 1984). In a recent study, this theory was tested experimentally and the health-related behaviours of medical students were evaluated both before and during a stressful examination period. The results showed that the students reported a deterioration in mood in terms of anxiety and depression and changes in their behaviour in terms of decreases in exercise, alcohol consumption and food intake (Ogden and Mtandabari 1997). The authors concluded that acute exposure to stress resulted in changes in health-related behaviours in a direction negative to health but that had only a minimal influence on the students' ability to perform satisfactorily. Obviously chronic stress may have more damaging effects on longer term changes in behaviour.

Illness as a stressor

Being ill itself could be a stressful event. If this is the case then the stress following illness also has implications for the health of individuals. Such stress may influence individuals' behaviour in terms of their likelihood to seek help, their compliance with interventions and medical recommendations, and also adopting healthy lifestyles. Therefore, stress may cause behaviour changes, which are related to the health status of the individual.

Stress and changes in physiology

The physiological consequences of stress and their effect on health have been studied extensively. Research indicates that stress causes physiological changes that have implications for promoting both the onset of illness and its progression.

Stress and illness onset

Stress may be related to illness via the physiological pathway in the following ways:

- Stress may cause an increase in acid secretion in the stomach, which can cause ulcers.
- Stress causes an increase in catecholamines, which cause an increase in blood clot formation thereby increasing the chances of a heart attack.
- An increase in catecholamines can lead to kidney disease.
- Heart attacks can also be promoted by stress via an increase in cardiovascular response and the increased chances of injury or damage to arteries via plaque formation and fat deposits.
- Stress causes an increase in corticosteroids, which can lead to arthritis.
- Stress causes increases in catecholamines and corticosteroids, which effect the immune system, thereby making the individual more susceptible to infection.

Stress and illness progression

Kiecolt-Glaser and Glaser (1986) argue that stress causes a decrease in the hormones produced to fight carcinogens and repair DNA. In particular, cortisol decreases the number of active T-cells, which could increase the rate of tumour development. This suggests that stress whilst ill could exacerbate the illness through physiological changes. Such stress may occur independently to the illness. However, stress may also be a result of the illness itself such as relationship breakdown, changes in occupation or simply the distress from a diagnosis. Therefore, if the illness is appraised as being stressful, this itself may be damaging to the chances of recovery.

Beliefs and physiological changes

It has also been suggested that beliefs may themselves have a direct effect on physiology. Kamen and Seligman (1987) reported that an internal, stable, global attributional style (i.e. a pessimist approach to life whereby the individual blames themselves when things go wrong) predicted poor health in later life. This was supported by Seligman *et al.* 1988 who argued that pessimism may be related to health through a decrease in T-cells and immunosuppression. The authors argued that this was not mediated through behavioural change but was indicative of a direct effect of attributional style and beliefs on physiology. In a further study, Greer *et al.* (1979) suggested that denial and a fighting spirit, not hopelessness, predicted survival for breast cancer, suggesting again that beliefs might have a direct effect on illness and recovery (see Chapter 13 for a discussion of cancer). The possible links between beliefs and physiological changes have been specifically studied within the field of psychoneuroimmunology (PNI).

Psychoneuroimmunology (PNI)

PNI is based on the prediction that an individual's psychological state can influence their immune system via the nervous system. This perspective provides a scientific basis for the 'mind over matter', 'think yourself well' and 'positive thinking, positive health' approaches to life. PNI can be understood in terms of (1) conditioning the immune system, (2) measuring immune changes and (3) psychological state and immunity.

Conditioning the immune system

Originally it was believed that the immune system was autonomous and did not interact with any other bodily systems. However, research indicates that this is not the case and that not only does the immune system interact with other systems, but it can be conditioned to respond in a particular way using the basic rules of classical and operant conditioning. The early work in this area was carried out by Ader and Cohen (1975, 1981) and showed that changes in the immune system brought about by an immunosuppressive drug could be paired with a sweet taste. This meant that after several pairings, the sweet taste itself began to bring about immunosuppression. These results were important for two reasons. First they confirmed that the immune system could be manipulated. Second, the results opened up the area for PNI and the possibility that psychological factors could change an individual's immune response.

Measuring immune changes

Although it is accepted that the immune system can be changed, measuring such changes has proved to be problematic. The four main markers of immune function used to date have been as follows: (1) tumour growth, which is mainly used in animal research, (2) wound healing, which can be used in human research by way of a removal of a small section of the skin and can be monitored to follow the healing process, (3) secretory immunoglobulin A (sIgA), which is found in saliva and can be accessed easily and without pain or discomfort to the subject and (4) natural killer cell cytoxicity (NKCC), T lymphocytes and T helper lymphocytes, which are found in the blood. All these markers have been shown to be useful in the study of immune functioning (see Chapter 13 for a discussion of immunity and longevity). However, each approach to measurement has its problems. For example, both wound healing and tumour growth present problems of researcher accuracy, and the degree of linkage between all of these markers and subsequent health have been questioned. In addition, the measurement of immune function raises questions such as 'How long after an event should the immune system marker be assessed?' (i.e. is the effect immediate or delayed?), 'How can baseline measures of the immune system be taken?' (i.e. does actually taking blood/saliva, etc., cause changes in immune functioning?) and 'Are changes in immune functioning predictive of changes in health?' (i.e. if we measure changes in a marker do we really know that this will impact on health in the long term?).

Psychological state and immunity

Research has focused on the capacity of psychological factors to change immune functioning. In particular, it has examined the role of mood, thought suppression and stress:

- Mood – studies indicate that positive mood is associated with better immune functioning (as measured by sIgA), that negative mood is associated with poorer functioning (Stone *et al.* 1987) and that humour appears to be specifically beneficial (Dillon *et al.* 1985).
- Thought suppression – there is evidence that certain coping styles such as suppression and denial may relate to illness onset and progression (e.g. Kune *et al.* 1991; Gross and Levenson 1997). There is also evidence that encouraging thought expression through writing or disclosure groups may decrease autonomic system activity (Pennebaker 1993), increase NKCC activity (Futterman *et al.* 1992) and increase lymphocyte activity (Pennebaker *et al.* 1988; Petrie *at al.* 1998).
- Stress – research has indicated an association between stress and immunity in terms of tumour growth (Laudenslager *et al.* 1983), lymphocyte activity (Kiecolt Glaser *et al.* 1986), and sIgA (McClelland *et al.* 1972). However, although most researchers accept that psychological state does impact on immune function, different studies use different immune markers, different populations and different ways of inducing changes in psychological state. Further, some studies rely on naturalistic designs whilst others involve laboratory based experiments. Therefore, generalized conclusions remain problematic.

Therefore, stress may influence health and illness via a behavioural pathway involving changes in health-related behaviours such as smoking, alcohol consumption and eating or via a physiological pathway involving changes in stress hormones. Further, it is possible that stress may influence health via the immune system. This has been studied within the framework of PNI and an exploration of how individuals' psychological state may impact upon their health via changes in immune function.

Which factors mediate the stress–illness link?

The relationship between stress and illness is not straightforward, and there is much evidence to suggest that several factors may mediate the stress–illness link. These factors are as follows:

- *Exercise*: this can cause a decrease in stress (see Chapter 7).
- *Gender*: there is some evidence for gender differences in the stress response and the role of stress in promoting illness. Stoney *et al.* (1987) argued that men respond more strenuously to stressors than women. It has also been argued that women show smaller increases in blood pressure during stressful tasks (Stoney, *et al.* 1990). This indicates that

gender may determine the stress response to a stressful event and consequently the effect of this response on the illness or health status of the individual.
- *Coping styles*: coping styles (or behavioural patterns) have been defined as follows: problem-solving (e.g. forming a plan of action), problem avoidance (e.g. refusing to think about the problem), wishful thinking (e.g. dreaming about better times), emotional social support (e.g. talking to people about feelings), instrumental social support (e.g. talking to people for advice), cognitive restructuring (e.g. redefining the problem), distraction (e.g. drinking, taking drugs). Some of these coping styles are regarded as approach styles (e.g. problem-solving, social support) and some are avoidance coping (e.g. wishful thinking, problem avoidance). The individual's type of coping style may well mediate the stress–illness link and determine the extent of the effect of the stressful event on their health status (see Chapter 3 for a discussion of coping).
- *Life events*: these may mediate the stress–illness link.
- *Type A behaviour/type A personality*: it has been suggested that this may influence the individual's response to a stressful situation and the effect of this response on health (see Chapter 13 for a discussion of type A behaviour).
- *Social support*: increased social support has been related to a decreased stress response and a subsequent reduction in illness.
- *Actual or perceived control*: control over the stressor may decrease the effects of stress on the individual's health status.

Social support and control will now be examined in greater detail.

Social support

What is social support?

Social support has been defined in a number of ways. Initially, it was defined according to the number of friends that were available to the individual. However, this has been developed to include not only the number of friends supplying social support, but the satisfaction with this support (Sarason *et al.* 1983). Wills (1985) has defined several types of social support.

- *esteem support*, whereby other people increase one's own self-esteem;
- *informational support*, whereby other people are available to offer advice;
- *social companionship*, which involves support through activities;
- *instrumental support*, which involves physical help.

The term 'social support' is generally used to refer to the perceived comfort, caring, esteem or help one individual receives from others (e.g. Wallston *et al.* 1983).

Does social support affect health?

A number of studies have examined whether social support influences the health status of the individual. Lynch (1977) reported that widowed, divorced or single individuals have higher mortality rates from heart disease than married people and suggested that heart disease and mortality are related to lower levels of social support. However, problems with this study include the absence of a direct measure of social support and the implicit assumption that marriage is an effective source of social support.

Berkman and Syme (1979) reported the results of a prospective study whereby they measured social support in 4700 men and women aged 30–69, whom they followed up for 9 years. They found that increased social support predicted a decrease in mortality rate. This indicates a role for social support in health. Research has also indicated that birth complications are lower in women who have high levels of social support, again suggesting a link between social support and health status (Oakley 1992). Research has also examined the effects of social support on immune functioning and consequently health. For example, Arnetz *et al.* (1987) examined the immune function of 25 women who were either employed ($n = 8$) or unemployed ($n = 17$). The unemployed group received either standard economic benefits only or received benefits as well as a psychosocial support programme. The results showed that those unemployed subjects who received the psychosocial support showed better immune functioning than the subjects who received benefits only. It would seem that social support reduced immuno-suppression, thus promoting health.

How does social support influence health?

If social support does influence or mediate the stress–illness link, then what are the possible mechanisms? Two theories have been developed to explain the role of social support in health status:

1 The *main effect hypothesis* suggests that social support itself is beneficial and that the absence of social support is itself stressful. This suggests that social support mediates the stress–illness link, with its very presence reducing the effect of the stressor and its absence itself acting as a stressor.
2 The *stress buffering hypothesis* suggests that social support helps individuals to cope with stress, therefore mediating the stress–illness link by buffering the individual from the stressor; social support influences the individual's appraisal of the potential stressor. This process, which has been described using *social comparison theory*, suggests that the existence of other people enables individuals exposed to a stressor to select an appropriate coping strategy by comparing themselves with others. For example, if an individual was going through a stressful life event, such as divorce, and existed in a social group where other people had dealt with divorces, the experiences of others would help them to choose a

FOCUS ON RESEARCH 10.1

TESTING A THEORY – SOCIAL SUPPORT AND HEALTH

A study to examine the effects of a stressor (unemployment) and social support on health among East German refugees (Schwarzer *et al.* 1994).

This study examined the relationship between social support and health. It is interesting because it accessed a naturally occurring stressor.

Background

Research suggests that stress may influence health either via changes in health-related behaviour and/or via a physiological pathway. However, the relationship between stress and illness is not automatic, and appears to be mediated by factors such as coping style, perceived control over the stressor and social support. This study examined the effects of stress on health in East German refugees and evaluated which factors were related to their health complaints. In particular, the study focused on employment status and social support.

Methodology

Subjects In 1989, prior to the opening of the Berlin Wall, the authors launched the study to examine the experiences of being a refugee/migrant in West Berlin. The authors recruited East German migrants who were living in temporary accommodation in West Berlin. The subjects were asked to take part in three waves of data collection; Autumn/Winter, 1989, Summer, 1990, Summer, 1991. A total of 235 migrants took part in all three stages of data collection. Of these, 62 per cent were defined as refugees (arrived before the opening of the wall) and 38 per cent were legal immigrants (arrived after the opening of the wall).

Design The study involved a longitudinal design and data were collected at three time points.

Measures The subjects completed the following measures:

- *Employment status*: this was recorded at the three time points and subjects were coded as 'always jobless' (jobless throughout the study), 'job hunt successful' (jobless at the beginning but employed by the end) and 'never jobless' (employed throughout the study). Seven subjects who were employed at the beginning and lost their jobs were excluded from the analysis as their numbers were too small.
- *Social support*: the subjects were asked to rate statements on a 4-point Likert scale relating to (1) 'received social support', which

referred to their retrospective assessment of actual behaviours, such as 'Friends and relatives have helped me look for a job', and (2) 'perceived social support', which referred to their anticipation of social support in the future when in times of need, such as 'There are people on whom I can rely when I need help'.

- *Ill-health*: the subjects were asked to rate a series of physical symptoms relating to (1) heart complaints, (2) pains in the limbs, (3) stomach complaints, and (4) exhaustion.

Results

The effect of employment on ill-health

The results were analysed to examine overall differences between the groups (always jobless/job hunt successful/never jobless) and showed that at all three time points the subjects who remained unemployed reported a greater number of physical symptoms than the other subject groups. This difference was also related to gender, with men who were always jobless reporting more ill-health than other individuals.

The effects of employment and social support on ill-health

The results were also analysed to examine the effect of social support on ill-health. The results showed that social support had only a small effect on ill-health in those subjects who were employed but had a much larger effect on those who had always been jobless. Within the 'always jobless' group, those who reported higher levels of social support reported far fewer physical symptoms than those who reported lower social support. In addition, subjects who were both unemployed and reported low social support reported more ill-health than all the other subjects.

The effects of employment on social support

The results were also analysed to examine the long-term effects of employment on both social support and ill-health. The results suggest that employment is related to both ill-health and social support and that the relationship between employment and social support is reciprocal over time (i.e. employment influences social support, and social support influences employment).

Conclusion

The results from this study provide support for the relationship between stress (unemployment) and health and suggest that this relationship is mediated by social support. Therefore, ill-health was greatest in those subjects who were both unemployed and who reported low social support. In addition, the results suggest that although social support may act as a mediating factor, it is itself related to employment status, with individuals gaining social support from work colleagues.

suitable coping strategy. The stress buffering hypothesis has also been described using role theory. This suggests that social support enables individuals to change their role or identity according to the demands of the stressor. Role theory emphasizes an individual's role and suggests that the existence of other people offers choices as to which role or identity to adopt as a result of the stressful event.

Control

The effect of control on the stress–illness link has also been extensively studied.

What is control?

Control has been studied within a variety of different psychological theories.

1 *Attributions and control.* Kelley's (1967, 1972) attributional theory examines control in terms of attributions for causality (see Chapter 2 for a discussion of attribution theory). If applied to a stressor, the cause of a stressful event would be understood in terms of whether the cause was controllable by the individual or not. For example, failure to get a job could be understood in terms of a controllable cause (e.g. 'I didn't perform as well as I could in the interview', 'I should have prepared better') or an uncontrollable cause (e.g. 'I am stupid', 'the interviewer was biased').
2 *Self-efficacy and control.* Control has also been discussed by Bandura in his self-efficacy theory (Bandura 1977). Self-efficacy refers to an individual's confidence to carry out a particular behaviour. Control is implicit in this concept.
3 *Categories of control.* Five different types of control have been defined by Thompson (1986): behavioural control (e.g. avoidance), cognitive control (e.g. reappraisal of coping strategies), decisional control (e.g. choice over possible outcome), informational control (e.g. the ability to access information about the stressor) and retrospective control (e.g. could I have prevented that event from happening).
4 *The reality of control.* Control has also been subdivided into perceived control (e.g. 'I believe that I can control the outcome of a job interview') and actual control (e.g. 'I can control the outcome of a job interview'). The discrepancy between these two factors has been referred to as illusory control (e.g. 'I control whether the plane crashes by counting throughout the journey'). However, within psychological theory, most control relates to perceived control.

Does control affect the stress response?

Research has examined the extent to which the controllability of the stressor influences the stress response to this stressor, both in terms of the subjective experience of stress and the accompanying physiological changes.

1 *Subjective experience*. Corah and Boffa (1970) examined the relationship between the controllability of the stressor and the subjective experience of stress. Subjects were exposed to a loud noise (the experimental stressor) and were either told about the noise (the stressor was predictable) or not (an unpredictable stressor). The results indicated that if the noise was predictable, there was a decrease in subjective experiences of stress. The author argued that the predictability enables the subject to feel that they have control over the stressor, and that this perceived control reduces the stress response. Baum *et al.* (1981) further suggested that if a stressor is predicted there is a decrease in the stress response, and reported that predictability or an expectation of the stress, enables the individual to prepare their coping strategies.
2 *Physiological changes*. Research has also examined the effect of control on the physiological response to stress. For example, Meyer *et al.* (1985) reported that if a stressor is regarded as uncontrollable the release of corticosteroids is increased.

Does control affect health?

If control influences the stress response, does control also influence the effect of stress on health and illness? This question has been examined by looking at both animal and human models.

Animal research

Seligman and Visintainer (1985) reported the results of a study whereby rats were injected with live tumour cells and exposed to either controllable or uncontrollable shocks. The results indicated that the uncontrollable shocks resulted in promotion of the tumour growth. This suggests that controllability may influence the stress response, which may then promote illness. In a further study, the relationship between control and coronary heart disease was studied in monkeys (Manuk *et al.* 1986). Some breeds of monkey exist in social hierarchies with clearly delineated roles. The monkeys are categorized as either dominant or submissive. Usually this hierarchy is stable. However, the authors introduced new members to the groups to create an unstable environment. They argued that the dominant monkeys show higher rates of coronary heart disease in the unstable condition than the dominant monkeys in the stable condition, or the submissive monkeys in the stable condition. It is suggested that the dominant monkeys have high expectations of control, and are used to experiencing high levels of control. However, in the unstable condition, there is a conflict between their expectations of control and the reality, which the authors argued results in an increase in coronary heart disease. These animal models are obviously problematic in that many assumptions are made about the similarities between the animals' experience of control and that of humans. However, the results indicate an association between control and health in the predicted direction.

Human research

Human models have also been used to examine the effect of control on the stress–illness link. For example, the job strain model was developed to examine the effects of control on coronary heart disease (e.g. Karasek and Theorell 1990). The three factors involved in the model are (1) psychological demands of the job in terms of workload, (2) the autonomy of the job, reflecting control, and (3) the satisfaction with the job. This model has been used to predict coronary heart disease in the USA (Karasek *et al.* 1988), and in Sweden (Karasek *et al.* 1981). The results of these studies suggest that a combination of high workload (i.e. high demand), low satisfaction and low control are the best predictors of coronary heart disease.

How does control mediate the stress–illness link?

A number of theories have been developed to explain how control influences health and mediates the stress–illness link.

- *Control and preventative behaviour.* It has been suggested that high control enables the individual to maintain a healthy lifestyle by believing 'I can do something to prevent illness'.
- *Control and behaviour following illness.* It has also been suggested that high control enables the individual to change behaviour after illness. For example, even though the individual may have low health status following an illness, if they believe there is something they can do about their health they will change their behaviour.
- *Control and physiology.* It has been suggested that control directly influences health via physiological changes.
- *Control and personal responsibility.* It is possible that high control can lead to a feeling of personal responsibility and consequently personal blame and learned helplessness. These feelings could lead either to no behaviour change or to unhealthy behaviours resulting in illness.

The possible benefits of low control

Most theories of the relationship between control and stress suggest that high control (such as predictability, responsibility, etc.) relates to a reduction in stress and is therefore beneficial to health. However, in certain situations a perception of low control may result in lowered stress. For example, flying in a plane can be made less stressful by acknowledging that there is nothing one can do about the possibility of crashing. To an extent this perception of helplessness may be less stressful than attempting to control an uncontrollable situation.

Control and social support in stress and illness

Haynes *et al.* (1980) carried out a study to examine the interrelationship between perceived control and social support and their effects on the stress–illness link. They examined the prevalence of coronary heart disease in women and compared this prevalence between working and non-working women. In addition, they measured aspects of work such as job demand, social support and perceived control over work. The results showed that the working women were not more likely to have coronary heart disease than the non-working women, suggesting that job demand is not simply a predictor of coronary heart disease. However, within the working women, those women who reported low perceived control over their work were more likely to have coronary heart disease than those who reported high perceived control, suggesting that within that group of people with high job demand, low control was a predictor of illness, supporting the predicted association between social support and health. In addition, within the group of working women, those who showed low work support were also more likely to have coronary heart disease, supporting the research on social support and its relationship to illness. The study also looked at how many children both the working and the non-working women had and related this to coronary heart disease. The results showed that a higher number of children increased the risk of coronary heart disease in the working women, but not in the non-working women. The authors argued that the number of children may be a contributor to job demand, but that this increased coronary heart disease in working women but not in the non-working women. The results for this study are shown in Fig. 10.3.

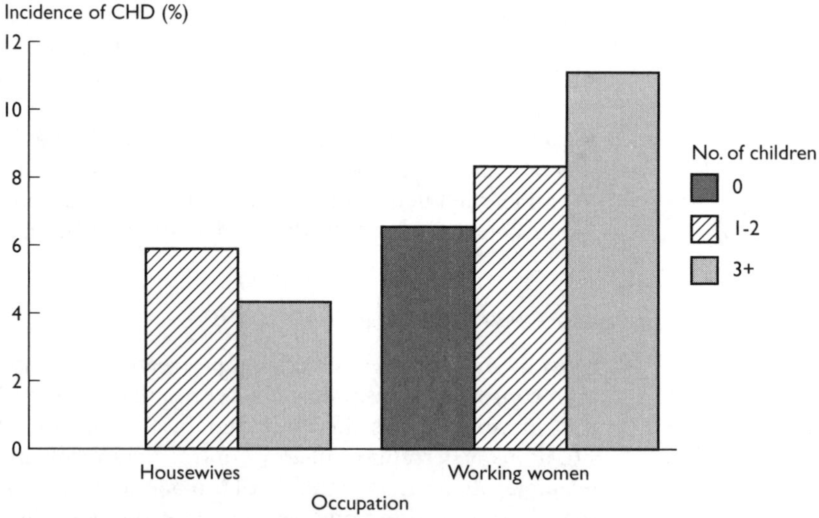

Figure 10.3 Incidence of CHD by number of children: the role of work stress on illness in women

To conclude

This chapter has examined the different models of stress and the relationship between stress and illness. Early models of stress regarded stress as an automatic response to an external stressor. However, the introduction of the concept of appraisal suggested that stress was best understood as an interaction between the individual and the outside world. Accordingly, a stress response would be elicited if an event was appraised as stressful. Theories of the stress–illness link suggest that stress may cause illness through either a behavioural pathway or one relating to physiological changes. The behavioural pathway involves changes in health behaviours such as smoking, alcohol consumption, eating and exercise, whereas the physiological pathway involves changes in factors such as stress hormones. Further, the area of PNI provides some insights into how an individual's psychological state might directly influence health. This chapter has also examined the factors that mediate the stress–illness link, including social support and control.

? Questions

1 Stress is an automatic response to external stressors. Discuss.

2 Discuss the role of appraisal in the stress response.

3 Stress causes illness. Discuss.

4 Discuss the possible factors that mediate the stress–illness link.

5 Describe a study designed to assess the potential effect of perceived control on the development of illness.

▶ For discussion

Consider the ways you cope with stress and discuss the extent to which these are either beneficial or detrimental to your health.

Assumptions in health psychology

The stress research highlights some of the assumptions in health psychology.

1 *The problem of mind–body split.* Although much of the stress research examines how the mind may influence the body (e.g. appraisal

relates to the release of stress hormones, social support relates to resulting stress-related illnesses), how this process occurs is unclear. In addition, although these relationships suggest an interaction between the mind and the body, they still define them as separate entities which influence each other, not as the same entity.

2 *The problem of progress*. It is often assumed that the most recent theories are better than earlier theories. Therefore, models including appraisal, social support, etc., are better than those describing stress as a knee jerk reaction to a stressor. Perhaps these different theories are not necessarily better than each other, but are simply different ways of describing the stress process.

3 *The problem of methodology*. It is assumed that methodology is neutral and separate to the data collected. For example, factors such as hardiness, self-efficacy and control exist before they are measured. Perhaps however, methodology is not so neutral, and that asking subjects questions relating to these factors actually encourages them to see themselves/the world in terms of hardiness, self-efficacy and control.

Further reading

Johnston, D. (1992) The management of stress in the prevention of coronary heart disease, in S. Maes, H. Leventhal and M. Johnston (Eds), *International Review of Health Psychology*. London: Wiley.

This chapter reviews the literature relating to the role of stress on CHD and evaluates the effectiveness of interventions aimed at reducing stress in individuals.

Maes, S., Vingerhoets, A. and van Heck, G. (1987) The study of stress and disease: some developments and requirements, *Social Science and Medicine*, 6: 567–78.

This paper examines the role of stress in the onset, course and outcome of disease and discusses the different models that have been developed to describe the stress–illness link.

Vingehoets, A. and Perski, A. (2000) The psychobiology of stress, in A. Kaptein, A. Appels and K. Orth-Gómer (eds) *Psychology in Medicine*. Houten: Bohn Stafleu Von Loghum.

This chapter provides an easily accessible overview of the physiological aspects of stress.

CHAPTER 11

Pain

Chapter overview

This chapter examines early models of pain and their description of pain as a sensation. It then examines the increasing emphasis on a role for psychology in pain and the development of the gate control theory, which examined factors such as previous experience and affect in the individual's perception of pain. Then the research assessing psychological factors in either increasing or exacerbating pain is discussed and the use of psychological factors in pain reduction is described. Finally, the chapter examines the problems with pain measurement and the ways in which pain can be assessed.

This chapter covers:

- Early pain theories – pain as a sensation
- The gate control theory of pain – pain as a perception
- The role of psychosocial factors in pain perception
- Pain treatment – a role for psychology?
- Measuring pain

Early pain theories – pain as a sensation

Early models of pain described pain within a biomedical framework as an automatic response to an external factor. Descartes, perhaps the earliest writer on pain, regarded pain as a response to a painful stimulus. He described a direct pathway from the source of pain (e.g. a burnt finger) to an area of the brain which detected the painful sensation. Von Frey (1895) developed the *specificity theory of pain*, which again reflected this very simple stimulus–response model. He suggested that there were specific sensory receptors which transmit touch, warmth and pain, and that each receptor was sensitive to specific stimulation. This model was similar to that described by Descartes in that the link between the cause of pain and the brain was seen as direct and automatic. In a similar vein, Goldschneider (1920) developed a further model of pain called the *pattern theory*. He suggested that nerve impulse patterns determined the degree of pain and that messages from the damaged area were sent directly to the brain via these nerve impulses. Therefore these three models of pain describe pain in the following ways:

- Tissue damage causes the sensation of pain.
- Psychology is involved in these models of pain only as a consequence of pain (e.g. anxiety, fear, depression). Psychology has no causal influence.
- Pain is an automatic response to an external stimuli. There is no place for interpretation or moderation.
- The pain sensation has a single cause.
- Pain was categorized into being either psychogenic pain or organic pain. Psychogenic pain was considered to be 'all in the patient's mind' and was a label given to pain when no organic basis could be found. Organic pain was regarded as being 'real pain' and was the label given to pain when some clear injury could be seen.

Including psychology in theories of pain

The early simple models of pain had no role for psychology. However, psychology came to play an important part in understanding pain through the twentieth century. This was based on several observations:

First, it was observed that medical treatments for pain (e.g. drugs, surgery) were, in the main, only useful for treating acute pain (i.e. pain with a short duration). Such treatments were fairly ineffective for treating chronic pain (i.e. pain which lasts for a long time). This suggested that there must be something else involved in the pain sensation which was not included in the simple stimulus response models.

It was also observed that individuals with the same degree of tissue damage differed in their reports of the painful sensation and or painful responses. Beecher (1956) observed soldiers' and civilians' requests for pain relief in a hospital during the Second World War. He reported that although soldiers and civilians often showed the same degree of injury,

80 per cent of the civilians requested medication, whereas only 25 per cent of the soldiers did. He suggested that this reflected a role for the meaning of the injury in the experience of pain; for the soldiers, the injury had a positive meaning as it indicated that their war was over. This meaning mediated the pain experience.

The third observation was phantom limb pain. The majority of amputees tend to feel pain in an absent limb. This pain can actually get worse after the amputation, and continues even after complete healing. Sometimes the pain can feel as if it is spreading and is often described as a hand being clenched with the nails digging into the palm (when the hand is missing) or the bottom of the foot being forced into the ankle (when the foot is missing). Phantom limb pain has no physical basis because the limb is obviously missing. In addition, not everybody feels phantom limb pain and those who do, do not experience it to the same extent. Further, even individuals who are born with missing limbs sometimes report phantom limb pain.

These observations, therefore, suggest variation between individuals. Perhaps this variation indicates a role for psychology.

The gate control theory of pain

Melzack and Wall (1965, 1982; Melzack 1979), developed the gate control theory of pain (GCT), which represented an attempt to introduce psychology into the understanding of pain. This model is illustrated in Fig. 11.1. It suggested that although pain could still be understood in terms of a stimulus–response pathway, this pathway was complex and mediated by a network of interacting processes. Therefore, the GCT integrated psychology into the traditional biomedical model of pain and described not only a role for physiological causes and interventions, but also allowed for psychological causes and interventions.

Input to the gate

Melzack and Wall suggested that a gate existed at the spinal cord level, which received input from the following sources:

- *Peripheral nerve fibres*. The site of injury (e.g. the hand) sends information about pain, pressure or heat to the gate.
- *Descending central influences from the brain*. The brain sends information related to the psychological state of the individual to the gate. This may reflect the individual's behavioural state (e.g. attention, focus on the source of the pain); emotional state (e.g. anxiety, fear, depression); and previous experiences or self-efficacy (e.g. I have experienced this pain before and know that it will go away) in terms of dealing with the pain.
- *Large and small fibres*. These fibres constitute part of the physiological input to pain perception.

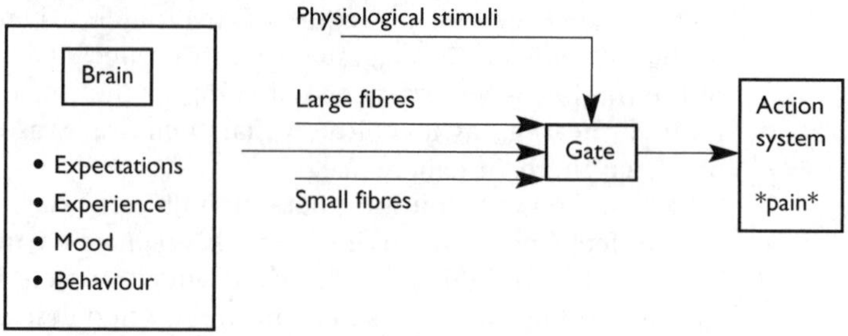

Figure 11.1 The gate control theory of pain

Output from the gate

The gate integrates all of the information from these different sources and produces an output. This output from the gate sends information to an action system, which results in the perception of pain.

How does the GCT differ from earlier models of pain?

The GCT differs from earlier models in a number of fundamental ways.

- *Pain as a perception.* According to the GCT, pain is a perception and an experience rather than a sensation. This change in terminology reflects the role of the individual in the degree of pain experienced. In the same way that psychologists regard vision as a perception, rather than a direct mirror image, pain is described as involving an active interpretation of the painful stimuli.
- *The individual as active not passive.* According to the gate control theory, pain is determined by central and peripheral fibres. Pain is seen as an active process as opposed to a passive one. The individual no longer just responds passively to painful stimuli, but actively interprets and appraises this painful stimuli.
- *The role of individual variability.* Individual variability is no longer a problem in understanding pain but central to the GCT. Variation in pain perception is understood in terms of the degree of opening or closing of the gate.
- *The role for multiple causes.* The GCT suggests that many factors are involved in pain perception, not just a singular physical cause.
- *Is pain ever organic?* The GCT describes most pain as a combination of physical and psychological. It could, therefore, be argued that within this model, pain is never totally either organic or psychogenic.
- *Pain and dualism.* The GCT attempts to depart from traditional dualistic models of the body and suggests an interaction between the mind and body.

What opens the gate?

The more the gate is opened the greater the perception of pain. Melzack and Wall suggest that several factors can open the gate:

- *physical factors*, such as injury or activation of the large fibres;
- *emotional factors*, such as anxiety, worry, tension and depression;
- *behavioural factors*, such as focusing on the pain or boredom.

What closes the gate?

Closing the gate reduces pain perception. The gate control theory also suggests that certain factors close the gate.

- *physical factors*, such as medication, stimulation of the small fibres;
- *emotional factors*, such as happiness, optimism or relaxation;
- *behavioural factors*, such as concentration, distraction or involvement in other activities.

Problems with the GCT

The gate control theory represented an important advancement on previous simple stimulus response theories of pain. It introduced a role for psychology and described a multidimensional process rather than a simple linear one. However, there are several problems with the theory.

First, there is no evidence to illustrate the existence of a gate or the interaction between the three components. Second, although the input from the site of physical injury is mediated and moderated by experience and other psychological factors, the model still assumes an organic basis for pain. This integration of physiological and psychological factors can explain individual variability and phantom limb pain to an extent, but, because the model still assumes some organic basis it is still based around a simple stimulus response process.

Third, the GCT attempted to depart from traditional dualistic models of health by its integration of the mind and the body. However, although the GCT suggests some integration or interaction between mind and body, it still sees them as separate processes. The model suggests that physical processes are influenced by the psychological processes, but that these two sets of processes are distinct.

The role of psychosocial factors in pain perception

The GCT was a development from previous theories in that it allowed for the existence of mediating variables, and emphasized active perception rather than passive sensation. The GCT and the subsequent attempts at evaluating the different components of pain perception reflect a *three-process model* of pain. The components of this model are: physiological processes, subjective-affective-cognitive processes and behavioural processes. Physiological processes involve factors such as tissue damage, the release of endorphins and changes in heart rate. The subjective-affective-cognitive and behavioural processes are described in more detail below.

Subjective-affective-cognitive processes

Learning processes

Classical conditioning

Research suggests that classical conditioning may have an effect on the perception of pain. As described by theories of associative learning, an individual may associate a particular environment with the experience of pain. For example, if an individual associates the dentist with pain due to past experience, the pain perception may be enhanced when attending the dentist due to this expectation. In addition, because of the association between these two factors, the individual may experience increased anxiety when attending the dentist, which may also increase pain. Jamner and Tursky (1987) examined the effect of presenting migraine sufferers with words associated with pain. They found that this presentation increased both anxiety and pain perception and concluded that the words caused a change in mood, which caused a change in the subject's perception of pain.

Operant conditioning

Research suggests that there is also a role for operant conditioning in pain perception. Individuals may respond to pain by showing pain behaviour (e.g. resting, grimacing, limping, staying off work). Such pain behaviour may be positively reinforced (e.g. sympathy, attention, time of work), which may itself increase pain perception (see below).

Anxiety

Anxiety also appears to influence pain perception. Fordyce and Steger (1979) examined the relationship between anxiety and acute and chronic pain. They reported that anxiety has a different relationship to these two types of pain. In terms of acute pain, pain increases anxiety, the successful treatment for the pain then decreases the pain which subsequently decreases the anxiety. This can then cause a further decrease in the pain. Therefore, because of the relative ease with which acute pain can be treated, anxiety relates to this pain perception in terms of a cycle of pain reduction. However, the pattern is different for chronic pain. Because treatment has very little effect on chronic pain, this increases anxiety, which can further increase pain. Therefore, in terms of the relationship between anxiety and chronic pain, there is a cycle of pain increase. Research has also shown a direct correlation between high anxiety levels and increased pain perception in children with migraines and sufferers of back pain and pelvic pain (Feuerstein *et al.* 1987; McGowan *et al.* 1998).

Neurosis

It has also been suggested that personality, in particular neurosis, may be related to pain perception. Hysteria, hypochondriasis and depression have been labelled the neurotic triad. Sternbach *et al.* (1973) reported that an increase in the neurotic triad is related to an increase in chronic pain and can be related to less sleep, reduced social and work life and feelings of exhaustion. Further, in a meta-analysis of the literature on chronic pelvic pain, McGowan *et al.* (1998) reported consistent differences between women with chronic pelvic pain and pain-free groups in their levels of neurotism, depression and psychopathology.

Cognitive states

One of the most important factors that influences pain is the cognitive state of the individual. Beecher (1956), in his study of soldiers' and civilians' requests for medication, was one of the first people to examine this and asked the question: 'What does pain mean to the individual?' Beecher argued that differences in pain perception were related to the meaning of pain for the individual. In Beecher's study, the soldiers benefited from their pain. This has been described in terms of secondary gains whereby the pain may have a positive reward for the individual.

Behavioural processes

Pain behaviour and secondary gains

The way in which an individual responds to the pain can itself increase or decrease the pain perception. In particular, research has looked at pain behaviours which have been defined by Turk *et al.* (1985) as facial or audible expression (e.g. clenched teeth and moaning), distorted posture or movement (e.g. limping, protecting the pain area), negative affect (e.g. irritability, depression) or avoidance of activity (e.g. not going to work, lying down). It has been suggested that pain behaviours are reinforced through attention, the acknowledgement they receive and through secondary gains, such as not having to go to work. Positively reinforcing pain behaviour may increase pain perception. Pain behaviour can also cause a lack of activity and muscle wastage, no social contact and no distraction leading to a sick role, which can also increase pain perception.

Recent developments in theories of pain

Recently, there has been an increasing interest in the role of cognitions in pain perception. In particular, research has emphasized the role of self-efficacy in pain perception and reduction. Turk *et al.* (1983) suggest that increased pain self-efficacy may be an important factor in determining the degree of pain perception. In addition, the concept of pain locus of control has been developed to emphasize the role of individual cognitions in pain perception (Manning and Wright 1983; Dolce 1987; Litt 1988). Within these models, the role of the stimuli in the external world is diminishing and pain is increasingly considered a consequence of self-control and self-regulation. Consequently, pain management and reduction is discussed in terms of cognitive strategies.

Pain treatment – a role for psychology?

If psychology is involved in the perception of pain, then research has suggested that psychology can also be involved in the treatment of pain. There are several methods of pain treatment, which reflect an interaction between psychology and physiological factors:

- *Biofeedback* has been used to enable the individual to exert voluntary control over their bodily functions. Biofeedback aims to decrease anxiety and tension and therefore to decrease pain.
- *Relaxation* methods aim to decrease anxiety and stress and consequently to decrease pain.
- *Operant conditioning* is related to increased pain perception and can therefore also be used in pain treatment to reduce pain. Some aspects of pain treatment aim to positively reinforce compliance and non-pain behaviour, thereby decreasing secondary gains and decreasing pain.
- A *cognitive* approach to pain treatment involves factors such as attention diversion (i.e. encouraging the individual not to focus on the pain) and imagery (i.e. encouraging the individual to have positive, pleasant thoughts). Both these factors appear to decrease pain.
- *Hypnosis* has also been shown to reduce pain. However, whether this is simply a result of attention diversion or not is unclear.

Multidisciplinary pain clinics

Recently, multi-disciplinary pain clinics have been set up that adopt a multidisciplinary approach to pain treatment and attempt to challenge factors which cause or exacerbate pain. The goals set by such clinics include:

- *Improving physical and lifestyle functioning*: this involves improving muscle tone, improving self-esteem, improving self-efficacy, improving distraction and decreasing boredom, pain behaviour and secondary gains.

FOCUS ON RESEARCH 11.1

PUTTING THEORY INTO PRACTICE – TREATING CHRONIC PAIN

A study to examine the effectiveness of cognitive behavioural treatment for chronic pain (Basler and Rehfisch 1990).

This is an interesting paper, as it illustrates how a theoretical approach can be used as a basis for clinical practice. The paper emphasizes pain as a perception and suggests that treatment interventions can focus on the different factors that contribute to this perception. In addition, the paper highlights the role of adherence in treatment success, which has implications for understanding placebos and compliance with medical/clinical recommendations.

Background

What is the cognitive–behavioural approach to pain?
A cognitive–behavioural approach to pain regards pain as a perception that involves an integration of four sources of pain-related information:

- *Cognitive,* e.g. the meaning of the pain ('it will prevent me from working').
- *Emotional,* e.g. the emotions associated with the pain ('I am anxious that it will never go away').
- *Physiological,* e.g. the impulses sent from the site of physical damage.
- *Behavioural,* e.g. pain behaviour that may increase the pain (such as not doing any exercise) and pain behaviour which may decrease the pain (such as doing sufficient exercise).

The cognitive–behavioural approach to pain therefore aims to reduce pain by focusing on these different sources of pain-related information.

The central role of self-control
In particular, the cognitive–behavioural approach to pain aims to improve the individual's self-control over the pain. Turk and Rudy (1986) summarize the objectives of interventions to improve self-control as follows:

- *Combat demoralization.* Chronic pain sufferers may become demoralized and feel helpless. They are taught to reconceptualize their problems so that they can be seen as manageable.
- *Enhance outcome efficacy.* If patients have previously received several forms of pain treatment, they may believe that nothing works. They

are taught to believe in the cognitive behavioural approach to pain treatment and that with their cooperation the treatment will improve their condition.

- *Foster self-efficacy*. Chronic pain sufferers may see themselves as passive and helpless. They are taught to believe that they can be resourceful and competent.
- *Break up automatic maladaptive coping patterns*. Chronic pain sufferers may have learnt emotional and behavioural coping strategies that may be increasing their pain, such as feeling consistently anxious, limping or avoiding exercise. They are taught to monitor these feelings and behaviours.
- *Skills training*. Once aware of the automatic emotions and behaviours that increase their pain, pain sufferers are taught a range of adaptive coping responses.
- *Self-attribution*. Chronic pain sufferers may have learnt to attribute any success to others and failure to themselves. They are taught to accept responsibility for the success of the treatment.
- *Facilitate maintenance*. Any effectiveness of the cognitive behavioural treatment should persist beyond the actual treatment intervention. Therefore, pain sufferers are taught how to anticipate any problems and to consider ways of dealing with these problems.

Within this model of pain treatment, Basler and Rehfisch (1990) set out to examine the effectiveness of a cognitive behavioural approach to pain. In addition, they aimed to examine whether such an approach could be used within general practice.

Methodology

Subjects Sixty chronic pain sufferers, who had experienced chronic pain in the head, shoulder, arm or spine for at least 6 months, were recruited for the study from general practice lists in West Germany. Subjects were allocated to either (1) the immediate treatment group (33 subjects started the treatment and 25 completed it) or (2) the waiting list control group (27 subjects were allocated to this group and 13 completed all measures).

Design All subjects completed measures at baseline (time 1), after the 12-week treatment intervention (time 2) and at 6-month follow-up (time 3). Subjects in the control group completed the same measures at comparable time intervals.

Measures At times 1, 2 and 3, all subjects completed a 14-day pain diary, which included measures of:

- *Intensity of pain*: the subjects rated the intensity of their pain from 'no pain' to 'very intense pain' every day.
- *Mood*: for the same 14 days, subjects also included in the diary measures of their mood three times a day.

- *Functional limitation*: the subjects also included measures of things they could not do within the 14 days.
- *Pain medication*: the subjects also recorded the kind and quantity of pain medication.

The subjects also completed the following measures:

- *The state–trait anxiety inventory*, which consists of 20 items and asks subjects to rate how frequently each of the items occurs.
- *The Von Zerssen Depression Scale* (Von Zerssen 1976), which consists of 16 items describing depressive symptoms (e.g. 'I can't help crying').
- *General bodily symptoms*: the subjects completed a checklist of 57 symptoms, such as 'nausea' and 'trembling'.
- *Sleep disorders due to pain*: the subjects were asked to rate problems they experienced in sleep onset, sleep maintenance and sleep quality.
- *Bodily symptoms due to pain attacks*: the subjects rated 13 symptoms for their severity during pain attacks (e.g. heart rate increase, sweating).
- *Pain intensity* over the last week was also measured.

In addition, at 6-month follow-up (time 2), subjects who had received the treatment were asked which of the recommended exercises they still carried out and the physicians rated the treatment outcome on a scale from 'extreme deterioration' to 'extreme improvement'.

The treatment intervention The treatment programme consisted of 12 weekly 90-minute sessions, which were carried out in a group with up to 12 patients. All subjects in the treatment group received a treatment manual. The following components were included in the sessions:

- *Education*. This component aimed to educate the subjects about the rationale of cognitive behaviour treatment. The subjects were encouraged to take an active part in the programme, they received information about the vicious circle of pain, muscular tension, demoralization and about how the programme would improve their sense of self-control over their thoughts, feelings and behaviour.
- *Relaxation*. The subjects were taught how to control their responses to pain using progressive muscle relaxation. They were given a home relaxation tape, and were also taught to use imagery techniques and visualization to distract themselves from pain and to further improve their relaxation skills.
- *Modifying thoughts and feelings*. The subjects were asked to complete coping cards to describe their maladaptive thoughts and adaptive coping thoughts. The groups were used to explain the role of fear, depression, anger and irrational thoughts in pain.
- *Pleasant activity scheduling*. The subjects were encouraged to use distraction techniques to reduce depression and pain perception. They were encouraged to shift their focus from those activities they could no longer perform to those that they could enjoy. Activity goals

were scheduled and pleasant activities were reinforced at subsequent groups.

Results

The results were analysed to examine differences between the two groups (treatment *vs* control) and to examine differences in changes in the measures (from time 1 to time 2 and at follow-up) between the two groups.

Time 1 to time 2
The results showed significantly different changes between the two groups in all their ratings. Compared with the control group, the subjects who had received cognitive behavioural treatment reported lower pain intensity, lower functional impairment, better daily mood, fewer bodily symptoms, less anxiety, less depression, fewer pain-related bodily symptoms and fewer pain-related sleep disorders.

Time 1 to time 2 to time 3
When the results at 6-month follow-up were included, again the results showed significant differences between the two groups on all variables except daily mood and sleep disorders.

The role of adherence
The subjects in the treatment condition were then divided into those who adhered to the recommended exercise regimen at follow-up (adherers) and those who did not (non-adherers). The results from this analysis indicate that the adherers showed an improvement in pain intensity at follow-up compared with their ratings immediately after the treatment intervention, whilst the non-adherers ratings at follow-up were the same as immediately after the treatment.

Conclusion

The authors conclude that the study provides support for the use of cognitive–behavioural treatment for chronic pain. The authors also point to the central role of treatment adherence in predicting improvement. They suggest that this effect of adherence indicates that the improvement in pain was a result of the specific treatment factors (i.e. the exercises) not the non-specific treatment factors (contact with professionals, a feeling of doing something). However, it is possible that the central role for adherence in the present study is similar to that discussed in Chapter 12 in the context of placebos, with treatment adherence itself being a placebo effect.

- *Decreasing reliance on drugs and medical services*: this involves improving personal control, decreasing the sick role and increasing self-efficacy.
- *Increasing social support and family life*: this aims to increase optimism and distraction and decrease boredom, anxiety, sick role behaviour and secondary gains.

Placebos and pain reduction

Placebos have been defined as inert substances that cause symptom relief (see Chapter 12). Traditionally, placebos were used in randomized control trials to compare an active drug with the effects of simply taking something. However, placebos have been shown to have an effect on pain relief. Beecher (1955) suggested that 30 per cent of chronic pain sufferers experience pain relief after taking placebos. In the 1960s Diamond *et al.* (1960) carried out several sham operations to examine the effect of placebos on pain relief. A sham heart bypass operation involved the individual believing that they were going to have a proper operation, being prepared for surgery, being given a general anaesthetic, cut open and then sewed up again without any actual bypass being carried out. The individual therefore believed that they had had an operation and had the scars to prove it. This procedure obviously has serious ethical problems. However, the results suggested that angina pain can actually be reduced by a sham operation by comparable levels to an actual operation for angina. This suggests that the expectations of the individual changes their perception of pain, again providing evidence for the role of psychology in pain perception.

Measuring pain

Whether it is to examine the causes or consequences of pain or to evaluate the effectiveness of a treatment for pain, pain needs to be measured. This has raised several questions and problems. For example: 'Are we interested in the individual's own experience of the pain?' (i.e. what someone says is all important), 'What about denial or self-image?' (i.e. someone might be in agony but deny it to themselves and to others), 'Are we interested in a more objective assessment?' (i.e. can we get over the problem of denial by asking someone else to rate their pain?) and 'Do we need to assess a physiological basis to pain?' These questions have resulted in three different perspectives on pain measurement: self-reports, observational assessments and physiological assessments, which are very similar to the different ways of measuring health status (see Chapter 14). In addition, these different perspectives reflect the different theories of pain.

Self-reports

Self-report scales of pain rely on the individual's own subjective view of their pain level. They take the form of visual analogue scales (e.g. How severe is your pain? Rated from 'not at all' (0) to 'extremely' (100)), verbal scales (e.g. Describe your pain: no pain, mild pain, moderate pain, severe pain, worst pain) and descriptive questionnaires (e.g. the McGill Pain Questionnaire (MPQ); Melzack 1975). The MPQ attempts to access the more complex nature of pain and asks individuals to rate their pain in terms of three dimensions: sensory (e.g. flickering, pulsing, beating), affective (e.g. punishing, cruel, killing) and evaluative (e.g. annoying, miserable, intense). Some self-report measures also attempt to access the impact that the pain is having upon the individuals' level of functioning and ask whether the pain influences the individuals' ability to do daily tasks such as walking, sitting and climbing stairs.

Observational assessment

Observational assessments attempt to make a more objective assessment of pain and are used when the patients' own self-reports are considered unreliable or when they are unable to provide them. For example, observational measures would be used for children, some stroke sufferers and some terminally ill patients. In addition, they can provide an objective validation of self-report measures. Observational measures include an assessment of the pain relief requested and used, pain behaviours (such as limping, grimacing and muscle tension) and time spent sleeping and/or resting.

Physiological measures

Both self-report measures and observational measures are sometimes regarded as unreliable if a supposedly 'objective' measure of pain is required. In particular, self-report measures are open to the bias of the individual in pain and observational measures are open to errors made by the observer. Therefore, physiological measures are sometimes used as an index of pain intensity. Such measures include an assessment of inflammation and measures of sweating, heart rate and skin temperature. However, the relationship between physiological measures and both observational and self-report measures is often contradictory, raising the question 'Are the individual and the rater mistaken or are the physiological measurements not measuring pain?'

To conclude

Early biomedical models of pain suggested that pain was a simple response to external stimuli and within this model categorized the individual as a passive responder to external factors. Such models had no causal role for psychology. However, the gate control theory, developed in the 1960s and 1970s by Melzack and Wall, included psychological factors. As a result, pain was no longer understood as a sensation but as an active perception. Due to this inclusion of psychological factors into pain perception, research has examined the role of learning, anxiety, cognitions and pain behaviour in either decreasing or exacerbating pain. As psychological factors appeared to have a role to play in eliciting pain perception, multidisciplinary pain clinics have been set up to use psychological factors in its treatment.

? Questions

1 Pain is a response to painful stimuli. Discuss.

2 To what extent does the gate control theory of pain depart from biomedical models of pain?

3 What are the implications of the GCT of pain for the mind–body debate?

4 Pain is a perception. Discuss.

5 To what extent can psychological factors be used to reduce pain perception?

6 Self-report is the only true way of measuring pain. Discuss.

7 Develop a research protocol to examine the role of secondary gains in pain perception.

For discussion

Consider the last time you experienced pain (e.g. period pain, headache, sports injury) and discuss the potential cognitive, emotional and behavioural factors that may have exacerbated the pain.

Assumptions in health psychology

The research into pain highlights some of the assumptions underlying health psychology.

1 *The mind–body split.* Early models of pain regarded the physical aspects of pain as 'real' and categorized pain as either 'organic' or 'psychogenic'. Such models conceptualized the mind and body as separate and conform to a dualistic model of individuals. Recent models of

pain have attempted to integrate the mind and the body by examining pain as a perception that is influenced by a multitude of different factors. However, even within these models the mind and the body are still regarded as separate.

2 *The problem of progression*. Over the last 100 years, different theories have been developed to explain pain. It is often assumed that changes in theoretical perspective over time represents improvement with the recent theories reflecting a better approximation to the truth of 'what pain really is'. However, perhaps these different theories can also be used themselves as data to show how psychologists have thought in the past and how they now think about individuals. For example, in the past pain was seen as a passive response to external stimuli; therefore, individuals were seen as passive responders. However, today pain is increasingly seen as a response to the individual's self-control – pain is a sign of either successful or failed self-control. Therefore, contemporary individuals are seen as having self-control, self-management and self-mastery. Perhaps the different theories over time reflect different (not necessarily better) versions of individuality.

Further reading

Horn, S. and Munafo, M. (1997) *Pain: Theory, Research and Intervention*. Buckingham: Open University Press.

This book provides a more detailed overview of the pain literature.

Karoly, P. and Jensen, M.P. (1987) *Multimethod Assessment of Chronic Pain*. New York: Pergamon Press.

This book provides a comprehensive and critical overview of the complex area of pain assessment.

Weinsenberg, M. (1987) Psychological intervention for the control of pain, *Behaviour Research and Therapy*, 25: 401.

This paper examines how theories of pain perception can be used to reduce the pain experience.

CHAPTER 12

The interrelationship between beliefs, behaviour and health – the example of placebos

Chapter overview

The study of placebos is a good illustration of many of the issues central to health psychology. This chapter examines problems with defining placebos and then assesses the different theories concerning how they work, highlighting the central role for patient expectations. It then outlines the implications of placebos for the different areas of health psychology discussed in the rest of this book, such as health beliefs and illness cognitions, health behaviours, stress, pain and illness and places this within a discussion of the relationship between the mind and body and the interrelationship between beliefs, behaviour and health and illness.

This chapter covers:

- What is a placebo?
- How do placebos work?
- The central role of patient expectations
- Cognitive dissonance theory
- The role of placebo effects in health psychology

What is a placebo?

Placebos have been defined as follows:

- Inert substances which cause symptom relief (e.g. 'My headache went away after having a sugar pill').
- Substances that cause changes in a symptom not directly attributable to specific or real pharmacological action of a drug or operation (e.g. 'After I had my hip operation I stopped getting headaches').
- Any therapy that is deliberately used for its non-specific psychological or physiological effects (e.g. 'I had a bath and my headache went away').

These definitions illustrate some of the problems with understanding placebos. For example:

- What are specific/real versus non-specific/unreal effects? For example, 'My headaches went after the operation, is this an unreal effect (it wasn't predicted) or a real effect (it definitely happened)?'
- Why are psychological effects non-specific? (e.g. 'I feel more relaxed after my operation – is this a non-specific effect?).
- Are there placebo effects in psychological treatments? For example, 'I specifically went for cognitive restructuring therapy and ended up simply feeling less tired. Is this a placebo effect or a real effect?'

The problems inherent in the distinctions between specific versus non-specific effects and physiological versus psychological effects are illustrated by examining the history of apparently medically inert treatments.

A history of inert treatments

For centuries, individuals (including doctors and psychologists) from many different cultural backgrounds have used (and still use) apparently inert treatments for various different conditions. For example, medicines such as wild animal faeces and the blood of a gladiator were supposed to increase strength, and part of a dolphin's penis was supposed to increase virility. These so-called 'medicines' have been used at different times in different cultures but have no apparent medical (active) properties. In addition, treatments such as bleeding by leeches to decrease fever or travelling to religious sites such as Lourdes in order to alleviate symptoms have also continued across the years without any obvious understanding of the processes involved. Faith healers are another example of inert treatments ranging from Jesus Christ, Buddha and Krishna. The tradition of faith healers has persisted, although our understanding of the processes involved is very poor.

Such apparently inert interventions, and the traditions involved with these practices, have lasted over many centuries. In addition, the people involved in these practices have become famous and have gained a degree of credibility. Furthermore, many of the treatments are still believed in. Perhaps, the maintenance of faith both in these interventions and in the people carrying out the treatments suggests that they were actually successful, giving the treatments themselves some validity. Why were they successful? It is possible that there are medically active substances in some of these traditional treatments that were not understood in the past and are still not understood now (e.g. gladiators' blood may actually contain some still unknown active chemical). It is also possible that the effectiveness of some of these treatments can be understood in terms of modern-day placebo effects.

Modern-day placebos

Recently placebos have been studied more specifically and have been found to have a multitude of effects. For example, placebos have been found to increase performance on a cognitive task (Ross and Buckalew 1983), to be effective in reducing anxiety (Downing and Rickles 1983), and Haas *et al.* (1959) listed a whole series of areas where placebos have been shown to have some effect, such as allergies, asthma, cancer, diabetes, enuresis, epilepsy, multiple sclerosis, insomnia, ulcers, obesity, acne, smoking and dementia.

Perhaps one of the most studied areas in relation to placebo effects is pain. Beecher (1955), in an early study of the specific effects of placebos in pain reduction, suggested that 30 per cent of chronic pain sufferers show relief from a placebo when using both subjective (e.g. 'I feel less pain') and objective (e.g. 'You are more mobile') measures of pain. In addition, Diamond *et al.* (1960) reported a sham operation for patients suffering from angina pain. They reported that half the subjects with angina pain were given a sham operation, and half of the subjects were given a real heart bypass operation. The results indicated that pain reduction in both groups was equal, and the authors concluded that the belief that the individual had had an operation was sufficient to cause pain reduction and alleviation of the angina.

Placebos – to be taken out of an understanding of health?

Since the 1940s, research into the effectiveness of drugs has used randomized controlled trials and placebos to assess the real effects of a drug versus the unreal effects. Placebos have been seen as something to take out of the health equation. However, if placebos have a multitude of effects as discussed above, perhaps, rather than being taken out they should be seen as central to health status. For this reason it is interesting to examine how placebos work.

How do placebos work?

If placebos have a multiple number of possible effects, what factors actually mediate these changes? Several theories have been developed to try and understand the process of placebo effects. These theories can be described as *non-interactive* theories in that they examine individual characteristics, characteristics of the treatment and characteristics of the health professional, or *interactive* theories in that they involve an examination of the processes involved in the interactions between patients, the treatment and the health professionals.

Non-interactive theories

Characteristics of the individual

Individual trait theories suggest that certain individuals have characteristics that make them susceptible to placebo effects. Such characteristics have been described as emotional dependency, extraversion, neurosis and being highly suggestible. Research has also suggested that individuals who respond to placebos are introverted. However, many of the characteristics described are conflicting and there is little evidence to support consistent traits as predictive of placebo responsiveness.

Characteristics of the treatment

Other researchers have focused on treatment characteristics and have suggested that the characteristics of the actual process involved in the placebo treatment relates to the effectiveness or degree of the placebo effect. For example, if a treatment is perceived by the individual as being serious, the placebo effect will be greater. Accordingly, surgery, which is likely to be perceived as very serious, has the greatest placebo effect, followed by an injection, followed by having two pills versus one pill. Research has also looked at the size of the pill and suggests that larger pills are more effective than small pills in eliciting a change.

Characteristics of the health professional

Research has also looked at the characteristics of the health professional suggesting that the kind of professional administering the placebo treatment may determine the degree of the placebo effect. For example, higher professional status and higher concern have been shown to increase the placebo effect.

Problems with the non-interactive theories

Theories that examine only the patient, only the treatment or only the professional ignore the interaction between patient and health professional that occurs when a placebo effect has taken place. They assume that these factors exist in isolation and can be examined independently of each other. However, if we are to understand placebo effects then perhaps theories of the interaction between health professionals and patients described within the literature (see Chapter 4) can be applied to understanding placebos.

Interactive theories

It is therefore necessary to understand the process of placebo effects as an active process, which involves patient, treatment and health professional variables. Placebo effects should be conceptualized as a multi-dimensional process that depends on an interaction between a multitude of different factors. To understand this multidimensional process, research has looked at possible mechanisms of the placebo effect.

Experimenter bias

Experimenter bias refers to the impact that the experimenter's expectations can have on the outcome of a study. For example, if an experimenter was carrying out a study to examine the effect of seeing an aggressive film on a child's aggressive behaviour (a classic social psychology study) the experimenter's expectations may themselves be responsible for changing the child's behaviour (by their own interaction with the child), not the film.

This phenomenon has been used to explain placebo effects. For example, Gracely *et al.* (1985) examined the impact of doctors' beliefs about the treatment on the patients' experience of placebo-induced pain reduction. Subjects were allocated to one of three conditions and were given either an analgesia (a pain killer), a placebo, or naloxone (an opiate antagonist, which increases the pain experience). The patients were therefore told that this treatment would either reduce, have no effect, or increase their pain. The doctors giving the drugs were themselves allocated to one of two conditions. They either believed that the patients would receive one of three of these substances (a chance of receiving a pain killer), or that the patient would receive either a placebo or naloxone (no chance of receiving a pain killer). Therefore, one group of doctors believed that there was a chance that the patient would be given analgesia and would show pain reduction, and the other half of doctors believed that there was no chance that the patient would receive some form of analgesia. In fact, all subjects were given a placebo. This study, therefore, manipulated both the patients' beliefs about the kind of treatment they had received and the doctors' beliefs about the kind of treatment they were administering.

The results showed that the subjects who were given the drug treatment by the doctor who believed they had a chance to receive the analgesia, showed a decrease in pain whereas the patients whose doctor believed that they had no chance of receiving the pain killer showed no effect. This suggests that if the doctors believed that the subjects may show pain reduction, this belief was communicated to the subjects who actually reported pain reduction. However, if the doctors believed that the subjects would not show pain reduction, this belief was also communicated to the subjects who accordingly reported no change in their pain experience. This study highlights a role for an interaction between the doctor and the patient and is similar to the effect described as experimenter bias described within social psychology. Experimenter bias suggests that the experimenter is capable of communicating their expectations to the subjects who respond in accordance with these expectations. Therefore, if applied to placebo effects, subjects show improvement because the health professionals expect them to.

Patient expectations

Research has also looked at the expectations of the patient. Ross and Olson (1981) examined the effects of patients' expectations on recovery following a placebo. They suggested that most patients experience spontaneous recovery following illness as most illnesses go through periods of spontaneous change and that patients attribute these changes to the treatment. Therefore, even if the treatment is a placebo, any change will be understood in terms of the effectiveness of this treatment. This suggests that because patients want to get better and expect to get better, any changes that they experience are attributed to the drugs they have taken. However, Park and Covi (1965) gave sugar pills to a group of neurotic patients and actually told the patients that the pills were sugar pills and would therefore have no effect. The results showed that the patients still showed some reduction in their neuroticism. It could be argued that in this case, even though the patients did not expect the treatment to work, they still responded to the placebo. However, it could also be argued that these patients would still have some expectations that they would get better otherwise they would not have bothered to take the pills. Jensen and Karoly (1991) also argue that patient motivation plays an important role in placebo effects, and differentiate between patient motivation (the desire to experience a symptom change) and patient expectation (a belief that a symptom change would occur). In a laboratory study, they examined the relative effects of patient motivation and patient expectation of placebo-induced changes in symptom perception following a 'sedative pill'. The results suggested a role for patient expectation but also suggested that higher motivation was related to a greater placebo effect.

Reporting error

Reporting error has also been suggested as an explanation of placebo effects. In support of previous theories that emphasize patient expectations, it has been argued that patients expect to show improvement following medical intervention, want to please the doctor and therefore show inaccurate reporting by suggesting that they are getting better, even when their symptoms remain unchanged. (In fact the term 'placebo' is derived from the latin meaning 'I will please'.) It has also been suggested that placebos are a result of reporting error by the doctor. Doctors also wish to see an improvement following their intervention, and may also show inaccurate measurement. The theory of reporting error therefore explains placebo effects in terms of error, misrepresentation, or misattributions of symptom changes to placebo. However, there are problems with the reporting error theory in that not all symptom changes reported by the patients or reported by the doctor are positive. Several studies show that patients report negative side-effects to placebos, both in terms of subjective changes, such as drowsiness, nausea, lack of concentration, and also objective changes such as sweating, vomiting and skin rashes. All these factors would not be pleasing to the doctor and therefore do not support the theory of reporting error as one of demand effects. In addition, there are also objective changes to placebos in terms of heart rate and blood pressure, which cannot be understood either in terms of the patient's desire to please the doctor, or the doctor's desire to see a change.

Conditioning effects

Traditional conditioning theories have also been used to explain placebo effects (Wickramasekera 1980). It is suggested that patients associate certain factors with recovery and an improvement in their symptoms. For example, the presence of doctors, white coats, pills, injections and surgery are associated with improvement, recovery, and with effective treatment. According to conditioning theory, the unconditioned stimulus (treatment) would usually be associated with an unconditioned response (recovery). However, if this unconditioned stimulus (treatment) is paired with a conditioned stimulus (e.g. hospital, a white coat), the conditioned stimulus can itself elicit a conditioned response (recovery, the placebo effect). The conditioned stimulus might be comprised of a number of factors, including the appearance of the doctor, the environment, the actual site of the treatment, or simply taking a pill. This stimulus may then elicit placebo recovery. For example, people often comment that they feel better as soon as they get into a doctor's waiting room, that their headache gets better before they have had time to digest a pill, that symptoms disappear when a doctor appears. According to conditioning theory, these changes would be examples of placebo recovery. Several reports provide support for conditioning theory. For example, research suggests that taking a placebo drug is more effective in a hospital setting when given by a doctor, than if taken at home given by someone who is not associated with the medical profession. This suggests that placebo effects require an interaction between the patient and their environment. In addition, placebo pain reduction is more effective with clinical and real pain than with experimentally created pain. This suggests that experimentally created pain does not elicit the association with the treatment environment, whereas the real pain has the effect of eliciting memories of previous experiences of treatment, making it more responsive to placebo intervention.

Anxiety reduction

Placebos have also been explained in terms of anxiety reduction. Downing and Rickles (1983) argued that placebos decrease anxiety, thus helping the patient to recover. In particular, such a decrease in anxiety is effective in causing pain reduction (Sternbach 1978). For example, according to the gate control theory, anxiety reduction may close the gate and reduce pain, whereas increased anxiety may open the gate and increase pain (see Chapter 11). Placebos may decrease anxiety by empowering the individual and encouraging them to feel that they are in control of their pain. This improved sense of control, may lead to decreased anxiety, which itself reduces the pain experience. Placebos may be particularly effective in chronic pain by breaking the anxiety–pain cycle (see Chapter 11). The role of anxiety reduction is supported by reports that placebos are more effective in reducing real pain than reducing experimental pain, perhaps because real pain elicits a greater degree of anxiety, which can be alleviated by the placebo, whereas experimentally induced pain does not make the individual anxious. However, there are problems with the anxiety reducing theory of placebos. Primarily, there are many other effects of placebos besides pain reduction. In addition, Butler and Steptoe (1986) reported that although placebos increased lung function in asthmatics, this increase was not related to anxiety.

Physiological theories

Physiologists have also developed theories to explain placebo effects, with specific focus on pain reduction. Levine *et al.* (1978) have argued that placebos increase endorphin (opiate) release – the brain's natural pain killers – which therefore decreases pain. Evidence for this comes in several forms. Placebos have been shown to create dependence, withdrawal and tolerance, all factors which are similar to those found in abstinent heroine addicts, suggesting that placebos may well increase opiate release. In addition, results suggest that placebo effects can be blocked by giving naloxone, which is an opiate antagonist. This indicates that placebos may increase the opiate release, but that this opiate release is blocked by naloxone, supporting the physiological theory of placebos. However, the physiological theories are limited as pain reduction is not the only consequence of placebos.

The central role of patient expectations

Galen is reported to have said about the physician 'He cures most in whom most are confident' (quoted by Evans 1974). In accordance with this, all theories of placebo effects described so far involve the patient expecting to get better. Experimenter bias theory describes the expectation of the

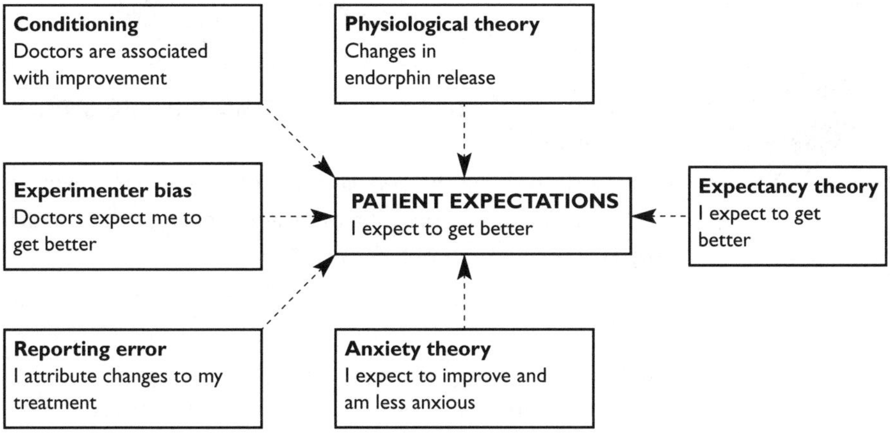

Figure 12.1 The central role of patient expectations in placebo effects

doctor, which is communicated to the patient, changing the patient's expectation. Expectancy effects theory describes directly the patients' expectations derived from previous experience of successful treatment. Reporting error theory suggests that patients expect to show recovery and therefore inaccurately report recovery, and theories of misattribution argue that patients' expectations of improvement are translated into understanding spontaneous changes in terms of the expected changes. In addition, conditioning theory requires the individual to expect the conditioned stimuli to be associated with successful intervention and anxiety reduction theory describes the individual as feeling less anxious after a placebo treatment because of the belief that the treatment will be effective. Finally, even the physiological theory assumes that the individual will expect to get better. The central role of patient expectations is illustrated in Fig. 12.1.

Ross and Olson (1981) summarize the placebo effects as follows:

- the direction of placebo effects parallels the effects of the drug under study;
- the strength of the placebo effect is proportional to that of the active drug;
- the reported side-effects of the placebo drug and the active drug are often similar;
- the time needed for both the placebo and the active drug to become active are often similar.

As a result, they conclude that 'most studies find that an administered placebo will alter the recipient's condition (or in some instances self-report of the condition) in accordance with the placebo's expected effects' (Ross and Olson 1981: 419). Therefore, according to the above theories, placebos work because the patient and the health professionals expect them to work. This emphasizes the role of expectations and regards

FOCUS ON RESEARCH 12.1

TESTING A THEORY – 'DOING AS YOU'RE TOLD' AS A PLACEBO

A study to examine the role of adhering to medical treatment in predicting recovery from a heart attack – taking pills (whether active or not) as a placebo (Horwitz *et al.* 1990).

For a long time, medicine has regarded adherence (compliance) with medical recommendations to be important for recovery: 'take these drugs and you will get better'. However, this study suggests that simply adhering to medical recommendations to take pills may be beneficial to recovery following a heart attack, regardless of whether the pills taken are active pills or placebo pills. This has implications for understanding the relationship between the mind and body ('I believe that I have taken my medication' is related to actually getting better) and for understanding the central role of beliefs and expectations in health and illness.

Background

Random controlled trials (RCTs) have been used since the 1940s to assess the effectiveness of drugs compared with placebos. For these trials, subjects are randomly allocated to either the experimental condition (and receive the real drug) or the control condition (and receive the placebo drug). Placebo drugs are used as a comparison point in order to distinguish the 'real' effects of the chemically active drug from both the 'placebo effects' and changes that may spontaneously happen over time. The RCT methodology acknowledges that changes in symptoms may occur following a placebo drug, but regards these as less important than the real changes that occur following the real drug. However, in 1982, data from the Coronary Drug Project was published which suggested that the best predictor of mortality in men who had survived a heart attack was not taking the lipid-lowering drug compared with taking the placebo drug, but adherence to taking any drug at all (whether an active drug or a placebo drug). The results indicated that adherers had lower mortality at 5 years than the non-adherers in both the experimental and the placebo groups. Horwitz *et al.* (1990) set out to examine whether adherence was a good predictor of risk of death in a large Beta-Blocker Heart Attack Trial (BHAT 1982) and to evaluate whether any effects of adherence could be explained by social and behavioural characteristics (e.g. were the non-adherers also the smokers with stressful lives?).

Methodology

Horwitz *et al.* reported a reanalysis of the data collected as part of the Beta-Blocker Heart Attack Trial, which was a multi-centre, randomized, double-blind trial comparing proprandol (a beta-blocker) with a placebo drug in patients who had survived an acute heart attack (this is known as secondary data analysis).

Subjects The original study included 3837 men and women aged 30–69 years who were reassessed every 3 months for an average of 25 months. The data from 1082 men in the experimental condition (who had received the beta-blocker) and 1094 men in the placebo condition were analysed (all women and those men who had not completed the psychosocial measures were excluded from the analysis). Follow-up data was analysed for 12 months.

Design The study was prospective with subjects completing initial measures 6 weeks after hospital discharge and completing subsequent follow-up measures every 3 months.

Measures Measures were taken of (1) psychosocial factors, (2) adherence and (3) clinical characteristics:

- *Psychosocial factors.* The subjects completed a structured interview 6 weeks after discharge. The answers to this were grouped to form four psychosocial variables: levels of life stress, social isolation, depression and type A behaviour pattern. In addition, data were collected concerning their health practices both at baseline and at follow-up (e.g. smoking, alcohol use, diet, physical activity other than work).
- *Adherence.* For each follow-up interval (3 months) adherence was calculated as the amount of medication divided by the amount prescribed. The subjects were divided into poor adherers (taking less than or equal to 75 per cent of prescribed medication) and good adherers (taking more than 75 per cent of prescribed medication).
- *Clinical characteristics.* Measures were also taken of the clinical severity of the heart attack (congestive heart failure, severity of heart attack, age) and sociodemographic features (ethnicity, marital status, education).
- *Mortality.* Mortality was measured after 12 months.

Results

Adherence and mortality

The results were analysed to examine the relationship between adherence and mortality, and showed that, compared with patients with good adherence, those with poor adherence were twice as likely to have died at 1-year follow-up. This association was also present when the data were analysed according to treatment category (i.e. for both the experimental group and the control group). Therefore, regardless of what the drug was (whether a beta-blocker or a placebo), taking it as recommended halved the subjects' chances of dying.

The role of psychosocial and clinical factors
The results showed that death after 1 year was higher for those subjects who had a history of congestive heart failure, were not married, and had high social isolation and high life stress. In addition, those who had died after 1 year were more likely to have been smokers at baseline and less likely to have given up smoking during the follow-up. However, even when the data were analysed to take into account these psychosocial and clinical factors, adherence was still strongly associated with mortality at 1 year.

Conclusion

These results therefore indicate a strong link between adherence to medical recommendations and mortality, regardless of the type of drug taken. This effect does not appear to be due to psychosocial or clinical factors (the non-adherers did not simply smoke more than the adherers). Therefore 'doing as the doctor suggests' appears to be beneficial to health, but not for the traditional reasons ('the drugs are good for you') but perhaps because by taking medication, the patient expects to get better. The authors concluded in a review article that 'perhaps the most provocative explanation for the good effect of good adherence on health is the one most perplexing to clinicians: the role of patient expectancies or self efficacy'. They suggested that 'patients who expect treatment to be effective engage in other health practices that lead to improved clinical outcomes' (Horwitz and Horwitz 1993). In addition, they suggested that the power of adherence may not be limited to taking drugs but may also occur with adherence to recommendations of behaviour change. Adherence may be a measure of patient expectation, with these expectations influencing the individual's health status – adherence is an illustration of the placebo effect and a reflection of the complex interrelationship between beliefs, behaviour and health.

placebo effects as an interaction between individuals and between individuals and their environment.

The cognitive dissonance theory of placebos, however, developed by Totman (1976, 1987), attempted to remove patient expectations from the placebo equation and emphasized justification and dissonance.

Cognitive dissonance theory

Totman placed his cognitive dissonance theory of placebos in the following context: 'Why did faith healing last for such a long time?' and 'Why are many of the homeopathic medicines, which have no medically active content, still used?' He argued that faith healing has lasted and homeopathic medicines are still used because they work. In answer to his question why this might be, Totman suggested that the one factor that all of these medically inert treatments have in common, is that they required an investment by the individual in terms of money, dedication, pain, time or inconvenience. He argued that if medically inactive drugs were freely available they would not be effective and that if an individual lived around the corner to Lourdes then a trip to Lourdes would have no effect on their health status.

The effect of investment

Totman suggested that this investment results in the individual having to go through two processes: (1) the individual needs to justify their behaviour and (2) the individual needs to see themselves as rational and in control. If these two factors are in line with each other (e.g. I spent money on a treatment and it worked), then the individual experiences low dissonance. If however, there is a conflict between these two factors (e.g. I spent money on a treatment and I do not feel any better), the individual experiences a state of high dissonance. Totman argued that high justification (it worked) results in low guilt and low dissonance (e.g. I can justify my behaviour, I am rational and in control). However, low justification (it didn't work) results in high guilt and high dissonance (e.g. I cannot justify my behaviour, I am not rational or in control). How does this relate to placebo effects and changes in symptoms?

Justification and changes in symptoms

If an individual travels far and pays a lot of money to see a faith healer then they need to justify this behaviour. Also they need to see themselves as being rational and in control. If they have put a lot of investment into seeing a faith healer and the faith healer has no effect on their health status, then they will not be able to see themselves as being rational and in control, and will therefore be in a state of high dissonance. The best way to resolve this dissonance according to Totman is for there to be an outcome that enables the individual to be able to justify their behaviour and to see themselves as rational and in control. In terms of the faith healer, the best outcome would be an improvement in health status. This would enable the individual to justify their behaviour and to enable them to maintain a sense of self as one who is rational and

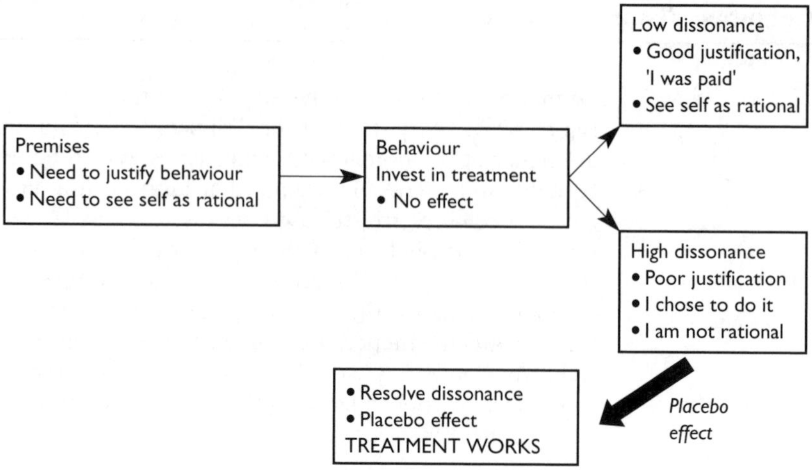

Figure 12.2 Cognitive dissonance theory of placebo effects

sensible. Totman argued that when in a state of high dissonance, unconscious regulating mechanisms are activated, which may cause physical changes that improve the health of the individual, which enables the individual to justify their behaviour, and this resolves the dissonance. Totman therefore suggested that for a placebo effect to occur, the individual does not require an expectation that they will get better, but a need to find justification for their behaviour and a state of cognitive dissonance to set this up. Totman's model is illustrated in Fig. 12.2.

Evidence for the role of justification

Research has examined whether a need for justification does in fact relate to symptom perception. Zimbardo (1969) evaluated the effects of *post-hoc* justification on hunger and thirst. Subjects were asked not to eat or drink for a length of time, and were divided into two groups. Group one were offered money if they managed to abstain from eating and drinking, providing these subjects with good justification for their behaviour. Group two were simply asked not to eat or drink for a length of time, but were given no reason or no incentive, and therefore had no justification. Having good justification for their behaviour, group 1 were not in a state of dissonance; they were able to justify not eating and still maintain a sense of being rational and in control. Group two had no justification for their behaviour and were therefore in a state of high dissonance, as they were performing a behaviour for very little reason. Therefore in order to resolve this dissonance it was argued that group two needed to find a justification for their behaviour. At the end of the period of abstinence all subjects were allowed to eat and drink as much as they wished. The results showed that group two (those in high dissonance) ate and drank less when free food was available to them than group one (those in low dissonance).

The results were interpreted as follows. The subjects in group two, being in a state of high dissonance, needed to find a justification for their behaviour and justified their behaviour by believing 'I didn't eat because I was not hungry'. They therefore ate and drank less when food was available. The subjects in group one, being in a state of low dissonance, had no need to find a justification for their behaviour as they had a good justification 'I didn't eat because I was paid not to'. They therefore ate more when the food was offered. The results of this study have been used to suggest that high dissonance influenced the subject's physiological state, and the physiological state changed in order to resolve the problem of dissonance.

Research has also examined the effects of justification on placebo-induced pain reduction. Totman (1987) induced pain in a group of subjects using heat stimulation. Subjects were then offered the choice of a drug in order to reduce pain. In fact this drug was a placebo. Half of the subjects were offered money to take part in the study, and half were offered no money. Totman argued that because one group were offered an incentive to carry out the study and to experience the pain they had a high justification for their behaviour, they therefore had high justification and were in a state of low dissonance. The other group, however, were offered no money and therefore had low justification for subjecting themselves to a painful situation; they therefore had low justification and were in a state of high dissonance. Totman argued that this group needed to find some kind of justification to resolve this state of dissonance. If the drug worked, Totman argued that this would provide them with justification for subjecting themselves to the experiment and for choosing to take the drug. The results showed that the group in a state of high dissonance experienced less pain following the placebo than the group in low dissonance. Totman argued that this suggests that being in a state of low justification activated the individual's unconscious regulating mechanisms, which caused physiological changes to reduce the pain, providing the group with justification for their behaviour, which therefore eradicated their state of dissonance.

An example of Totman's theory

The following example illustrates the relationship between justification, the need to see oneself as rational and in control, and the problem of dissonance between these two factors.

Walking to Lourdes in order to improve one's health status involves a degree of investment in that behaviour in terms of time, money, etc. If the visit to Lourdes has no effect, then the behaviour begins to appear irrational and unjustified. If the individual can provide justification for their behaviour, for example 'I was paid to go to Lourdes', then they will experience low dissonance. If, however, the individual can find no justification for their visit to Lourdes and therefore believes 'I chose to do it and it didn't work', they remain in a state of high dissonance. Dissonance is an uncomfortable state to be in and the individual is motivated to remove this state. Changing the outcome (e.g. 'I feel better following my visit to Lourdes') removes this dissonance and the individual can believe, 'I chose to do it and it worked'. Therefore, according to cognitive dissonance theory, dissonance can be resolved by the placebo having an effect on the individual's health status by activating unconscious regulating mechanisms.

Support for cognitive dissonance theory

The following factors provide support and evidence for cognitive dissonance theory:

- ◆ The theory can explain all placebo effects, not just pain.
- ◆ The theory does not require patient expectations, but choice. This helps to explain those reported instances where the individual does not appear to expect to get better.
- ◆ The theory suggests that the individual needs commitment to the medical procedure, which explains why the individual may need to show some investment (e.g. pain, time, money) in order to get better. This can explain some of the proposed effects of treatment characteristics, individual characteristics and therapist characteristics.

Problems with cognitive dissonance theory

However, there are several problems with cognitive dissonance theory:

- ◆ Much of the research examining the effects of justification has involved giving money to subjects to enable them to provide justification for their behaviour. It is possible that providing subjects with money increases their anxiety and therefore increases pain perception.
- ◆ It is also possible that the experimenter's attempt to persuade the individual to participate, itself also increases anxiety.
- ◆ Cognitive dissonance theory has mainly been tested using acute pain, which has been elicited in a laboratory setting. Whether the results are transferable to 'real life' is questionable.
- ◆ Totman argues that patient expectations are not necessary. However, an individual must expect some changes following the intervention, otherwise they would not make the original investment. It is also possible that paying subjects to participate changes their expectations of a successful outcome.
- ◆ Totman does not explain what these unconscious regulating mechanisms may be.

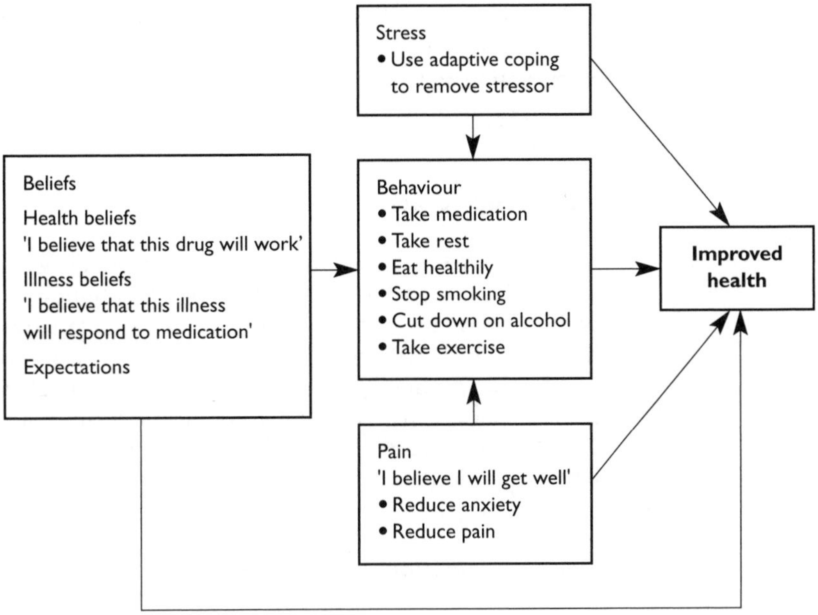

Figure 12.3 The interrelationship between beliefs, behaviour and health

The role of placebo effects in health psychology

Placebos have implications for many areas of health psychology and illustrate how these different areas may interact. These are outlined in terms of the areas of health psychology described in this book, which provides additional insights into possible mechanisms of the placebo effect. The interactions between these different areas are illustrated in Fig. 12.3.

Health beliefs

For a placebo to have an effect, the individual needs to have a belief that the intervention will be effective. For example, a placebo in the form of a pill will work if the individual subscribes to a medical model of health and illness and believes that traditional medical interventions are effective. A placebo in the form of herbal tea may only be effective if the individual believes in alternative medicines and is open to non-traditional forms of intervention. Furthermore, the conditioning effects, reporting error and misattribution process may only occur if the individual believes that health professionals in white coats can treat illness, that hospitals are where people get better and that medical interventions should produce positive results. Patients' beliefs may themselves be a mechanism for explaining placebo effects. Perhaps the belief about a treatment has either a direct effect on health through physiological changes, or an indirect effect via behavioural change. For example, the belief that a treatment intervention will work, may directly influence the individual's immune system or alternatively may promote a change in lifestyle.

Illness cognitions

For a placebo to have an effect, the individual needs to hold particular beliefs about their illness. For example, if an illness is seen as long lasting without episodes of remission, times of spontaneous recovery may not happen, which will therefore not be explained in terms of the effectiveness of the treatment. Likewise, if an individual believes that their illness has a medical cause then a placebo in the form of a pill would be effective. However, if the individual believes that their illness is caused by their lifestyle, a pill placebo may not be effective.

Health professionals' health beliefs

Placebos may also be related to the beliefs of the health professionals. For example, a doctor may need to believe in the intervention for it to have an effect. If the doctor believes that an illness is the result of lifestyle, and can be cured by changes in that lifestyle, then a placebo in the form of a medical intervention may not work, as the doctor's expectation of failure may be communicated to the patient. Furthermore, theories of health professionals' health beliefs and their role in doctor–patient communication illustrate a useful emphasis on interaction rather than individual characteristics.

Health-related behaviours

A placebo may function via changes in health-related behaviour. If an individual believes that they have taken something or behaved in a way that may promote good health, they may also change other health-related behaviours (e.g. smoking, drinking, exercise), which may also improve their health. Furthermore, the choice to take a medication may itself be seen as a health-related behaviour, and may be predicted by theories of behaviour and behaviour change.

Stress

Placebos also have implications for understanding responses to stress. If placebos have an effect either directly (physiological change) or indirectly (behaviour change) then this is in parallel with theories of stress. In addition, placebos may function by reducing any stress caused by illness.

The belief that an individual has taken control of their illness (perceived control) may reduce the stress response reducing any effects this stress may have on the illness.

Pain

Placebo-induced pain reduction may be mediated either by physiological changes, such as opiate release, or by anxiety reduction. Both of these changes can be explained in terms of the gate control theory of pain, which suggests that the experience of pain is a result of an interaction between psychological (beliefs, anxiety) and physiological (opiates) processes. Previous experience and expectation are also implicated in pain reduction. Perhaps, placebo-induced pain reduction may also be mediated by patient expectations and previous experience about the efficacy of the treatment intervention.

Implications for dualism

Placebos indicate that an individual's symptoms and health status may be influenced by their expectations, beliefs and previous experience. These factors are central to health psychology in its attempt to challenge the traditional biomedical approach to health and illness. If an individual's psychological state can influence their health, then perhaps the mind and body should not be seen as separate entities but as interacting. This is, in part, in contradiction to dualistic models of the individual. However, this interaction still assumes that the mind and body are distinct; to interact with each other, they still need to be defined as separate.

To conclude

Placebos have been shown to have a multitude of effects ranging from pain relief to changing cognitive state. Many theories have been developed in an attempt to explain how placebos work, and these can be categorized as non-interactive theories, which focus on the characteristics of either the patient, the health professional or the treatment, and interactive theories, which regard placebo effects as arising from interaction between these different variables. In particular, most explanations of placebos point to a central role for expectations both of the patient and the health professional. These theories suggest that if a patient expects to get better, then this expectation will influence their health. Therefore, through expectancies, it is possible that patient and doctor expectations, anxiety, conditioning, opiates and cognitive dissonance could interact with each other. However, how this interaction would actually influence health remains unclear. Finally, placebos have many implications for the areas of health psychology examined in this book. They indicate that beliefs, behaviours, stress, pain and illness may not be separate areas, requiring separate theories and research, but may be interrelated, and that rather than being a factor to be taken out of an understanding of health the placebo effect may itself play a central role in determining health status.

Questions

1 Discuss the evidence for the possible theories of the placebo effect.

2 Placebos are all in the mind. Discuss.

3 Placebos are a useful treatment for pain. Discuss.

4 Discuss the role of patient expectations in improvements in health.

5 Discuss the implications of theories of placebos for the interrelationship between beliefs, behaviours and health.

6 Design a research study to illustrate the role of expectations in recovery from an acute illness.

For discussion

Consider the last time you took any medication (e.g. pain killer, antibiotics, etc.). To what extent were any subsequent changes due to the placebo effect?

Assumptions in health psychology

The research into placebo effects highlights some of the assumptions in health psychology:

1 *The mind–body split.* Placebos suggest an interaction between the mind and the body – expecting to get better may produce both subjective ('I feel better') and objective ('You did not have another heart attack') changes in the individual's physical well-being. This is in line with health psychology's aim at challenging traditional dualistic models. However, implicit in the interaction between the mind and body is a definition of these two factors being separate in order to interact.

2 *Dividing up the soup.* Health psychology discusses variables such as beliefs, expectations, anxiety, behaviour and health as separate facets of individuals. It then examines how these factors interact and emphasizes the complex interrelationships between them all

(e.g. beliefs create changes in behaviour, behaviours cause changes in health, emotions cause changes in behaviours). However, perhaps individuals are not made up of these separate factors but are a blurred 'soup' of undefined and unseparated 'everything'. Within this soup all the factors are one as they are not undifferentiated. Health psychology takes the soup and divides it up into different separate factors as if these different factors exist. It then discusses how they relate to each other. However, the discussion of how they interrelate can only occur because health psychology has separated them up in the first place. Perhaps, psychological theory creates separate 'things' in order to look at the relationship between these 'things'. Without the original separation there would be no need for a discussion of interaction – it would be obvious that 'things' were related as they would be as one!

Further reading

Critelli, J.W. and Neumann, K.F. (1984) The placebo: conceptual analysis of a construct in transition, *American Psychologist*, 39: 32–9.

This paper provides a theoretical discussion on placebos and analyses the role of placebos in health and illness.

Totman, R.G. (1987) *The Social Causes of Illness*. London: Souvenir Press.

This book provides an interesting perspective on placebos and the interrelationship between beliefs, behaviours and health.

CHAPTER 13

Psychology throughout the course of illness: the examples of HIV, cancer and coronary heart disease

Chapter overview

This chapter examines the role that psychology plays at each stage of an illness, from illness onset, to its progression, to the psychological consequences and longevity. It does not aim to be a comprehensive overview of the immense literature on illness, but to illustrate the possible varied role of psychology in illness. The chapter uses the examples of HIV, cancer and coronary heart disease, although these psychological factors are relevant to a multitude of other chronic and acute illnesses. It suggests that, rather than being seen as a passive response to biomedical factors, such chronic illnesses are better understood in terms of a complex interplay of physiological and psychological processes.

This chapter covers:

- What is HIV?
- The role of psychology in the study of HIV
- Susceptibility/progression/longevity and HIV
- What is cancer?
- The role of psychology in cancer
- Initiation/maintenance/consequences and the alleviation of symptoms and cancer
- What is coronary heart disease?
- The role of psychology in coronary heart disease
- Risk factors and rehabilitation and coronary heart disease

HIV and AIDS

This section examines the history of HIV, what HIV is and how it is transmitted. It then evaluates the role of psychology in understanding HIV in terms of attitudes to HIV and AIDS, susceptibility to HIV and AIDS, progression from HIV to AIDS and longevity. A detailed discussion of condom use in the context of HIV and AIDS can be found in Chapter 8.

The history of HIV

AIDS (Acquired Immune Deficiency Syndrome) was identified as a new syndrome in 1981. At that time, it was regarded as specific to homosexuality and was known as GRIDS (gay-related immune deficiency syndrome). As a result of this belief a number of theories were developed to try and explain the occurrence of this new illness amongst homosexuals. These ranged from the suggestion that AIDS may be a response to the over-use of recreational drugs such as 'poppers' or to over-exposure to semen, and they focused on the perceived lifestyles of the homosexual population. In 1982, however, AIDS occurred in haemophiliacs. As haemophiliacs were seen not to have lifestyles comparable with the homosexual population, scientists started to reform their theories about AIDS and suggested, for the first time, that perhaps AIDS was caused by a virus. Such a virus could reach haemophiliacs through their use of Factor VIII, a donated blood clotting agent.

The HIV virus was first isolated in 1983. However, there is debate as to whether this was achieved by Gallo in the USA or/and Montagnier in France. Both these researchers were looking for a retro-virus, having examined a cat retro-virus that caused leukaemia and appeared to be very similar to what they thought was causing this new illness. In 1984, the Human Immuno-Deficiency virus type 1 (HIV 1) was identified, and in 1985 HIV 2 was identified in Africa.

What is HIV?

The structure of HIV

The HIV virus is a retro-virus, a type of virus containing RNA. There are three types of retro-virus: oncogenic retro-viruses which cause cancer, foamy retro-viruses which have no effect at all on the health status of the individual, and lentiviruses, or slow viruses, which have slow long-term effects. HIV is a lentivirus.

The HIV virus is structured with an outer coat and an inner core. The RNA is situated in the core and contains eight viral genes, which encode the proteins of the envelope and the core, and also contains enzymes, which are essential for replication.

The transmission of HIV

In order to be transmitted from one individual to the next, the HIV virus generally needs to come into contact with cells that have CD4 molecules on their surface. Such cells are found within the immune system and are called T-helper cells. The process of transmission of the HIV virus follows the following stages:

1 HIV binds to the CD4 molecule of T-helper cell.
2 HIV virus is internalized into the cytoplasm of the cell.
3 The cell itself generates a pro-viral DNA, which is a copy of the host cell.
4 This pro-virus enters the nucleus of the host cell.
5 The host cell produces new viral particles, which it reads off from the viral code of the viral DNA.
6 These viral particles bud off and infect new cells.
7 Eventually, after much replication, the host T-helper cell dies.

The progression from HIV to AIDS

The progression from HIV to HIV disease and AIDS varies in time. AIDS reflects a reduction in T-helper cells and specifically those that are CD4-positive T-cells. This causes immune deficiency and the appearance of opportunistic infections. The progression from initial HIV sero-conversion through to AIDS tends to go through the following stages:

1 the initial viral seroconversion illness;
2 an asymptomatic stage;
3 enlargement of the lymph nodes, onset of opportunistic infections;
4 AIDS-related complex (ARC);
5 AIDS.

The prevalence of HIV and AIDS

Because of the recent identification of HIV and AIDS and due to the long disease-free interval from seroconversion to AIDS, data on the prevalence and incidence of HIV and AIDS are limited. However, estimates of the number of cases globally show that 30.6 million people are living with HIV/AIDS and 11.7 million have died from HIV/AIDS. By continent, data concerning the prevalence of reported incidences of AIDS from the late 1970s to the end of 1994 indicate the following case statistics: Africa, 350,000; USA, 400,000; Europe, 127,000; Americas (excluding USA), 123,000; Asia, 20,000; Oceania, 5000; total, 1,025,000. In the UK, from 1982 to March 1997, 32,200 people have been diagnosed as HIV+, of whom 15,500 have progressed to AIDS and 12,800 have died from HIV/AIDS-related diseases. In terms of current data, in the UK there are 16,000 people living with a diagnosed HIV infection and in 1997 the following numbers of new cases were reported across the world: North America, 44,000; Caribbean, 47,000; Latin America, 180,000; Western Europe, 30,000; North Africa and Middle East, 19,000; sub-Saharan Africa, 4 million; Eastern Europe and Central Asia, 100,000; East Asia and Pacific, 180,000; South and South East Asia, 1.3 million; Australia and New Zealand, 600.

The role of psychology in the study of HIV

HIV is transmitted mostly because of people's behaviour (e.g. sexual intercourse, needle use). Health psychology has studied HIV in terms of attitudes to HIV, changing these attitudes, and examining predictors of behaviour. The following observations suggest that psychology has an additional role to play in HIV:

- Not everyone exposed to HIV virus becomes HIV positive. This suggests that psychological factors may influence an individual's susceptibility to the HIV virus.
- The time for progression from HIV to AIDS is variable. Psychological factors may have a role in promoting the replication of the HIV virus and the progression from being HIV-positive to having AIDS.
- Perhaps not everyone with HIV dies from AIDS. Psychological factors may have a role to play in determining the longevity of the individual.

The potential role of psychological factors in understanding HIV and AIDS is shown in Fig. 13.1.

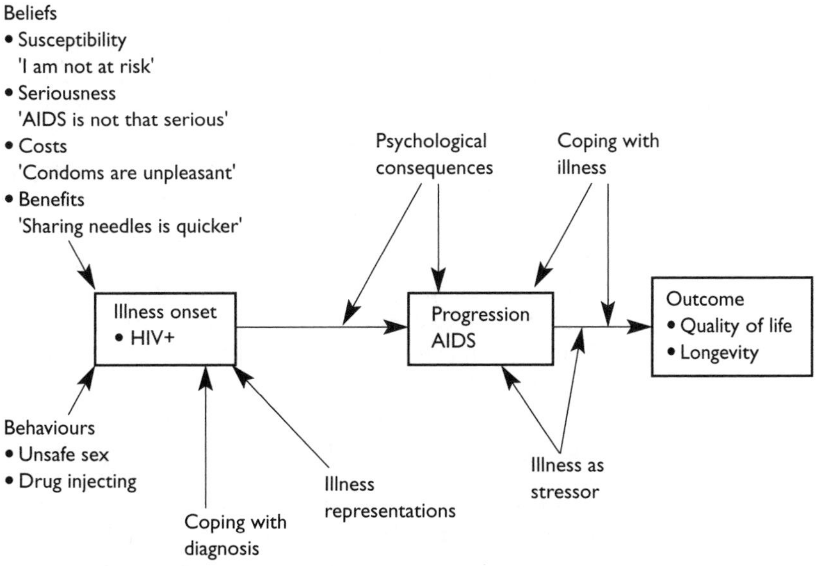

Figure 13.1 The potential role of psychology in HIV

The role of psychology in AIDS in terms of (1) attitudes to AIDS, (2) susceptibility to AIDS, (3) progression from HIV to AIDS and (4) longevity will now be examined.

Attitudes to AIDS

Research has examined attitudes to HIV and the relationship between these attitudes and behaviour. As AIDS is a new disease, the research into attitudes reflects not only differences in these attitudes between individuals but also changes in attitude across time.

Research has asked the question, 'Do people feel vulnerable to the HIV virus?' Temoshok *et al.* (1987) carried out a survey of people living in a number of different cities in America and asked these people whether AIDS was seen as a personal health concern. The proportions responding 'yes' were as follows: San Francisco, 33 per cent; New York, 57 per cent; Miami, 50 per cent; and Los Angeles, 47 per cent.

It is interesting to note that subjects in San Francisco, which has the highest incidence of HIV-positive individuals in the USA, reported seeing HIV as less of a personal health concern than those living in other cities. There are two possible explanations for this, which raise questions about the complex interrelationship between knowledge, education, personal experience and attitudes. First, by living in a city with high levels of HIV and high exposure to health education on information around HIV and AIDS, knowledge of the disease is increased. This knowledge makes people feel less vulnerable because they believe they can do something about it. Alternatively however, perhaps being exposed to AIDS and HIV, and death following AIDS, increases the sense of fear and denial in individuals living in cities where there is a high prevalence of the illness. Feeling less vulnerable may reflect this denial.

Many studies in the UK have also examined individuals' perception of risk and its relationship to knowledge. Research in the late 1980s and early 1990s indicated that although knowledge about transmission of HIV was high, many college students reported being relatively invulnerable to HIV. Abrams *et al.* (1990: 49) reported that 'young people have a strong sense of AIDS invulnerability which seems to involve a perception that they have control over the risk at which they place themselves'. Woodcock *et al.* (1992) examined young people's interpretations of their personal risk of infection and suggested that although some subjects acknowledged that they were at risk, this was often dismissed because it was in the past and 'it would show by now'. However, many subjects in this study denied that they were at risk and justified this in terms of beliefs such as 'it's been blown out of proportion', 'AIDS is a risk you take in living', 'partners were (or are) not promiscuous', or partners came from geographical areas that were not regarded as high-risk (e.g. the New Forest in Southern England was considered a low-risk area and Glasgow, a high-risk area) (see Chapter 8 for a discussion of risk perception and condom use).

Another question that has been asked about HIV is, 'Does the sexuality and sexual behaviour of individuals influence their beliefs about HIV?'

Temoshok *et al.* (1987) examined gay, bisexual and heterosexual men's beliefs about HIV. The results suggested that gay and bi-sexual men believe that AIDS was more important than heterosexual men. This group showed higher levels of knowledge about HIV, reported having been concerned about HIV for a longer period of time, reported feeling more susceptible to HIV, and reported feeling that their chances of getting HIV were higher than the heterosexual population.

Some researchers have also looked at how teenagers and students view HIV, as they tend to be particularly sexually active. Price *et al.* (1985) found that this group of individuals, despite being high risk and sexually active, reported low levels of knowledge and said that they were less likely to get AIDS.

Attitudes and behaviour change

Research has specifically examined the relationship between beliefs about HIV and behaviour change. Temoshok *et al.* (1987) reported that perceived risk of AIDS was not related to changes in sexual behaviour. However, they reported that anti-gay attitudes and fear were related to a change in sexual behaviour. Several studies have also looked at the change in risky sexual behaviour in gay men. Curran *et al.* (1985), McKusick *et al.* (1990) and Martin (1987) suggested that there has been a reduction in such behaviour in gay men, reflecting their attitudes and beliefs about HIV. Likewise Simkins and Ebenhage (1984) examined the sexual behaviour of heterosexual college students and reported no changes in their behaviour. This again reflects their attitudes towards HIV with their reports of being at low risk.

The interrelationship between knowledge, attitudes and behaviour

The relationship between knowledge and beliefs about HIV is a complex one. Health education campaigns assume that improving knowledge will change attitudes and therefore change behaviour. In terms of HIV, one behaviour that is targeted by health educational campaigns is safer sex (see Chapter 8 for a discussion of condom use). However, whether increasing knowledge actually increases the practice of safer sex is questionable. There are several possible consequences of knowledge:

- It is possible that increasing knowledge increases fear in the individual, which may then cause denial, resulting in no effect on behaviour or even a detrimental effect on behaviour.
- Alternatively, improved knowledge may improve the individual's perception of reality and their perception of risk, which could therefore cause a change in behaviour as the individual is not experiencing fear.
- It is also possible that improving knowledge may increase the awareness of the seriousness of the illness, which could cause individuals who actually contract the illness to be blamed for this (victim blaming). Fear and victim blaming themselves can also have a complicated

interaction with other beliefs and also on the safer sex practices of individuals. Fear and victim blaming may be related to denial, or behavioural change, or prejudice, or helplessness, or a feeling of lack of control.

Therefore, promoting safer sex may be more complicated than simply increasing knowledge (see Chapter 8 for a discussion of sex education influences).

Psychology and susceptibility to the HIV virus

Psychology may also have a role to play in an individual's susceptibility to the HIV virus once exposed to it. Several studies have examined the possibility that not all those individuals who come into contact with HIV, become HIV-positive, and have suggested several reasons for this. One train of thought argues that the lifestyle of an individual may increase their chances of contracting HIV once exposed to the virus. Van Griensven *et al.* (1986) suggested that the use of other drugs, such as nitrates and cannabis, increase the chance of contracting HIV once exposed to the virus. Lifson *et al.* (1989) also argued that the existence of other viruses, such as herpes simplex and cytomegalovirus (CMV), in the bloodstream may increase the chances of contracting HIV. These viruses are also thought to be associated with unsafe sex and injecting drugs. Therefore, unhealthy behaviours may not only be related to exposure to the HIV virus but also the likelihood that an individual will become HIV-positive. However, much of the lifestyle literature surrounding susceptibility to HIV virus was based on the beliefs about HIV that existed during the 1980s, when HIV was still regarded as a homosexual illness. It therefore focused on the lifestyles of homosexuals and made generalizations about this lifestyle in order to explain susceptibility to the virus.

Psychology and the progression from HIV to AIDS

Research has also examined the role of psychology in the progression from HIV to AIDS. It has been argued that HIV provides a useful basis for such research for the following reasons: (1) there are large numbers of individuals who can be identified at the asymptomatic stage of their illness allowing an analysis of disease progression from a symptom-free stage; (2) as people with HIV tend to be young the problem of other co-existing diseases can be avoided; and (3) the measurement of disease progression using numbers of CD4 T-helper cells is accurate (Taylor *et al.* 1998).

This research points to roles for both lifestyle and psychological state in the progression of the illness. First, in terms of lifestyle, it has been suggested that injecting drugs further stimulates the immune system, which may well influence replication, and thereby points to a role for drug use not only in contracting the virus but also for its replication. In addition, research has also indicated that replication of the HIV virus may be influenced by further exposure to the HIV virus, suggesting a role for unsafe sex and drug use in its progression. Furthermore, it has been suggested that contact with drugs, which may have an immuno-suppressive effect, or other viruses, such as herpes complex and CMV, may also be related to an increase in replication. Second, in terms of psychological factors, Sodroski *et al.* (1984) suggested that stress or distress may well increase the replication of the HIV virus, causing a quicker progression to AIDS. This has been tentatively supported by the research of Solomon and Temoshok (1987), who argued that social homophobia may well cause stress in individuals who have contracted HIV, which could exacerbate their illness. Furthermore, research from the Multi Center AIDS Cohort Study (MACS) in the USA has suggested a role for forms of cognitive adjustment to bereavement and illness progression (Reed *et al.* 1994; 1999; Bower *et al.* 1998). In the first part of this study, 72 men who were HIV-positive, asymptomatic and half of whom had recently experienced the death of a close friend or primary partner, completed measures of their psychosocial state (HIV specific expectancies, mood state and hopelessness) and had the number of their CD4 T-helper cells recorded. They were then followed up over a 6-year period. The results showed that about half of the sample showed symptoms over the follow-up period. However, the rate and extent of the disease progression was not consistent for everyone. In particular, the results showed that symptom development was predicted by baseline HIV specific expectancies, particularly in those who had been bereaved. Therefore, it would seem that having more negative expectancies of HIV progression is predictive of actual progression (Reed *et al.* 1999). In the second part of this study, 40 HIV-positive men who had recently lost a close friend or partner to AIDS were interviewed about how they made sense of this death. These interviews were then classified according to whether the individual had managed to find meaning in the death in line with Taylor's cognitive adaptation theory of coping (Taylor 1983) (see Chapter 3). An example of meaning would be 'What his death did was snap a certain value into my behaviour, which is "Listen you don't know how long you've got. You've just lost another one. Spend more time with the people that mean something to you".' The results showed that those who had managed to find meaning maintained their levels of CD4 T-helper cells at follow-up, where as those who did not find meaning showed a decline. Therefore, both an individual's behaviour and his or her psychological state appear to relate to the progression from HIV to AIDS.

Psychology and longevity

Research has also examined the role of psychological factors in longevity following infection with HIV. In particular, this has looked at the direct effects of beliefs and behaviour on the state of immunosuppression of the individual (see Chapter 10 for a discussion of PNI). In 1987, Solomon *et al.* studied 21 AIDS patients and examined their health status and the

FOCUS ON RESEARCH 13.1

TESTING A THEORY – PSYCHOLOGY AND IMMUNE FUNCTIONING

A study to examine the role of psychosocial factors such as coping style, life stress and social support on immune functioning in HIV-positive homosexual men (Goodkin *et al.* 1992).

This study examined the relationship between psychosocial factors and the physical health of HIV-positive men. Models of the relationship between psychological factors and physical health suggest that the link between psychology and health may be via behaviour change (e.g. feeling stressed increases smoking behaviour) and/or via direct physiological changes (e.g. feeling stressed causes a release of stress hormones). This study is based on the belief that psychological variables such as coping style, stress and social support may influence health and illness directly through changes in the individual's physiology (their immune system) regardless of behaviour.

Background

Research has suggested that psychosocial factors may be associated with changes in natural killer cell cytotoxicity (NKCC), which is an important defence against infections and cancer growth. For example, lowered NKCC has been shown in medical students under stress, bereaved individuals, and those with major depressive disorder. In addition, research has suggested that social support, active coping style and joy may be related to changes in NKCC in patients with breast cancer. Although, the research into NKCC in still in its early stages and is somewhat controversial, Goodkin *et al.* (1992) aimed to examine the relationship between psychosocial factors and NKCC in HIV-positive men.

Methodology

Subjects Sixty-two asymptomatic HIV-positive homosexual men from Miami volunteered for the study. They were recruited from the University of Miami School of Medicine Clinical Research Unit, community-based HIV-related service agencies, community physicians, advertisements in magazines and referrals from other studies. Subjects were excluded from the study if they were taking anti-viral medication, had a history of alcohol/substance abuse, a history of psychiatric

disorder, or had a severe head trauma. All subjects were aware of their HIV-positive status and either had no symptoms or a sign of physical infection of no more than three months. Their average age was 33.8 years; 72.6 per cent were native English speakers; nearly half had a first degree; the majority were in full-time employment; 66.1 per cent described themselves as exclusively homosexual; 51.6 per cent were single; 30.6 per cent were in a monogamous relationship and the remainder were either in an open relationship, divorced or widowed.
Design The study was cross-sectional with all subjects completing all measures once.
Measures The subjects completed the following psychosocial, behavioural control and physiological measures.

1 *Psychosocial measures.*
  - *Life Experience Survey*: this assesses the count and impact of life events over the previous 6 months. For the present study, the authors focused on the number of life events and categorized subjects as either mild (0–5), moderate (6–10), high (11–15) or very high (>15).
  - *Social Provisions Scale*: this measures the individual's perception of available social support. The authors used a shortened 20-item version and computed a total 'perceived social support' score.
  - *The Coping Orientations to Problems Experienced scale*: this is a 57-item scale, which measures coping strategies. The present study examined these items in terms of (i) active coping (made up of all the problem focused strategies, such as planning, suppression of competing activities, restraint coping, seeking instrumental support, active coping, and three of the emotion-focused scales, such as seeking emotional support, positive reinterpretation, acceptance); (ii) disengagement/denial (which is made up of behavioural and mental disengagement items and denial); (iii) focus on and venting emotions; and (iv) turning to religion (see Chapter 3 for a discussion of coping).
  - *Profile of Mood States*: this is a 65-item scale of mood-related items. The present study computed a composite 'emotional distress score' composed of items relating to anxiety, depression, fatigue, and confusion.

2 *Measures to control for behaviour.* Subjects completed measures of diet (using a food frequency questionnaire), alcohol and substance use (e.g. marijuana, cocaine, LSD, nitrate inhalants, amphetamines and opiods), smoking behaviour and prescribed medication. These were included in order to determine whether any differences in immune status were due to the psychosocial or behavioural factors. Measures of blood proteins, vitamins and minerals were also taken.

3 *Physiological measures.* Measurements were taken of (i) anti HIV-1 antibody to confirm the subjects' HIV-positive status and (ii) NKCC.

Results

Individual variables and NKCC
The results were first analysed to examine how individual variables were related to NKCC. The results showed that active coping and retinol A (a dietary source of vitamin A) were associated with improved NKCC and that alcohol use was associated with decreased NKCC. There was a trend for a relationship between focus on and venting emotions and improved NKCC, but no effect for social support, life stressors and emotional distress.

Predicting NKCC
All variables were then entered into the analysis to examine the best predictors of NKCC. The results showed that although the control behaviour variables (diet and alcohol) accounted for most of the variance in NKCC, active coping remained predictive of improved NKCC.

Conclusion

The authors conclude that active coping is related to improved immune functioning in terms of NKCC in HIV-positive men. In addition, immune functioning was also related to diet (vitamin A) and alcohol use. This supports the prediction that psychosocial variables may influence health and illness. However, the results indicate that the link between psychological variables and health status is probably via both a behavioural pathway (i.e. changes in health-related behaviours) *and* a direct physiological pathway (i.e. changes in immune functioning).

relationship of this health status to predictive baseline psychological variables. At follow-up, they found that survival was predicted by their general health status at baseline, their health behaviours, hardiness, social support, type C behaviour (self-sacrificing, self-blaming, not emotionally expressive) and coping strategies. In a further study, Solomon and Temoshok (1987) reported an additional follow-up of AIDS patients. They argued that a positive outcome was predicted by perceived control over illness at baseline, social support, problem-solving, help-seeking behaviour, low social desirability and the expression of anger and hostility. This study indicated that type C behaviour was not related to longevity.

More recently, Reed *et al.* (1994) examined the psychological state of 78 gay men who had been diagnosed with AIDS in terms of their self-reported health status, psychological adjustment and psychological responses to HIV, well-being, self-esteem and levels of hopelessness. In addition, they completed measures of 'realistic acceptance', which reflected statements such as 'I tried to accept what might happen', 'I prepare for the worst' and 'I go over in my mind what I say or do about this problem'. At follow-up, the results showed that two-thirds of the men had died. However, survival was predicted by 'realistic acceptance' at baseline with those who showed greater acceptance of their own death living longer. Therefore, psychological state may also relate to longevity.

Conclusion

The study of HIV and AIDS illustrates the role of psychology at different stages of an illness. Psychological factors are important not only for attitudes and beliefs about HIV and the resulting behaviour, but may also be involved in an individual's susceptibility to contracting the virus, the replication of the virus once it has been contracted and their subsequent longevity.

Cancer

This section examines what cancer is, looks at its prevalence and then assesses the role of psychology in understanding cancer in terms of the initiation and promotion of cancer, the psychological consequences of cancer, dealing with the symptoms of cancer, longevity and the promotion of a disease-free interval.

What is cancer?

Cancer is defined as an uncontrolled growth of abnormal cells, which produces tumours called neoplasms. There are two types of tumours: *benign* tumours, which do not spread throughout the body, and *malignant* tumours, which show metastasis (the process of cells breaking off from the tumour and moving elsewhere). There are three types of cancer cells: *carcinomas*, which constitute 90 per cent of all cancer cells and which originate in tissue cells; *sarcomas*, which originate in connective tissue; and *leukaemias*, which originate in the blood.

The prevalence of cancer

In 1991, it was reported that there were six million new cases of cancer in the world every year, and that one-tenth of all deaths in the world are caused by cancer. In 1989, it was reported that cancers are the second leading cause of death in the UK and accounted for 24 per cent of all deaths in England and Wales in 1984 (Smith and Jacobson 1989). The main causes of cancer mortality among men in England and Wales (1984) are lung cancer (36 per cent), colorectal cancer (11 per cent), prostate cancer (9 per cent); and among women are breast cancer (20 per cent), lung cancer (15 per cent), colorectal cancer (14 per cent), ovarian cancer

(6 per cent), cervical cancer (3 per cent). While the overall number of cancer deaths do not appear to be rising, the incidence of lung cancer deaths in women has risen over the past few years.

The role of psychology in cancer

A role for psychology in cancer was first suggested by Galen in AD 200–300, who argued for an association between melancholia and cancer, and also by Gedman in 1701, who suggested that cancer might be related to life disasters. Eighty-five per cent of cancers are thought to be potentially avoidable. Psychology therefore plays a role in terms, attitudes and beliefs about cancer and predicting behaviours, such as smoking and diet, which are implicated in its initiation (details of these behaviours can be found in Chapters 2, 5, 6 and 7). In addition, sufferers of cancer report psychological consequences, which have implications for their quality of life. The role of psychology in cancer is also illustrated by the following observations:

- ◆ Cancer cells are present in most people but not everybody gets cancer; in addition although research suggests a link between smoking and lung cancer, not all heavy smokers get lung cancer. Perhaps psychology is involved in the susceptibility to cancer.
- ◆ All those who have cancer do not always show progression towards death at the same rate. Perhaps psychology has a role to play in the progression of cancer.
- ◆ Not all cancer sufferers die of cancer. Perhaps psychology has a role to play in longevity.

The potential role of psychology in understanding cancer is shown in Fig. 13.2.

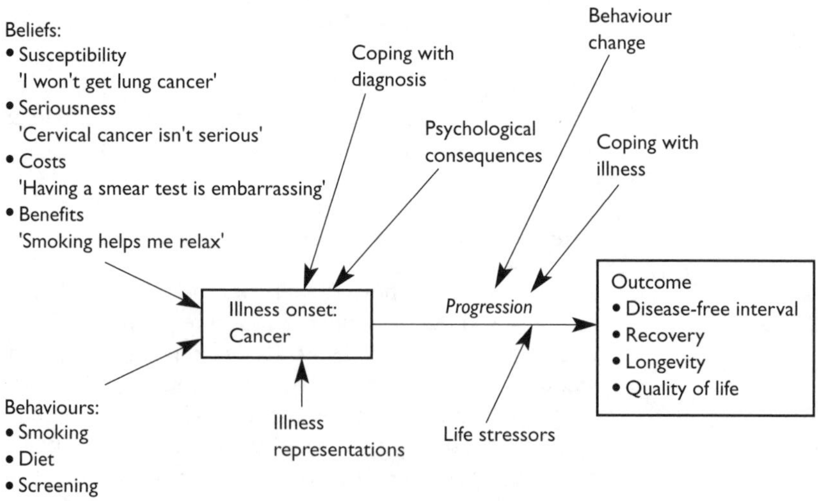

Figure 13.2 The potential role of psychology in cancer

The role of psychology in cancer will now be examined in terms of (1) the initiation and promotion of cancer, (2) the psychological consequences of cancer, (3) dealing with the symptoms of cancer and (4) longevity and promoting a disease-free interval.

The psychosocial factors in initiation and promotion of cancer

1 *Behavioural factors*. Behavioural factors have been shown to play a role in the initiation and promotion of cancer. Smith and Jacobson (1989) reported that 30 per cent of cancers are related to tobacco use, 35 per cent are related to diet, 7 per cent are due to reproductive and sexual behaviour and 3 per cent are due to alcohol. These behaviours can be predicted by examining individual health beliefs (see Chapters 2, 5 and 9).
2 *Stress*. Stress has also been shown to have a role to play in cancer. Laudenslager *et al.* (1983) reported a study that involved exposing cancer-prone mice to stress (shaking the cage). They found that if this stressor could be controlled there was a decrease in the rate of tumour development. However, if the stressor was perceived as uncontrollable this resulted in an increase in the development. This suggests a role for stress in the initiation of cancer. However, Sklar and Anisman (1981) argued that an increase in stress increased the promotion of cancer not its initiation (see Chapter 10 for a discussion of the relationship between stress and illness).
3 *Life events*. It has also been suggested that life events play a role in cancer (see Chapter 10 for a discussion of life events). A study by Jacobs and Charles (1980) examined the differences in life events between families who had a cancer victim and families who did not. They reported that in families who had a cancer victim there were higher numbers who had moved house, higher numbers who had changed some form of their behaviour, higher numbers who had had a change in health status other than the cancer person, and higher numbers of divorces indicating that life events may well be a factor contributing to the onset of cancer. However, the results from a meta-analysis by Petticrew *et al.* (1999) do not support this suggestion. They identified 29 studies, from 1966 to 1997, which met their inclusion criteria (adult women with breast cancer, group of cancer-free controls, measure of stressful life events) and concluded that although several individual studies report a relationship between life events and breast cancer, when methodological problems are taken into account and when the data across the different studies is merged 'the research shows no good evidence of a relationship between stressful life events and breast cancer'.
4 *Control*. Control also seems to play a role in the initiation and promotion of cancer and it has been argued that control over stressors and control over environmental factors may be related to an increase in the onset of cancer (see Chapter 10 for a discussion of control and the stress–illness link).
5 *Coping styles*. Coping styles are also important. If an individual is subjected to stress, then the methods they use to cope with this stress

may well be related to the onset of cancer. For example, maladaptive, disengagement coping strategies, such as smoking and alcohol, may have a relationship with an increase in cancer (see Chapter 3 for a discussion of coping).

6 *Depression*. Bieliauskas (1980) highlighted a relationship between depression and cancer and suggests that chronic mild stress, but not clinical depression may be related to cancer.
7 *Personality*. Over the past few years there has been some interest in the relationship between personality and cancer. Temoshok and Fox (1984) argued that individuals who develop cancer have a 'type C personality'. A type C personality is described as passive, appeasing, helpless, other focused and unexpressive of emotion. Eysenck (1990) described 'a cancer-prone personality', and suggests that this is characteristic of individuals who react to stress with helplessness and hopelessness, and individuals who repress emotional reactions to life events. An early study by Kissen (1966) supported this relationship between personality and cancer and reported that heavy smokers who develop lung cancer have a poorly developed outlet for their emotions, perhaps suggesting type C personality. In 1987, Shaffer *et al.* carried out a prospective study to examine the predictive capacity of personality and its relationship to developing cancer in medical students over 30 years. At follow-up they described the type of individual who was more likely to develop cancer as having impaired self-awareness, being self-sacrificing, self-blaming and not being emotionally expressive. The results from this study suggest that those individuals who had this type of personality were 16 times more likely to develop cancer than those individuals who did not. However, the relationship between cancer and personality is not a straightforward one. It has been argued that the different personality types predicted to relate to illness are not distinct from each other and also that people with cancer do not consistently differ from either healthy people or people with heart disease in the predicted direction (Amelang and Schmidt-Rathjens 1996).
8 *Hardiness*. Kobasa *et al.* (1982) described a coping style called 'hardiness', which has three components: control, commitment and challenge. Low control suggests a tendency to show feelings of helplessness in the face of stress. Commitment is defined as the opposite of alienation: individuals high in commitment find meaning in their work, values and personal relationships. Individuals high in challenge regard potentially stressful events as a challenge to be met with expected success. Hardiness may be protective in developing cancer.

Psychological consequences of cancer

Emotional responses

Up to 20 per cent of cancer patients may show severe depression, grief, lack of control, personality change, anger and anxiety. Pinder *et al.* (1993) examined the emotional responses of women with operable breast cancer and reported that these can differ widely from little disruption of mood to clinical states of depression and anxiety. The emotional state of breast cancer sufferers appears to be unrelated to the type of surgery they have (Kiebert *et al.* 1991), whether or not they have radiotherapy (Hughson *et al.* 1987) and is only effected by chemotherapy in the medium term (Hughson *et al.* 1986). However, persistent deterioration in mood does seem to be related to previous psychiatric history (Dean 1987), lack of social support (Bloom 1983), age, and lack of an intimate relationship (Pinder *et al.* 1993). Pinder *et al.* (1993) also reported that in sufferers with advanced cancer, psychological morbidity was related to functional status (how well the patient functioned physically) and suggested that lowered functional status was associated with higher levels of depression, which was also related to lower social class.

Cognitive responses

Research has also examined cognitive responses to cancer and suggests that a 'fighting spirit' is negatively correlated with anxiety and depression whilst 'fatalism', 'helplessness' and 'anxious preoccupation' is related to lowered mood (Watson *et al.* 1991). Taylor (1983) examined the cognitive adaptation of 78 women with breast cancer. She reported that these women responded to their cancer in three ways. First, they made a search for meaning, whereby the cancer patients attempted to understand why they had developed cancer. Meanings that were reported included stress, hereditary factors, ingested carcinogens such as birth control pills, environmental carcinogens such as chemical waste, diet, and a blow to the breast. Second, they also attempted to gain a sense of mastery by believing that they could control their cancer and any relapses. Such attempts at control included meditation, positive thinking, and a belief that the original cause is no longer in effect. Third, the women began a process of self-enhancement. This involved social comparison, whereby the women tended to analyse their condition in terms of others they knew. Taylor argued that they showed 'downward comparison', which involved comparing themselves to others worse off, thus improving their beliefs about their own situation. According to Taylor's theory of cognitive adaptation, the combination of meaning, mastery and self-enhancement creates illusions which are a central component of attempts to cope. This theory is discussed in more detail in Chapter 3.

Psychology and the alleviation of symptoms

Psychology also has a role to play in the alleviation of symptoms of cancer, and in promoting quality of life (see Chapter 14 for a discussion of quality of life theory and measurement). Cartwright *et al.* (1973) described the experiences of cancer sufferers, which included very distressing pain, breathing difficulties, vomiting, sleeplessness, loss of bowel and bladder control, loss of appetite, and mental confusion. Psychosocial interventions have therefore been used to attempt to alleviate some of the symptoms of the cancer sufferer and to improve their quality of life.

1 *Pain management.* One of the main roles of psychology is in terms of pain management, and this has taken place through a variety of different pain management techniques (see Chapter 11). For example, biofeedback and hypnosis have been shown to decrease pain. Turk and Rennert (1981) encouraged patients with cancer to describe and monitor their pain, encouraged them to develop coping skills, taught them relaxation skills, encouraged them to do positive imagery and to focus on other things. They reported that these techniques were successful in reducing the pain experience.
2 *Social support interventions.* Social support interventions have also been used through the provision of support groups, which emphasize control, meaningful activities and aim to reduce denial and promote hope. It has been suggested that although this intervention may not have any effect on longevity it may improve the meaningfulness of the cancer patient's life.
3 *Treating nausea and vomiting.* Psychology has also been involved in treating the nausea and vomiting experienced by cancer patients. Cancer patients are often offered chemotherapy as a treatment for their cancer, which can cause anticipatory nausea, vomiting and anxiety. Respondent conditioning and visual imagery, relaxation, hypnosis and desensitization have been shown to decrease nausea and anxiety in cancer patients. Redd (1982) and Burish *et al.* (1987) suggested that 25–33 per cent of cancer patients show conditioned vomiting and 60 per cent show anticipatory anxiety. It is reported that relaxation and guided imagery may decrease these problems.
4 *Body image counselling.* The quality of life of cancer patients may also be improved through altered body image counselling, particularly following the loss of a breast and more generally in dealing with the grief at loss of various parts of the body.
5 *Cognitive adaptation strategies.* Research also suggests that quality of life may also be improved using cognitive adaptation strategies. Taylor (1983) used such strategies to improve patients' self-worth, their ability to be close to others, and the improvement in the meaningfulness of their lives. Such methods have been suggested to involve self-transcendence and this has again been related to improvement in well-being and decrease in illness-related distresses.
6 *The work of the Simontons.* Simonton and Simonton (1975) are well known for applying psychosocial factors and interventions for improving the quality of life of cancer patients using a whole-person approach. This involves the following processes: (1) relaxation, which aims to decrease muscle tension and therefore decrease pain; (2) mental imagery, whereby cancer patients are encouraged to focus on something positive (this aims to develop a belief in the ability to recover, therefore decreasing pain, tension and fear); and (3) exercise programmes, which aim to increase the sense of well-being. In 1975, Simonton and Simonton encouraged a positive attitude towards treatment using whole-person

approach among 152 cancer patients for 18 months, and argued that this intervention predicted a good response of treatment and reduced side-effects. These methods are also currently being used in the Bristol clinic in the UK.

Adjuvant psychological therapy

Greer *et al.* (1992) suggested that, in addition to physical interventions, patients with breast cancer should be offered adjuvant psychological therapy. This involves encouraging cancer patients to examine the personal meaning of their cancer and what they can do to cope with it (see **Focus on research 13.2**).

Psychological factors in longevity

The final question about the role of psychology in cancer is its relationship to longevity; do psychosocial factors influence longevity?

Cognitive responses and longevity

Greer *et al.* (1979) carried out a prospective study in which they examined the relationship between cognitive responses to a breast cancer diagnosis and disease-free intervals. Using semi-structured interviews, they defined three types of responders: those with 'fighting spirit', those who showed denial of the implications of their disease and those who showed a hopeless/helpless response. The authors reported that the groups who showed either 'fighting spirit' or 'denial' had a longer disease-free interval than the other groups. In addition, at a further 15-year follow-up, both a fighting spirit and denial approach also predicted longevity. However, there were problems with this study. At baseline the authors did not measure several important physiological prognostic indicators, such as lymph node involvement, as these measures were not available at the time. These physiological factors may have contributed to both the disease-free interval and the survival of the patients.

Life stress and disease-free interval

In a case control study, Ramirez *et al.* (1989) examined the relationship between life stress and relapse in operable breast cancer. The life events and difficulties occurring during the disease-free interval were recorded in 50 women who had developed their first recurrence of breast cancer and 50 women who were in remission. The two subject groups were matched for the main physical and pathological factors believed to be associated with prognosis and for the socio-demographic variables believed to be related to life events and difficulties. The results showed that life events rated as severe were related to first recurrence of breast cancer. However, the study was cross-sectional in nature, which has implications for determining causality.

FOCUS ON RESEARCH 13.2

PUTTING THEORY INTO PRACTICE – TREATING CANCER SYMPTOMS

A random controlled trial to examine the effects of adjuvant psychological therapy on the psychological sequelae of cancer (Greer *et al.* 1992).

Research has examined the psychological consequences of having cancer. This study examined changes in cancer patients' psychological state as a result of adjuvant psychological therapy (APT). The study used a random controlled trial design in order to compare changes in measures of quality of life in patients receiving APT with those receiving no therapy.

Background

Evidence suggests that a substantial minority of cancer patients show psychological ill-health, particularly in terms of depression and anxiety. As a result, a number of psychotherapeutic procedures have been developed to improve cancer patients' emotional well-being. However, evaluating the effectiveness of such procedures raises several ethical and methodological problems, and these are addressed by Greer *et al.* (1992). These are: (1) the ethical considerations of having a control group (can patients suffering from psychological distress not be given therapy?); (2) the specificity of any psychological intervention (terms such as counselling and psychotherapy are vague and any procedure being evaluated should be clarified); and (3) the outcome measures chosen (many measures of psychological state include items that are not appropriate for cancer patients, such as weight loss and fatigue, which may change as a result of the cancer not the individuals' psychological state). The authors of this study aimed to examine the effects of APT on the psychological state of cancer patients in the light of these problems.

Methodology

Subjects A total of 174 patients attending the Royal Marsden Hospital in the UK were recruited for the study using the following criteria: (1) any form of cancer except cerebral tumours and benign skin cancers; (2) a life expectancy of at least 12 months; (3) aged 18–74 years;

(4) no obvious intellectual impairments, psychotic illness or suicide risk; (5) residence within 65 km of the hospital; and (6) psychological morbidity defined above a set of cut-off points for anxiety, depression, helplessness and below a cut-off point for fighting spirit. Altogether, 153 subjects completed the baseline and 8-week measures and 137 completed all measures.

Design All subjects completed measures of their psychological state at baseline. They were then allocated to either the experimental group (and received 8 weeks of APT) or the control group. The subjects then completed follow-up measures at 8 weeks and 4 months.

Measures Subjects completed the following measures at baseline (before randomization), at 8 weeks and 4 months follow-up:

- *The Hospital Anxiety and Depression scale.*
- *The Mental Adjustment to Cancer scale*: this measures four dimensions of adjustment – fighting spirit, helplessness, anxious preoccupation, fatalism.
- *The Psychosocial Adjustment to Illness scale*: this measures health care orientation, work adjustment, domestic environment, sexual relationships, extended family relationships, the social environment, psychological distress.
- *Rotterdam symptom checklist*: this measures quality of life in terms of both physical and psychological symptoms.

The intervention The subjects were randomly allocated to either the experimental (APT) or the control group. ATP is a cognitive behavioural treatment developed specifically for cancer patients. Therapy involved approximately eight 1-hour weekly sessions with individual patients and their spouses (if appropriate). However, many patients in the present study did not attend all these sessions and several received additional sessions throughout the 4 months. The therapy focused on the personal meaning of the cancer for the patient, examined their coping strategies and emphasized the current problems defined jointly by the therapist and the patient. APT uses the following cognitive behavioural techniques:

- Identifying the patient's strengths and using these to develop self-esteem, overcome feelings of helplessness, promote fighting spirit.
- Teaching patients to identify any automatic thoughts underlying their anxiety and depression and developing means to challenge these thoughts.
- Teaching patients how to use imagination and role play as a means of coping with stressors.
- Encouraging patients to carry out activities that give them a sense of pleasure and achievement in order to promote a sense of control.
- Encouraging expression of emotions and open communication.
- Teaching relaxation to control anxiety.

Results

The results showed that at 8 weeks the patients receiving the APT had significantly higher scores on fighting spirit and significantly lower scores on helplessness, anxious preoccupation, fatalism, anxiety, psychological symptoms and orientation towards health care than the control patients. At 4 months, patients receiving the APT had significantly lower scores than the controls on anxiety, psychological symptoms and psychological distress.

Conclusion

The authors concluded that APT improves the psychological well-being of cancer patients who show increased psychological problems and that some of these improvements persist for up to 4 months. They suggest that APT relates to 'improvement in the psychological dimension of the quality of life of cancer patients'.

Personality/coping style and longevity

In 1991, Eysenck and Grossarth-Maticek reported a study whereby they selected 'at-risk' individuals who were healthy (the controls) and another group of individuals (the experimental group) who showed conflict-avoiding and emotion-suppression type personality (a type C/cancer-prone personality). The experimental group received cognitive behavioural therapy in an attempt to change how they dealt with stress. At follow-up, the authors reported that this group showed a decrease in mortality rate compared with the controls who did not receive the cognitive behavioural therapy. In a further study by Temoshok and Fox (1984), the results from a 15-year follow-up of women with breast cancer indicated that poor outcome was associated with a passive, helplessness coping style. However, it has been questioned as to whether the personality styles predicted to be associated with different illnesses are distinct (Amelang and Schmidt-Rathjens 1996).

There is no relationship between psychological factors and longevity

However, not all research has pointed to an association between psychological factors and longevity. Barraclough *et al.* (1992) measured the severe life events, social difficulties and depression at baseline in a group of breast cancer patients, and followed them up after 42 months. Of a total of 204 subjects, 26 died and 23 per cent relapsed. However, the results showed no relationship between these outcomes and the psychosocial factors measured at baseline. These results caused debate in the light of earlier studies and it has been suggested that the absence of a relationship between life events and outcome may be due to the older age of the women in Barraclough and co-workers' study, the short follow-up period used, and the unreported use of chemotherapy (Ramirez *et al.* 1992).

Conclusion

Psychology appears to have a role to play in understanding cancer, not only in terms of beliefs and behaviours, which may be related to the onset of cancer, but also in terms of psychological consequences, the treatment of symptoms, improving quality of life, disease-free intervals and longevity.

Coronary heart disease (CHD)

This section examines what coronary heart disease is and the role of psychology in understanding CHD in terms of predicting and changing behavioural risk factors and the rehabilitation of sufferers.

What is CHD?

Coronary heart disease is caused by hardening of the arteries (atherosclerosis), which are narrowed by fatty deposits. This can result in angina (pain) or a heart attack (myocardial infarction).

The prevalence of CHD

Coronary heart disease is responsible for 33 per cent of deaths in men under 65 and 28 per cent of all deaths. It is the leading cause of death in the UK and accounted for 4300 deaths in men and 2721 deaths in women per million in 1992. It has been estimated that CHD cost the UK National Health Service (NHS) about £390 million in 1985–86. The highest death rates from CHD are found in men and women in the manual classes, and men and women of Asian origin. In middle age, the death rate is up to five times higher for men than for women; this evens out, however, in old age when CHD is the leading cause of death for both men and women.

Risk factors for CHD

Many risk factors for CHD have been identified. Some of these are regarded as (1) *non-modifiable*, such as educational status, social mobility, social class, age, gender, family history and race, or (2) *modifiable*, such as smoking behaviour, obesity, sedentary lifestyle, perceived work stress and type A behaviour. However, whether some of the latter can be changed is debatable.

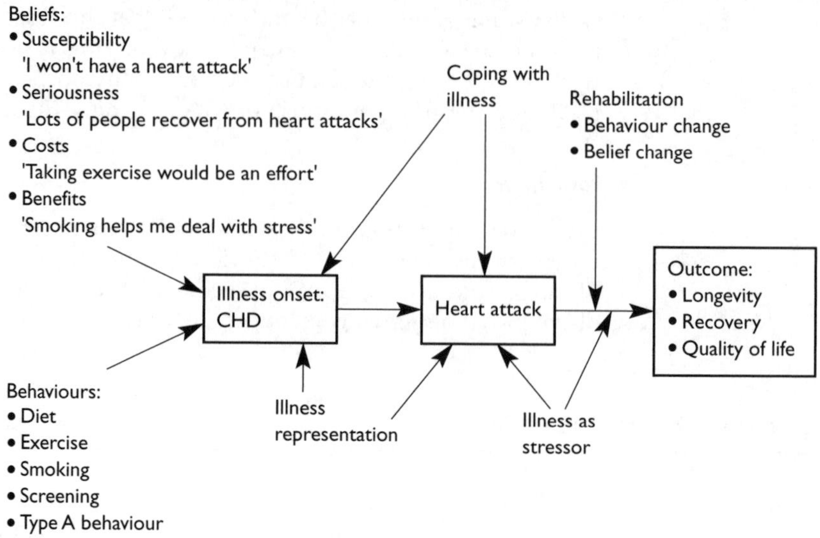

Figure 13.3 The potential role of psychology in CHD

The role of psychology in CHD

Psychology has a role to play in CHD, both in predicting and changing the behavioural risk factors (e.g. diet, smoking, exercise) and in developing rehabilitation programmes and preventing reinfarction (see Fig. 13.3).

The role of psychology will now be examined in terms of (1) predicting and changing behavioural risk factors and (2) the rehabilitation of sufferers.

Predicting and changing behavioural risk factors

1 *Smoking.* One in four deaths from CHD is thought to be caused by smoking. Smoking more than 20 cigarettes a day increases the risk of CHD in middle age threefold. In addition, stopping smoking can halve the risk of another heart attack in those who have already had one.
2 *Diet.* Diet, in particular cholesterol levels, has also been implicated in CHD. It has been suggested that the 20 per cent of a population with the highest cholesterol levels are three times more likely to die of heart disease than the 20 per cent with the lowest levels. Cholesterol levels may be determined by the amount of saturated fat consumed (derived mainly from animal fats). Cholesterol reduction can be achieved through a reduction in total fats and saturated fats, an increase in polyunsaturated fats and an increase in dietary fibre.
3 *High blood pressure.* High blood pressure is also a risk factor for CHD – the higher the blood pressure the greater the risk. It has been suggested that a 10 mmHg decrease in a population's average blood pressure could reduce the mortality attributable to heart disease by 30 per cent.

Blood pressure appears to be related to a multitude of factors such as genetics, obesity, alcohol intake and salt consumption.

Other possible behavioural risk factors include exercise, coffee, alcohol and soft water consumption. The risk factors for CHD can be understood and predicted by examining an individual's health beliefs (see Chapters 2 and 5). Psychology, therefore, has a role to play in CHD by understanding and possibly changing these behavioural risk factors.

4 *Type A behaviour*. Type A behaviour is probably the most extensively studied risk factor for coronary heart disease. Friedman and Rosenman (1959) initially defined type A behaviour in terms of excessive competitiveness, impatience, hostility and vigorous speech. Using a semi-structured interview, three types of type A behaviour were identified. Type A1 reflected vigour, energy, alertness, confidence, loud speaking, rapid speaking, tense clipped speech, impatience, hostility, interrupting, frequent use of the word 'never' and frequent use of the word 'absolutely'. Type A2 was defined as being similar to type A1, but not as extreme, and type B was regarded as relaxed, showing no interruptions and quieter (e.g. Rosenman 1978).

The Jenkins activity survey was developed in 1971 to further define type A behaviour. Support for a relationship between type A behaviour and coronary heart disease using the Jenkins activity survey has been reported by a number studies (Rosenman *et al.* 1975; Jenkins *et al.* 1979; Haynes *et al.* 1980). However, research has also reported no relationship between type A behaviour and CHD. For example, Johnston *et al.* (1987) used Bortner's (1969) questionnaire to predict heart attacks in 5936 men aged 40–59 years, who were randomly selected from British general practice lists. All subjects were examined at the start of the study for the presence of heart disease and completed the Bortner questionnaire. They were then followed up for morbidity and mortality from heart attack and for sudden cardiac death for an average of 6.2 years. The results showed that non-manual workers had higher type A scores than manual workers and that type A score decreased with age. However, at follow-up the results showed no relationship between type A behaviour and heart disease.

5 *Stress*. Stress has also been studied extensively as a predictor of coronary heart disease. In the 1980s, Karasek developed his job demand–job control model of stress, which was further developed by Karasek and Theorell (1990). This model argues that personal control over a stressor and job stress predicts coronary heart disease which is described within 'the job demand control hypothesis', within which he defines the term job strain. According to the model, there are two aspects of job strain: *job demands*, which reflect conditions that effect performance, and *job autonomy*, which reflects the control over the speed or the nature of decisions made within the job. Karasek's job demand and control hypothesis suggests that high job demands and low job autonomy (control) predicts coronary heart disease.

Recently, Karasek and co-workers developed the job demand control hypothesis to include social support. Within this context, social support is defined as either *emotional support*, involving trust between colleagues and social cohesion, or *instrumental social support* involving the provision of extra resources and assistance. It is argued that high social support mediates and moderates the effects of low control and high job demand. A study was carried out (see Karasek and Theorell 1990) in which subjects were divided into low social support and high social support groups, and their decisional control and the demands of their job were measured. The results indicated that subjects in the high social support group showed fewer symptoms of CHD than those subjects in the low social support group. In addition, within those groups high job control and low job demands predicted fewer CHD symptoms.

Psychology and rehabilitation of CHD sufferers

Psychology also plays a role in the rehabilitation of individuals who have suffered a heart attack. Rehabilitation programmes have been developed to encourage CHD sufferers to modify their risk factors, such as exercise, type A behaviour, smoking, diet and stress.

Modifying exercise

Most rehabilitation programmes emphasize the restoration of physical functioning through exercise with the assumption that physical recovery will in turn promote psychological and social recovery. Meta-analyses of these exercise-based programmes have suggested that they may have favourable effects on cardiovascular mortality (e.g. Oldridge *et al.* 1988). However, such meta-analyses are problematic as there is a trend towards publishing positive results, thereby influencing the overall picture. In addition, whether these exercise-based programmes influence risk factors other than exercise, such as smoking, diet and type A behaviour, is questionable.

Modifying type A behaviour

The recurrent coronary prevention project was developed by Friedman *et al.* (1986) in an attempt to modify type A behaviour. This programme was based on the following questions: Can type A behaviour be modified? If so, can such modification reduce the chances of a re-occurrence of a heart attack? The study involved 1000 subjects and a 5-year intervention. Subjects had all suffered a heart attack and were allocated to one of three groups: cardiology counselling, type A behaviour modification, or no treatment. Type A behaviour modification involved discussions of the beliefs and values of type A, discussing methods of reducing work demands, relaxation and education about changing the cognitive framework of the individuals. At 5 years, the results showed that the type A modification group showed a reduced re-occurrence of heart attacks, suggesting that not only can type A behaviour be modified but that when modified there may be a reduction of reinfarction. However, the relationship between type A behaviour and CHD is still controversial, with recent discussions suggesting that type A may at times be protective against CHD.

Modifying general lifestyle factors

In addition, rehabilitation programmes have been developed which focus on modifying other risk factors such as smoking and diet. For example, van Elderen *et al.* (1994) developed a health education and counselling programme for patients with cardiovascular disease after hospitalization, with weekly follow-ups by telephone. Thirty CHD sufferers and their partners were offered the intervention and were compared with a group of 30 control patients who received standard medical care only. The results showed that after 2 months, the patients who had received health education and counselling reported a greater increase in physical activity and a greater decrease in unhealthy eating habits. In addition, within those subjects in the experimental condition (receiving health education and counselling), those whose partners had also participated in the programme showed greater improvements in their activity and diet and, in addition, showed a decrease in their smoking behaviour. At 12 months, subjects who had participated in the health education and counselling programme maintained their improvement in their eating behaviour. The authors concluded that, although this study involved only a small number of patients, the results provide some support for including health education in rehabilitation programmes.

Modifying stress

Stress management involves teaching individuals about the theories of stress, encouraging them to be aware of the factors that can trigger stress, and teaching them a range of strategies to reduce stress, such as 'self-talk', relaxation techniques and general life management approaches, such as time management and problem-solving. Stress management has been used successfully to reduce some of the risk factors for CHD disease, including raised blood pressure (Johnston *et al.* 1993), blood cholesterol (Gill *et al.* 1985) and type A behaviour (Roskies *et al.* 1986). Further, some studies also indicate that it can reduce angina, which is highly predictive of heart attack and/or death. For example, Gallacher *et al.* (1997) randomly allocated 452 male angina patients to receive either stress management or no intervention at all. The results showed that at 6-month follow-up, those who had received stress management reported a reduced frequency of chest pain when resting. In a similar trial, Bundy *et al.* (1998) examined both the independent and the combined effect of stress management and exercise on angina compared with a control group taken from a waiting list. The results indicated that those who undertook both stress management and exercise reported fewer angina attacks and reduced reliance on medication. Therefore, stress management appears to reduce angina, which in turn could reduce the occurrence of myocardial infarctions.

Conclusion

CHD is a common cause of death in the western world. It illustrates the role of psychology in illness in terms of identifying and changing risk factors (e.g. smoking, diet, exercise, type A behaviour and stress) in order to prevent CHD and developing programmes to modify them in individuals who already have the disease.

To conclude

Illnesses such as HIV, cancer and coronary heart disease illustrate the role of psychology throughout the course of an illness. For example, psychological factors play a role in illness onset (e.g. health beliefs, health behaviours, personality, coping mechanisms), illness progression (e.g. psychological consequences, adaptation, health behaviours) and longevity (e.g. health behaviours, coping mechanisms, quality of life). These psychological factors are also relevant to a multitude of other chronic and acute illnesses, such as diabetes, asthma, chronic fatigue syndrome and multiple sclerosis. This suggests that illness is best conceptualized, not as a biomedical problem, but as complex interplay of physiological and psychological factors.

? Questions – AIDS

1 Discuss the role of psychological factors in the progression to full-blown AIDS.

2 AIDS kills. Discuss.

3 Discuss the role of responsibility in HIV disease.

? Questions – Cancer

1 Discuss the validity of the Type C personality.

2 Changing one's lifestyle can prevent lung cancer.

3 Discuss the role of psychological factors in longevity.

? Questions – CHD

1 CHD is the fault of the patient. Discuss.

2 CHD is an inevitable product of lifestyle. Discuss.

3 To what extent can a reinfarction be prevented?

▶ For discussion

In the light of the literature on HIV, cancer and CHD discuss the possible role of psychological factors throughout the course of an alternative chronic illness (e.g. diabetes, multiple sclerosis).

Assumptions in health psychology

An examination of the role of psychological factors in illness highlights some of the assumptions in health psychology:

1 *The mind–body split.* By examining the role of psychology in illness, it is implicitly assumed that psychology and illness (the body) are separate. This promotes a model of an individual who has a physical and a mental world which interact but are separate. Although this interaction is an attempt at a holistic approach to health and illness, it is still intrinsically dualistic.

2 *Correlational studies.* Many of the research studies carried out in health psychology are cross-sectional (i.e. they examine the relationship between variables measured at the same time). For example, 'What is the relationship between coping style and immune status?', and 'What is the relationship between life stressors and illness?' Studies using cross-sectional designs often make statements about causality (e.g. 'coping style causes changes in immune status', 'stressors cause illness'). However, it is quite possible that the relationship between these variables is either causal in the opposite direction (e.g. illness causes high reports of stressors, 'I am now ill and remember the last six months differently'), or non-existent (e.g. 'I am ill and I have had lots of stressful events in my life recently but they are unrelated' (the third variable problem)). Prospective studies are used as an attempt to solve this problem, but even prospective studies only examine the correlation between variables – it is still difficult to talk about causality.

Further reading

Cooper, C.L. (Ed.) (1984) *Psychosocial Stress and Cancer*. Chichester: Wiley and Sons.
This book provides a useful review of the literature on the role of psychology in cancer aetiology and disease-free intervals.

Mulder, C.L. and Antoni, M.H. (1992) Psychosocial correlates of immune status and disease progression in HIV-1 infected homosexual men: review of preliminary findings and commentary, *Psychology and Health*, 6: 175–92.
This paper reviews the literature on the role of behavioural and psychological factors in the course of HIV infection. It is a good introduction to psychoneuroimmunology.

Steptoe, A. (1981) *Psychological Factors in Cardiovascular Disorders*. New York: Academic Press.
This book provides a comprehensive overview of the theories and research into the role of behavioural risk factors in CHD.

CHAPTER 14

Measuring health status

Chapter overview

This chapter examines the different ways in which health status has been measured from mortality rates to quality of life. In addition, it describes the ways in which quality of life has been used in research both in terms of the factors that predict quality of life (quality of life as an outcome variable) and the association between quality of life and longevity (quality of life as a predictor).

This chapter covers:

- Mortality rates
- Morbidity rates
- Measures of functioning
- Subjective health status
- Quality of life measures
- Predicting quality of life
- Quality of life and longevity

Mortality rates

At its most basic, a measure of health status takes the form of a very crude mortality rate, which is calculated by simply counting the number of deaths in one year compared with either previous or subsequent years. The question asked is, 'Has the number of people who have died this year gone up, gone down or stayed the same?' An increase in mortality rate can be seen as a decrease in health status and a decrease as an increase in health status. This approach, however, requires a denominator, a measure of who is at risk. The next most basic form of mortality rate therefore includes a denominator reflecting the size of the population being studied. Such a measure allows for comparisons to be made between different populations: more people may die in a given year in London when compared with Bournemouth, but London is simply bigger. In order to provide any meaningful measure of health status, mortality rates are corrected for age (Bournemouth has an older population and therefore we would predict that more people would die each year) and sex (men generally die younger than women and this needs to be taken into account). Furthermore, mortality rates can be produced to be either age specific such as infant mortality rates, or illness specific such as sudden death rates. As long as the population being studied is accurately specified, corrected and specific, mortality rates provide an easily available and simple measure: death is a good reliable outcome.

Morbidity rates

Laboratory and clinical researchers and epidemiologists may accept mortality rates as the perfect measure of health status. However, the juxtaposition of social scientists to the medical world has challenged this position to raise the now seemingly obvious question, 'Is health really only the absence of death?' In response to this, there has been an increasing focus upon morbidity. However, in line with the emphasis upon simplicity inherent within the focus on mortality rates, many morbidity measures still use methods of counting and recording. For example, the expensive and time-consuming production of morbidity prevalence rates involve large surveys of 'caseness' to simply count how many people within a given population suffer from a particular problem. Likewise, sickness absence rates simply count days lost due to illness and caseload assessments count the number of people who visit their general practitioner or hospital within a given time frame. Such morbidity rates provide details at the level of the population in general. However, morbidity is also measured for each individual using measures of functioning.

Measures of functioning

Measures of functioning ask the question, 'To what extent can you do the following tasks?' and are generally called activity of daily living scales (ADLs). For example, Katz *et al.* (1970) designed the index of activities of daily living to assess levels of functioning in the elderly. This was developed for the therapist and/or carer to complete and asked the rater to evaluate the individual on a range of dimensions including bathing, dressing, continence and feeding. ADLs have also been developed for individuals themselves to complete and include questions such as, 'Do you or would you have any difficulty: washing down/cutting toenails/running to catch a bus/going up/down stairs?' Measures of functioning can either be administered on their own or as part of a more complex assessment involving measures of subjective health status.

Subjective health status

Over recent years, measures of health status have increasingly opted for measures of subjective health status, which all have one thing in common: they ask the individuals themselves to rate their health. Some of these are referred to simply as subjective health measures, others are referred to as either quality of life scales or health-related quality of life scales. However, the literature in the area of subjective health status and quality of life is plagued by two main questions: 'What is quality of life?' and 'How should it be measured?'

What is quality of life?

Reports of a Medline search on the term 'quality of life' indicate a surge in its use from 40 citations (1966–1974), to 1907 citations (1981–1985), to 5078 citations (1986–1990) (Albrecht 1994). Quality of life is obviously in vogue. However, to date there exists no consensus as to what it actually is. For example, it has been defined as 'the value assigned to duration of life as modified by the impairments, functional states, perceptions and social opportunities that are influenced by disease, injury, treatment or policy' (Patrick and Ericson 1993), 'a personal statement of the positivity or negativity of attributes that characterise one's life' (Grant *et al.* 1990) and by the World Health Organization as 'a broad ranging concept affected in a complex way by the person's physical health, psychological state, level of independence, social relationships and their relationship to the salient features in their environment' (WHOQOL Group 1993). Furthermore, the problems with definition have resulted in a range of ways of operationalizing quality of life. For example, following the discussions about an acceptable definition of quality of life, the European Organisation for Research on Treatment of Cancer operationalized quality of life in terms of 'functional status, cancer and treatment specific symptoms, psychological distress, social interaction, financial/economic impact, perceived health status and overall quality of life' (Aaronson *et al.* 1993). In line with this, their measure consisted of items that reflected these different dimensions. Likewise, the researchers who worked on the Rand Corporation health batteries operationalized quality of life in terms of 'physical functioning, social functioning, role limitations due to physical problems, role limitations due to emotional problems, mental health, energy/vitality, pain and general health perception', which formed the basic dimensions of their scale (e.g. Stewart and Ware 1992). Furthermore, Fallowfield (1990) defined the four main dimensions of quality of life as psychological (mood, emotional distress, adjustment to illness), social (relationships, social and leisure activities), occupational (paid and unpaid word) and physical (mobility, pain, sleep and appetite).

Creating a conceptual framework

In response to the problems of defining quality of life, researchers have recently attempted to create a clearer conceptual framework for this construct. In particular, researchers have divided quality of life measures either according to who devises the measure or in terms of whether the measure is considered objective or subjective.

Who devises the measure?

Browne *et al.* (1997) differentiated between the standard needs approach and the psychological processes perspective. The first of these is described as being based on the assumption that 'a consensus about what constitutes a good or poor quality of life exists or at least can be discovered through investigation' (p. 738). In addition, the standard needs approach assumes that needs rather than wants are central to quality of life and that these needs are common to all, including the researchers. In contrast, the psychological processes approach considers quality of life to be 'constructed from individual evaluations of personally salient aspects of life' (p. 737). Therefore, Browne *et al.* (1997) conceptualized measures of quality of life as being devised either by researchers or by the individuals themselves.

Is the measure objective or subjective?

Muldoon *et al.* (1998) provided an alternative conceptual framework for quality of life based on the degree to which the domains being rated can be objectively validated. They argued that quality of life measures should be divided into those that assess objective functioning and those that assess subjective well-being. The first of these reflects those measures that describe an individual's level of functioning, which they argue must be validated against directly observed behavioural performance, and the second describes the individual's own appraisal of their well-being.

Therefore, some progress has been made to clarify the problems surrounding measures of quality of life. However, until a consensus among researchers and clinicians exists it remains unclear what quality of life is, and whether quality of life is different to subjective health status and health-related quality of life. In fact, Annas (1990) argued that we should stop using the term altogether. However, 'quality of life', 'subjective health status' and 'health-related quality of life' continue to be used and their measurement continues to be taken. The range of measures developed will now be considered in terms of (1) unidimensional measures and (2) multidimensional measures.

How should it be measured?

Unidimensional measures

Many measures focus on one particular aspect of health. For example, Goldberg (1978) developed the general health questionnaire (GHQ), which assesses mood by asking questions such as: 'Have you recently: Been able to concentrate on whatever you're doing/Spent much time chatting to people/Been feeling happy or depressed?' The GHQ is available as long forms, consisting of either 30, 28 or 20 items, and a short form, which consists of 12 items. Whilst the short form is mainly used to explore mood in general and provides results as to an individual's relative mood (i.e. is the person better or worse than usual?), the longer forms have been used to detect 'caseness' (i.e. is the person depressed or not?). Other unidimensional measures include the following: the hospital anxiety and depression scale (HAD) (Zigmond and Snaith 1983) and the Beck depression inventory (BDI) (Beck *et al.* 1961), both of which focus on mood; the McGill pain questionnaire, which assesses pain levels (Melzack 1975); measures of self-esteem, such as the self-esteem scale (Rosenberg 1965) and the self-esteem inventory (Coopersmith 1967); measures of social support (e.g. Sarason *et al.* 1983, 1987); measures of satisfaction with life (e.g. Diner *et al.* 1985); and measures of symptoms (e.g. deHaes *et al.* Knippenberg 1990). Therefore, these unidimensional measures assess health in terms of one specific aspect of health and can be used on their own or in conjunction with other measures.

Multidimensional measures

Multidimensional measures assess health in the broadest sense. However, this does not mean that such measures are always long and complicated. For example, researchers often use a single item such as, 'would you say your health is: excellent/good/fair/poor' or 'rate your current state of health' on a scale ranging from 'poor' to 'perfect'. Further, some researchers simply ask respondents to make a relative judgement about their health on a scale from 'best possible' to 'worst possible'. Although these simple measures do not provide as much detail as longer measures, they have been shown to correlate highly with other more complex measures and to be useful as an outcome measure (Idler and Kasl 1995).

In the main, researchers have tended to use composite scales. Because of the many ways of defining quality of life, many different measures have been developed. Some focus on particular populations, such as the elderly (Lawton 1972, 1975), children (Maylath 1990), or those in the last year of life (Lawton *et al.* 1990). Others focus on specific illnesses, such as diabetes (Brook *et al.* 1981), arthritis (Meenan *et al.* 1980), or heart disease (Rector *et al.* 1993). In addition, generic measures of quality of life have also been developed, which can be applied to all individuals. These include: the Nottingham Health Profile (NHP) (Hunt *et al.* 1986), the short form 36 (SF36) (Ware and Sherbourne 1992), and the sickness impact profile (SIP) (Bergner *et al.* 1981). All of these measures have been criticized for being too broad and therefore resulting in a definition of quality of life that is all encompassing, vague and unfocused. In contrast, they have also been criticized for being too focused and for potentially missing out aspects of quality of life that may be of specific importance to the individual concerned. In particular, it has been suggested that by asking individuals to answer a pre-defined set of questions and to rate statements that have been developed by researchers, the individual's own concerns may be missed. This has led to the development of individual quality of life measures.

Individual quality of life measures

Measures of subjective health status ask the individual to rate their own health. This is in great contrast to measures of mortality, morbidity and most measures of functioning, which are completed by carers, researchers or an observer. However, although such measures enable individuals to rate their own health, they do not allow them to select the dimensions along which to rate it. For example, a measure that asks about an individual's work life assumes that work is important to this person, but they might not want to work. Furthermore, one that asks about family life, might be addressing the question to someone who is glad not to see their family. How can one set of individuals who happen to be researchers know what is important to the quality of life of another set of individuals? In line with this perspective, researchers have developed individual quality of life measures, which not only ask the subjects to rate their own health status but also to define the dimensions along which it should be rated. One such measure, the schedule for evaluating individual quality of life (SEIQoL) (McGee *et al.* 1991; O'Boyle *et al.* 1992) asks subjects to select five areas of their lives that are important to them, to weight them in terms of their importance and then to rate how satisfied they currently are with each dimension (see **Focus on research 14.1**).

FOCUS ON RESEARCH 14.1

PUTTING THEORY INTO PRACTICE – EVALUATING HIP REPLACEMENT SURGERY

Individual quality of life in patients undergoing hip replacement (O'Boyle *et al.* 1992).

This is an interesting paper as it illustrates how a measurement tool, developed within a psychological framework, can be used to evaluate the impact of a surgical intervention. In addition, it compared the use of composite scales with an individual quality of life scale.

Background

There are a multitude of measures of quality of life available, most of which ask patients to rate a set of statements that a group of researchers consider to reflect quality of life. However, whether this approach actually accesses what the patient thinks is unclear. Therefore, O'Boyle *et al.* (1992) devised their own measure of quality of life and this asks the patients themselves to decide what is important to them. It is called the schedule for the evaluation of individual quality of life (SEIQoL). In addition, the authors wanted to compare the results using SEIQoL with those of more traditional assessment tools: 'We wanted to know whether SEIQoL could answer the question "What does the patient think".'

Methodology

Subjects Consecutive patients attending a hospital in Dublin for osteoarthritis of the hip were asked to participate. These were matched to control subjects from local general practices in terms of age, sex and class. The study consisted of 20 subjects, who underwent hip replacement operation, and 20 controls.
Design The study used a repeated measures design with measures completed before (baseline) and after (6-month follow-up) unilateral total hip replacement surgery.
Measures The subjects completed the following measures at baseline and follow-up:

- *Individual quality of life*: this involved the following stages. First, the subjects were asked to list the five areas of life that they considered to be most important to their quality of life. Second, the subjects were then asked to rate each area for their status at the present time ranging from 'as good as could possibly be' to 'as bad as could possibly be'. Finally, in order to weight each area of life, the subjects were presented with 30 randomly generated profiles of hypothetical people labelled with the five chosen areas and were asked to rate the quality of life of each of these people. These three ratings were then used to compute total quality of life score (i.e. adding up each current rating and multiplied by weighting per area).

- *Global health status*: the subjects completed the McMaster health index questionnaire, which assesses physical, social and emotional functioning (Chambers *et al.* 1982).
- *Disease specific health status*: subjects completed the arthritis impact scale that assesses nine aspects of functioning: mobility, physical activity, dexterity, household activities, social activity, activities of daily living, pain, anxiety and depression (Meenan *et al.* 1980).

Results The results were analysed in terms of the areas of life selected as part of the individual quality of life scale and to assess the impact of the hip replacement operation in terms of changes in all measures from baseline to follow-up and differences in these changes between the patients and the controls.

- Areas of life selected: Social/leisure activities and family were nominated most frequently by both groups. Happiness, intellectual function and living conditions were nominated least frequently. Health was nominated more frequently by the control than the patients who rated independence and finance more frequently.
- The impact of the hip replacement operation: The results showed that all measures of quality of life improved following the hip replacement operation.

Conclusion

The authors concluded that their individual quality of life measure can be used to elicit the views of patients and in addition can detect changes in quality of life over time. In addition, they argued that 'a major advantage of a patient centred measure such as SEIQol especially with elicited cues is that it is applicable across all patients, illnesses and diseases and is not specific to any one culture'. Therefore, this study illustrates the usefulness of an individual quality of life measure in evaluating the effectiveness of a surgical procedure.

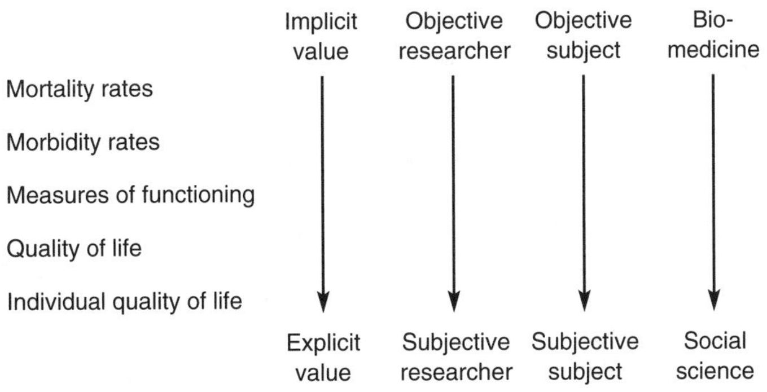

Figure 14.1 A shift in perspective in measuring health

Therefore, health status can be assessed in terms of mortality rates, morbidity, levels of functioning and subjective health measures. Subjective health measures overlap significantly with measures of quality of life and health-related quality of life. These different measures illustrate a shift between a number of perspectives (see Fig. 14.1).

A shift in perspective

Value

The shift from mortality rates to subjective health measures represents a shift from implicit value to attempts to make this value explicit. For example, mortality and morbidity measures assume that what they are measuring is an absolute index of health. The subjects being studied are not asked, 'Is it a bad thing that you cannot walk upstairs' or the relatives asked, 'Did they want to die?' Subjective health measures attempt to make the value within the constructs being studied explicit by asking, 'To what extent are you prevented from doing the things you would like to do?'

Subjectivity of the subject

Mortality and morbidity measures are assumed to be objective scientific measures that access a reality which is uncontaminated by bias. In contrast, the subjective measures make this bias the essence of what they are interested in. For example, mortality data are taken from hospital records or death certificates, and morbidity ratings are often made by the health professionals rather than the individuals being studied. However, subjective health measures ask the individual for their own experiences and beliefs in terms of 'How do you rate your health?' or 'How do you feel?'

They make no pretence to be objective and rather than attempting to exclude the individuals' beliefs they make them their focus.

Subjectivity of the researcher

In addition, there is also a shift in the ways in which measures of health status conceptualize the researcher. For example, mortality and morbidity rates are assumed to be consistent regardless of who collected them; the researcher is assumed to be an objective person. Subjective measures, however, attempt to address the issue of researcher subjectivity. For example, self-report questionnaires and the use of closed questions aim to minimize researcher input. However, the questions being asked and the response frames given are still chosen by the researcher. In contrast, the individual quality of life scale (O'Boyle *et al.* 1992) in effect presents the subject with a blank sheet and asks them to devise their own scale.

Definition of health

Finally, such shifts epitomize the different perspectives of biomedicine and health psychology. Therefore, if health status is regarded as the presence or absence of death, then mortality rates provide a suitable assessment tool. Death is a reliable outcome variable and mortality is appropriately simple. If, however, health status is regarded as more complex than this, more complex measures are needed. Morbidity rates account for a continuum model of health and illness and facilitate the assessment of the more grey areas, and even some morbidity measures accept the subjective nature of health. However, if health psychology regards health status as made up of a complex range of factors that can only be both chosen and evaluated by the individuals themselves, then it could be argued that it is only measures that ask the individuals themselves to rate their own health which are fully in line with a health psychology model of what health means.

Using quality of life in research

Quality of life measures, in the form of subjective health measures and both simple and composite scales, play a central role in many debates within health psychology, medical sociology, primary care and clinical medicine. Most funded trials are now required to include a measure of quality of life among their outcome variables, and interventions that only focus on mortality are generally regarded as narrow and old-fashioned. However, a recent analysis of the literature suggested that the vast majority of published trials still do not report data on quality of life (Sanders *et al.* 1998). For example, following an assessment of the Cochrane Controlled Trials Register from 1980 to 1997, Sanders *et al.* reported that although the frequency of reporting quality of life data had increased from 0.63 per cent to 4.2 per cent for trials from all disciplines, from 1.5 per cent to 8.2 per cent for cancer trials and from 0.34 per cent to 3.6 per cent for cardiovascular trials, less than 5 per cent of all trials reported data on quality of life. Furthermore, they showed that this proportion was below 10 per cent even for cancer trials. In addition, they indicated that whilst 72 per cent of the trials used established measures of quality of life, 22 per cent used measures developed by the authors themselves. Therefore, it would seem that although quality of life is in vogue and is a required part of outcome research, it still remains underused. For those trials that do include a measure of quality of life, it is used mainly as an outcome variable and the data are analysed to assess whether the intervention has an impact on the individual's health status, including their quality of life.

Quality of life as an outcome measure

Research has examined how a range of interventions influence an individual's quality of life using a repeated measures design. For example, a trial of breast reduction surgery compared women's quality of life before and after the operation (Klassen *et al.* 1996). The study involved 166 women who were referred for plastic surgery, mainly for physical reasons and their health status was assessed using the SF36 to assess general quality of life, the 28-item GHQ to assess mood and Rosenberg's self-esteem scale. The results showed that the women reported significantly lower quality of life both before and after the operation than a control group of women in the general population and further, that the operation resulted in a reduction in the women's physical, social and psychological functioning including their levels of 'caseness' for psychiatric morbidity. Accordingly, the authors concluded that breast reduction surgery is beneficial for quality of life and should be included in NHS purchasing contracts.

Quality of life has also been included as an outcome variable for disease-specific randomized controlled trials. For example, Grunfeld *et al.* (1996) examined the relative impact of providing either hospital (routine care) or primary care follow-ups for women with breast cancer. The study included 296 women with breast cancer who were in remission and randomly allocated them to receive follow-up care either in hospital or by their general practitioner. Quality of life was assessed using some of the dimensions from the SF36 and the HAD scale. The results showed that general practice care was not associated with any deterioration in quality of life. In addition, it was not related to an increased time to diagnose any recurrence of the cancer. Therefore, the authors concluded that general practice care of women in remission from breast cancer is as good as hospital care.

Other studies have explored the impact of an intervention for a range of illnesses. For example, Shepperd *et al.* (1998) examined the relative effectiveness of home versus hospital care for patients with a range of problems, including hip replacement, knee replacement and hysterectomy. Quality of life was assessed using tools such as the SF36 and disease-specific measures, and the results showed no differences between the two groups at a 3-months follow-up. Therefore, the authors concluded that if there are no significant differences between home and hospital care in terms of quality of life, then the cost of these different forms of care becomes an important factor.

Problems with using quality of life as an outcome measure

Therefore, research uses quality of life as an outcome measure for trials that have different designs and are either focused on specific illnesses or involve a range of problems. However, there are the following problems with such studies.

- Different studies use different ways of measuring quality of life: generalizing across studies is difficult.
- Some studies use the term 'quality of life' while others use the term 'subjective health status': generalizing across studies is difficult.
- Some studies report results from the different measures of quality of life, which are in the opposite direction to each other: drawing conclusions is difficult.
- Some studies report the results from quality of life measures, which are in the opposite direction to mortality or morbidity data: deciding whether an intervention is good or bad is difficult.

Quality of life as a predictor of longevity

Most research using quality of life explores its predictors and therefore places this variable as the end-point. However, it is possible that quality of life may also be a predictor of future events. In particular, quality of life could be seen as a predictor of longevity. To date, there are no studies that have directly addressed this possibility, although there are some studies which indirectly suggest an association between quality of life and longevity. For example, several studies indicate that mortality is higher in the first 6 months after the death of a spouse, particularly from heart disease or suicide (e.g. Kaprio *et al.* 1987; Schaefer *et al.* 1995; Martikainen and Valkonen 1996). It is possible that this could relate to a lowering of quality of life. Further, some studies suggest a link between life events and longevity (see Chapter 13). Perhaps these links could also be explained by quality of life. Therefore, quality of life may not only be an outcome variable in itself but a predictor of further outcomes in the future.

To conclude

This chapter has explored the different ways of measuring health status. In particular, it has examined the use of mortality rates, morbidity rates, measures of functioning, measures of subjective health status and quality of life. It has then described how the shift from mortality rates to quality of life reflects a shift from implicit to explicit value, an increasing subjectivity on behalf of both the subject being studied and the researcher, and a change in the definition of health from a biomedical dichotomous model to a more complex psychological one. Further, it has explored definitions of quality of life and the vast range of scales that have been developed to assess this complex construct and their use in research.

? Questions

1 Mortality rates are the most accurate measure of health status. Discuss.

2 The views of the subject get in the way of measuring health. Discuss.

3 The views of the researcher get in the way of measuring health. Discuss.

4 To what extent is quality of life a useful construct?

5 Should all outcome research include an assessment of quality of life?

▶ For discussion

Consider the last time you felt that your quality of life was reduced. What did this mean to you and would this be addressed by the available measures?

Assumptions in health psychology

The measurement of health status highlights some of the assumptions in health psychology:

1 *The problem of methodology.* It is assumed that methodology is separate to the data being collected. Accordingly, it is assumed that subjects experience factors as important to their quality of life even before they have been asked about them. It is possible that items relating to family life, physical fitness and work may only become important once the individual has been asked to rate them.

2 *The problem of the mind–body split.* Although much outcome research examines both mortality and quality of life, it is often assumed that these two factors are separate. Therefore, research explores the impact of an intervention either on an individual's quality of life or on their longevity. Very little relationship assesses the impact of quality of life itself on longevity. Therefore, factors influencing the mind are deemed to be separate to those influencing the body.

3 *The problem of progress.* Mortality rates were very much in vogue at the beginning of the century whereas quality of life measures are in vogue at the end of the century. This shift is mainly regarded as an improvement in the way in which we understand health status. However, rather than being an improvement, perhaps it simply reflects a change of the way in which we make sense of what health is.

Further reading

Bowling, A. (1991) *Measuring Health: A Review of Quality of Life Measurement Scales*. Buckingham: Open University Press.

This is an extremely comprehensive overview of the different scales that have been developed to assess quality of life. It also includes two interesting chapters on what quality of life is and theories of measurement.

Browne, J., McGee, H.M. and O'Boyle, C.A. (1997) Conceptual approaches to the assessment of quality of Life, *Psychology and Health*, 12: 737–51.

This paper explores a possible way of conceptualizing quality of life and presents a way forward for future research.

Joyce, C.R.B., O'Boyle, C.A. and McGee, H.M. (Eds) (1999) *Individual Quality of Life*. London: Harwood.

This edited book provides details on the conceptual and methodological principles of quality of life and focuses on individual measures. It then provides some examples of using these measures, together with some ideas for future directions.

CHAPTER 15

The assumptions of health psychology

Chapter overview

This book has highlighted a range of assumptions within health psychology. This chapter outlines these assumptions and points towards the possibility of studying a discipline as a means to understanding the changing nature of the individual.

The assumptions of health psychology

Throughout this book, several assumptions central to health psychology have been highlighted. These include the following:

The mind–body split

Health psychology sets out to provide an integrated model of the individual by establishing a holistic approach to health. Therefore, it challenges the traditional medical model of the mind–body split and provides theories and research to support the notion of a mind and body that are one. For example, it suggests beliefs influence behaviour, which in turn influences health; that stress can cause illness and that pain is a perception rather than a sensation. In addition, it argues that illness cognitions relate to recovery from illness and coping relates to longevity. However, does this approach really represent an integrated individual? Although all these perspectives and the research that has been carried out in their support indicate that the mind and the body interact, they are still defined as separate. The mind reflects the individuals' psychological states (i.e. their beliefs, cognitions, perceptions), which influence but are separate to their bodies (i.e. the illness, the body, the body's systems).

Dividing up the soup

Health psychology describes variables such as beliefs (risk perception, outcome expectancies, costs and benefits, intentions, implementation intentions), emotions (fear, depression, anxiety) and behaviours (smoking, drinking, eating, screening) as separate and discrete. It then develops models and theories to examine how these variables interrelate. For example, it asks, 'What beliefs predict smoking?', 'What emotions relate to screening?' Therefore, it separates out 'the soup' into discrete entities and then tries to put them back together. However, perhaps these different beliefs, emotions and behaviours were not separate until psychology came along. Is there really a difference between all the different beliefs? Is the thought 'I am depressed' a cognition or an emotion? When I am sitting quietly thinking, am I behaving? Health psychology assumes differences and then looks for association. However, perhaps without the original separation there would be nothing to separate!

The problem of progression

This book has illustrated how theories, such as those relating to addictions, stress and screening, have changed over time. In addition, it presents new developments in the areas of social cognition models and PNI. For example, early models of stress focused on a simple stimulus response approach.

Nowadays we focus on appraisal. Furthermore, nineteenth-century models of addiction believed that it was the fault of the drug. In the early twenty-first century, we see addiction as being a product of learning. Health psychology assumes that these shifts in theory represent improvement in our knowledge about the world. We know more than we did a hundred years ago and our theories are more accurate. However, perhaps such changes indicate different, not better, ways of viewing the world. Perhaps these theories tell us more about how we see the world now compared with then, rather than simply that we have got better at seeing the world.

The problem of methodology

In health psychology we carry out research to collect data about the world. We then analyse this data to find out how the world is, and we assume that our methodologies are separate to the data we are collecting. In line with this, if we ask someone about their implementation intentions it is assumed that they have such intentions before we ask them. Further, is we ask someone about their anxieties we assume that they have an emotion called anxiety, regardless of whether or not they are talking to us or answering our questionnaire. However, how do we know that our methods are separate from the data we collect? How do we know that these objects of research (beliefs, emotions and behaviours) exist prior to when we study them? Perhaps by studying the world we are not objectively examining what is really going on but are actually changing and possibly even creating it.

The problem of measurement

In line with the problem of methodology is the problem of measurement. Throughout the different areas of health psychology researchers develop research tools to assess quality of life, pain, stress, beliefs and behaviours. These tools are then used by the researchers to examine how the subjects in the research feel/think/behave. However, this process involves an enormous leap of faith – that our measurement tool actually measures something out there. How do we know this? Perhaps what the tool measures is simply what the tool measures. A depression scale may not assess 'depression' but only the score on the scale. Likewise, a quality of life scale may not assess quality of life but simply how someone completes the questionnaire.

Integrating the individual with their social context

Psychology is traditionally the study of the individual. Sociology is traditionally the study of the social context. Recently, however, health psychology has made moves to integrate this individual with their social world. To do this they turn to social epidemiology (i.e. explore class, gender and ethnicity), social psychology (i.e. turn to subjective norms) or social constructionism (i.e. turn to qualitative methods). Therefore, health psychologists access either the individuals' location within their social world via their demographic factors or ask the individuals for their beliefs about the social world. However, does this really integrate the individual with the social world? A belief about the social context is still an individual's belief. Can psychology really succeed with this integration? Would it still be psychology if it did?

Data are collected in order to develop theories; these theories are not data

Health psychologists collect data and develop theories about the individual, for example theories about smoking, eating, stress and pain. These theories are then used to tell us something about the world. However, these theories could also be used as data, and in the same way that we study the world we could study our theories about the world. Perhaps this would not tell us about the world *per se* but about how we see it. Furthermore, changes in theories could also tell us about the way in which we see the world has changed. Likewise we could study our methods and our measurement tools. Do these also tell us something about the changing psychology of the past hundred years?

Theories concerning different areas of health psychology are distinct from each other

This book has outlined many theories relating to stress, pain and health behaviours, but has not examined parallels within these theories. Perhaps there are patterns within these different theories that reflect 'umbrella' changes within health psychology. Perhaps also these changes indicate consistent shifts in the way psychological theory describes the individual.

Studying a discipline

Therefore there are many assumptions underlying the discipline of health psychology. Acknowledging and understanding these assumptions provides the basis of a more critical perspective on research. Findings from research are not taken for granted and theories can be seen within their inherent limitations. However, these assumptions themselves provide a basis for research – research into how a discipline has changed. In addition, this kind of research can provide insights into how the focus of that discipline (the individual) has also changed. This approach provides a basis for a social study of a discipline. In the same way that sociologists study scientists, biographers study authors and literary theorists study literature, a discipline can also be studied.

Further reading

Ogden, J. (1995) Psychosocial theory and the creation of the risky self, *Social Science and Medicine*, 40: 409–15.

This paper examines the changes in psychological theory during the twentieth century and relates them to discussions about risk and responsibility for health and illness.

Ogden, J. (1995) Changing the subject of health psychology, *Psychology and Health*, 10: 257–65.

This paper addresses some of the assumptions in health psychology and discusses the interrelationship between theory, methodology and the psychological individual.

Ogden, J. (1997) The rhetoric and reality of psychosocial theories: a challenge to biomedicine? *Journal of Health Psychology*, 2: 21–9.

This paper explores health psychology's apparent challenge to biomedicine.

Ogden, J. (2000) *Health and Construction of the Individual*. London: Routledge.

This book explores how both psychological and sociological theory construct the individual through an exploration of methodology, measurement, theory and the construction of boundaries.

Methodology glossary

Between-subjects design: this involves making comparisons between different groups of subjects; for example males *vs* females, those who have been offered a health-related intervention *vs* those who have not.

Case-control design: this involves taking a group of subjects who show a particular characteristic (e.g. lung cancer – the dependent variable), selecting a control group without the characteristic (e.g. no lung cancer) and retrospectively examining these two groups for the factors that may have caused this characteristic (e.g. did those with lung cancer smoke more than those without?).

Condition: experimental studies often involve allocating subjects to different conditions; for example, information *vs* no information, relaxation *vs* no relaxation, active drug *vs* placebo *vs* control condition.

Cross-sectional design: a study is described as being cross-sectional if the different variables are measured at the same time as each other.

Dependent variable: the characteristic that appears to change as a result of the independent variable; for example, changing behavioural intentions (the independent variable) causes a change in behaviour (the dependent variable).

Experimental design: this involves a controlled study in which variables are manipulated in order to specifically examine the relationship between the independent variable (the cause) and the dependent variable (the effect); for example, does experimentally induced anxiety change pain perception?

Independent variable: the characteristic that appears to cause a change in the dependent variable; for example, smoking (the independent variable) causes lung cancer (the dependent variable).

Likert scale: variables can be measured on a scale marked by numbers (e.g. 1 to 5) or terms (e.g. never/seldom/sometimes/often/very often). The subject is asked to mark the appropriate point.

Longitudinal design: this involves measuring variables at a baseline and then following up the subjects at a later point in time (sometimes called prospective or cohort design).

Prospective design: this involves following subjects up over a period of time (sometimes called longitudinal or cohort design).

Qualitative study: this involves methodologies such as interviews in order to collect data from subjects. Qualitative data is a way of describing the variety of beliefs, interpretations and behaviours from a heterogenous subject group without making generalizations to the population as a whole. It is believed that qualitative studies are more able to access the subjects' beliefs without contaminating the data with the researcher's own expectations. Qualitative data are described in terms of themes and categories.

Quantitative study: this involves collecting data in the form of numbers using methodologies such as questionnaires and experiments. Quantitative data are a way of describing the beliefs, interpretations and behaviours of a large population and generalizations are made about the population as a whole. Quantitative data are described in terms of frequencies, means and statistically significant differences and correlations.

Randomly allocated: subjects are randomly allocated to different conditions in order to minimize the effects of any individual differences; for example, to ensure that subjects who receive the drug *vs* the placebo *vs* nothing are equivalent in age and sex. If all the subjects who received the placebo happened to be female, this would obviously influence the results.

Repeated-measures design: this involves asking subjects to complete the same set of measures more than once; for example, before and after reading a health information leaflet.

Subjects: these are the individuals who are involved in the study. They may also be referred to as participants, clients, respondents or cases.

Variable: a characteristic that can be measured (e.g. age, beliefs, fitness).

Visual analogue scale: variables such as beliefs are sometimes measured using a 100 mm line with anchor points at each end (such as not at all confident/extremely confident). The subject is asked to place a cross on the line in the appropriate point.

Within-subjects design: this involves making comparisons within the same group of subjects: How do subjects respond to receiving an invitation to attend a screening programme? How does a belief about smoking relate to the subjects' smoking behaviour?

References

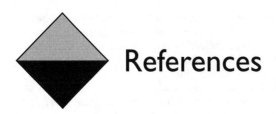

Aaronson, N.K., Ahmedzai, S., Bergman, B. *et al.* (1993) The European Organisation for research and treatment of cancer QLQ-C30: a quality of life instrument for use in international clinical trials in oncology, *Journal for the National Cancer Institute*, 85: 365–76.

Abraham, C. and Sheeran, P. (1993) In search of a psychology of safer-sex promotion; beyond beliefs and text, *Health Education Research: Theory and Practice*, 8: 245–54.

Abraham, C. and Sheeran, P. (1994) Modelling and modifying young heterosexuals' HIV preventive behaviour: a review of theories, findings and educational implications, *Patient Education and Counselling*, 23: 173–86.

Abraham, C., Sheeran, P., Abrams, D., Spears, R. and Marks, D. (1991) Young people learning about AIDS: a study of beliefs and information sources, *Health Education Research: Theory and Practice*, 6: 19–29.

Abraham, S.C.S., Sheeran, P., Abrams, D. and Spears, R. (1994) Exploring teenagers' adaptive and maladaptive thinking in relation to the threat of HIV infection, *Psychology and Health*, 7: 253–72.

Abraham, S.C.S., Sheeran, P., Abrams, D. and Spears, R. (1996) Health beliefs and teenage condom use: a prospective study, *Psychology and Health*, 11: 641–55.

Abrams, D., Abraham, C., Spears, R. and Marks, D. (1990) AIDS invulnerability: relationships, sexual behaviour and attitudes among 16–19 year-olds, in P. Aggleton, P. Davies and G. Hart (eds), *AIDS: Individual, Cultural and Policy Dimensions*, pp. 35–52. London: Falmer Press.

Abrams, K., Allen, L. and Gray, J. (1992) Disordered eating attitudes and behaviours, psychological adjustment and ethnic identity: A comparison of black and white female college students, *International Journal of Eating Disorders*, 14: 49–57.

Ader, R. and Cohen, N. (1975) Behaviourally conditioned immuno suppression, *Psychosomatic Medicine*, 37: 333–40.

Ader, R. and Cohen, N. (1981) Conditioned immunopharmacologic responses, in R. Ader (ed.), *Psychoneuroimmunology*. New York: Academic Press.

Aggleton, P. (1989) HIV/AIDS education in schools; constraints and possibilities, *Health Education Journal*, 48: 167–71.

Aggleton, P. and Homans, H. (1988) *Social Aspects of AIDS*. London: Falmer Press.

Ahmed, S., Waller, G. and Verduyn, C. (1994) Eating attitudes among Asian school girls: the role of perceived parental control, *International Journal of Eating Disorders*, 15: 91–7.

Ajzen, I. (1985) From intention to actions: A theory of planned behavior, in J. Kuhl and J. Beckman (eds), *Action-control: From Cognition to Behavior*, pp. 11–39. Heidelberg: Springer.

Ajzen, I. (1988) *Attitudes, Personality and Behavior*. Chicago, IL: Dorsey Press.

Ajzen, I. and Fishbein, M. (1970) The prediction of behaviour from attitudinal and normative beliefs, *Journal of Personality and Social Psychology*, 6: 466–87.

Ajzen, I. and Madden, T.J. (1986) Prediction of goal-directed behavior: Attitudes, intentions, and perceived behavioral control, *Journal of Experimental Social Psychology*, 22: 453–74.

Akan, G.E. and Grilo, C.M. (1995) Sociocultural influences on eating attitudes and behaviors, body image, and psychological functioning: a comparison of African-American, Asian-American and Caucasian college women, *International Journal of Eating Disorders*, 18: 181–7.

Alagna, S.W. and Reddy, D.M. (1984) Predictors of proficient technique and successful lesion detection in breast self-examination, *Health Psychology*, 3: 113–27.

Albrecht, G.L. (1994) Subjective health status, in C. Jenkinson (ed.), *Measuring Health and Medical Outcomes*, pp. 7–26. London: UCL Press.

Allied Dunbar National Fitness Survey (1992) *A Report on Activity Patterns and Fitness Levels*. London: Sports Council and Health Education Authority.

Amelang, M. and Schmidt-Rathjens, C. (1996) Personality, cancer and coronary heart disease: Further evidence on a controversial issue, *British Journal of Health Psychology*, 1: 191–205.

Anderson, H.R., Freeling, P. and Patel, S.P. (1983) Decision making in acute asthma, *Journal of the Royal College of General Practitioners*, 33: 105–8.

Annas, G.J. (1990) Quality of life in the courts: Early spring in fantasyland, in J.J. Walter and T.A. Shannon (eds), *Quality of Life: The New Medical Dilemma*. New York: Paulist Press.

Appleton, P.L. and Pharoah, P.O.D. (1998) Partner smoking behaviour change is associated with women's smoking reduction and cessation during pregnancy, *British Journal of Health Psychology*, 3: 361–74.

Armstrong, D. (1995) The rise of Surveillance Medicine, *Sociology of Health and Illness*, 17: 393–404.

Arnetz, B.B., Wasserman, J., Petrini, B. *et al.* (1987) Immune function in unemployed women, *Psychosomatic Medicine*, 49: 3–12.

Ashworth, H.W. (1963) An experiment in presymptomatic diagnosis, *Journal of the Royal College of General Practice*, 6: 71.

Attie, I. and Brooks-Gunn, J. (1989) Development of eating problems in adolescent girls: a longitudinal study, *Developmental Psychology*, 25: 70–9.

Autorengruppe Nationales Forschungsprogramm (1984) *Wirksamkeit der Gemeindeorientierten Pravention Kardiovascularer Krankheiten (Effectiveness of community-orientated prevention of cardiovascular diseases)*. Bern: Hans Huber.

Baer, P.E., Garmezy, L.B., McLaughlin, R.J., Pokorny, A.D. and Wernick, M.J. (1987) Stress, coping, family conflict, and adolescent alcohol use, *Journal of Behavioral Medicine*, 10: 449–66.

Bagozzi, R.P. (1993) On the neglect of volition in consumer research: a critique and proposal, *Psychology and Marketing*, 10: 215–37.

Bagozzi, R.P. and Warshaw, P.R. (1990) Trying to consume, *Journal of Consumer Research*, 17: 127–40.

Bain, D.J.G. (1977) Patient knowledge and the content of the consultation in general practice, *Medical Education*, 11: 347–50.

Bandura, A. (1977) Self efficacy: Toward a unifying theory of behavior change, *Psychological Review*, 84: 191–215.

Bandura, A. (1986) *Social foundations of thought and action*. Englewood Cliffs, NJ: Prentice Hall.

Bandura, A., Ross, D. and Ross, S.A. (1963) Imitation of film mediated aggressive models, *Journal of Abnormal and Social Psychology*, 66: 3–11.

Bandura, A., Reese, L. and Adams, N.E. (1982) Micro-analysis of action and fear arousal as a function of differential levels of perceived self efficacy, *Journal of Personality and Social Psychology*, 43: 5–21.

Bandura, A., Cioffi, D., Taylor, C.B. and Brouillard, M.E. (1988) Perceived self efficacy in coping with cognitive stressors and opioid activation, *Journal of Personality and Social Psychology*, 55: 479–88.

Barraclough, J., Pinder, P., Cruddas, M. *et al.* (1992) Life events and breast cancer prognosis, *British Medical Journal*, 304: 1078–81.

Basler, H.D. and Rehfisch, H.P. (1990) Follow up results of a cognitive behavioural treatment for chronic pain in a primary care setting, *Psychology and Health*, 4: 293–304.

Baucom, D.H. and Aiken, P.A. (1981) Effect of depressed mood on eating among obese and nonobese dieting and nondieting persons, *Journal of Personality and Social Psychology*, 41: 577–85.

Baum, A., Fisher, J.D. and Solomon, S. (1981) Type of information, familiarity and the reduction of crowding stress, *Journal of Personality and Social Psychology*, 40: 11–23.

Beck, A.T., Mendelson, M., Mock, J. *et al.* (1961) Inventory for measuring depression, *Archives of General Psychiatry*, 4: 561–71.

Beck, K.H. and Lund, A.K. (1981) The effects of health threat seriousness and personal efficacy upon intentions and behaviour, *Journal of Applied Social Psychology*, 11: 401–15.

Becker, M.H. (ed.) (1974) The health belief model and personal health behavior, *Health Education Monographs*, 2: 324–508.

Becker, M.H. and Rosenstock, I.M. (1984) Compliance with medical advice, in A. Steptoe and A. Mathews (eds), *Health Care and Human Behaviour*. London: Academic Press.

Becker, M.H. and Rosenstock, I.M. (1987) Comparing social learning theory and the health belief model, in W.B. Ward (ed.), *Advances in Health Education and Promotion*, pp. 245–9. Greenwich, CT: JAI Press.

Becker, M.H., Kaback, M., Rosenstock, I. and Ruth, M. (1975) Some influences on public participation in a genetic screening program, *Journal of Community Health*, 1: 3–14.

Becker, M.H., Maiman, L.A., Kirscht, J.P., Haefner, D.P. and Drachman, R.H. (1977) The health belief model and prediction of dietary compliance: A field experiment, *Journal of Health and Social Behaviour*, 18: 348–66.

Beecher, H.K. (1955) The powerful placebo, *The Journal of the American Medical Association*, 159: 1602–6.

Beecher, H.K. (1956) Relationship of significance of wound to the pain experienced, *Journal of the American Medical Association*, 161: 1609–13.

Belar, C.D. and Deardorff, W.W. (1995) *Clinical Health Psychology in Medical Settings: A Practitioner's Guidebook*. Hyattsville, MD: APA.

Belloc, N.B. (1973) Relationship of health practices and mortality, *Preventative Medicine*, 2: 67–81.

Belloc, N.B. and Breslow, L. (1972) Relationship of physical health status and health practices, *Preventative Medicine*, 1: 409–21.

Benwell, M.E., Balfour, D.J. and Anderson, J.M. (1988) Evidence that nicotine increases the density of (-)-[^{3}H] nicotine binding sites in human brain, *Journal of Neurochemistry*, 50: 1243–7.

Bergner, M., Bobbitt, R.A., Carter, W.B. and Gilson, D. (1981) The sickness impact profile: Development and final revision of a health status measure, *Medical Care*, 19: 787–805.

Berkman, L.F. and Syme, S.L. (1979) Social networks, lost resistance and mortality: a nine year follow up study of Alameda County residents, *American Journal of Epidemiology*, 109: 186–204.

Berry, D.C., Michas, I.C., Gillie, T. and Forster, M. (1997) What do patients want to know about their medicines, and what do doctors want to tell them? A comparative study, *Psychology and Health*, 12: 467–80.

Beta-Blocker Heart Attack Trial Research Group (BHAT) (1982) A randomized trial of propranolol in patients with acute myocardial infarction. I. Mortality results, *Journal of the American Medical Association*, 247: 1707–14.

Bieliauskas, L.A. (1980) Life stress and aid seeking, *Journal of Human Stress*, 6: 28–36.

Biener, L., Abrams, D.B., Follick, M.J. and Dean, L. (1989) A comparative evaluation of a restrictive smoking policy in a general hospital, *American Journal of Public Health*, 79: 192–5.

Bishop, G.D. and Converse, S.A. (1986) Illness representations: a prototype approach, *Health Psychology*, 5: 95–114.

Black, R.B. (1989) A 1 and 16 month follow up of prenatal diagnosis patients who lost pregnancies, *Prenatal Diagnosis*, 9: 795–804.

Blackburn, G.L. and Kanders, B.S. (1987) Medical evaluation and treatment of the obese patient with cardiovascular disease, *American Journal of Cardiology*, 60: 55–8.

Blair, S.N., Ellsworth, N.M., Haskell, W.L. *et al.* (1981) Comparison of nutrient intake in middle aged men and women runners and controls, *Medicine, Science and Sports and Exercise*, 13: 310–15.

Blair, S.N., Kohl, H.W., Paffenbarger, R.S. *et al.* (1989) Physical fitness and all-cause mortality: A prospective study of healthy men and women, *Journal of the American Medical Association*, 262: 2395–401.

Blair, S.N., Kohl, H.W., Gordon, N.F. and Paffenbarger, R.S. (1992) How much physical activity is good for health? *Annual Review of Public Health*, 13: 99–126.

Blaxter, M. (1990) *Health and Lifestyles*. London: Routledge.

Bloom, J.R. (1983) Social support, accommodation to stress and adjustment to breast cancer, *Social Science and Medicine*, 16: 1329–38.

Bloom, J.R. and Monterossa, S. (1981) Hypertension labelling and sense of well-being, *American Journal of Public Health*, 71: 1228–32.

Blundell, J. and Macdiarmid, J. (1997) Fat as a risk factor for over consumption: satiation, satiety and patterns of eating, *Journal of the American Dietetic Association*, 97: S63–S69.

Blundell, J.E., Lawton, C.L., Cotton, J.R. and Macdiarmid, J.I. (1996) Control of human appetite: Implications for the intake of dietary fat, *Annual Review of Nutrition*, 16: 285–319.

Boldero, J., Moore, S. and Rosenthal, D. (1992) Intention, context, and safe sex: Australian adolescent's responses to AIDS, *Journal of Applied Social Psychology*, 22: 1374–98.

Bolton-Smith, C. and Woodward, M. (1994) Dietary composition and fat to sugar ratios in relation to obesity, *International Journal of Obesity*, 18: 820–8.

Borland, R., Owens, N., Hill, D. and Chapman, S. (1990) Changes in acceptance of workplace smoking bans following their implementation: a prospective study, *Preventative Medicine*, 19: 314–22.

Borland, R., Owens, N. and Hocking, B. (1991) Changes in smoking behaviour after a total work place ban, *Australian Journal of Public Health*, 15: 130–4.

Bortner, R.W. (1969) A short rating scale as a potential measure of pattern A behaviour, *Journal of Chronic Disease*, 22: 87–91.

Bouchard, C., Trembley, A., Despres, J.P. *et al.* (1990) The response to long term overfeeding in identical twins, *New England Journal of Medicine*, 322: 1477–82.

Boulton, M., Schramm Evans, Z., Fitzpatrick, R. and Hart, G. (1991) Bisexual men: women, safer sex, and HIV infection, in P. Aggleton, P.M. Davies and G. Hart (eds), *AIDS: Responses, Policy and Care*. London: The Falmer Press.

Bower, J.E., Kemeny, M.E., Taylor, S.E., Visscher, B.R. and Fahey, J.L. (1998) Cognitive processing, discovery of meaning, CD 4 decline, and AIDS-related mortality among bereaved HIV-seropositive men, *Journal of Consulting and Clinical Psychology*, 66: 979–86.

Boyd, B. and Wandersman, A. (1991) Predicting undergraduate condom use with the Fishbein and Ajzen and the Triandis attitude-behaviour models: implications for public health interventions, *Journal of Applied Social Psychology*, 21: 1810–30.

Boyer, C.B. and Kegles, S.M. (1991) AIDS risk and prevention among adolescents, *Social Science and Medicine*, 33: 11–23.

Boyle, C.M. (1970) Differences between patients' and doctors' interpretations of common medical terms, *British Medical Journal*, 2: 286–9.

Bradley, C. (1985) Psychological aspects of diabetes, in D.G.M.M. Alberti and L.P. Drall (eds), *Diabetes Annual*. Amsterdam: Elsevier.

Bray, G.A. (1986) Effects of obesity on health and happiness, in K.D. Brownell and J.P. Foreyt (eds), *Handbook of Eating Disorders: Physiology, Psychology and Treatment of Obesity, Anorexia and Bulimia*. New York: Basic Books.

Breslow, L. and Enstrom, J. (1980) Persistance of health habits and their relationship to mortality, *Preventive Medicine*, 9: 469–83.

Brewin, C.R. (1984) Perceived controllability of life events and willingness to prescribe psychotropic drugs, *British Journal of Social Psychology*, 23: 285–7.

Brickman, P., Rabinowitz, V.C., Karuza, J. *et al.* (1982) Models of helping and coping, *American Psychologist*, 37: 368–84.

Brodie, D.A., Slade, P.D. and Rose, H. (1989) Reliability measures in disturbing body image, *Perceptual and Motor Skills*, 69: 723–32.

Brook, R.H., Berman, D.M., Lohr, K.N. *et al.* (1981) *Conceptualisation and Measurement of Health for Adults, Vol. 7, Diabetes Mellitus*. Santa Monica, CA: Rand Corporation.

Brown, R.A., Lichtenstein, E., McIntyre, K. and Harrington-Kostur, J. (1984) Effects of nicotine fading and relapse prevention on smoking cessation, *Journal of Consulting and Clinical Psychology*, 52: 307–8.

Brown, T.A., Cash, T.F. and Mikulka, P.J. (1990) Attitudinal body-image assessment: Factor analysis of the Body Self Relations Questionnaire, *Journal of Personality Assessment*, 55: 135–44.

Browne, J.P., McGee, H.M. and O'Boyle, C.A. (1997) Conceptual approaches to the assessment of quality of life, *Psychology and Health*, 12: 737–51.

Brownell, K.D. (1989) Weight control and your health, in *World Book Encyclopedia*.

Brownell, K.D. (1990) *The LEARN Programme for Weight Control*. Dallas, TX: American HealthPub.

Brownell, K.D. and Steen, S.N. (1987) Modern methods for weight control: the physiology and psychology of dieting, *The Physician and Sports Medicine*, 15: 122–37.

Brownell, K.D. and Wadden, T.A. (1991) The heterogeneity of obesity: Fitting treatments to individuals, *Behaviour Therapy*, 22: 153–77.

Brownell, K.D. and Wadden, T.A. (1992) Etiology and treatment of obesity: Understanding a serious, prevalent and refractory disorder, *Journal Consulting and Clinical Psychology*, 60: 435–42.

Brownell, K.D., Marlatt, G.A., Lichtenstein, E. and Wilson, G.T. (1986a) Understanding and preventing relapse, *American Psychologist*, 41: 765–82.

Brownell, K.D., Greenwood, M.R.C., Stellar, E. and Shrager, E.E. (1986b) The effects of repeated cycles of weight loss and regain in rats, *Physiology and Behaviour*, 38: 459–64.

Brownell, K.D., Steen, S.N. and Wilmore, J.H. (1989) Weight regulation practices in athletes: Analysis of metabolic and health effects, *Medical Science and Sports Exercise*, 7: 125–32.

Brubaker, C. and Wickersham, D. (1990) Encouraging the practice of testicular self examination: a field application of the theory of reasoned action, *Health Psychology*, 9: 154–63.

Bruch, H. (1974) *Eating Disorders: Obesity, Anorexia and the Person Within*. New York: Basic Books.

Bucknall, C.A., Morris, G.K. and Mitchell, J.R.A. (1986) Physicians' attitudes to four common problems: hypertension, atrial fibrillation, transient ischaemic attacks, and angina pectoris, *British Medical Journal*, 293: 739–42.

Bull, R.H., Engels, W.D., Engelsmann, F. and Bloom, L. (1983) Behavioural changes following gastric surgery for morbid obesity: A prospective, controlled study, *Journal of Psychosomatic Research*, 27: 457–67.

Bullen, B.A., Reed, R.B. and Mayer, J. (1964) Physical activity of obese and non-obese adolescent girls appraised by motion picture sampling, *American Journal of Clinical Nutrition*, 4: 211–33.

Bundy, C., Carroll, D., Wallace, L. and Nagle, R. (1998) Stress management and exercise training in chronic stable angina pectoris, *Psychology and Health*, 13: 147–55.

Burish, T.G., Carey, M.P., Krozely, M.G. and Greco, F.F. (1987) Conditioned side-effects induced by cancer chemotherapy: prevention through behavioral treatment, *Journal of Consulting and Clinical Psychology*, 55: 42–8.

Burke, P. (1992) The ethics of screening, in C.R. Hart and P. Burke (eds), *Screening and Surveillance in General Practice*. London: Churchill Livingstone.

Butler, C. and Steptoe, A. (1986) Placebo responses: An experimental study of psychophysiological processes in asthmatic volunteers, *British Journal of Clinical Psychology*, 25: 173–83.

Butterfield, W.J.H. (1968) *Priorities in Medicine*. London: Nuffield.

Byrne, D., Jazwinski, C., DeNinno, J.A. and Fisher, W.A. (1977) Negative sexual attitudes and contraception, in D. Byrne and L.A. Byrne (eds), *Exploring Human Sexuality*. New York: Crowell.

Calnan, M. (1987) *Health and Illness: The Lay Perspective*. London: Tavistock.

Campion, M.J., Brown, J.R., McCance, D.J. *et al.* (1988) Psychosexual trauma of an abnormal cervical smear, *British Journal of Obstetrics and Gynaecology*, 95: 175–81.

Cancer Research Campaign (1991) *Smoking Policy and Prevalence Among 16–19 Year Olds*. London: HMSO.

Cannon, W.B. (1932) *The Wisdom of the Body*. New York: Norton.

Cappell, H. and Greeley, J. (1987) Alcohol and tension reduction: An update on research and theory, in H.T. Blane and K.E. Leonard (eds), *Psychological Theories of Drinking and Alcoholism*, pp. 15–54. New York: Guilford Press.

Carey, M.P., Kalra, D.L., Carey, K.B., Halperin, S. and Richard, C.S. (1993) Stress and unaided smoking cessation: a prospective investigation, *Journal of Consulting and Clinical Psychology*, 61: 831–8.

Cartwright, A., Hockey, L. and Anderson, J.L. (1973) *Life Before Death*. London: Routledge.

Carver, C.S., Scheier, M.F. and Weintraub, J.K. (1989) Assessing coping strategies: A theoretically based approach, *Journal of Personality and Social Psychology*, 56: 267–83.

Caspersen, C.J., Powell, K.E. and Christenson, G.M. (1985) Physical activity, exercise, and physical fitness. Definitions and distinctions for health-related research, *Public Health Reports*, 100: 126–31.

Catania, J.A., Coates, T.J., Kegeles, S.M. *et al.* (1989) Implications of the AIDS risk-reduction model for the gay community: The importance of perceived sexual enjoyment and help seeking behaviors, in V.M. Mays, G.W. Albee and S.F. Schneider (eds), *Primary Prevention of AIDS*, pp. 242–61. Newbury Park, CA: Sage.

Central Statistical Office (1994) *Social Trends 24*. London: HMSO.

Chambers, L.W., McDonald, L.A., Tugwell, P. *et al.* (1982) The McMaster health index questionnaire as a measure of quality of life for patients with rheumatoid arthritis, *Journal of Rheumatology*, 9: 780–4.

Champion, V.L. (1990) Breast self examination in women 35 and older – A prospective study, *Journal of Behavioural Medicine*, 13: 523–38.

Chan, J.M., Rimm, E.B., Colditz, G.A., Stampfer, M.J. and Willett, W.C. (1994) Obesity, fat distribution and weight gain as risk factors for clinical diabetes in men, *Diabetes Care*, 17: 961–9.

Charlton, A. (1984) Children's opinion about smoking, *Journal of the Royal College of General Practitioners*, 34: 483–7.

Charlton, A. (1992) Children and tobacco, *British Journal of Cancer*, 66: 1–4.

Charlton, A. and Blair, V. (1989) Predicting the onset of smoking in boys and girls, *Social Science and Medicine*, 29: 813–18.

Coates, T.J., Jeffrey, R.W. and Wing, R.R. (1978) The relationship between a person's relative body weight and the quality and quantity of food stored in their homes, *Addictive Behaviours*, 3: 179–84.

Cockburn, J., Staples, M., Hurley, S.F. and DeLuise, T. (1994) Psychological consequences of screening mammography, *Journal of Medical Screening*, 1: 7–12.

Cohen, J.B., Severy, L.J. and Ahtola, O.T. (1978) An extended expectancy value approach to contraceptive alternatives, *Journal of Population Studies*, 1: 22–41.

Cohen, S. and Lichtenstein, E. (1990) Partner behaviours that support quitting smoking, *Journal of Consulting and Clinical Psychology*, 58: 304–9.

Cohen, S., Mermelstein, R., Kamarck, T. and Hoberman, N.H. (1985) Measuring the functional components of social support, in I. Sarason and B. Sarason (eds), *Social Support: Theory, Research, and Applications*, pp. 73–94. Dordrecht, Netherlands: Martinus Nijhoff.

Cole, S. and Edelmann, R. (1988) Restraint, eating disorders and the need to achieve in state and public school subjects, *Personality and Individual Differences*, 8: 475–82.

Collins, M.E. (1991) Body figure perceptions and preferences among preadolescent children, *International Journal of Eating Disorders*, 10: 199–208.

Conner, M., Fitter, M. and Fletcher, W. (1999) Stress and snacking: A diary study of daily hassles and between-meal snacking, *Psychology and Health*, 14: 51–63.

Conway, T.L., Vickers, R.R., Ward, H.W. and Rahe, R.H. (1981) Occupational stress and variation in cigarette, coffee and alcohol consumption, *Journal of Health and Social Behaviour*, 22: 155–65.

Cools, J., Schotte, D.E. and McNally, R.J. (1992) Emotional arousal and overeating in restrained eaters, *Journal of Abnormal Psychology*, 101: 348–51.

Cooper, Z. and Fairburn, C.G. (1987) The eating disorder examination: A semi-structured interview for the assessment of the specific psychopathology of eating disorder, *International Journal of Eating Disorders*, 6: 1–8.

Cooper, P.J., Taylor, M.J., Cooper, Z. and Fairburn, C.G. (1987) The development and validation of the body shape questionnaire, *International Journal of Eating Disorders*, 6: 485–94.

Coopersmith, S. (1967) *The Antecedents of Self-esteem*. San Francisco: WH Freeman. Reprinted in 1981.

Corah, W.L. and Boffa, J. (1970) Perceived control, self observation and responses to aversive stimulation, *Journal of Personality and Social Psychology*, 16: 1–4.

Counts, C.R. and Adams, H.E. (1985) Body image in bulimia, dieting and normal females, *Journal of Psychopathology and Behavioral Assessment*, 7: 289–300.

Crichton, E.F., Smith, D.L. and Demanuele, F. (1978) Patients' recall of medication information, *Drug Intelligence and Clinical Pharmacy*, 12: 591–9.

Crisp, A., Palmer, R. and Kalucy, R. (1976) How common is Anorexia Nervosa? A prevalence study, *British Journal of Psychiatry*, 128: 549–54.

Crisp, A.H., Hsu, L., Harding, B. and Hartshorn, J. (1980) Clinical features of anorexia. A study of consecutive series of 102 female patients, *Journal of Psychosomatic Research*, 24: 179–91.

Cummings, K., Hellmann, R. and Emont, S.L. (1988) Correlates of participation in a worksite stop-smoking contest, *Journal of Behavioral Medicine*, 11: 267–77.

Curran, J.W., Morgan, W.M., Hardy, A.M. *et al.* (1985) The epidemiology of AIDS: Current status and future prospects, *Science*, 229: 1352–7.

Cvetkovich, G. and Grote, B. (1981) Psychosocial maturity and teenage contraceptive use: an investigation of decision-making and communication skills, *Population and Environment*, 4: 211–26.

Danaher, B.G. (1977) Rapid smoking and self-control in the modification of smoking behaviour, *Journal of Consulting and Clinical Psychology*, 45: 1068–75.

Davies, D.L. (1962) Normal drinking in recovered alcohol addicts, *Quarterly Journal of Studies on Alcohol*, 23: 94–104.

Dean, C. (1987) Psychiatric morbidity following mastectomy: preoperative predictors and types of illness, *Journal of Psychosomatic Research*, 31: 385–92.

Dean, C., Roberts, M.M., French, K. and Robinson, S. (1984) Psychiatric morbidity after screening for breast cancer, *Journal of Epidemiology and Community Health*, 40: 71–5.

deHaes, J.C.J.M. and van Knippenberg, F.C.E. (1985) The quality of life of cancer patients: A review of the literature, *Social Science and Medicine*, 20: 809–17.

deHaes, J.C.J.M., van Knippenberg, F.C. and Neigt, J.P. (1990) Measuring psychological and physical distress in cancer patients: structure and application of the Rotterdam symptom checklist, *British Journal of Cancer*, 62: 1034–8.

Dekker, F.W., Kaptein, A.A., van der Waart, M.A.C. and Gill, K. (1992) Quality of self care of patients with asthma, *Journal of Asthma*, 29: 203–8.

DeLamater, J. and MacCorquodale, P. (1978) Premarital contraceptive use: a test of two models, *Journal of Marriage and the Family*, 40: 235–47.

DeLamater, J. and MacCorquodale, P. (1979) *Premarital Sexuality: Attitudes, Relationships, Behavior*. Madison, WI: University of Wisconsin Press.

Department of Health (DoH) (1991) *The Health of the Nation*. London: HMSO.

Department of Health (DoH) (1995) *Obesity: Reversing the Increasing Problem of Obesity in England*, a report from the Nutrition and Physical Activity Task Forces. London: HMSO.

Department of Health and Human Services (1980) Prescription drug products: patient package insert requirements, *Federal Register*, 45: 60754–817.

Department of Health and Welsh Office (1989) *General Practice in the National Health Service: A New Contract*. London: HMSO.

Diamond, E.G., Kittle, C.F. and Crockett, J.F. (1960) Comparison of internal mammary artery ligation and sham operation for angina pectoris, *American Journal of Cardiology*, 5: 483–6.

Dickinson, A. (1980) *Contemporary Animal Learning Theory*. Cambridge: Cambridge University Press.

DiClemente, C.C. (1986) Self-efficacy and the addictive behaviors, *Journal of Social and Clinical Psychology*, 4: 303–15.

DiClemente, C.C. and Prochaska, J.O. (1982) Self-change and therapy change of smoking behavior: A comparison of processes of change in cessation and maintenance, *Addictive Behaviours*, 7: 133–42.

DiClemente, C.C. and Prochaska, J.O. (1985) Processes and stages of change: Coping and competence in smoking behavior change, in F. Shiffman and T.A. Wills (eds), *Coping and Substance Abuse*, pp. 319–43. New York: Academic Press.

DiClemente, C.C. and Hughes, S.O. (1990) Stages of change profiles in outpatient alcoholism treatment, *Journal of Substance Abuse*, 2: 217–35.

DiClemente, C.C., Prochaska, J.O. and Gilbertini, M. (1985) Self-efficacy and the stages of self-change of smoking, *Cognitive Therapy and Research*, 9: 181–200.

DiClemente, C.C., Prochaska, J.O., Fairhurst, S.K. *et al.* (1991) The process of smoking cessation: An analysis of precontemplation, contemplation, and preparation stages of change, *Journal of Consulting and Clinical Psychology*, 59: 295–304.

Diedericks, J.P. *et al.* (1991) Predictors of return to former leisure and social activities in MI patients, *Journal of Psychosomatic Research*, 35: 687–96.

Dillon, K.M., Minchoff, B. and Baker, K.H. (1985–1986) Positive emotional states and enhancement of the immune system, *International Journal of Psychiatry in Medicine*, 15: 13–17.

Diner, E., Emmons, R.A., Larson, R.J. and Griffen, S. (1985) The satisfaction with life scale, *Journal of Personality Assessment*, 49: 71–6.

Dishman, R.K. (1982) Compliance/adherence in health-related exercise, *Health Psychology*, 1: 237–67.

Dishman, R.K. and Gettman, L.R. (1980) Psychobiologic influences on exercise adherence, *Journal of Sport Psychology*, 2: 295–310.

Dishman, R.K., Sallis, J.F. and Orenstein, D.M. (1985) The determinants of physical activity and exercise, *Public Health Reports*, 100: 158–72.

Dolan, B., Lacey, J. and Evans, C. (1990) Eating behaviour and attitudes to weight and shape in British women from three ethnic groups, *British Journal of Psychiatry*, 157: 523–8.

Dolce, J.J. (1987) Self efficacy and disability beliefs in the behavioral treatment of pain, *Behavior Research and Therapy*, 25: 289–96.

Doll, R. and Hill, A.B. (1954) The mortality of doctors in relation to their smoking habits. A preliminary report, *British Medical Journal,* 1: 1451–55.

Doll, R. and Peto, R. (1981) *The Causes of Cancer*. New York: Oxford University Press.

Dornbusch, S., Carlsmith, J., Duncan, P. *et al.* (1984) Sexual maturation, social class and the desire to be thin among adolescent females, *Developmental and Behavioural Paediatrics,* 5: 475–82.

Downing, R.W. and Rickels, K. (1983) Physician prognosis in relation to drug and placebo response in anxious and depressed psychiatric outpatients, *The Journal of Nervous and Mental Disease,* 171: 182–5.

Drenowski, A., Kurt, C. and Krahn, D. (1994) Body weight and dieting in adolescence: impact of socioeconomic status, *International Journal of Eating Disorders,* 16: 61–5.

Duncan, I. (1992) (ed.) *Guidelines for Clinical Practice and Programme Management*. Oxford: NHS Cervical Screening Programme.

Durnin, J.V.G.A., Lonergan, M.E., Good, J. and Ewan, A. (1974) A cross sectional nutritional and anthropometric study with an interval of 7 years on 611 young adolescent school children, *British Journal of Nutrition,* 32: 169–79.

Edholm, O.G., Fletcher, J.G., Widdowson, E.M. and McCance, R.A. (1955) The food intake and individual expenditure of individual men, *British Journal of Nutrition,* 9: 286–300.

Edwards, G. and Gross, M. (1976) Alcohol dependence: Provisional description of a clinical syndrome, *British Medical Journal,* i: 1058–61.

Edwards, N. (1954) The theory of decision making, *Psychological Bulletin,* 51: 380–417.

Egbert, L.D., Battit, G.E., Welch, C.E. and Bartlett, M.K. (1964) Reduction of postoperative pain by encouragement and instruction of patients, *The New England Journal of Medicine,* 270: 825–7.

Egger, G., Fitzgerald, W., Frape, G. *et al.* (1983) Result of a large scale media antismoking campaign in Australia: North Coast 'Quit For Life' Programme, *British Medical Journal,* 286: 1125–8.

Eisler, I. and Szmukler, G. (1985) Social class as a confounding variable in the eating attitudes test, *Journal of Psychiatric Research,* 19: 171–6.

Engel, G.L. (1977) The need for a new medical model: A challenge for biomedicine, *Science,* 196: 129–35.

Engel, G.L. (1980) The clinical application of the biopsychosocial model, *American Journal of Psychiatry,* 137: 535–44.

Etzwiler, D.D. (1967) Who's teaching the diabetic? *Diabetes,* 16: 111–17.

Evans, F.J. (1974) The power of the sugar pill, *Psychology Today,* April: 55–9.

Eysenck, H.J. (1990) The prediction of death from cancer by means of personality/stress questionnaire: too good to be true? *Perceptual Motor Skills,* 71: 216–18.

Eysenck, H.J. and Grossarth-Maticek, R. (1991) Creative novation behaviour therapy as a prophylactic treatment for cancer and coronary heart disease. Part II – Effects of treatment, *Behavioral Research and Therapy,* 29: 17–31.

Fallowfield, L. (1990) *The Quality of Life: The Missing Measurement in Health Care*. London: Souvenir Press.

Fallowfield, L.J., Rodway, A. and Baum, M. (1990) What are the psychological factors influencing attendance, non-attendance and re-attendance at a breast screening centre? *Journal of the Royal Society of Medicine,* 83: 547–51.

Farooqi, I.S., Jebb, S.A., Cook, G. *et al.* (1999) Effects of recombinant leptin therapy in a child with leptin deficiency, *New England Journal of Medicine,* 16: 879–84.

Farquhar, J.W., Fortmann, S.P., Flora, J.A. *et al.* (1990) Effects of communitywide education on cardiovascular disease risk factors: The Stanford Five-City Project, *Journal of the American Medical Association*, 264: 359–65.

Ferster, C.B., Nurnberger, J.I. and Levitt, E.B. (1962) The control of eating, *Journal of Mathetics*, 1: 87–109.

Festinger L. (1957) *A Theory of Cognitive Dissonance*. Evanston, Ill: Row, Peterson.

Feuerstein, M., Carter, R.L. and Papciak, A.S. (1987) A prospective analysis of stress and fatigue in recurrent low back pain, *Pain*, 31: 333–44.

Fife-Schaw, C.R. and Breakwell, G.M. (1992) Estimating sexual behaviour parameters in the light of AIDS: a review of recent UK studies of young people, *Aids Care*, 4: 187–201.

Fiore, M.C., Novotny, T.F., Pierce, J.P. *et al.* (1990) Methods used to quit smoking in the United States: Do cessation programs help? *Journal of the American Medical Association*, 263: 2760–5.

Fishbein, M. (1967) Attitude and the prediction of behavior, in M. Fishbein (ed.), *Readings in Attitude Theory and Measurement*. New York: Wiley.

Fishbein, M. and Ajzen, I. (1975) *Belief, Attitude, Intention, and Behavior: An Introduction to Theory and Research*. Reading, MA: Addison-Wesley.

Fisher, W.A. (1984) Predicting contraceptive behavior among university men: the role of emotions and behavioral intentions, *Journal of Applied Social Psychology*, 14: 104–23.

Fitzpatrick, R. (1993) Scope and measurement of patient satisfaction, in R. Fitzpatrick and A. Hopkins (eds), *Measurement of Patients' Satisfaction with their Care*. London. Royal College of Physicians of London.

Flannelly, G., Anderson, D., Kitchener, H.C. *et al.* (1994) Management of women with mild and moderate cervical dyskaryosis, *British Medical Journal*, 308: 1399–403.

Flay, B.R. (1985) Psychosocial approaches to smoking prevention: A review of findings, *Health Psychology*, 4: 449–88.

Flegal, K.M., Harlan, W.R. and Landis, J.R. (1988) Secular trends in body mass index and skinfold thickness with socioeconomic factors in young adult women, *American Journal of Clinical Nutrition*, 48: 535–43.

Flowers, P., Smith, J.A., Sheeran, P. and Beail, N. (1997) Health and romance: understanding unprotected sex in relationships between gay men, *British Journal of Health Psychology*, 2: 73–86.

Flowers, P., Smith, J.A., Sheeran, P. and Beail, N. (1998) 'Coming Out' and sexual debut: Understanding the social context of HIV risk-related behaviour, *Journal of Community & Applied Social Psychology*, 8: 409–21.

Fordyce, W.E. and Steger, J.C. (1979) Chronic pain, in O.F. Pomerleau and J.P. Brady (eds), *Behavioral Medicine: Theory and Practice*, pp. 125–53. Baltimore: Williams and Wilkins.

Forrest, A.P.M. (1986) Breast cancer screening. *Report to the Health Ministers of England, Wales, Scotland and Northern Ireland*. London: HMSO.

Foucault, M. (1979) *The History of Sexuality, Vol. 1: An Introduction*. London: Allen and Lane.

Freeling, P. (1965) Candidates for exfoliative cytology of the cervix, *Journal of the Royal College of General Practitioners*, 10: 261.

Freeman, R.F., Thomas, C.D., Solyom, L. and Hunter, M.A. (1984) A modified video camera for measuring body image distortion: Technical description and reliability, *Psychological Medicine*, 14: 411–16.

Freidson, E. (1970) *Profession of Medicine*. New York: Dodds Mead.

Friedman, L.A. and Kimball, A.W. (1986) Coronary heart disease mortality and alcohol consumption in Framingham, *American Journal of Epidemiology*, 124: 481–9.

Friedman, M. and Rosenman, R.H. (1959) Association of specific overt behavior pattern with blood and cardiovascular findings, *Journal of American Medical Association*, 169: 1286–97.

Friedman, M., Thoresen, C., Gill, J. *et al.* (1986) Alteration of Type A behavior and its effects on cardiac recurrences in post myocardial infarction patients: Summary results of the recurrent coronary prevention project, *American Heart Journal*, 112: 653–65.

Furstenberg, F., Shea, J., Allison, P., Herceg-Baron, R. and Webb, D. (1983) Contraceptive continuation among adolescents attending family planning clinics, *Family Planning Perspectives*, 15: 211–17.

Futterman, A.D., Kemeny, M.E., Shapiro, D., Polonsky, W. and Fahey, J.L. (1992) Immunological variability associated with experimentally-induced positive and negative affective states, *Psychological Medicine*, 22: 231–8.

Gallacher, J.E.J., Hopkinson, C.A., Bennett, P., Burr, M.L. and Elwood, P.C. (1997) Effect of stress management on angina, *Psychology and Health*, 12: 523–32.

Gardner, R.M., Martinez, R. and Sandoval, Y. (1987) Obesity and body image: an evaluation of sensory and non-sensory components, *Psychological Medicine*, 17: 927–32.

Garn, S.M., Bailey, S.M., Solomon, M.A. and Hopkins, P.J. (1981) Effects of remaining family members on fatness prediction, *American Journal of Clinical Nutrition*, 34: 148–53.

Garner, D.M. (1991) *EDI-2: Professional Manual*. Odessa, FL: Psychological Assessment Resources Inc.

Garrow, J. (1984) *Energy Balance and Obesity in Man*. New York: Elsevier.

Geis, B.D. and Gerrard, M. (1984) Predicting male and female contraceptive behaviour: a discriminant analysis of groups in high, moderate, and low in contraceptive effectiveness, *Journal of Personality and Social Psychology*, 46: 669–80.

General Household Survey (GHS) (1992) OPCS: London.

General Household Survey (GHS) (1993) OPCS: London.

General Household Survey (GHS) (1994) OPCS: London.

George, W.H. and Marlatt, G.A. (1983) Alcoholism: The evolution of a behavioral perspective, in M. Galanter (ed.), *Recent Developments in Alcoholism*, Vol. 1, pp. 105–38. New York: Plenum Press.

Gerrard, M., Gibbons, F.X., Benthin, A.C. and Hessling, R.M. (1996) A longitudinal study of the reciprocal nature of risk behaviors and cognitions in adolescents: what you do shapes what you think and vice versa, *Health Psychology*, 15: 344–54.

Giannetti, V.J., Reynolds, J. and Rihen, T. (1985) Factors which differentiate smokers from ex-smokers among cardiovascular patients: A discriminant analysis, *Social Science and Medicine*, 20: 241–5.

Gibbons, F.X., Gerrard, M., Ouelette, J. and Burzette, R. (1998) Cognitive antecedents to adolescent health risk: Discriminating between behavioural intention and behavioural willingness, *Psychology and Health*, 13: 319–39.

Gilbert, D.G. and Spielberger, C.D. (1987) Effects of smoking on heart rate, anxiety, and feelings of success during social interaction, *Journal of Behavioral Medicine*, 10: 629–38.

Gill, J.J., Price, V.A. and Friedman, M. (1985) Reduction of Type A behavior in healthy middle-aged American military officers, *American Heart Journal*, 110: 503–14.

Gillies, P.A. and Galt, M. (1990) Teenage smoking – fun or coping? in J.A.M. Wimbust and S. Maes (eds), *Lifestyles and Health: New Developments in Health Psychology*. DSWO/LEIDEN. Netherlands: University Press.

Gleghorn, A.A., Penner, L.A., Powers, P.S. and Schulman, R. (1987) The psychometric properties of several measures of body image, *Journal of Psychopathology and Behavioral Assessment*, 9: 203–18.

Goddard, E. (1990) *Why Children Start Smoking*. London: HMSO.

Godin, G., Valois, P., Lepage, L. and Desharnais, R. (1992) Predictors of smoking behaviour: An application of Ajzen's theory of planned behaviour, *British Journal of Addiction*, 87: 1335–43.

Gold, R.S., Skinner, M.J., Grant, P.J. and Plummer, D.C. (1991) Situational factors and thought processes associated with unprotected intercourse in gay men, *Psychology and Health*, 5: 259–78.

Goldberg, D.P. (1978) *Manual of the General Health Questionnaire*. Windsor: NFER-Nelson.

Goldschneider, A. (1920) *Das Schmerz Problem*. Berlin: Springer.

Gollwitzer, P.M. (1993) Goal achievement: the role of intentions, in W. Stroebe and M. Hewstone (eds), *European Review of Social Psychology*, 4: 141–85.

Gollwitzer, P.M. and Brandstatter, V. (1997) Implementation intentions and effective goal pursuit, *Journal of Personality and Social Psychology*, 73: 186–99.

Gomel, M., Oldenburg, B., Lemon, J., Owen, N. and Westbrook, F. (1993) Pilot study of the effects of a workplace smoking ban on indices of smoking, cigarette craving, stress and other health behaviours, *Psychology and Health*, 8: 223–9.

Goodkin, K., Blaney, T., Feaster, D. *et al.* (1992) Active coping style is associated with natural killer cell cytotoxicity in asymptomatic HIV–I seropositive homosexual men, *Journal of Psychosomatic Research*, 36: 635–50.

Gould, G.M. (1900) A system of personal biologic examination. The condition of adequate medical and scientific conduct of life, *Journal of the American Medical Association*, 35: 134.

Gracely, R.H., Dubner, R., Deeter, W.R. and Wolskee, P.J. (1985) Clinical expectations influence placebo analgesia, *Lancet*, i: 43.

Graham, H. (1987) Women's smoking and family health, *Social Science and Family Health*, 25: 47–56.

Grant, A. and Elbourne, D. (1989) Fetal movement counting to assess fetal well-being, in I. Chalmers, M. Enkin and M.J.N.C. Keirse (eds), *Effective Care in Pregnancy and Childbirth*, pp. 440–54. Oxford: Oxford University Press.

Grant, M., Padilla, G.V., Ferrell, B.R. and Rhiner, M. (1990) Assessment of quality of life with a single instrument, *Seminars in Oncology Nursing*, 6: 260–70.

Gray, J., Ford, K. and Kelly, L. (1987) The prevalence of bulimia in a Black college population, *International Journal of Eating Disorders*, 6: 733–40.

Greeno, C.G. and Wing, R.R. (1994) Stress-induced eating, *Psychological Bulletin*, 115: 444–64.

Greer, S., Morris, T.E. and Pettingale, K.W. (1979) Psychological responses to breast cancer: Effect on outcome, *Lancet*, 2: 785–7.

Greer, S., Moorey, S., Baruch, J.D.R. *et al.* (1992) Adjuvant psychological therapy for patients with cancer: a prospective randomised trial, *British Medical Journal*, 304: 675–80.

Gregg, I. (1966) The recognition of early chronic bronchitis, *Journal of the American Medical Association*, 176: 1114–16.

Grilo, C.M., Shiffman, S. and Wing, R.R. (1989) Relapse crisis and coping among dieters, *Journal of Consulting and Clinical Psychology*, 57: 488–95.

Grimes, D.S. (1988) Value of a negative cervical smear, *British Medical Journal*, 296: 1363.

Gross, J. and Levenson, R.W. (1997) Hiding feelings: The acute effects of inhibiting negative and positive emotion, *Journal of Abnormal Psychology*, 106: 95–103.

Grunberg, N.E., Winders, S.E. and Wewers, M.E. (1991) Gender differences in tobacco use, *Health Psychology*, 10: 143–53.

Grunfeld, E., Mant, D., Yudkin, P. *et al.* (1996) Routine follow up of breast cancer in primary care: randomised trial, *British Medical Journal*, 313: 665–9.

Gupta, N. and Jenkins, D.G. Jr (1984) Substance use as an employee response to the work environment, *Journal of Vocational Behaviour*, 24: 84–93.

Haas, H., Fink, H. and Hartfelder, G. (1959) *Das placeboproblem. Fortschritte der Arzneimittelforschung*, 1: 279–354.

Hall, A. and Brown, L.B. (1982) A comparison of the attitudes of young anorexia nervosa patients and non patients with those of their mothers, *British Journal of Psychology*, 56: 39–48.

Hall, J.A., Epstein, A.M. and McNeil, B.J. (1989) Multidimensionality of health status in an elderly population: Construct validity of a measurement battery, *Medical Care*, 27: 168–77.

Hall, S.M., Hall, R.G. and Ginsberg, D. (1990) Cigarette dependence, in A.S. Bellack, M. Hersen and A.E. Kazdin (eds), *International Handbook of Behavior Modification and Therapy*, 2nd edn, pp. 437–47. New York: Plenum Press.

Halmi, K.A., Stunkard, A.J. and Mason, E.E. (1980) Emotional responses to weight reduction by three methods: diet, jejunoileal bypass, and gastric, *American Journal of Clinical Nutrition*, 33: 446–51.

Hamilton, K. and Waller, G. (1993) Media influences on body size estimation in anorexia and bulimia: an experimental study, *British Journal of Psychiatry*, 162: 837–40.

Hamm, P.B., Shekelle, R.B. and Stamler, J. (1989) Large fluctuations in body weight during young adulthood and twenty five year risk of coronary death in men, *American Journal of Epidemiology*, 129: 312–18.

Hannah, M.C., Happer, J.L. and Mathews, J.D. (1985) Twin concordance for a binary trait. Nested analysis of never smoking and ex smoking traits and unnested analysis of a committed smoking trait, *American Journal of Human Genetics*, 37: 153–65.

Hart, J.T. (1971) The inverse care law, *Lancet*, i: 405–12.

Hart, J.T. (1987) *Hypertension*, 2nd edn. Edinburgh: Churchill Livingstone.

Havelock, C., Edwards, R., Cuzlick, J. and Chamberlain, J. (1988) The organisation of cervical screening in general practice, *Journal of the Royal College of General Practitioners*, 38: 207–11.

Haynes, R.B., Sackett, D.L. and Taylor, D.W. (eds) (1979) *Compliance in Health Care*. Baltimore: Johns Hopkins University Press.

Haynes, R.B. (1982) Improving patient compliance: An empirical review, in R.B. Stuart (ed.), *Adherence, Compliance and Generalisation in Behavioral Medicine*. New York: Brunner/Mazel.

Haynes, R.B., Sackett, D.L. and Taylor, D.W. (1978) Increased absenteeism from work after detection and labeling of hypertension patients, *New England Journal of Medicine*, 299: 741.

Haynes, S.G., Feinleib, M. and Kannel, W.B. (1980) The relationship of psychosocial factors to coronary heart disease in the Framingham study. III: Eight year incidence of coronary heart disease, *American Journal of Epidemiology*, 111: 37–58.

Hays, R.D. and Stewart, A.L. (1990) The structure of self-reported health in chronic disease patients, *Psychological Assessment*, 2: 22–30.

He, Y., Lam, T.H., Li, L.S. *et al.* (1994) Passive smoking at work as a risk factor for coronary heart disease in Chinese women who have never smoked, *British Medical Journal*, 308: 380–4.

Heatherton, T.F. and Baumeister, R.F. (1991) Binge eating as an escape from self awareness, *Psychological Bulletin*, 110: 86–108.

Heatherton, T.F., Polivy, J. and Herman, C.P. (1991) Restraint, weight loss and variability of body weight, *Journal of Abnormal Psychology*, 100: 78–83.

Heatherton, T.F., Herman, C.P., Polivy, J.A., King, G.A. and McGree, S.T. (1988) The (Mis)measurement of Restraint: An Analysis of Conceptual and Psychometric Issues, *Journal of Abnormal Psychology*, 97: 19–28.

Heider, F. (1944) Social perception and phenomenal causality, *Psychological Review*, 51: 358–74.

Heider, F. (1958) *The Psychology of Interpersonal Relations*. New York: John Wiley.

Helman, C. (1978) Feed a cold starve a fever – folk models of infection in an English suburban community and their relation to medical treatment, *Culture Medicine and Psychiatry*, 2: 107–37.

Herman, C.P. and Polivy, J.A. (1984) A boundary model for the regulation of eating, in A.J. Stunkard and E. Stellar (eds), *Eating and its Disorders*, pp. 141–56. New York: Raven Press.

Herman, C.P. and Polivy, J.A. (1989) Restraint and excess in dieters and bulimics, in K.M. Pirke and D. Ploog (eds), *The Psychobiology of Bulimia*. Berlin: Springer-Verlag.

Herman, C.P., Polivy, J.A. and Esses, V.M. (1987) The illusion of counter-regulation, *Appetite*, 9: 161–9.

Herman, P. and Mack, D. (1975) Restrained and unrestrained eating, *Journal of Personality*, 43: 646–60.

Herold, D.M. and Conlon, E.J. (1981) Work factors as potential causal agents of alcohol abuse, *Journal of Drug Issues*, 11: 337–56.

Herold, E.S. (1981) Contraceptive embarrassment and contraceptive behaviour among young single women, *Journal of Youth and Adolescence*, 10: 233–42.

Herold, E.S. and Samson, M. (1980) Differences between women who begin pill use before and after first intercourse: Ontario, Canada, *Family Planning Perspectives*, 12: 304–5.

Herold, E.S. and McNamee, J.E. (1982) An explanatory model of contraceptive use among young women, *Journal of Sex Research*, 18: 289–304.

Herzlich, C. (1973) *Health and Illness*. London: Academic Press.

Hibscher, J.A. and Herman, C.P. (1977) Obesity, dieting, and the expression of 'obese' characteristics, *Journal of Comparative Physiological Psychology*, 91: 374–80.

Hill, D., Gardner, G. and Rassaby, J. (1985) Factors predisposing women to take precautions against breast and cervix cancer, *Journal of Applied Social Psychology*, 15(1): 59–79.

Hill, A.J. and Bhatti, R. (1995) Body shape perception and dieting in preadolescent British Asian girls: links with eating disorders, *International Journal of Eating Disorders*, 17: 175–83.

Hill, A.J., Weaver, C. and Blundell, J.E. (1990) Dieting concerns of 10 year old girls and their mothers, *British Journal of Clinical Psychology*, 29: 346–8.

Hill, A.J., Draper, E. and Stack, J. (1994) A weight on children's minds: body shape dissatisfactions at 9 years old, *International Journal of Obesity*, 18: 383–9.

Hingson, R.W., Strunin, L., Berlin, M. and Heeren, T. (1990) Beliefs about AIDS, use of alcohol and drugs and unprotected sex among Massachusetts adolescents, *American Journal of Public Health*, 80: 295–9.

Hinton, C. (1992) Breast cancer, in C.R. Hart and P. Burke (eds), *Screening and Surveillance in General Practice*. London: Churchill Livingstone.

Hite, S. (1976) *The Hite Report*. New York: Macmillan.

Hite, S. (1981) *The Hite Report on Male Sexuality*. New York: A.A. Knopf.

Hite, S. (1987) *The Hite Report on Women and Love*. London: Penguin.

Hodgkins, S. and Orbell, S. (1998) Can protection motivation theory predict behaviour? A longitudinal study exploring the role of previous behaviour, *Psychology and Health*, 13: 237–50.

Holland, J., Ramazanoglu, C. and Scott, S. (1990a) Managing risk and experiencing danger: Tensions between government AIDS health education policy and young women's sexuality, *Gender and Education*, 2: 125–46.

Holland, J., Ramazanoglu, C., Scott, S., Sharpe, S. and Thompson, R. (1990b) Sex, gender and power: Young women's sexuality in the shadow of AIDS, *Sociology of Health and Illness*, 12: 336–50.

Holleb, A.I., Venet, L., Day, E. and Hayt, S. (1960) Breast cancer detection by routine physical examinations, *New York Journal of Medicine*, 60: 823–7.

Holmes, T.H. and Rahe, R.H. (1967) The social readjustment rating scale, *Journal of Psychosomatic Research*, 11: 213–18.

Hooykaas, C., van der Linden, M.M.D., van Doornum, G.J.J., van der Velde, F.W., van der Pligt, J. and Coutinho, R.A. (1991) Limited changes in sexual behaviour of heterosexual men and women with multiple partners in the Netherlands, *AIDS Care*, 3: 21–30.

Hopkinson, G. and Bland, R.C. (1982) Depressive syndromes in grossly obese women, *Canadian Journal of Psychiatry*, 27: 213–15.

Hoppe, R. and Ogden, J. (1996) The effect of selectively reviewing behavioural risk factors on HIV risk perception, *Psychology and Health*, 11: 757–64.

Hoppe, R. and Ogden, J. (1997) Practice nurse's beliefs about obesity and weight related interventions in primary care, *International Journal of Obesity*, 21: 141–6.

Horne, R. (1997) Representations of medication and treatment: advances in theory and measurement, in K.J. Petrie and J. Weinman (eds), *Perceptions of Health and Illness: Current Research and Applications*. London: Harwood Academic Press.

Horne, R., Weinman, J. and Hankins, M. (1999) The beliefs about medicines questionnaire: the development and evaluation of a new method for assessing the cognitive representation of medication, *Psychology and Health*, 14: 1–24.

Hornick, J.P., Doran, L. and Crawford, S.H. (1979) Premarital contraceptive usage among male and female adolescents, *Family Coordinator*, 28: 181–90.

Horwitz, R.I. and Horwitz, S.M. (1993) Adherence to treatment and health outcome, *Archives of International Medicine*, 153: 1863–8.

Horwitz, R.I., Viscoli, C.M., Berkman, L. *et al.* (1990) Treatment adherence and risk of death after a myocardial infarction, *Lancet*, 336(8714): 542–5.

Hughson, A., Cooper, A., McArdle, C. and Smith, D. (1987) Psychosocial effects of radiotherapy after mastectomy, *British Medical Journal,* 294: 1515–16.

Hughson, A., Cooper, A., McArdle, C. and Smith, D. (1986) Psychological impact of adjuvant chemotherapy in the first two years after mastectomy, *British Medical Journal,* 293: 1268–72.

Hunt, S.M., McEwen, J. and McKenna, S.P. (1986) *Measuring Health Status.* Beckenham: Croom Helm.

Idler, E.L. and Kasl, S.V. (1995) Self ratings of health: Do they predict change in function as ability? *Journals of Gerontology Series B-Psychological Sciences and Social Sciences,* 50B: S344–S353.

Illich, I. (1974) *Medical Nemesis.* London: Caldar Boyars.

Ingham, R., Woodcock, A. and Stenner, K. (1991) Getting to know you . . . Young people's knowledge of their partners at first intercourse, *Journal of Community and Applied Social Psychology,* 1: 117–32.

Ingledew, D.K., Markland, D. and Medley, A.R. (1998) Exercise motives and stages of change, *Journal of Health Psychology,* 3(4): 477–89.

Isen, A.M., Rosenzweig, A.S. and Young, M.J. (1991) The influence of positive affect on clinical problem solving, *Medical Decision Making,* 11: 221–7.

Jacobs, T.J. and Charles, E. (1980) Life events and the occurrence of cancer in children, *Psychosomatic Medicine,* 42: 11–24.

Jamner, L.D. and Tursky, B. (1987) Syndrome-specific descriptor profiling: A psychophysiological and psychophysical approach, *Health Psychology,* 6: 417–30.

Janis, I. (1958) *Psychological Stress.* New York: Wiley.

Janis, I.L. and Mann, L. (1977) *Decision Making: A Psychological Analysis of Conflict, Choice, and Commitment.* New York: Free Press.

Janz, N.K. and Becker, M.H. (1984) The health belief model: a decade later, *Health Education Quarterly,* 11: 1–47.

Jellinek, E.M. (1960) *The Disease Concept in Alcoholism.* New Brunswick, NJ: Hill House Press.

Jenkins, C.D., Zyzanski, S.J. and Rosenman, R.H. (1979) *The Jenkins Activity Survey for Health Prediction.* New York: The Psychological Corporation.

Jensen, M.P. and Karoly, P. (1991) Motivation and expectancy factors in symptom perception: A laboratory study of the placebo effect, *Psychosomatic Medicine,* 53: 144–52.

Johnson, J.E. and Leventhal, H. (1974) Effects of accurate expectations and behavioural instructions on reactions during a noxious medical examination, *Journal of Personality and Social Psychology,* 29: 710–18.

Johnson, J.H. (1986) *Life Events as Stressors in Childhood and Adolescence.* Newbury Park, CA: Sage.

Johnston, D.W., Cook, D.G. and Shaper, A.G. (1987) Type A behaviour and ischaemic heart disease in middle aged British men, *British Medical Journal,* 295: 86–9.

Johnston, D.W., Gold, A., Kentish, J. *et al.* (1993) Effect of stress management on blood pressure in mild primary hypertension, *British Medical Journal,* 306: 963–6.

Johnston, M. (1980) Anxiety in surgical patients, *Psychological Medicine,* 10: 145–52.

Johnston, M. and Vogele, C. (1993) Benefits of psychological preparation for surgery: a meta analysis, *Annals of Behavioural Medicine,* 15: 245–56.

Johnston, M. and Kennedy, P. (1998) Editorial: Special issue on clinical health psychology in chronic conditions, *Clinical Psychology and Psychotherapy,* 5: 59–61.

Johnston, M., Morrison, V., Macwalter, R. and Partridge, C. (1999) Perceived control, coping and recovery from disability following stroke, *Psychology and Health*, 14: 181–366.

Jonas, K., Stroebe, W. and Eagly, A. (1993) Adherence to an exercise program. Unpublished manuscript, University of Tubingen.

Jones, F., Harris, P. and Waller, H. (1998) Expectations of an exercise prescription scheme: An exploratory study using repertory grids, *British Journal of Health Psychology*, 3: 277–89.

Jones, R. (1992) Gastrointestinal disorders, in C.R. Hart and P. Burke (eds), *Screening and Surveillance in General Practice*, pp. 283–90. London: Churchill Livingstone.

Joseph, J.G., Montgomery, S.B., Emmons, C.A. *et al.* (1987) Magnitude and determinants of behaviour risk reduction: Longitudinal analysis of a cohort at risk for AIDS, *Psychological Health*, 1: 73–96.

Kalucy, R.S., Crisp, A.H. and Harding, B. (1977) A study of 56 families with anorexia nervosa, *British Journal of Medical Psychology*, 50: 381–95.

Kamen, L.P. and Seligman, M.E.P. (1987) Explanatory style and health, *Current Psychological Research and Reviews*, 6: 207–18.

Kaprio, J., Koskenvuo, M. and Rita, H. (1987) Mortality after bereavement: a prospective study of 95,647 widowed persons, *American Journal of Public Health*, 77: 283–7.

Karasek, R. and Theorell, T. (1990) *Healthy Work. Stress, Productivity and the Reconstruction of Working Life*. New York: Basic Books.

Karasek, R.A., Baker, D., Marxer, F., Ahlbom, A. and Theorell, T. (1981) Job decision latitude, job demands and cardiovascular disease: A prospective study of Swedish men, *American Journal of Public Health*, 71: 694–705.

Karasek, R.A., Theorell, T., Schwartz, J. *et al.* (1988) Job characteristics in relation to the prevalence of myocardial infarction in the U.S. HES and HANES, *American Journal of Public Health*, 78: 910–18.

Kasl, S.V. and Cobb, S. (1966) Health behaviour, illness behaviour, and sick role behaviour: II. Sick role behaviour, *Archives of Environmental Health*, 12: 531–41.

Katz, S., Downs, T.D., Cash, H.R. and Grotz, R.C. (1970) Progress in development of the index of ADL, *Gerontology*, 10: 20–30.

Kelley, H.H. (1967) Attribution theory in social psychology, in D. Levine (ed.), *Nebraska Symposium on Motivation*, pp. 192–238. Lincoln: University of Nebraska Press.

Kelley, H.H. (1971) Attribution: *Perceiving the Causes of Behaviour*. New York: General Learning Press.

Keys, A., Brozek, J., Henscel, A., Mickelson, O. and Taylor, H.L. (1950) *The Biology of Human Starvation*. Minneapolis, MN: University of Minnesota Press.

Kiebert, G., de Haes, J. and van der Velde, C. (1991) The impact of breast conserving treatment and mastectomy on the quality of life of early stage breast cancer patients: A review, *Journal of Clinical Oncology*, 9: 1059–70.

Kiecolt-Glaser, J.K. and Glaser, R. (1986) Psychological influences on immunity, *Psychosomatics*, 27: 621–4.

Killen, J.D., Maccoby, N. and Taylor, C.B. (1984) Nicotine gum and self-regulation training in smoking relapse prevention, *Behaviour Therapy*, 15: 234–48.

Killen, J.D., Fortmenn, S.P., Newman, B. and Vardy, A. (1990) Evaluation of a treatment approach combining nicotine gum with self-guided behavioral treatments for smoking relapse prevention, *Journal of Consulting and Clinical Psychology*, 58: 85–92.

King, A.C., Haskell, W.L., Taylor, C.B., Kraemer, H.C. and DeBusk, R.F. (1991) Group- *vs* home-based exercise training in healthy older men and women: A community-based clinical trial, *Journal of the American Medical Association*, 266: 1535–42.

King, A.C., Blair, S.N., Bild, D.E. *et al.* (1992) Determinants of physical activity and interventions in adults, *Medicine and Science in Sports and Exercise*, 24: S221–S237.

King, J.B. (1982) The impact of patients' perceptions of high blood pressure on attendance at screening: an attributional extension of the health belief model, *Social Science and Medicine*, 16: 1079–92.

Kinlay, S. (1988) High cholesterol levels: is screening the best option? *Medical Journal of Australia*, 148: 635–7.

Kinsey, A., Pomeroy, W. and Martin, C. (1948) *Sexual Behaviour in the Human Male*. London: Saunders.

Kirkley, B.G., Burge, J.C. and Ammerman, M.P.H. (1988) Dietary restraint, binge eating and dietary behaviour patterns, *International Journal of Eating Disorders*, 7: 771–8.

Kissen, D.M. (1966) The significance of personality in lung cancer in men, *Annals of the New York Academy of Sciences*, 125: 820–6.

Klassen, A., Fitzpatrick, R., Jenkinson, C. and Goodacre, T. (1996) Should breast reduction surgery be rationed? A comparison of the health status of patients before and after treatment: postal questionnaire survey, *British Medical Journal*, 313: 454–7.

Klesges, R.C. and Klesges, L. (1988) Cigarette smoking as a dieting strategy in a University population, *International Journal of Eating Disorders*, 7: 413–19.

Kobasa, S.C., Maddi, S.R. and Puccetti, M.C. (1982) Personality and exercise as buffers in the stress-illness relationship, *Journal of Behavioral Medicine*, 5: 391–404.

Kral, J.G. (1983) Surgical therapy. Contemporary issues in Clinical Nutrition, *Obesity*, 4: 25–38.

Krantz, D.S., Glass, D.C., Contrada, R. and Miller, N.E. (1981) *Behavior and Health. National Science Foundations Second Five Year Outlook on Science and Technology*. Washington, DC: US Government Printing Office.

Kristiansen, C.M. (1985) Value correlates of preventive health behaviour, *Journal of Personality and Social Psychology*, 49: 748–58.

Kuczmarski, R.J. (1992) Prevalence of overweight and weight gain in the United States, *American Journal of Clinical Nutrition*, 55: 495–502.

Kune, G.A., Kune, S., Watson, L.F. and Bahnson, C.B. (1991) Personality as a risk factor in large bowel cancer: Data from the Melbourne Colorectal Cancer Study, *Psychological Medicine*, 21: 29–41.

Lader, D. and Matheson, J. (1991) *Smoking among Secondary School Children in England 1990: An Enquiry Carried out by the Social Survey Division of OPCS*. London: HMSO.

Laessle, R.G., Tuschl, R.J., Kotthaus, B.C. and Pirke, K.M. (1989) Behavioural and biological correlates of dietary restraint in normal life, *Appetite*, 12: 83–94.

Lancet (1985) Cancer of the cervix – death by incompetence (Editorial), *Lancet*, ii: 363–4.

Lando, H.A. (1977) Successful treatment of smokers with a broad-spectrum behavioral approach, *Journal of Consulting and Clinical Psychology*, 45: 361–6.

Lando, H.A. and McGovern, P.G. (1982) Three-year data on a behavioural treatment for smoking: A follow-up note, *Addictive behaviours*, 7: 177–81.

Lang, A.R. and Marlatt, G.A. (1982) Problem drinking: A social learning perspective, in R.J. Gatchel, A. Baum and J.E. Singer (eds), *Handbook of Psychology and Health. Vol. 1. Clinical Psychology and Behavioral Medicine: Overlapping Disciplines*, pp. 121–69. Hillsdale, NJ: Erlbaum.

Langlie, J.K. (1977) Social networks, health beliefs, and preventative health behaviour, *Journal of Health and Social Behaviour*, 18: 244–60.

Larkin, J.C. and Pines, H.A. (1979) No fat persons need to apply: experimental studies on the overweight stereotype and hiring preference, *Sociology of Work and Occupations*, 6: 312–27.

Larsson, G., Spangberg, L., Lindgren, S. and Bohlin, A.B. (1990) Screening for HIV in pregnant women: a study of maternal opinion, *AIDS Care*, 2: 223–8.

Lashley, M.E. (1987) Predictors of breast self examination practice among elderly women, *Advances in Nursing Science*, 9: 25–34.

Last, J.M. (1963) The clinical iceberg in England and Wales, *Lancet*, 2: 28–31.

Lau, R.R. (1995) Cognitive representations of health and illness, in D. Gochman (ed.), *Handbook of Health Behavior Research, Vol. I*. New York: Plenum.

Lau, R., Bernard, J.M. and Hartman, K.A. (1989) Further explanations of common sense representations of common illnesses, *Health Psychology*, 8: 195–219.

Laudenslager, M.L., Ryan, S.M., Drugan, R.C., Hyson, R.L. and Maier, S.F. (1983) Coping and immunosuppression: Inescapable but not escapable shock suppresses lymphocyte proliferation, *Science*, 221: 568–70.

Lawton, M.P. (1972) The dimensions of morale, in D. Kent, R. Kastenbaum and S. Sherwood (eds), *Research, Planning and Action for the Elderly*. New York: Behavioral Publications.

Lawton, M.P. (1975) The Philadelphia Geriatric Center Moral Scale: a revision, *Journal of Gerontology*, 30: 85–9.

Lawton, M.P., Moss, M. and Glicksman, A. (1990) The quality of life in the last year of life of older persons, *The Millbank Quarterly*, 68: 1–28.

Lazarus, R.S. (1975) A cognitively oriented psychologist looks at biofeedback, *American Psychologist*, 30: 553–61.

Lazarus, R.S. and Cohen, F. (1973) Active coping processes, coping dispositions, and recovery from surgery, *Psychosomatic Medicine*, 35: 375–89.

Lazarus, R.S. and Cohen, J.B. (1977) Environmental stress, in L. Altman and J.F. Wohlwill (eds), *Human Behavior and the Environment: Current Theory and Research*, Vol. 2, pp. 89–127. New York: Plenum.

Lazarus, R.S. and Launier, R. (1978) Stress related transactions between person and environment, in L.A. Pervin and M. Lewis (eds), *Perspectives in International Psychology*, pp. 287–327. New York: Plenum.

Lazarus, R.S. and Folkman, S. (1987) Transactional theory and research on emotions and coping, *European Journal of Personality*, 1: 141–70.

Leck, I. (1986) An epidemiological assessment of neonatal screening for the dislocation of the hip, *Journal of the Royal College of Physicians*, 20: 56–62.

Lerner, R.M. and Gellert, E. (1969) Body build identification, preference and aversion in children, *Developmental Psychology*, 1: 456–62.

Leventhal, H. and Nerenz, D. (1985) The assessment of illness cognition, in P. Karoly (ed.), *Measurement Strategies in Health Psychology*, pp. 517–54. New York: Wiley and Sons.

Leventhal, H., Meyer, D. and Nerenz, D. (1980) The common sense representation of illness danger, in S. Rachman (ed.), *Medical Psychology*, 2: 7–30.

Leventhal, H., Prohaska, T.R. and Hirschman, R.S. (1985) Preventive health behavior across the life span, in J.C. Rosen and L.J. Solomon (eds), *Prevention in Health Psychology*. Hanover, NH: University Press of New England.

Leventhal, H., Benyamini, Y., Brownlee, S. *et al.* (1997) Illness representations: theoretical foundations, in K.J. Petrie and J.A. Weinman (eds), *Perceptions of Health and Illness*, pp. 1–18. Amsterdam: Harwood.

Levine, J.D., Gordon, N.C. and Fields, H.L. (1978) The mechanism of placebo analgesia, *Lancet*, 2: 654–7.

Ley, P. (1981) Professional non-compliance: a neglected problem. *British Journal of Clinical Psychology*, 20: 151–4.

Ley, P. (1988) *Communicating with patients*, London: Croom Helm.

Ley, P. (1989) Improving patients' understanding, recall, satisfaction and compliance, in A. Broome (ed.), *Health Psychology*, London: Chapman and Hall.

Ley, P. and Morris, L.A. (1984) Psychological aspects of written information for patients, in S. Rachman (ed.), *Contributions to Medical Psychology*, pp. 117–49, Oxford: Pergamon Press.

Lichtenstein, E. and Brown, R.A. (1983) Current trends in the modification of cigarette dependence, in A.S. Bellack, M. Hersen and A.E. Kazdin (eds), *International Handbook of Behavior Modification and Therapy*. New York: Plenum.

Lichtenstein, E. and Glasgow, R. (1992) Smoking cessation: What have we learnt over the past decade? *Journal of Consulting and Clinical Psychology*, 60: 518–27.

Lichtenstein, E., Weiss, S.M., Hitchcock, J.L. *et al.* (1986) Task force 3: Patterns of smoking relapse, *Health Psychology*, 5 (sppl): 29–40.

Lifson, A., Hessol, N., Rutherford, G.W. *et al.* (1989) *The Natural History of HIV Infection in a Cohort of Homosexual and Bisexual men: Clinical manifestations, 1978–1989. In the Vth International Conference on AIDS*, Montreal, September.

Lindemann, C. (1977) Factors affecting the use of contraception in the nonmarital context, in R. Gemme and C.C. Wheeler (eds), *Progress in Sexology*. New York: Plenum Press.

Lissner, L., Odell, P.M., D'Agostino, R.B. *et al.* (1991) Variability of body weight and health outcomes in the Framingham population, *New England Journal of Medicine*, 324: 1839–44.

Litt, M.D. (1988) Self efficacy and perceived control: Cognitive mediators of pain tolerance, *Journal of Personality and Social Psychology*, 54: 149–60.

Loro, A.D. and Orleans, C.S. (1981) Binge eating in obesity: Preliminary findings and guidelines for behavioural analysis and treatment, *Addictive Behaviours*, 7: 155–66.

Lowe, C.S. and Radius, S.M. (1982) Young adults' contraceptive practices: an investigation of influences, *Adolescence*, 22: 291–304.

Ludwig, A.M. and Stark, L.H. (1974) Alcohol craving: Subjective and situational aspects, *Quarterly Journal of Studies on Alcohol*, 35: 899–905.

Luker, K. (1975) *Taking Chances: Abortion and the Decision not to Contracept*. Berkeley, CA: University of California Press.

Lundgren, B. (1981) Breast cancer in Sweden by single oblique-view mammography. *Reviews of Endocrine-related Cancer* (suppl. 10): 67–70.

Lynch, J.J. (1977) *The Broken Heart: The Medical Consequences of Loneliness*. New York: Basic Books.

MacKenzie, I. (1965) Breast cancer following multiple fluoroscopies, *British Journal of Cancer*, 19: 1–18.

MacLean, U., Sinfield, D., Klein, S. and Harnden, B. (1984) Women who decline breast screening, *Journal of Epidemiology and Community Health*, 24: 278–83.

MacWhinney, D.R. (1973) Problem-solving and decision making in primary medical practice, *Proceeds of the Royal Society of Medicine*, 65: 934–8.

Maddi, S. and Kobasa, S.G. (1984) *The Hardy Executive, Health Under Stress.* Homewood, IL: Dow Jones-Irwin.

Maddox, G.L. and Liederman, V. (1969) Overweight as a social disability with medical implications, *Journal of Medical Education*, 44: 214–20.

Maeland, J.G. and Havik, O.E. (1987) Psychological predictors for return for work after a myocardial infarction, *Journal of Psychosomatic Research*, 31: 471–81.

Mann, J.M., Chin, J., Piot, P. and Quinn, T. (1988) The international epidemiology of AIDS, in *The Science of AIDS*, pp. 51–61. New York: W.H. Freeman.

Manning, M.M. and Wright, T.L. (1983) Self efficacy expectancies, outcome expectancies and the persistence of pain control in child birth, *Journal of Personality and Social Psychology*, 45: 421–31.

Manuck, S.B., Kaplan, J.R. and Matthews, K.A. (1986) Behavioural antecedents of coronary heart disease and atherosclerosis, *Arteriosclerosis*, 6: 1–14.

Mapes, R. (1980) (ed.) *Prescribing Practice and Drug Usage*. London: Croom Helm.

Marcus, B.H., Rakowski, W. and Rossi, J.S. (1992) Assessing motivational readiness and decision-making for exercise, *Health Psychology*, 22: 3–16.

Marks, D.F., Brucher-Albers, N.C., Donker, F.J.S. *et al.* (1998) Health Psychology 2000: The development of professional health psychology, *Journal of Health Psychology*, 3: 149–60.

Marlatt, G.A. (1978) Craving for alcohol, loss of control and relapse: A cognitive behavioral analysis, in P.E. Nathan, G.A. Marlatt and T. Loberg (eds), *Alcoholism: New Directions in Behavioral Research and Treatment*. New York: Plenum.

Marlatt, G.A. and Gordon, J.R. (1985) *Relapse Prevention*. New York: Guilford Press.

Marteau, T.M. (1989) Psychological costs of screening, *British Medical Journal*, 291: 97.

Marteau, T.M. (1993) Health related screening: Psychological predictors of uptake and impact, in S. Maes, H. Leventhal and M. Johnston (eds), *International Review of Health Psychology*, Vol. 2, pp. 149–74. Chichester: John Wiley.

Marteau, T.M. and Baum, J.D. (1984) Doctors' views on diabetes, *Archives of Disease in Childhood*, 56: 566–70.

Marteau, T.M. and Johnston, M. (1990) Health professionals: a source of variance in health outcomes, *Psychology and Health*, 5: 47–58.

Marteau, T.M. and Riordan, D.C. (1992) Staff attitudes to patients: The influence of causal attributions for illness, *British Journal of Clinical Psychology*, 31: 107–10.

Marteau, T.M., van Duijn, M. and Ellis, I. (1992) Effects of genetic screening on perceptions of health: a pilot study, *Journal of Medicine and Genetics*, 24: 24–6.

Martikainen, P. and Valkonen, T. (1996) Mortality after death of spouse in relation to duration of bereavement in Finland, *Journal of Epidemiology Community Health*, 50(3): 264–8.

Martin, J.E., Dubbert, P.M., Kattell, A.D. *et al.* (1984) Behavioral control of exercise in sedentary adults. Studies 1 through 6, *Journal of Consulting and Clinical Psychology*, 52: 795–811.

Martin, J.L. (1987) The impact of AIDS on the gay male sexual behavior patterns in New York City, *American Journal of Public Health*, 77: 578–81.

Mason, E.E. (1987) Morbid obesity: Use of vertical banded gastroplasty, *Surgical Clinics of North America*, 67: 521–37.

Mason, J.W. (1975) A historical view of the stress field, *Journal of Human Stress*, 1: 22–36.

Masters, W. and Johnson, V. (1966) *Human Sexual Response*. Boston: Little Brown.

Matarazzo, J.D. (1980) Behavioral health and behavioral medicine: Frontiers for a new health psychology, *American Psychologist*, 35: 807–17.

Matarazzo, J.D. (1984) Behavioral health: A 1990 challenge for the health sciences professions, in J.D. Matarazzo, N.E. Miller, S.M. Weiss, J.A. Herd and S.M. Weiss (eds), *Behavioral Health: A Handbook of Health Enhancement and Disease Prevention*, pp. 3–40. New York: John Wiley.

Maylath, N.S. (1990) Development of the children's Health Rating Scale, *Health Education Quarterly*, 17: 89–97.

McCann, I.L. and Holmes, D.S. (1984) Influence of aerobics on depression, *Journal of Personality and Social Psychology*, 46: 1142–7.

McClelland, D., Davis, W., Kalin, R. and Wanner, E. (1972) *The Drinking Man*. New York: Free Press.

McCormick, J. (1989) Cervical smears: A questionable practice? *Lancet*, 2: 207–9.

McCormick, N., Izzo, A. and Folcik, J. (1985) Adolescents' values, sexuality, and contraception in a rural New York county, *Adolescence*, 20: 385–95.

McCusker, J., Stoddard, J.G., Zapka, M.Z. and Meyer, K.H. (1989) Predictors of AIDS preventive behaviour among homosexually active men: a longitudunal study, *AIDS*, 3: 443–6.

McDonald, D.G. and Hodgdon, J.A. (1991) *Psychological Effects of Aerobic Fitness Training: Research and Theory*. New York: Springer.

McGee, H.M., O'Boyle, C.A., Hickey, A., O'Malley, K. and Joyce, C.R. (1991) Assessing the quality of life of the individual: The SEIQoL with a healthy and a gastroenterology unit population, *Psychological Medicine*, 21: 749–59.

McGowan, L.P.A., Clarke-Carter, D.D. and Pitts, M.K. (1998) Chronic pelvic pain: A meta-analytic review, *Psychology and Health*, 13: 937–51.

McIntosh, P. and Charlton, V. (1985) *The Impact of the Sport for All Policy 1966–1984 and a Way Forward*. London: The Sports Council.

McKeown, T. (1979) *The Role of Medicine*. Oxford: Blackwell.

McKusick, L., Coates, T.J., Morin, S.F., Pollack, L. and Hoff, C. (1990) Longitudinal predictors of reduction in unprotected anal intercourse among gay men in San Francisco: The AIDS behavioral research project, *American Journal of Public Health*, 80: 978–83.

McLelland, D.C., Alexander, C. and Marks, E. (1982) The need for power, stress, immune function, and illness among male prisoners, *Journal of Abnormal Psychology*, 91(1): 61–71.

McNair, D., Lorr, M. and Droppleman, L. (1971) *Manual for the Profile of Mood States*. San Diego: Educational and Industrial Testing Service.

McNeil, A.D., Jarvis, M.J., Stapleton, J.A. *et al.* (1988) Prospective study of factors predicting uptake of smoking in adolescents, *Journal of Epidemiology and Community Health*, 43: 72–8.

McNeil, B.J., Pauker, S.G., Sox, H.C. and Tversky, A. (1982) On the elicitation of preferences for alternative therapies, *New England Journal of Medicine*, 306: 1259–62.

McReynolds, W.T. (1982) Towards a psychology of obesity: Review of research on the role of personality and level of adjustment, *International Journal of Eating Disorders*, 2: 37–57.

Meadows, J., Jenkinson, S., Catalan, J. and Gazzard, B. (1990) Voluntary HIV testing in the antenatal clinic: Differing uptake rates for individual counselling midwives, *Aids Care*, 2: 229–33.

Mechanic, D. (1962) *Students under Stress: A Study in the Social Psychology of Adaptation*. Glencoe, IL: Free Press of Glencoe.

Meenan, R.F., Gertman, P.M. and Mason, J.H. (1980) Measuring health status in arthritis: the arthritis impact measurement scales, *Arthritis Rheumatology*, 23: 146–52.

Melzack, R. (1975) The McGill pain questionnaire: Major properties and scoring methods, *Pain*, 1: 277–99.

Melzack, R. (1979) *The Puzzle of Pain*. New York: Basic Books.

Melzack, R. and Wall, P.D. (1965) Pain mechanisms: a new theory, *Science*, 150: 971–9.

Melzack, R. and Wall, P.D. (1982) *The Challenge of Pain*. New York: Basic Books.

Metler, F.A., Hempelmann, L.H. and Dutton, A.M. (1969) Breast neoplasias in women treated with X-rays for acute postpartum mastitis, *Journal of the National Cancer Institute*, 43: 803–22.

Meyer, D., Leventhal, H. and Guttman, M. (1985) Common-sense models of illness: The example of hypertension, *Health Psychology*, 4: 115–35.

Michaud, C., Kahn, J.P., Musse, N. *et al.* (1990) Relationships between a critical life event and eating behaviour in high school students, *Stress Medicine*, 6: 57–64.

Miller, P. (1975) A behavioral intervention program for chronic public drunkenness offenders, *Archives of General Psychiatry*, 32: 915–18.

Miller, S.M., Brody, D.S. and Summerton, J. (1987) Styles of coping with threat: Implications for health, *Journal of Personality and Social Psychology*, 54: 142–8.

Minuchin, S., Rosman, B.L. and Baker, L. (1978) *The Anorectic Family in Psychosomatic Families: Anorexia Nervosa in Context*, pp. 51–73. London: Harvard University Press.

Misselbrook, D. and Armstrong, D. (2000). How do patients respond to presentation of risk information? A survey in General Practice of willingness to accept treatment for hypertension.

Moatti, J.-P., Le Gales, C., Seror, J., Papiernik, E. and Henrion, R. (1990) Social acceptability of HIV screening among pregnant women, *AIDS Care*, 2: 213–22.

Montague, C.T., Farooqi, I.S., Whitehead, J.P. *et al.* (1997) Congenital leptin deficiency is associated with severe early onset obesity in humans, *Nature*, 387: 903–8.

Moos, R.H. and Schaefer, J.A. (1984) The crisis of physical illness: An overview and conceptual approach, in R.H. Moos (ed.), *Coping with physical illness: New Perspectives*, Vol. 2, pp. 3–25. New York: Plenum.

Moos, R.H. and Swindle, R.W. Jr. (1990) Stressful life circumstances: Concepts and measures, *Stress Medicine*, 6: 171–8.

Morgan, W.P. and O'Connor, P.J. (1988) Exercise and mental health, in R.K. Dishman (ed.), *Exercise Adherence: Its Impact on Public Health*, pp. 91–121. Champaign, IL: Human Kinetics.

MORI (1984) *Public Attitudes Towards Fitness: Research Study Conducted for Fitness Magazine*. London: MORI.

Morris, J.N. (1964) *Uses of Epidemiology*, 2nd edn. Edinburgh: Churchill Livingstone.

Morris, J.N., Pollard, R., Everitt, M.G. and Chave, S.P.W. (1980) Vigorous exercise in leisure-time protection against coronary heart disease, *Lancet*, 2: 1207–10.

Morrison, D.M. (1985) Adolescent contraceptive behaviour: a review, *Psychological Bulletin*, 98: 538–68.

Mosbach, P. and Leventhal, H. (1988) Peer group identification and smoking: Implications for intervention, *Journal of Abnormal Psychology*, 97: 238–45.

Moss-Morris, R., Petrie, K.J. and Weinman, J. (1996) Functioning in chronic fatigue syndrome: do illness perceptions play a regulatory role? *British Journal of Health Psychology*, 1: 15–26.

Muir, J., Mant, D., Jones, L. and Yudkin, P. (1994) Effectiveness of health checks conducted by nurses in primary care: results of the OXCHECK study after one year, *British Medical Journal*, 308: 308–12.

Muldoon, M.F., Barger, S.D., Flory, J.D. and Manuck, S.B. (1998) What are quality of life measurements measuring? *British Medical Journal*, 316: 542–5.

Mullen, P.D., Green, L.W. and Persinger, G.S. (1985) Clinical trials of patient education for chronic conditions: a comparative meta analysis of intervention types, *Preventive Medicine*, 14: 753–81.

Mumford, D.B., Whitehouse, A.M. and Platts, M. (1991) Sociocultural correlates of eating disorders among Asian school girls in Bradford, *British Journal of Psychiatry*, 158: 222–8.

Murray, M. and McMillan, C. (1993) Health beliefs, locus of control, emotional control and women's cancer screening behaviour, *British Journal of Clinical Psychology*, 32: 87–100.

Murray, M., Swan, A.V., Bewley, B.R. and Johnson, M.R.D. (1984) The development of smoking during adolescence – the MRC/Derbyshire smoking study, *International Journal of Epidemiology*, 12: 185–92.

Murray, S., Narayan, V., Mitchell, M. and Witte, H. (1993) Study of dietetic knowledge among members of the primary health care team, *British Journal of General Practice*, 43: 229–31.

Nathoo, V. (1988) Investigation of non-responders at a cervical screening clinic in Manchester, *British Medical Journal*, 296: 1041–2.

Newell, A. and Simon, H.A. (1972) *Human Problem Solving*. Englewood Cliffs, New Jersey: Prentice Hall.

NHS Centre for Reviews and Dissemination (1997) *Systematic Review of Interventions in the Treatment and Prevention of Obesity*. York: University of York.

Norman, P. and Fitter, M. (1989) Intention to attend a health screening appointment: Some implications for general practice, *Counselling Psychology Quarterly*, 2: 261–72.

Norman, P. and Conner, M. (1993) The role of social cognition models in predicting attendance at health checks, *Psychology and Health*, 8: 447–62.

Norman, P. and Smith, L. (1995) The theory of planned behaviour and exercise: an investigation into the role of prior behaviour, behavioural intentions and attitude variability, *European Journal of Social Psychology*, 25: 403–15.

Norman, P. and Conner, M. (1996) The role of social cognition models in predicting health behaviours: Future directions, in M. Conner and P. Norman (eds), *Predicting Health Behaviour: Research and Practice with Social Cognition Models*, pp. 197–225. Buckingham: Open University Press.

Norman, P., Conner, M. and Bell, R. (1999) The theory of planned behavior and smoking cessation, *Health Psychology*, 18: 89–94.

Normandeau, S., Kalinins, I., Jutras, S. and Hanigan, D. (1998) A description of 5 to 12 year old children's conception of health within the context of their daily life, *Psychology and Health*, 13: 883–96.

Oakley, A. (1992) *Social Support and Motherhood*. Oxford: Basil Blackwell.

O'Boyle, C., McGee, H., Hickey, A., O'Malley, K. and Joyce, C.R.B. (1992) Individual quality of life in patients undergoing hip replacements, *Lancet*, 339: 1088–91.

O'Brien, S. and Lee, L. (1990) Effects of videotape intervention on Pap smear knowledge, attitudes and behavior. Special issue: Behavioural research in cancer, *Behaviour Changes*, 7: 143–50.

Ogden, J. (1993) The measurement of restraint – confounding success and failure? *International Journal of Eating Disorders*, 13: 69–76.

Ogden, J. (1994) The effects of smoking cessation, restrained eating, and motivational states on food intake in the laboratory, *Health Psychology*, 13: 114–21.

Ogden, J. (1995a) Cognitive and motivational consequence of dieting, *European Eating Disorders Review*, 24: 228–41.

Ogden, J. (1995b) Changing the subject of health psychology, *Psychology and Health*, 10: 257–65.

Ogden, J. (1995c) Psychosocial theory and the creation of the risky self, *Social Science and Medicine*, 40: 409–15.

Ogden, J. (1999) Body dissatisfaction, *Counselling News*, January: 20–1.

Ogden, J. and Wardle, J. (1990) Control of eating and attributional style, *British Journal of Clinical Psychology*, 29: 445–6.

Ogden, J. and Wardle, J. (1991) Cognitive and emotional responses to food, *International Journal of Eating Disorders*, 10: 297–311.

Ogden, J. and Greville, L. (1993) Cognitive changes to preloading in restrained and unrestrained eaters as measured by the Stroop task, *International Journal of Eating Disorders*, 14: 185–95.

Ogden, J. and Fox, P. (1994) An examination of the use of smoking for weight control in restrained and unrestrained eaters, *International Journal of Eating Disorders*, 16: 177–86.

Ogden, J. and Knight, D. (1995) Attributions for illness and treatment interventions in community nurses, *Journal of Advanced Nursing*, 22: 290–3.

Ogden, J. and Mundray, K. (1996) The effect of the media on body satisfaction: the role of gender and size, *European Eating Disorders Review*, 4: 171–82.

Ogden, J. and Mtandabari, T. (1997) Examination stress and changes in mood and health related behaviours, *Psychology and Health*, 12: 289–99.

Ogden, J. and Chanana, A. (1998) Explaining the effect of ethnicity in body dissatisfaction and dieting: finding a role for values, *International Journal of Obesity*, 22: 641–7.

Ogden, J. and Elder, C. (1998) The role of family status and ethnic group on body image and eating behaviour, *International Journal of Eating Disorders*, 23: 309–15.

Ogden, J. and Thomas, D. (1999) The role of familial values in understanding the impact of social class on weight concern, *International Journal of Eating Disorders*, 25: 273–9.

Ogden, J. and Steward, J. (in press) The role of the mother/daughter relationship in explaining weight concern, *International Journal of Eating Disorders*.

Ogden, J., Andrade, J., Eisner, M. *et al.* (1997) To treat? To befriend? To prevent? Patients' and GPs' views of the doctor's role, *Scandinavian Journal of Primary Health Care*, 15: 114–17.

Ogden, J., Boden, J., Caird, R. *et al.* (2000) You're depressed; no I'm not: GPs' and patients' different models of depression, *British Journal of General Practice*, 49: 123–4.

Ogden, J., Bandara, I., Cohen, H. *et al.* (submitted) GPs' and patients' models of obesity: Whose problem is it anyway?

Oldridge, N.B. and Jones, N.L. (1983) Improving patient compliance in cardiac exercise rehabilitation: Effects of written agreement and self-monitoring, *Journal of Cardiac Rehabilitation*, 3: 257–62.

Oldridge, N.B., Guyatt, G.H., Fischer, M.E. and Rimm, A.A. (1988) Cardiac rehabilitation after myocardial infarction. Combined experience of randomised clinical trials, *Journal of the American Medical Association*, 260(7): 945–50.

Orbach, S. (1978) *Fat is a Feminist Issue – the Anti-diet Guide to Weight Loss*. New York: Paddington Press.

Orbell, S., Hodgkins, S. and Sheeran, P. (1997) Implementation intentions and the theory of planned behaviour, *Personality and Social Psychology Bulletin*, 23: 945–54.

Orford, J. (1985) *Excessive Appetites: A Psychological View of Addictions*. Chichester: John Wiley.

Orford, J. and Velleman, R. (1991) The environmental intergenerational transmission of alcohol problems: A comparison of two hypotheses, *British Journal of Medical Psychology*, 64: 189–200.

Orton, M., Fitzpatrick, R., Fuller, A. *et al.* (1991) Factors affecting women's responses to an invitation to attend for a second breast cancer screening examination, *British Journal of General Practice*, 41: 320–3.

Owens, R.G., Daly, J., Heron, K. and Leinster, S.J. (1987) Psychological and social characteristics of attenders for breast screening, *Psychology and Health*, 1: 320–3.

Paffenbarger, R.S. Jr. and Hale, W.E. (1975) Work activity and coronary heart mortality, *New England Journal of Medicine*, 292: 545–50.

Paffenbarger, R.S., Wing, A.L. and Hyde, R.T. (1978) Physical activity as an index of heart attack risk in college alumni, *American Journal of Epidemiology*, 108: 161–75.

Paffenbarger, R.S. Jr., Wing, A.L., Hyde, R.T. and Jung, D.L. (1983) Physical activity and incidence of hypertension in college alumni, *American Journal of Epidemiology*, 117: 245–57.

Paffenbarger, R.S., Hyde, R.T., Wing, A.L. and Hsieh, C.C. (1986) Physical activity, all-cause mortality, and longevity of college alumni, *New England Journal of Medicine*, 314: 605–13.

Paisley, C.M. and Sparks, P. (1998) Expectations of reducing fat intake: the role of perceived need within the theory of planned behaviour, *Psychology and Health*, 13: 341–53.

Palmer, A.G., Tucker, S., Warren, R. and Adams, M. (1993) Understanding women's responses for cervical intra-epithelial neoplasia, *British Journal of Clinical Psychology*, 32: 101–12.

Park, L.C. and Covi, L. (1965) Non blind placebo trial: an exploration of neurotic patients' responses to placebo when its inert content is disclosed, *Archives of General Psychiatry*, 12: 336–45.

Parker, D., Manstead, A.S. and Stradling, S.G. (1995) Extending the theory of planned behaviour: the role of personal norm, *British Journal of Social Psychology*, 34: 127–37.

Partridge, C.J. and Johnston, M. (1989) Perceived control and recovery from physical disability, *British Journal of Clinical Psychology*, 28: 53–60.

Patrick, D.L. and Ericson, P.E. (1993) *Health Status and Health Policy: Allocating Resources to Health Care*. Oxford: Oxford University Press.

Patterson, K.R. (1993) Population screening for diabetes, report from the professional Advisory Committee of the British Diabetic Association, *Diabetic Medicine*, 10: 777–81.

Paxton, S.J., Browning, C.J. and O'Connell, G. (1997) Predictors of exercise program participation in older women, *Psychology and Health*, 12: 543–52.

Pearse, I.H. and Crocker, L. (1943) *The Peckham Experiment*. London: Allen and Unwin.

Peele, S. (1984) The cultural context of psychological approaches to alcoholism: Can we control the effects of alcohol? *American Psychologist*, 39: 1337–51.

Pendleton, D., Schofield, T., Tate, P. and Havelock, P. (1984) *The Consultation: An Approach to Learning and Teaching*. Oxford: Oxford Medical Publications.

Pennebaker, J.W. (1983) Accuracy of symptom perception, in A. Baum, S.E. Taylor and J. Singer (eds), *Handbook of Psychology and Health*, Vol. 4. Hillsdale, NJ: Erlbaum.

Pennebaker, J.W. (1993) Social mechanisms of constraint, in D.M. Wegner and J.W. Pennebaker (eds), *Handbook of Mental Control*, pp. 200–19. Englewood Cliffs, NJ: Prentice Hall.

Pennebaker, J.W., Kiecolt-Glasser, J.K. and Glaser, R. (1988) Disclosure of trauma and immune function: Health implications for psychotherapy, *Journal of Consulting and Clinical Psychology*, 56: 239–45.

Perkins, K.A., Grobe, J.E., Stiller, R.L., Fonte, C. and Goettler, J.E. (1992) Nasal spray nicotine replacement suppresses cigarette smoking desire and behaviour, *Clinical Pharmacology and Therapeutics*, 52: 627–34.

Perquin, B., Baillet, F. and Wilson, J.F. (1976) Radiation therapy in the management of primary breast cancer, *American Journal of Roentgenology*, 127: 645–8.

Peto, R., Lopez, A.D., Boreham, J. *et al.* (1994) *Mortality from Smoking in Developed Countries 1950–2000*. Oxford: Oxford University Press.

Petrie, K.J., Booth, R.J. and Pennebaker, J.W. (1998) The immunological effects of thought suppression, *Journal of Personality and Social Psychology*, 75: 1264–72.

Petrie, K.J., Weinman, J.A., Sharpe, N. and Buckley, J. (1996) Role of patient's view of their illness in predicting return to work and functioning after myocardial infarction: longitudinal study, *British Medical Journal*, 312: 1191–4.

Petticrew, M., Fraser, J.M. and Regan, M. (1999) Adverse life-events and risk of breast cancer: A meta-analysis, *British Journal of Health Psychology*, 4: 1–17.

Pilkonis, P.A., Imler, S.D. and Rubinsky, P. (1985) Dimensions of life stress in psychiatric patients, *Journal of Human Stress*, 11: 5–10.

Pill, R. and Stott, N.C.H. (1982) Concepts of illness causation and responsibility: some preliminary data from a sample of working class mothers, *Social Science and Medicine*, 16: 315–22.

Pinder, K.L., Ramierz, A.J., Black, M.E. *et al.* (1993) Psychiatric disorder in patients with advanced breast cancer: Prevalence and associated factors, *European Journal of Cancer*, 29A: 524–7.

Pomerleau, O.F. and Brady, J.P. (1979) *Behavioral Medicine: Theory and Practice*. Baltimore: Williams and Wilkins.

Powell, D. and Khan, S. (1995) Racial differences in women's desire to be thin, *International Journal of Eating Disorders*, 17: 191–5.

Prentice, A.M. (1995) Are all calories equal? in Cottrell, R. (ed.), *Weight Control: The Current Perspective*. London: Chapman & Hall.

Prentice, A.M. and Jebb, S.A. (1995) Obesity in Britain: gluttony or sloth? *British Medical Journal*, 311: 437–9.

Price, J.H., Desmond, S. and Kukulka, G. (1985) High school students perceptions and misperceptions of AIDS, *Journal of School Health*, 55: 107–9.

Prochaska, J.O. and DiClemente, C.C. (1982) Transtheoretical therapy: toward a more integrative model of change, *Psychotherapy: Theory Research and Practice*, 19: 276–88.

Prochaska, J.O. and DiClemente, C.C. (1984) *The Transtheoretical Approach: Crossing Traditional Boundaries of Therapy*. Homewood, IL: Dow Jones Irwin.

Puska, P., Nissinen, A., Tuomilehto, J. *et al.* (1985) The community-based strategy to prevent coronary heart disease: Conclusions from ten years of the North Karelia Project, in L. Breslow, J.E. Fielding and L.B. Lave (eds), *Annual Review of Public Health*, Vol. 6, pp. 147–94. Palo Alto, CA: Annual Reviews Inc.

Quine, L., Rutter, D.R. and Arnold, L. (1998) Predicting safety helmet use among schoolboy cyclists: A comparison of the theory of planned behaviour and the health belief model, *Psychology and Health*, 13: 251–69.

Rains, P. (1971) *Becoming an Unwed Mother*. Chicago: Aldine.

Ramirez, A.J., Craig, T.J.K., Watson, J.P., Fentiman, I.S., North, W.R.S. and Rubens, R.D. (1989) Stress and relapse of breast cancer, *British Medical Journal*, 298: 291–3.

Ramirez, A.J., Watson, J.P., Richards, M.A. *et al.* (1992) Life events and breast cancer prognosis – letter to the editor, *British Medical Journal*, 304: 1632.

Rand, C.S.W. and MacGregor, A.M.C. (1991) Successful weight loss following obesity surgery and the perceived liability of morbid obesity, *International Journal of Obesity*, 15: 577–9.

Ravussin, E. and Bogardus, C. (1989) Relationship of genetics, age and physical activity to daily energy expenditure and fuel utilisation, *American Journal of Clinical Nutrition*, 49: 968–75.

Rector, T.S., Kubo, S.H. and Cohn, J.N. (1993) Validity of the Minnesota Living with Heart Failure Questionnaire as a measure of therapeutic response: effects of enalapril and placebo, *American Journal of Cardiology*, 71: 1006–7.

Redd, W.H. (1982) Behavioural analysis and control of psychosomatic symptoms in patients receiving intensive cancer treatment, *British Journal of Clinical Psychology*, 21: 351–8.

Redhead, I.H. (1960) The incidence of glycosuria and diabetes mellitus in general practice, *British Medical Journal*, 1: 695.

Reed, G.M., Kemeny, M.E., Taylor, S.E., Wang, H.-Y.J. and Visscher, B.R. (1994) Realistic acceptance as a predictor of decreased survival time in gay men with AIDS, *Health Psychology*, 13: 299–307.

Reed, G.M., Kemeny, M.E., Taylor, S.E. and Visscher, B.R. (1999) Negative HIV-specific expectancies and AIDS-related bereavement as predictors of symptom onset in asymptomatic HIV-positive gay men, *Health Psychology*, 18: 354–63.

Reelick, N.F., DeHaes, W.F.M. and Schuurman, J.H. (1984) Psychological side effects of the mass screening on cervical cancer, *Social Science and Medicine*, 18: 1089–93.

Reiss, I.L. and Leik, R.K. (1989) Evaluating strategies to avoid AIDS: numbers of partners versus use of condoms, *Journal of Sex Research*, 26: 411–33.

Reiss, I.L., Banwart, A. and Foreman, H. (1975) Premarital contraceptive usage: a study and some theoretical explorations, *Journal of Marriage and the Family*, 37: 619–30.

Rescorla, R.A. and Wagner, A.R. (1972) A theory of Pavlovian conditioning: variations in the effectiveness of reinforcement and non-reinforcement, in A.H. Black and W.F. Prokasy (eds), *Classical Conditioning 11: Current Research and Theory*, pp. 64–9. New York: Appleton-Century-Crofts.

Reynolds, B.D., Puck, M.H. and Robertson, A. (1974) Genetic counselling: an appraisal, *Clinical Genetics*, 5: 177–87.

Richard, R. and van der Pligt, J. (1991) Factors effecting condom use among adolescents, *Journal of Community and Applied Social Psychology*, 1: 105–16.

Riddle, P.K. (1980) Attitudes, beliefs, intentions, and behaviours of men and women toward regular jogging, *Research Quarterly for Exercise and Sport*, 51: 663–74.

Riegel, B.J. (1993) Contributions to cardiac invalidism after acute myocardial infarction, *Coronary Artery Disease*, 4: 569–78.

Rimer, B.K., Trock, B., Lermon, C. *et al.* (1991) Why do some women get regular mammograms? *American Journal of Preventative Medicine*, 7: 69–74.

Rippetoe, P.A. and Rogers, R.W. (1987) Effects of components of protection-motivation theory on adaptive and maladaptive coping with a health threat, *Journal of Personality and Social Psychology*, 52: 596–604.

Rissanen, A.M., Heliovaara, M., Knekt, P., Reunanen, A. and Aromaa, A. (1991) Determinants of weight gain and overweight in adult Finns, *European Journal of Clinical Nutrition*, 45: 419–30.

Rogers, R.W. (1975) A protection motivation theory of fear appeals and attitude change, *Journal of Psychology*, 91: 93–114.

Rogers, R.W. (1983) Cognitive and physiological processes in fear appeals and attitude change: A revised theory of protection motivation, in J.R. Cacioppo and R.E. Petty (eds), *Social Psychology: A Source Book*, pp. 153–76. New York: Guilford Press.

Rogers, R.W. (1985) Attitude change and information integration in fear appeals, *Psychological Reports*, 56: 179–82.

Rosenberg, M. (1965) *Society and the Adolescent Self Image*. Princeton, NJ: Princeton University Press.

Rosenman, R.H. (1978) Role of type A pattern in the pathogenesis of ischaemic heart disease and modification for prevention, *Advances in Cardiology*, 25: 34–46.

Rosenman, R.H., Brand, R.J., Jenkins, C.D. *et al.* (1975) Coronary heart disease in the western collaborative heart study: Final follow-up experience of $8^1/2$ years, *Journal of the American Medical Association*, 233: 872–7.

Rosenstock, I.M. (1966) Why people use health services, *Millbank Memorial Fund Quarterly*, 44: 94–124.

Roskies, E., Seraganian, P., Oseasohn, R. *et al.* (1986) The Montreal type A intervention project: Major findings, *Health Psychology*, 5: 45–69.

Ross, M. and Olson, J.M. (1981) An expectancy attribution model of the effects of placebos, *Psychological Review*, 88: 408–37.

Ross, S. and Buckalew, L.W. (1983) The placebo as an agent in behavioural manipulation: a review of the problems, issues and affected measures, *Clinical Psychology Review*, 3: 457–71.

Roth, H.P. (1979) Problems in conducting a study of the effects of patient compliance of teaching the rationale for antacid therapy, in S.J. Cohen (ed.), *New Directions in Patient Compliance*, pp. 111–26. Lexington, MA: Lexington Books.

Ruble, D.N. (1977) Premenstrual symptoms. A reinterpretation, *Science*, 197: 291–2.

Rucker, C.E. and Cash, T. (1992) Body images, body size perceptions and eating behaviors among African-American and white college women, *International Journal of Eating Disorders*, 12: 291–9.

Ruderman, A.J. and Wilson, G.T. (1979) Weight, Restraint, Cognitions and Counterregulation, *Behaviour Research and Therapy*, 17: 581–90.

Russell, M.A.H., Wilson, C., Taylor, C. and Baker, C.D. (1979) Effect of general practitioners' advice against smoking, *British Medical Journal,* 2: 231–5.

Sackett, D.L. and Holland, W.W. (1975) Controversy in the detection of disease, *Lancet,* ii: 357–9.

Sackett, D.L. and Haynes, R.B. (1976) *Compliance with Therapeutic Regimens.* Baltimore, MD: Johns Hopkins University Press.

Sallis, J.F., Haskell, W.L., Fortmann, S.P. *et al.* (1986) Predictors of adoption and maintenance of physical activity in a community sample, *Preventive Medicine,* 15: 331–41.

Salonen, J.T., Puska, P. and Tuomilehto, J. (1982) Physical activity and risk of myocardial infarction, cerebral stroke and death: A longitudinal study in eastern Finland, *American Journal of Epidemiology,* 115: 526–37.

Sanders, C., Egger, M., Donovan, J., Tallon, D. and Frankel, S. (1998) Reporting on quality of life in randomised controlled trials: bibliographic study, *British Medical Journal,* 317: 1191–4.

Santi, S., Best, J.A., Brown, K.S. and Cargo, M. (1991) Social environment and smoking initiation, *The International of the Addictions,* 25: 881–903.

Sarason, I.G., Johnson, J.H. and Siegel, J.M. (1978) Assessing the impact of life changes: the Life Experiences Survey, *Journal of Consulting Clinical Psychology,* 46: 932–46.

Sarason, I.G., Levine, H.M., Basham, R.B. *et al.* (1983) Assessing social support: the social support questionnaire, *Journal of Personality and Social Psychology,* 44: 127–39.

Sarason, I.G., Sarason, B.R., Shearin, E.N. and Pierce, G.R. (1987) A brief measure of social support: practical and theoretical implications, *Journal of Social and Personal Relationships,* 4: 497–510.

Savage, R. and Armstrong, D. (1990) Effect of a general practitioner's consulting style on patient's satisfaction: a controlled study, *British Medical Journal,* 301: 968–70.

Scambler, A., Scambler, G. and Craig, D. (1981) Kinship and friendship networks and women's demands for primary care, *Journal of the Royal College of General Practice,* 26: 746–50.

Schachter, S. (1968) Obesity and eating, *Science,* 161: 751–6.

Schachter, S. and Gross, L. (1968) Manipulated time and eating behaviour, *Journal of Personality and Social Psychology,* 10: 98–106.

Schachter, S. and Rodin, J. (1974) *Obese Humans and Rats.* Potomac, MD: Erlbaum.

Schaefer, C., Quesenberry, C.P. Jr. and Wi, S. (1995) Mortality following conjugal bereavement and the effects of a shared environment, *American Journal of Epidemiology,* 141: 1142–52.

Scheiderich, S.D., Freidbaum, D.M. and Peterson, L.M. (1983) Registered nurses' knowledge about diabetes mellitus, *Diabetes Care,* 6: 57–61.

Schifter, D.E. and Ajzen, I. (1985) Intention, perceived control, and weight loss: An application of the theory of planned behaviour, *Journal of Personality and Social Psychology,* 49: 843–51.

Schuckit, M.A. (1985) Genetics and the risk for alcoholism, *Journal of the American Medical Association,* 254: 2614–17.

Schwartz, G.E. and Weiss, S.M. (1977) *Yale Conference on Behavioral Medicine.* Washington DC: Department of Health, Education and Welfare; National Heart, Lung, and Blood Institute.

Schwartz, J.L. (1987) *Review and Evaluation of Smoking Cessation Methods: The United States and Canada, 1978–1985,* NIH Pub. No. 87–2940. Washington DC: National Cancer Institute.

Schwarzer, R. (1992) Self efficacy in the adoption and maintenance of health behaviors: Theoretical approaches and a new model, in R. Schwarzer (ed.), *Self Efficacy: Thought Control of Action*, pp. 217–43. Washington, DC: Hemisphere.

Schwarzer, R., Jerusalem, M. and Hahn, A. (1994) Unemployment, social support and health complaints: A longitudinal study of stress in East German refugees, *Journal of Community and Applied Social Psychology*, 4: 31–45.

Segal, L. (1994) *Straight Sex: The Politics of Pleasure*. London: Virago.

Seligman, M.E.P. and Visintainer, M.A. (1985) Turnout rejection and early experience of uncontrollable shock in the rat, in F.R. Brush and J.B. Overmier (eds) *Affect Conditioning and Cognition: Essays on the Determinants of Behavior*. Hillstate, NJ: Erlbaum.

Seligman, M.E., Peterson, C. and Vaillant, G.E. (1988) Pessimistic explanatory style is a risk factor for illness: A 35 year longitudinal study, *Journal of Personality and Social Psychology*, 55: 23–7.

Selvini, M. (1988) Self starvation: the last synthesis on anorexia nervosa, in M. Selvini and M. Selvini Palazzoli (eds), *The Work of Mara Selvini Palazzoli*, pp. 147–50. NJ: Jason Aronson.

Selye, H. (1956) *The Stress of Life*. New York: McGraw-Hill.

Seydel, E., Taal, E. and Wiegman, O. (1990) Risk appraisal, outcome and self efficacy expectancies: Cognitive factors in preventative behaviour related to cancer, *Psychology and Health*, 4: 99–109.

Shaffer, J.W., Graves, P.L., Swank, R.T. and Pearson, T.A. (1987) Clustering of personality traits in youth and the subsequent development of cancer among physicians, *Journal of Behavioural Medicine*, 10: 441–7.

Shafi, M.I. (1994) Management of women with mild dyskaryosis. Cytological surveillance avoids overtreatment, *British Medical Journal*, 309: 590–2.

Shapiro, S. (1977) Evidence on screening for breast cancer from a randomised trial, *Cancer*, 39: 2772–82.

Shapiro, S., Strax, P., Venet, L. and Venet, W. (1972) Changes in 5-year breast cancer mortality in a breast cancer screening programme, in *Seventh National Cancer Conference Proceedings*. New York: American Cancer Society Inc.

Shapiro, S., Venet, W. and Strax, P. *et al.* (1982) Ten to fourteen year effects of breast cancer screening on mortality, *Journal of the National Cancer Institute*, 62: 340–54.

Shaw, C., Abrams, K. and Marteau, T.M. (1999) Psychological impact of predicting individuals' risk of illness: A systematic review, *Social Science and Medicine*, 49: 1571–98.

Shea, S., Basch, C.E., Lantigua, R. and Wechsler, H. (1992) The Washington Heights-Inwood Healthy Heart Program: A third generation community-based cardiovascular disease prevention program in a disadvantaged urban setting, *Preventive Medicine*, 21: 201–17.

Sheeran, P. and Orbell, S. (1998) Implementation intentions and repeated behaviour: augmenting the predictive validity of the theory of planned behaviour, *European Journal of Social Psychology*, 28: 1–21.

Sheeran, P., White, D. and Phillips, K. (1991) Premarital contraceptive use: a review of the psychological literature, *Journal of Reproductive and Infant Psychology*, 9: 253–69.

Sheilds, J.S. (1962) *Monozygotic Twins: Brought up Apart and Brought up Together*. London: Oxford University Press.

Sheppard, B.H., Hartwick, J. and Warshaw, P.R. (1988) The theory of reasoned action: a meta analysis of past research with recommendations for modifications and future research, *Journal of Consumer Research*, 15: 325–43.

Shepperd, S., Harwood, D., Jenkinson, C. *et al.* (1998) Randomised controlled trial comparing hospital at home care with inpatient hospital care. I: three month follow up of health outcomes, *British Medical Journal,* 316: 1786–91.

Sherman, S.J., Barton, J., Chassin, L. and Pressin, C.C. (1982) Social image factors as motivators of smoking initiation in early and middle adolescence, *Child Development,* 53: 1499–511.

Sherr, L. (1987) An evaluation of the UK government health education campaign on AIDS, *Psychology and Health,* 1: 61–72.

Shiloh, S., Vinter, M. and Barak, A. (1997) Correlates of health screening utilisation: The roles of health beliefs and self-regulation motivation, *Psychology and Health,* 12: 301–17.

Shontz, F.C. (1975) *The Psychological Aspects of Physical Illness and Disability.* New York: Macmillan Co.

Shy, K.K., Luthy, D.A., Whitfield, M. *et al.* (1990) Effects of electronic fetal-heart-rate monitoring, as compared with periodic auscultation, on the neurologic development of premature infants, *New England Journal of Medicine,* 322: 588–93.

Sibinga, M.S. and Friedman, C.J. (1971) Complexities of parental understanding of phenylketonuria, *Paediatrics,* 48: 216–24.

Simkins, L. and Ebenhage, M. (1984) Attitudes towards AIDS, herpes II and toxic shock syndrome, *Psychological Reports,* 55: 779–86.

Simon, N. (1977) Breast cancer induced by radiation, *Journal of the American Medical Association,* 237: 789–90.

Simonton, O.C. and Simonton, S.S. (1975) Belief systems and the management of emotional aspects of malignancy, *Journal of Transpersonal Psychology,* 7: 29–47.

Simpson, W.M., Johnston, M. and McEwan, S.R. (1997) Screening for risk factors for cardiovascular disease: a psychological perspective, *Scottish Medical Journal,* 42: 178–81.

Sjostrom, L. (1980) Fat cells and body weight, in A.J. Stunkard (ed.), *Obesity,* pp. 72–100. Philadelphia: Saunders.

Skelton, J.A. and Pennebaker, J.W. (1982) The psychology of physical symptoms and sensations, in G.S. Sanders and J. Suls (eds), *Social Psychology of Health and Illness.* Hillsdale, NJ: Erlbaum.

Sklar, S.L. and Anisman, H. (1981) Stress and cancer, *Psychological Bulletin,* 89(3): 369–406.

Skrabanek, P. (1988) The physician's responsibility to the patient, *Lancet,* 1: 1155–7.

Slade, P.D. and Russell, G.F.M. (1973) Awareness of body dimensions in anorexia nervosa: Cross-sectional and longitudinal studies, *Psychological Medicine,* 3: 188–99.

Smith, A. and Chamberlain, J. (1987) Managing cervical screening, in *Institute of Health Service Management. Information Technology in Health Care.* London: Kluwer Academic.

Smith, A. and Jacobson, B. (1989) *The Nation's Health.* London: The King's Fund.

Smith, G.S. and Kraus, J.F. (1988) Alcohol and residential, recreational, and occupational injuries: A review of the epidemiologic evidence, in L. Breslow, J.E. Fielding and L.B. Lave (eds), *Annual Review of Public Health,* vol. 9. Palo Alto, CA: Annual Reviews.

Smith, L.M., Mullis, R.L. and Hill, W.E. (1995) Identity strivings within the mother daughter relationship, *Psychological Reports,* 76: 495–503.

Smith, R.A., Williams, D.K., Silbert, J.R. and Harper, P.S. (1990) Attitudes of mothers to neonatal screening for Duchenne muscular dystrophy, *British Medical Journal*, 300: 1112.

Sobel, M.B. and Sobel, L.C. (1976) Second year treatment outcome of alcoholics treated by individualized behaviour therapy: Results, *Behaviour Research and Therapy*, 14: 195–215.

Sobel, M.B. and Sobel, L.C. (1978) *Behavioral Treatment of Alcohol Problems*. New York: Plenum.

Sodroski, J.G., Rosen, C.A. and Haseltine, W.A. (1984) Trans-acting transcription of the long terminal repeat of human T lymphocyte viruses in infected cells, *Science*, 225: 381–5.

Solomon, G.F. and Temoshok, L. (1987) A psychoneuroimmunologic perspective on AIDS research: Questions, preliminary findings, and suggestions, *Journal of Applied Social Psychology*, 17: 286–308.

Solomon, G.F., Temoshok, L., O'Leary, A. and Zich, J.A. (1987) An intensive psychoimmunologic study of long-surviving persons with AIDS: Pilot work background studies, hypotheses, and methods, *Annals New York Academy of Sciences*, 46: 647–55.

Sonstroem, R. (1988) Psychological models, in R.K. Dishman (ed.), *Exercise Adherence: Its Impact on Public Health*. Champaign, Ill: Human Kinetics.

Sontag, S. (1988) *Illness as Metaphor*. Harmonsworth: Penguin.

Soutter, W.P. and Fletcher, A. (1994) Invasive cancer in women with mild dyskaryosis followed cytologically, *British Medical Journal*, 308: 1421–3.

Sparks, P. and Shepherd, R. (1992) Self-identity and the theory of planned behaviour: assessing the role of identification with 'green consumerism', *Social Psychology Quarterly*, 55: 388–99.

Sparks, P. (1994) Food choice and health: applying, assessing, and extending the theory of planned behaviour, in D.R. Rutter and L. Quine (eds), *Social Psychology and Health: European Perspectives*, pp. 25–46. Aldershot: Avebury.

Speisman, J.C., Lazarus, R.S., Mordkoff, A. and Davison, L. (1964) Experimental reduction of stress based on ego defense theory, *Journal of Abnormal and Social Psychology*, 68: 367–80.

Spencer, J.A. and Fremouw, M.J. (1979) Binge eating as a function of restraint and weight classification, *Journal of Abnormal Psychology*, 88: 262–7.

Spitzer, L. and Rodin, J. (1981) Human eating behaviour: a critical review of studies in normal weight and overweight individuals, *Appetite*, 2: 293–329.

Stanton, A.L. (1987) Determinants of adherence to medical regimens by hypertensive patients, *Journal of Behavioral Medicine*, 10: 377–94.

Steiger, H., Stotland, S., Ghadirian, A.M. and Whitehead, V. (1994) Controlled study of eating concerns and psychopathological traits in relatives of eating disorders probands: Do familial traits exist? *International Journal of Eating Disorders*, 18: 107–18.

Steinberg, H. and Sykes, E.A. (1985) Introduction to symposium on endorphins and behavioral processes: Review of literature on endorphins and exercise, *Pharmacology, Biochemistry and Behaviour*, 23: 857–62.

Steptoe, A., Kearsley, N. and Walters, N. (1993) Acute mood responses to maximal and submaximal exercise in active and inactive men, *Psychology and Health*, 8: 89–99.

Stern, J.S. (1984) Is obesity a disease of inactivity? in A.J. Stunkard and E. Stellar (eds), *Eating and Its Disorders*. New York: Raven Press.

Sternbach, R.A. (1964) The effects of instructional sets on autonomic responsivity, *Psychophysiology*, 1: 64–72.

Sternbach, R.A., Wolf, S.R., Murphy, R.W. and Akeson, W.H. (1973) Traits of pain patients: The low-back 'loser', *Psychosomatics*, 14: 226–9.
Sternbach, R.A. (ed.) (1978) *The Psychology of Pain*. New York: Raven Press.
Stewart, A.L. and Ware, J.E. (eds) (1992) *Measuring Functioning and Well Being: The Medical Outcomes Study Approach*. Durham, NC: Duke University Press.
Stoate, H. (1989) Can health screening damage your health? *Journal of the Royal College of General Practitioners*, 39: 193–5.
Stokes, J. and Rigotti, N. (1988) The health consequences of cigarette smoking and the internist's role in smoking cessation, *Annals of Internal Medicine*, 33: 431–60.
Stone, A.A. and Brownell, K.D. (1994) The stress-eating paradox: Multiple daily measurements in adult males and females, *Psychology and Health*, 9: 425–36.
Stone, A.A., Cox, D.S., Valdimarsdottir, H., Jandorf, L. and Neale, J.M. (1987) Evidence that secretory IgA antibody is associated with daily mood, *Journal of Personality and Social Psychology*, 52: 988–93.
Stoney, C.M., Davis, M.C. and Mathews, K.A. (1987) Sex differences in physiological responses to stress and coronary heart disease: A casual link? *Psychophysiology*, 24: 127–31.
Stoney, C.M., Mathews, K.A., McDonald, R.H. and Johnson, C.A. (1990) Sex differences in acute stress response: Lipid, lipoprotein, cardiovascular and neuroendocrine adjustments, *Psychophysiology*, 12: 52–61.
Story, M., French, S., Resnick, M. and Blum, R. (1995) Ethnic/racial and socioeconomic differences in dieting behaviours and body image perceptions in adolescents, *International Journal of Eating Disorders*, 18: 173–9.
Strax, P. (1978) Evaluation of screening programs for the early diagnosis of breast cancer, *Surgical Clinics of North America*, 58: 667–79.
Striegel-Moore, H., Shrieber, B., Pike, M., Wifley, E. and Rodin, J. (1995) Drive for thinness in Black and white preadolescent girls, *International Journal of Eating Disorders*, 18: 59.
Striegel-Moore, R., Silberstein, L. and Rodin, J. (1986) Towards an understanding of risk factors for bulimia, *American Psychologist*, 41: 246–63.
Stroop, J.R. (1935) Studies of interference in serial verbal reactions, *Journal of Experimental Psychology*, 18: 643–62.
Stuart, R.B. (1967) Behavioural control of overeating, *Behaviour Research and Therapy*, 5: 357–65.
Stuart, R.B. and Davis, B. (1972) *Slim Chance in a Fat World: Behavioral Control of Obesity*. Champaign, IL: Research Press.
Stunkard, A.J. (1958) The management of obesity, *New York State Journal of Medicine*, 58: 79–87.
Stunkard, A.J. (1984) The current status of treatment for obesity in adults, in A.J. Stunkard and E. Stellar (eds), *Eating and Its Disorders*. New York: Raven Press.
Stunkard, A.J. and Penick, S.B. (1979) Behaviour modification in the treatment of obesity: The problem of maintaining weight loss, *Archives on General Psychiatry*, 36: 801–6.
Stunkard, A., Sorenson, T. and Schlusinger, F. (1983) Use of the Danish Adoption Register for the study of obesity and thinness, in S. Kety, L.P. Rowland, R.L. Sidman and S.W. Matthysse (eds), *The Genetics of Neurological and Psychiatric Disorders*, pp. 115–20. New York: Raven.
Stunkard, A.J., Stinnett, J.L. and Smoller, J.W. (1986a) Psychological and social aspects of the surgical treatment of obesity, *American Journal of Psychiatry*, 143: 417–29.

Stunkard, A.J., Sorenson, T.I.A., Hanis, C. *et al.* (1986b) An adoption study of human obesity, *New England Journal of medicine*, 314: 193–8.

Stunkard, A.J., Harris, J.R. Pedersen, N.L. and McClearn, G.E. (1990) A separated twin study of body mass index, *New England Journal of Medicine*, 322: 1483–7.

Sumner, A., Waller, G., Killick, S. and Elstein, M. (1993) Body image distortion in pregnancy: a pilot study of the effects of media images, *Journal of Reproductive and Infant Psychology*, 11: 203–8.

Sussman, S., Dent, C., Stacy, A.W. *et al.* (1990) Peer group association and adolescent tobacco use, *Journal of Abnormal Psychology*, 99: 349–52.

Sutton, S.R. (1982) Fear-arousing communications: A critical examination of theory and research, in J.R. Eiser (ed.), *Social Psychology and Behavioural Medicine*, pp. 303–7. Chichester: John Wiley.

Sutton, S. (1998a) Predicting and explaining intentions and behavior: How well are we doing? *Journal of Applied Social Psychology*, 28: 1317–38.

Sutton, S. (1998b) How ordinary people in Great Britain perceive the health risks of smoking, *Journal of Epidemiological Community Health*, 52: 338–9.

Sutton, S. (1999) The psychological costs of screening, in J.S. Tobias and I.C. Henderson (eds), *New Horizons in Breast Cancer: Current Controversies, Future Directions*. London: Chapman and Hall.

Sutton, S. (in press) Interpreting cross-sectional data on stages of change, *Psychology and Health*.

Sutton, S.R. and Hallett, R. (1989) Understanding the effect of fear-arousing communications: The role of cognitive factors and amount of fear aroused, *Journal of Behavioral Medicine*, 11: 353–60.

Sutton, S., Saidi, G., Bickler, G. and Hunter, J. (1995) Does routine screening for breast cancer raise anxiety? Results from a three wave prospective study in England, *Journal of Epidemiology and Community Health*, 49: 413–18.

Sutton, S., McVey, D. and Glanz, A. (1999) A comparative test of the theory of reasoned action and the theory of planned behaviour in the prediction of condom use intentions in a national sample of English young people, *Health Psychology*, 18: 72–81.

Swan, A.V., Murray, M. and Jarrett, L. (1991) *Smoking Behaviour from Pre-adolescence to Young Adulthood*. Aldershot: Avebury.

Taylor, S.E. (1983) Adjustment to threatening events: A theory of cognitive adaptation, *American Psychologist*, 38: 1161–73.

Taylor, S.E. (1999) *Health Psychology*, 4th edn. New York: McGraw-Hill.

Taylor, S.E., Lichtman, R.R. and Wood, J.V. (1984) Attributions, beliefs about control, and adjustment to breast cancer, *Journal of Personality and Social Psychology*, 46: 489–502.

Taylor, S., Kemeny, M., Reed, G. and Bower, J. (1998) Psychosocial influence on course of disease: predictors of HIV progression, *Health Psychology Update*, 34: 7–12.

Temoshok, L. and Fox, B.H. (1984) Coping styles and other psychosocial factors related to medical status and to prognosis in patients with cutaneous malignant melanoma, in B.H. Fox and B.H. Newberry (eds), *Impact of Psychoendocrine Systems in Cancer and Immunity*, pp. 258–87. Toronto: C.J. Hogrefe.

Temoshok, L., Sweet, D.M. and Zich, J.A. (1987) A three city comparison of the public's knowledge and attitudes about AIDS, *Psychology and Health*, 1: 43–60.

Thompson, J.P., Palmer, R.L. and Petersen, S.A. (1988) Is there a metabolic component to counterregulation? *International Journal of Eating Disorders*, 7: 307–19.

Thompson, S.C. (1986) Will it hurt less if I can control it? A complex answer to a simple question, *Psychological Bulletin*, 90: 89–101.

Totman, R.G. (1976) Cognitive dissonance and the placebo response, *European Journal of Social Psychology*, 5: 119–25.

Totman, R.G. (1987) *The Social Causes of Illness*. London: Souvenir Press.

Trostle, J.A. (1988) Medical compliance as an ideology, *Social Science and Medicine*, 27: 1299–308.

Tuckett, D., Boulton, M., Olson, C. and Williams, A. (1985) *Meetings Between Experts*. London: Tavistock Publications.

Turk, D. and Rennert, K. (1981) Pain and the terminally ill cancer patient: a cognitive social learning perspective, in H. Sobel (ed.), *Journal of Behavior Therapy in Terminal Care*, New York: Ballinger.

Turk, D.C. and Rudy, T.E. (1986) Assessment of cognitive factors in chronic pain: A worthwhile enterprise? *Journal of Consulting and Clinical Psychology*, 54: 760–8.

Turk, D.C., Meichenbaum, D. and Genest, M. (1983) *Pain and Behavioral Medicine*. New York: Guilford Press.

Turk, D.C., Wack, J.T. and Kerns, R.D. (1985) An empirical examination of the 'pain-behaviour' construct, *Journal of Behavioral Medicine*, 8: 119–30.

US Department of Health and Human Services (USDHHS) (1990) *The Health Benefits of Smoking Cessation: A Report of the Surgeon General*. Rockville, MD: USDHHS.

US Environmental Protection Agency (1992) *Respiratory Health Effects of Passive Smoking: Lung Cancer and Other Disorders*. Washington, DC: US Environmental Protection Agency.

Upton, A.L., Beebe, G.W., Brown, J.W. *et al.* (1977) Report of NCI ad hoc working group on the risks associated with mammography in mass screening for the detection of breast cancer, *Journal of the National Cancer Institute*, 59: 479–93.

Valois, P., Desharnais, R. and Godin, G. (1988) A comparison of the Fishbein and the Triandis attitudinal models for the prediction of exercise intention and behavior, *Journal of Behavioral Medicine*, 11: 459–72.

van der Velde, F.W. and van der Pligt, J. (1991) AIDS related health behavior: Coping, protection motivation, and previous behavior, *Behavioral Medicine*, 14: 429–52.

van der Velde, F., Hookyas, C. and van der Pligt, J. (1992) Risk perception and behavior: pessimism, realism, and optimism about AIDS-related health behavior, *Psychology and Health*, 6: 23–38.

van Elderen, T., Maes, S. and van den Broek, Y. (1994) Effects of a health education programme with telephone follow-up during cardiac rehabilitation, *British Journal of Clinical Psychology*, 33: 367–78.

van Griensven, G.J.P., Teilman, R.A.P., Goudsmit, J. *et al.* (1986) Riskofaktoren en prevalentie van LAV/HTLV III antistoffen bij homoseksuele mannen in Nederland, *Tijdschrift voor Sociale Gezondheidszorg*, 64: 100–7.

van Strien, T., Frijters, J.E., Bergers, G.P. and Defares, P.B. (1986) Dutch eating behaviour questionnaire for the assessment of restrained, emotional, and external eating behaviour, *International Journal of Eating Disorders*, 5: 295–315.

van Zuuren, F.J. (1998) The effects of information, distraction and coping style on symptom reporting during preterm labor, *Psychology and Health*, 13: 49–54.

Velicer, W.F., DiClemente, C.C., Prochaska, J.O. and Brandenberg, N. (1985) A decisional balance measure for assessing and predicting smoking status, *Journal of Personality and Social Psychology*, 48: 1279–89.

Violanti, J., Marshall, J. and Howe, B. (1983) Police occupational demands, psychological distress and the coping function of alcohol, *Journal of Occupational Medicine*, 25: 455–8.

Von Frey, M. (1895) *Untersuchungen Über die Sinnesfunctionen der Menschlichen Haut Erste Abhandlung: Druckempfindung und Schmerz*. Leipzig: Hirzel.

Von Zerssen, D. (1976) *Klinische Selbestbeurteilungsskalen (KSb-S) aus dem Munchener Psychiatrischen Informations System (PSYCHIS Muenchen). Die Paranoid Depressivitats Skala*. Weinheim: Beltz.

Wadden, T.A. (1993) Treatment of obesity by moderate and severe calorie restriction: Results of clinical research trials, *Annals of Internal Medicine*, 119: 688–93.

Wadden, T.A., Stunkard, A.J. and Smoller, W.S. (1986) Dieting and depression: A methodological study, *Journal of Consulting and Clinical Psychology*, 64: 869–71.

Walker, W.B. and Franzini, L.R. (1985) Low-risk aversive group treatments, physiological feedback, and booster sessions for smoking cessation, *Behaviour Therapy*, 16: 263–74.

Waller, D., Agass, M., Mant, D. *et al.* (1990) Health checks in General Practice: another example of inverse care? *British Medical Journal*, 300: 1115–18.

Waller, G., Hamilton, K. and Shaw, J. (1992) Media influences on body size estimation in eating disordered and comparison subjects, *British Review of Bulimia and Anorexia Nervosa*, 6: 81–7.

Wallsten, T.S. (1978) *Three biases in the cognitive processing of diagnostic information*. Unpublished paper, Psychometric Laboratory, University of North Carolina, Chapel Hill, NC.

Wallston, B.S., Alagna, S.W., Devellis, B.M. and Devellis, R.F. (1983) Social support and physical illness, *Health Psychology*, 2: 367–91.

Wallston, K.A. and Wallston, B.S. (1982) Who is responsible for your health? The construct of health locus of control, in G.S. Sanders and J. Suls (eds), *Social Psychology of Health and Illness*, pp. 65–95. Hillsdale, NJ: Erlbaum.

Wallston, K.A., Wallston, B.S. and DeVeliis, R. (1978) Development of the multidimensional health locus of control (MHLC) scales, *Health Education Monographs*, 6: 160–70.

Wanebo, C.K., Johnson, K.G., Sato, K. and Thorslind, T.W. (1968) Breast cancer after the exposure to the atomic bombings of Hiroshima and Nagasaki, *New England Journal of Medicine*, 279: 667–71.

Wardle, J. (1980) Dietary restraint and binge eating, *Behaviour Analysis and Modification*, 4: 201–9.

Wardle, J. and Beales, S. (1986) Restraint, body image and food attitudes in children from 12 to 18 years, *Appetite*, 7: 209–17.

Wardle, J. and Beales, S. (1988) Control and loss of control over eating: An experimental investigation, *Journal of Abnormal Psychology*, 97: 35–40.

Wardle, J. and Marsland, L. (1990) Adolescent concerns about weight and eating: a social developmental perspective, *Journal of Psychosomatic Research*, 34: 377–91.

Wardle, J., Volz, C. and Golding, C. (1995) Social variation in attitudes to obesity in children, *International Journal of Obesity*, 19: 562–9.

Ware, J.E. and Sherbourne, C.D. (1992) The MOS 36 item short form health survey (SF-36). Conceptual framework and item selection, *Medical Care*, 30: 473–83.

Warren, C. and Cooper, P.J. (1988) Psychological effects of dieting, *British Journal of Clinical Psychology*, 27: 269–70.

Wason, P.C. (1974) The psychology of deceptive problems, *New Scientist*, 15 August: 382–5.

Watson, M. and Greer, S. (1983) Development of a questionnaire measure of emotional control, *Journal of Psychosomatic Research*, 27: 299–305.

Watson, M., Greer, S., Rowden, L. *et al.* (1991) Relationships between emotional control, adjustment to cancer and depression and anxiety in breast cancer patients, *Psychological Medicine*, 21: 51–7.

Weatherburn, P., Hunt, A.J., Davies, P.M., Coxon, A.P.M. and McManus, T.J. (1991) Condom use in a large cohort of homosexually active men in England and Wales, *AIDS Care*, 3: 31–41.

Weeks, J. (1985) *Sexuality and Its Discontents: Meanings, Myths and Modern Sexuality*. London: Routledge and Kegan Paul.

Weg, R.B. (1983) Changing physiology of aging, in D.S. Woodruff and J.E. Birren (eds), *Ageing: Scientific Perspectives and Social Issues*, 2nd edn. Monterey, CA: Brooks/Cole.

Weiner, B. (1986) *An Attributional Theory of Motivation and Emotion*. New York: Springer-Verlag.

Weinman, J. (1987) Diagnosis as problem-solving, in J. Weinman (ed.) *An Outline of Psychology as Applied to Medicine*, 2nd edn. London: J. Wright.

Weinman, J. and Petrie, K.J. (1997) Illness perceptions: A new paradigm for psychosomatics? *Journal of Psychosomatic Research*, 42: 113–16.

Weinman, J., Petrie, K.J., Moss-Morris, R. and Horne, R. (1996) The Illness perception questionnaire: a new method for assessing the cognitive representation of illness, *Psychology and Health*, 11: 431–46.

Weinstein, N. (1983) Reducing unrealistic optimism about illness susceptibility, *Health Psychology*, 2: 11–20.

Weinstein, N. (1984) Why it won't happen to me: perceptions of risk factors and susceptibility, *Health Psychology*, 3: 431–57.

Weinstein, N. (1987) Unrealistic optimism about illness susceptibility: conclusions from a community-wide sample, *Journal of Behavioural Medicine*, 10: 481–500.

Weinstein, N.D., Rothman, A.J. and Sutton, S.R. (1998) Stage theories of health behavior: conceptual and methodological issues, *Health Psychology*, 17: 290–9.

Weisman, C.S., Plichta, S., Nathanson, C.A., Ensminger, M. and Robertson, J.C. (1991) Consistency of condom use for disease prevention among adolescent users of oral contraceptives, *Family Planning Perspective*, 23: 71–4.

Weller, S.S. (1984) Cross cultural concepts of illness: Variables and validation, *American Anthropologist*, 86: 341–51.

Wellings, K., Field, J., Johnson, A.M. and Wadsworth, J. (1994) *Sexual Behaviour in Britain: The National Survey of Sexual Attitudes and Lifestyles*. Middlesex: Penguin Books.

Werner, P.D. and Middlestadt, S.E. (1979) Factors in the use of oral contraceptives by young women, *Journal of Applied Social Psychology*, 9: 537–47.

Whitaker, A., Davies, M., Shaffer, D. *et al.* (1989) The struggle to be thin: a survey of anorexic and bulimic symptoms in a non-referred adolescent population, *Psychological Medicine*, 19: 143–63.

Whitley, B.E. and Schofield, J.W. (1986) A meta-analysis of research on adolescent contraceptive use, *Population and Environment*, 8: 173–203.

WHOQOL Group (1993) *Measuring Quality of Life: The Development of a World Health Organisation Quality of Life Instrument (WHOQOL)*. Geneva: WHO.

Wickramasekera, I. (1980) A conditioned response model of the placebo effect: predictions from the model, *Biofeedback and Self Regulation*, 5: 5–18.

Wiebe, D.J. and McCallum, D.M. (1986) Health practices and hardiness as mediators in the stress-illness relationship, *Health Psychology*, 5: 425–38.

Wiedenfeld, S.A., O'Leary, A., Bandura, A. *et al.* (1990) Impact of perceived self efficacy in coping with stressors on immune function, *Journal of Personality and Social Psychology*, 59: 1082–94.

Wilkinson, C., Jones, J.M. and McBride, J. (1990) Anxiety caused by abnormal result of cervical smear test: a controlled trial, *British Medical Journal*, 300: 440.

Williams, S., Weinman, J.A., Dale, J. and Newman, S. (1995) Patient expectations: what do primary care patients want from their GP and how far does meeting expectations affect patient satisfaction? *Journal of Family Practice*, 12: 193–201.

Williamson, G.S. and Pearse, I.H. (1938) *Biologists in Search of Material*. London: Faber and Faber.

Wills, T.A. (1985) Supportive functions of interpersonal relationships, in S. Cohen and S.L. Syme (eds), *Social Support and Health*. Orlando, FL: Academic Press.

Wilson, D.M., Taylor, M.A., Gilbert, J.R. *et al.* (1988) A ramdomised trial of a family physician intervention for smoking cessation, *Journal of the American Medical Association*, 260: 1570–4.

Wilson, G.T. (1978) Alcoholism and aversion therapy: Issues, ethics, and evidence, in G. Marlatt and P. Nathan (eds), *Behavioral Approaches to Alcoholism*. New Brunswick, NJ: Journal of Studies on Alcohol.

Wilson, G.T. (1994) Behavioural treatment of obesity: Thirty years and counting, *Advances in Behavioural Research Therapy*, 16: 31–75.

Wilson, J.M.G. (1965) Screening criteria, in G. Teeling-Smith (ed.), *Surveillance and Early Diagnosis in General Practice*. London: Office of Health Economics.

Wing, R.R., Koeske, R., Epstein, L.H. *et al.* (1987) Long term effects of modest weight loss in Type II diabetic patients, *Archives of Internal Medicine*, 147: 1749–53.

Wolf, T.M. and Kissling, G.E. (1984) Changes in life-style characteristics, health, and mood of freshman medical students, *Journal of Medical Education*, 59: 806–14.

Wood, D.A., Kinmouth, A.L., Pyke, S.D.M. and Thompson, S.G. (1994) Randomised controlled trial evaluating cardiovascular screening and intervention in general practice: principal results of British family heart study, *British Medical Journal*, 308: 313–20.

Woodcock, A., Stenner, K. and Ingham, R. (1992) Young people talking about HIV and AIDS: Interpretations of personal risk of infection, *Health Education Research: Theory and Practice*, 7: 229–47.

Wooley, S.C. and Wooley, O.W. (1984) Should obesity be treated at all? in A.J. Stunkard and E. Stellar (eds), *Eating and Its Disorders*. New York: Raven Press.

World Health Organization (1947) *Constitution of the World Health Organization*. Geneva: WHO.

World Health Organization (1981) *Global strategy for Health for All by the year 2000*. Geneva: WHO.

Wyper, M.A. (1990) Breast self examination and Health Belief Model, *Research in Nursing and Health*, 13: 421–8.

Young, L. and Humphrey, M. (1985) Cognitive methods of preparing women for hysterectomy: does a booklet help? *British Journal of Clinical Psychology*, 24: 303–4.

Zigmond, A.S. and Snaith, R.P. (1983) The Hospital Anxiety and Depression Scale, *Acta Psychiatrica Scandinavica*, 67: 361–70.

Zimbardo, P.G. (1969) *The Cognitive Control of Motivation*. Illinois: Scott Foresman.

Zola, I.K. (1972) Medicine as an institution of social control, *Sociological Review*, 20: 487–504.

Index

Note: page numbers followed by *fig* refer to figures

SOCIAL PSYCHOLOGY AND HEALTH

Wolfgang Stroebe and Margaret S. Stroebe

This book discusses major topics of health psychology from a social psychological perspective. This approach reflects the significant changes which have taken place in conceptions of health and illness during recent decades and the move away from purely biomedical models of illness. In line with this broadening perspective, health psychology has become a dominant force in the health sciences, a field to which social psychological theory and research has much to offer. The book addresses two major factors detrimental to health and well-being, namely health impairing behaviors and stressful life events. The following key questions are discussed: which behavior patterns are detrimental to one's health? Why do people engage in health impairing behaviors even if they know about their negative effects? How can people be influenced to change their behavior? What are stressful life events and which mechanisms mediate the impact of these stresses on health? The book argues for an integrative approach that combines psychological, economic and environmental interventions to reduce behavioral risk factors.

Contents

Changing conceptions of health and illness – Determinants of health behavior: a social psychological analysis – Beyond persuasion: the modification of health behavior – Behavior and health: excessive appetites – Behavior and health: self-protection – Stress and health – Moderators of the stress-health relationship – The role of social psychology in health – References – Author index – Subject index.

204pp 0 335 09857 6 (Paperback) 0 335 09858 4 (Hardback)

LOSS AND BEREAVEMENT

Sheila Payne, Sandra Horn and Marilyn Relf

- How have people sought to understand loss and bereavement?
- What are the current theoretical approaches to loss and bereavement?
- What are the implications of these approaches for intentions?

This book aims to provide students with an understanding of important theoretical perspectives and specific models of adaptation to loss. It is assumed that loss and change are normal processes that occur within a social and cultural context, and the reader is introduced to historical and cultural perspectives which illustrate the diversity of approaches to loss. Major theoretical perspectives are explored to enable students to understand their origins and influence. The authors go on to review the development of common models used to conceptualize individual reactions to loss and provide a critique of these models, highlighting the assumptions that underpin them. Finally, they discuss how these conceptual models have actually been used in clinical and community interventions. This is a comprehensive text describing the variety of approaches available to understand the process of loss and bereavement.

Contents

144pp 0 335 20105 9 (Paperback) 0 335 20106 7 (Hardback)